THE NEW BUREAUCRACY

THE NEW BUREAUCRACY

Waste and Folly in
the Private Sector

Herschel Hardin

M&S

Canadian Cataloguing in Publication Data

Hardin, Herschel, 1936–
   The new bureaucracy

Includes index.
ISBN 0–7710–3914–X

1. Executives – North America.   2. Bureaucracy – North America.
3. Industrial management – North America.   4. Industrial productivity –
North America.   I. Title.

HD38.25.N67H3 1992   658.4'09   C91–095387–2

Printed and bound in Canada. The paper used in this book is acid-free.

McClelland & Stewart Inc.
The Canadian Publishers
481 University Avenue
Toronto, Ontario
M5G 2E9

Printed and bound in Canada by
John Deyell Company Limited.

CONTENTS

1

The New Bureaucracy

In the early 1980s, former CBC journalist Ken Colby hosted an extended series of television commercials for the Canadian Petroleum Association (CPA), aimed at influencing government policy in favour of the major oil companies. Newspaper, magazine, and radio ads were also used. Colby in this period also became director of government affairs for Norcen Energy, an oil and gas company controlled at the time by Conrad Black. The CPA campaign, in four carefully planned phases, included separate material for Quebeckers. Yves Corbeil, popular morning show host of the commercial TVA network, fronted the television campaign on the French side. The outlay, all told, came to $11 million.

There was some criticism of the manipulative nature of the CPA campaign, but the spending on the campaign and on the organization behind it wasn't brought into question. Even the protests about the mind-bending purpose of the commercials petered out quickly. The criticism had nowhere to go. Any individuals who were alarmed at the heavy hand of the CPA had neither the political weight nor the resources to make a difference.

At the same time, Colby's ex-employer, the CBC, was under attack as usual, in effect because most of the resources it used were collected through public-funding mechanisms. Later, Prime Minister Brian Mulroney and his cabinet would cut back the CBC's appropriation, and cut it back again, and again, in real terms, and with it the kind of work that CBC journalists had been doing.

Here was the unmentioned irony. The lavish expenditures on Colby, the propagandist, and on the organization behind him went unquestioned because they occurred in the "private sector." By contrast, expenditures on CBC journalism and other CBC broadcasting – on Colby the journalist –

were continually questioned because they occurred in the public sector. The fact that Colby might be paid much more handsomely for his time by the CPA than he was as a correspondent for the CBC, even as a senior reporter, also wasn't questioned, for the same reason. It made no difference that his propaganda function for the CPA was objectionable, as well as using up money from the economy, whereas his function as a CBC journalist was a highly valuable, democratic one. The oil-company corporate bureaucracy simply allocated the funds.

How did this misallocation of resources happen? Or perhaps one should ask, how did the oil-company bureaucracy get its power to misallocate economic resources and to manipulate public opinion so brazenly?

Private-enterprise ideology has a great deal to do with it. The ideology continually associates the public sector with the notion of "bureaucracy" and, by implication, the notion of waste. The federal civil service, for example, is denounced as an "infamous bureaucratic labyrinth" and its civil servants as "mushrooming mandarins." Calls are made, sometimes with great indignation, for "reining in" or "restraining" or "slashing" public spending, as if that spending were automatically wasteful in itself or, at best, of little usefulness. Commissions and task forces are periodically struck, amid great publicity, to advise on eliminating government duplication, waste, and inefficiencies – the Glassco Commission (reporting in 1962); the Nielsen Task Force (producing twenty-one volumes, 1985); in the United States, the Grace Commission (1984) and, before it, the Hoover Commission (1949). Colourful individual cases of waste, real and alleged, and even innocent but unusual expenditures (sometimes involving as little as $5,000), are pointed to with accusatory fingers. The perks of members of Parliament come under the gun. Public employees and public spending in general (eventually touching, say, the number of nurses available for heart-surgery work) and publicly financed organizations (here's where the CBC comes in) get painted with the same ideological brush.

Meanwhile, the possibility that the most extravagant waste and unproductive bureaucracy are in the private sector instead isn't allowed to come into it. The assumption is that the private sector looks after itself – the marketplace looks after it – and can't be wasteful by definition. Not just that, but private-sector officials – for example, the chairman of the Royal Bank of Canada or the president of the Canadian Chamber of Commerce – are the loudest in calling for public-sector cutbacks. Their advice on public-sector waste is actively sought after. The Nielsen Task Force had a "private sector advisory committee" and private-sector participants on each of the study teams. The Grace Commission was headed by a private-sector executive and a 161-member Executive Committee, which included heads of the largest U.S. corporations and accounting firms.

The reality hidden behind the ideology, however, is quite different. Waste in the private sector is large, ever-growing, and in many ways unchecked. It is structural waste, built into the way the private sector does things. Its abuses are breathtaking. Its juxtaposition to people doing productive and useful work in the much-abused public sector is replete with ironies. And atop this waste is as intrusive, sprawling, and self-indulgent a bureaucratic order as ever existed. This is the New Bureaucracy, a phenomenon of our times.

There is no mistaking its bureaucratic character, even if many people's idea of the word "bureaucracy" only extends as far as government red tape and the unsympathetic civil servant. Here are all the attributes of bureaucracy, full-blown: hierarchical organizations, size and complication, ranks of cadres, politicking behind the scenes, churning of paper and paper games, makework and waste at our expense, elaboration added to elaboration, intrusion into our lives, and the self-protection that comes from bureaucratic entrenchment.

The CPA case gives a hint of the bureaucracy at work. Colby and Corbeil, who appeared in the television commercials, were just a part of the bureaucratic machinery involved. There was the CPA itself, a large and well-financed industry lobby. Executive committees of the major oil companies were also involved, meeting to discuss their unhappiness with federal oil policy and the strategy to take. Among them would be officers in charge of "corporate communications," "external affairs," "government affairs," or "public relations," some of them as high in rank and in pay as vice-president. This was their bailiwick.

Many of the same oil companies in turn retained "public affairs consulting" firms in Ottawa. Then there were the advertising agencies (McLaughlin, Mohr, Massey in Toronto and Allard, Lesiège in Montreal) and the television production companies that filmed the commercials. Also involved was prominent Conservative pollster Allan Gregg and his Decima Research Ltd. polling and research firm.

But this kind of lavish propaganda campaign represents just a minute fragment of the structural waste in the private sector and its bureaucratic elaboration. First and foremost is executive life in corporations themselves, what American authors Mark Green and John Berry, in their book *The Challenge of Hidden Profits: Reducing Corporate Bureaucracy and Waste*, call the "corpocracy." Here we find extravagant and blown-up salaries and bonuses, self-serving devices like "golden parachutes," perks, and handholding by consultants that would make the court of a czar envious. Patronage is also not unknown. We also find the devices by which these executive orders entrench their bureaucratic life and security: lobbies, propaganda, and relations with politicians and governments.

"Paper entrepreneurialism" – the takeover games and other shuffling of paper assets – is another branch of this bureaucracy, one that mushroomed in the last decade. This branch has many sub-branches unto itself, reaching down like a root system into one corner and then another. Investment dealers, management consultants, commercial banks, institutional investors, lawyers, and accountants all are involved. They are the bureaucratic cadres of paper entrepreneurship.

Related to paper entrepreneurship, but a full-fledged bureaucratic world in themselves, are stock markets, which move shares back and forth in an endless churning by speculators and institutional investors. Sometimes a stock exchange floor is full of sound and fury. This surface excitement disguises just how routine, bureaucratic, and wasteful the inflated stock-exchange process has become, while the real productive work on which it battens takes place elsewhere. Its sub-branches are endless – not just stock-brokers, traders, and others sustained directly by the operation of exchanges, but also market watchers, analysts, newsletter publishers, financial writers, advertising and media cadres, regulators, sometimes police, right down to the television news announcer providing the Dow Jones and TSE stock indexes for the day, plus all the auxiliary back-up staff and suppliers.

Add to them futures exchanges and their commodity speculation, options trading, foreign-currency trading, bond trading and interest-rate speculation, the concoction of hybrid and synthetic financial "products" and a host of cadres who move such paper around. This is the derivative-paper branch of the New Bureaucracy.

Closely allied to the stock-exchange branch are the money managers. Institutional investors lead the way in this part of bureaucratic growth. Except for the most addicted individual speculators, the institutional money managers are perhaps the greatest paper-churners of them all. What some money managers win for their account in this manoeuvring, others lose. Nothing over all is gained except an expansion of the money managers' activity. Mutual funds are part of this branch. Financial counselling, a branch section, has also mushroomed in numbers and overheads.

The unkempt and unchecked growth of advertising and marketing is another part of the New Bureaucracy. Accelerated advertising expenditures ultimately cancel each other out, but the process, by its own momentum, keeps vendors of products locked into this waste. Television has brought a sea-change to advertising, turning it into an office of propaganda. In a way, this makes it the most pernicious of all branches of the New Bureaucracy. Like the other branches, it is certainly spendthrift. Its specific expenditures sometimes pass credibility.

Other branches of the New Bureaucracy form a confluence here. Corporate executives gloss their activities (institutional advertising) and propagandize their views (advocacy advertising) through this branch, without regard to what their spending on this propaganda might be doing to the democratic process. The money-manager branch has become a heavy user of advertising. The advertising, with its acculturating effect, incidentally enhances the image of what these cadres are doing and hence, also, entrenches the status of their bureaucracies themselves.

The advertising and marketing branch also acts as an agent for the growing takeover by corporate bureaucracies of sports and culture. Sports and culture are as far removed from the corporations' ostensible reason for existence (the production of goods or services) as random objects. There is no inherent connection between operating a brewery and operating as a rock-concert impresario or between a cigarette company and a theatre festival. But the New Bureaucracy, ideologically protected, knows no limits. It intrudes everywhere and dictates conditions, even imposing itself on generations-old events like "Hockey Night in Canada," now "Molson Hockey Night in Canada." Its bureaucratic warrens quietly multiply and inflate.

Like every ascendant bureaucracy, this one needs a screen of legitimacy to expand and impose itself. A new factor has been added. Never before, not even under the most systematic and pervasive dictatorship, has a bureaucracy had a propaganda medium like television to legitimize its expansion. But that would not be enough if journalism were independent and critical of that expansion. It isn't. Journalism is supine – not surprisingly, perhaps, because the media themselves are a part of the New Bureaucracy and financially dependent on its advertising branch. They give inordinate coverage to the New Bureaucracy's activities, particularly its stock exchanges, day after day, without ever questioning the economic usefulness of these activities, except incidentally. Some financially lucky reporters, like Ken Colby, even get to move through the revolving door into the highly lucrative bureaucratic mainstream of the corpocracy.

Most economists also play a role. Their doctrinaire and abstract views of the workings of the universe are based on the very free-enterprise dogma behind which the bureaucratic proliferation has taken place. "Think tanks," financially supported by the corporate and other branches, oblige as well. Their relationship with the New Bureaucracy is an intimate one. Such protective intellectual elaboration is part and parcel of bureaucratic development.

But despite the many exotic details of indulgence and waste, no grand conspiracy is involved in the expansion of the New Bureaucracy, just the day-to-day, incremental banality of bureaucratic development, buried in specifics.

So entrenched is the New Bureaucracy that its participants are able to perpetrate waste and abuses that, if committed by the old bureaucracy (civil service), would raise screams of horror and indignation. Bureaucratic power might be measured in just that ability to impose oneself without risk, where criticism can be ignored. Worse still, the new and powerful bureaucratic establishment infects the old, with government and public agencies picking up its bad habits.

The New Bureaucracy is most rampant in the United States, where the private-enterprise ideology which screens it is held sacrosanct. Most new extensions and practices of the bureaucracy take place in the United States first and are adopted in Canada and other countries later. Watching the bureaucratic elaboration at work in the United States is like watching cells multiply in a laboratory – exciting and awe-inspiring, if dreadful in its import – so fertile and well-nourished is this bureaucratic process in America. Its proliferation is dazzling. Its unending invention is comically inspired.

As the spin-off process outwards from the United States occurs, passing from one country to another, "globalization" becomes a byword. More and more, globalization consists of the expansion of the New Bureaucracy – by the New Bureaucracy and for the New Bureaucracy – putting it even further away from any community constraints. One Big Bureaucracy is what we are looking at now.

2

The Corporate Branch

Max Weber, the nineteenth-century German sociologist who first wrote about bureaucracies, if alive today, would be astonished at the sheer size of modern corporations. He would be even more astonished at how the people on the top rungs of these bureaucracies, the chief executives, have captured power for themselves and bathed in huge compensation and luxurious indulgences. The waste and misallocation of resources would bring him up with a start. As for the lobbying ranks of these corporate bureaucracies – grown to an inflated bureaucracy in their own right and messing up government – he would have simply raised his hands in the air, in disbelief.

Even in a middleweight country like Canada, there are corporate bureaucracies of stunning magnitude. BCE, a former telephone company, had assets of C$42 billion in 1990. Canadian Pacific Limited, which originally began as a railway, had assets of $20 billion. General Motors of Canada, a smaller organization by assets but leading the way in sales ($18 billion), isn't even a company unto itself, but a mere subsidiary of a much larger organization. Companies well down the list are no less impressive in their own right; many which rank lower than the top 400 measured by sales have assets in the hundreds of millions of dollars.

These companies, in turn, are growing ever larger. In many cases the bureaucratic structure is extended through takeovers – the swallowing up of other organizations. Occasionally the company being swallowed is larger than the swallower – a "reverse takeover" or a case of the fish swallowing the whale. Often, the bureaucracy disgorges what it has ingested, finding a swallowed company too troublesome or awkward, only to take over a different company later on. Something in their inner core – a kind of bureaucratic life force – impels these corporate hierarchies to expand and to increase the territory and personnel under their officers.

Similar bureaucratic structures are under the control of family or family-dominated holding companies. The largest, the Peter Bronfman Hees-Edper group, covers six hundred companies and C$100 billion in non-financial and financial assets. The annual sales of the ten largest non-financial companies in the group reached $42 billion in 1989, almost half of the federal government's revenue.

This, again, is for a small country. Corporations based in larger countries are even more imposing. The leader in 1990, General Motors, had US$180 billion in assets under its administration and $126 billion in sales. There were almost three hundred industrial corporations in the United States alone with assets over $1 billion that year, leaving aside the service sector and utilities. The largest U.S. bank, Citicorp, had financial assets of $217 billion, and the largest bank in the world, Dai-Ichi Kangyo Bank in Japan, had financial assets of $406 billion under its control.

Weber's appreciation of bureaucracy was inspired by his ideal of what government administration should be. He also realized, however, that the same kind of structures, with hierarchical lines of accountability, were required for business. The bureaucratic character of corporate life, even in the most dynamic and creative of corporations, is the nature of the beast. There has been no lack of comment on the phenomenon. Among many other observers, William H. Whyte, in his celebrated 1956 book *The Organization Man*, offered a vivid portrait of the individual in the corporate bureaucracy. John Kenneth Galbraith, in *The New Industrial State*, 1967, described how the chief administrators of these bureaucracies (collectively, the "technostructure") functioned by "group decision," where accommodation to organization was one of the most important skills. They weren't the grasping, crude industrial barons of the fabled American past, and "executive life, so far from being competitive and dangerous, is highly secure."

The similarity between the work of corporate administrators and government administrators is a commonplace. Executives in corporations hold endless meetings in offices (as much as 60 per cent of their time), work within committee structures, discuss subjects which are described and analyzed in paper documents, wrestle with information and communications, function by rank (laid out in organizational charts for greater clarity), and give orders which others down the line obey. Bureaucracy literally means rule by office, coming from the French word *bureau* meaning office and the Greek root *kratein*, to rule. *Bureau* in turn, derives from the same word for desk, originally a table covered with a cloth known as *burel*. "Rule by office" is how corporations work, and the image of the baize-covered table in the old French government *bureau* now summons up most of all the image of the corporate boardroom. Internal executive politics are as complicated and byzantine – can be more complicated and byzantine – than the jockeying within the most mystifying of government departments. Building of alliances and learning the rules of the game within the organization are crucial.

This similarity between corporate and government bureaucracy is most graphic in Japan. Management of a company has traditionally been seen as a bureaucratic and co-operative venture, "the government of a company," as an observer of Japanese corporate management put it. Major decisions are made committee style, with the cadres going over the details from every angle until a consensus is reached.

Leading positions in Japanese executive offices are often filled by people whose training and first careers were in government administration. The passage of people from the public service into corporate life, through the revolving door, isn't particular to Japan, but there it is regularized and works at the highest levels. It is called *amakaduri*, the "descent from heaven." Senior civil servants, on retirement at a relatively early age, descend to become leading executives of major corporations.

But corporate bureaucracies everywhere have a rare and particular advantage unto themselves. Civil servants have to answer to elected representatives who also, ultimately, control budgets. Executives and boards of widely held private corporations, on the other hand – the private-sector model – don't need to answer to anybody. Shareholdings are too fragmented for the average shareholder to have any influence. As long as the company keeps afloat, management usually reigns, although stock-market pressures may give them headaches, and a hostile takeover, if the company isn't too big, may depose them. Recently, institutional investors, who now hold large blocks of shares – bureaucracies in their own right – have begun to throw their weight around in jousting with the corporate cadres. Their leverage is limited.

The premise behind this bureaucratic arrangement – or cover for it – is that corporations have to contend against others in competitive markets, and this automatically looks after things. But market competition has its limits, especially where the dominant players are large, complex organizations with mercantile power and with a *modus vivendi* amongst themselves. Corporate cadres have plenty of room to play with. They can also shortchange shareholders to maintain that room. Through other bureaucratic devices, like lobbying and brand-name propaganda, they extend their leeway.

Two American scholars, Adolf Berle and Gardiner Means, described the phenomenon of management autonomy back in 1932, in their classic, *The Modern Corporation and Private Property*. The ordinary shareholder, they wrote, "is left with a mere symbol of ownership" while the substance is in the hands of management and a friendly board of directors. These groups, in relation to the small shareholder, are effectively "economic autocrats." They also "virtually dictate their own successors" through the proxy committee, becoming thereby a self-perpetuating body. Little did Berle and Means know. The bureaucratic corporation, still young in their day, became ever-more elaborate and ingenious, sophisticated, artful, and self-serving.

Most graphically, this bureaucratic process has spawned enormous salaries, perks, bonuses, severance payments, retirement packages, and luxuries of office, with year-to-year increases to raise eyebrows. In the 1980s in Canada, top executive compensation, including stock options and bonuses, went to Peter Munk, chairman and CEO of American Barrick. He pulled down C$4.6 million in 1988, according to the annual *Financial Post* survey. Garth Drabinsky, chairman of Cineplex Odeon at the time, pocketed $4.3 million in 1986 and $3.9 million in 1988. We used to count millionaires in terms of people who had accumulated $1 million, usually over several decades of striving. Now the *Financial Post* runs a separate box listing Canada's $1-million-a-year men. In 1990, a recession-troubled year, eleven executives made the list and, in 1988, a record eighteen made it, as compared to only six in 1986 and none at all in 1979.

Not only the top executives floated almost gravity-free in the salary stratosphere. Number twenty-five overall in the recession-battered 1990 list, R. A. Gusella of Sceptre Resources, pocketed C$758,00. This was 41 per cent more than the take of number twenty-five in 1986 ($538,000 for Texaco Canada's president).

The *Financial Post's* listings include only companies whose shares traded on American stock exchanges and which were required by U.S. law to disclose the relevant information. Just sixty-two were on the paper's 1990 list. This left out most of Canada's largest companies, including family dynasties (the Irving, Peter Bronfman, Eaton, Reichmann, Thomson, and Weston holdings), the major chartered banks, and wholly owned subsidiaries (such as General Motors, Chrysler, and IBM). If the whole corporate bureaucracy had been surveyed, the catalogue of outsized compensation would have been even more astounding.

Large annual pay increases, on a base that was already extraordinarily remunerative, became routine, regardless of what others were being paid. The exercise of stock options produced the really big money on top of that. The average wage, meanwhile, trailed the pace of inflation. In 1987, for example, a good year for stock options, compensation of top Canadian executives, as calculated by the *Financial Times of Canada* from the American data, increased an average 21 per cent. This was on top of a major increase, similarly enriched by stock options, the prior year. The average wage that year, by comparison, increased 3.8 per cent. Middle managers, next to the top executives in the hierarchy, benefitted from the overflow of the largesse.

Inflated as executive remuneration is in Canada, it pales next to what corporate administrators in the United States have arranged for themselves. Compensation, including stock options and bonuses, kept inflating and inflating further. When Chrysler chairman Lee Iacocca pulled down US$20.5 million in 1986, people could hardly believe it. It was close to double the highest CEO compensation the previous year of $12.7 million, itself astronomical (Iacocca, in 1985, took home $11.4 million). But the bureaucratic process simply extended this inflation in subsequent years.

Top of the heap in 1987, according to the annual *Business Week* score-card, appeared at first to be Jim Manzi, the chairman of Lotus, who took home US$26.3 million. Manzi wasn't even a founder or pioneer of the firm, but a former newspaperman and consultant who arrived as director of marketing. "The day when a fast-tracker makes his age in millions isn't far off," *Business Week* joked. No sooner said than almost done. A late return for Charles Lazarus, sixty-four, chairman of Toys 'R' Us Inc., had him pulling in $60 million in 1987, including bonuses and, most importantly, stock options.

By 1988, four executives – two from Walt Disney and two from RJR Nabisco – were snaffling more compensation than Iacocca had ever managed to extract in any one year. Top compensation went to Disney chairman Michael Eisner at US$40 million. Poor Lee Iacocca, exercising fewer stock options than in the past, had to settle for a paltry $3.7 million. In 1989, top CEO pay went to Craig McCaw of McCaw Cellular: $53.9 million. As if to mock even that, the next year, 1990, a recession year, saw two even larger compensation jackpots recorded. In the first, Steven Ross, co-chairman of Time Warner, cashed in various stock plans for a $75 million "bonus," for a total compensation of $78 million, on top of his 1989 take of $34 million. (Ross's defenders argued that the $75 million bonus reflected his performance over many years; even so, his compensation was extraordinary.) In the second case, Donald Pels, chairman of Lin Broadcasting, took home $186 million from stock options when his company was bought by McCaw Cellular. Yet to come, for a fiscal year ending in 1991: Anthony O'Reilly, chairman of H. J. Heinz, netted $75 million, of which $71.5 million was in stock options.

By the time one got to the low man of the top twenty-five in 1990 (all of them were men), the payout was down to a trifle – US$6.2 million. Five of the top twenty-five that year weren't even chief executives. Including long-term compensation, the *average* pay of the 730 executives covered in the annual *Business Week* survey was $1.95 million, and that was in a poor year. A record four hundred executives took home more than $1 million each.

Steven Ross's compensation arrangements were particularly celebrated. Ross, in the 1980s, was chairman of movie, cable, and recording company Warner Communications. He was widely known for his lavish living, shuttling celebrities by company helicopter from Manhattan to his estate one hundred miles away – company bodyguard always along for the security and long life of chairman Ross. The company also maintained a six-bedroom villa in Acapulco, set on a cliff overlooking the Pacific, for Ross and his guests. Then, at a heated 1987 board meeting, as *Fortune* described it, he arranged a contract that set the back lots buzzing. If the company's net income rose 10 per cent a year compounded annually, Ross, under the contract, would receive an average of US$14 million a year in compensation. (The entire U.S. Senate was paid only $9 million a year, *Fortune* observed.) If, on the other hand, Warner's stock and earnings remained flat, Ross would still get close to $6 million a year. Later it was disclosed that the contract was worth as much as $181 million over ten years, depending on the company's earnings and stock performance. This was carried over by the terms of Warner's subsequent merger with Time.

For most of the decade, executive compensation leapt ahead year to year by multiples of the inflation rate. In 1987 alone, a good year for cashing in stock options, the average increase was in the 48-59 per cent range as compared to a 4.4 per cent inflation rate. In the 1980s through to 1990 inclusive, CEO compensation covered by *Business Week's* annual survey (360 leading companies) grew about four-and-a-half times as fast as the pay of factory workers, compounded over the period.

Pay relationships provide another measure. In 1960, at the height of American business power, top CEOs were generously rewarded for their accomplishments – or at least for their bureaucratic status – with an average pay of US$190,383, as charted by *Business Week*. This was considered *premium* pay, forty-one times the average pay of a factory worker, thirty-eight times the salary of an average school teacher, and nineteen times an average engineer's pay. It already constituted an outlandish differential. By 1990, with U.S. manufacturing, a key sector, losing ground in the world, the same category of CEO compensation had nevertheless inflated to eighty-five times, sixty-three times, and forty times the average pay of a factory worker, teacher, and engineer respectively. Almost all this increase in the differential occurred in the 1980s. CEOs who earn 100-plus times the average worker's wage are now common. In the U.S. auto industry, according to *Business Month* magazine, the ratio was 192 to 1 in 1990. U.S. compensation expert Graef Crystal knew of a case where the CEO's pay was 1,800 times the average hourly worker's wage. "We haven't seen differentials this high since Herod was CEO of Judea," he joked. The maximum income tax rate, in the same period, had shrunk from 91 per cent to 33 per cent, puffing up the top corporate bureaucrats' take-home pay even more spectacularly.

Once entrenched, these privileged pay-outs become inviolate in the eye of the recipient (the executive) and his friends (his fellow board members). "For a company that makes a couple of billion dollars," one U.S. oil company director explained, "a $1 million paycheck is only a flyspeck." The pay-outs are so large that a Wall Street headhunter (executive personnel recruiting firm) nabbed $450,000 for reeling in an executive to head a corporate-finance unit. That wasn't the executive's salary, only the percentage commission the head-hunting firm received for finding the man. Another headhunter was given a $600,000 annual retainer by a company, not to fill a particular position but just to alert it if he came across an executive worth a special look.

Top corporate bureaucrats who lose their jobs because of takeovers or other events, also bathe in huge emoluments, in the form of "golden parachutes" and severance payments. Golden parachutes are special dispensations to executives who may leave or be kicked out after a takeover, hostile or friendly. These dispensations are pre-arranged by incumbent boards – in effect, in most cases, by the executives themselves through their boards. Executives so departed lose their bureaucratic security in the process, at least till they find another perch, but are more than assuaged financially for the inconvenience. (When the dispensation isn't pre-arranged, but is given to get rid of somebody without fuss and bother, it's called a "golden handshake.")

The record for floating a golden parachute in the United States, through to late 1988, belonged to Gerald Tsai, who was then chairman of a financial services company called Primamerica. He was blessed with US$46.8 million. He had been with the company for less than three years. An $8.6 million chunk of Tsai's payment was to pay the excise taxes on the rest of it – a device aptly referred to as "grossing up." He also stayed on with the new merged entity, as consultant and director of the executive committee, for a relatively paltry $250,000 per year plus office space, staff, and perks. Tsai's parachute was then topped by Ross Johnson and his second-in-command at RJR Nabisco with parachutes of $53 million and $45.7 million respectively (including final salary, bonus, stock-option pay-off, certain retirement benefits, and estimated future annuity payments). (Steven Ross, as CEO of Warner, arranged a golden parachute of up to $90 million for himself but, kept on after the Time-Warner merger, he didn't have to bother pulling the rip cord.)

Other golden parachutes, if not quite so large, weren't shabby, either. Parachute number ten on the U.S. list for 1988 – a good year, because of all the takeovers and leveraged buyouts – came in at US$7.5 million (average for the top ten parachutes: $26 million). "Parachutes A-Popping," quipped

Fortune, of the use of the device. Even well-placed minor-leaguers could fashion broad parachutes for themselves. The chairman of medium-sized Ponderosa Inc., a restaurant chain, had a $12 million golden parachute arranged, *circa* 1985-1986, just in case he was booted out because of the chain's poor financial performance; the parachute was more than double the profits of the company at the time.

Golden parachutes also help the jettisoned corporate executive float down in Canada. Ex-Cineplex chairman Garth Drabinsky, for example, took home C$4.5 million in a severance package, plus $893,000 in a salary remainder, or $5.4 million in total, when he lost control of the company. (Drabinsky, the previous year, had been obliged to take a pay cut to a measly $1.6 million). His second-in-command was floated down with $4.2 million. Bernard Isautier, who briefly headed Polysar, cashed in stock options estimated at a reported $20 million when Nova Corp., in 1988, bought Polysar at a huge premium price.

Other permutations and combinations can also amount to extraordinary dispensations on leaving a company. In 1985 in Canada, when Imasco took over Genstar, two Genstar executives stood to make some $40 million each in a combination of salary, shares they held in a private partnership and stock options garnered over the years. Even an investment friend of theirs called it "absolutely outrageous." They hadn't even taken a risk, the friend complained.

"Clearly, it's an enormous amount of money," said departing Revlon chairman Michel Bergerac in 1985 of his then record parachute of US$35 million. "Whether it should be less or more, how do you judge those things? I don't know." Bureaucratic equilibrium decides. Another nice part of it is that floating down with a golden parachute doesn't stop the recipient from starting another job the next day at a lucrative salary, plus bonuses, plus stock options, while keeping the proceeds of the parachute anyway.

Ordinary severance payments have also become extraordinary – not least for dismal and sometimes reprobate executives leaving horrible messes behind. The unwritten rule is that losers leave quietly, but with their bank accounts bulging. So people who get the boot for having messed up, sometimes in the most questionable circumstances, end up being rewarded instead of punished. When CEO Frank Lorenzo was pushed out of Continental Airlines Holdings (Texas Air) in 1990, he was paid US$14 per share for his stock; the trading price the day before the deal was announced was below $5 a share. It was the only way to get Lorenzo out, a board member explained. Lorenzo's total cash-out, with the premium and severance payments added: $30.5 million. If, moreover, by some stroke of fate, a jettisoned executive doesn't get the inflated bureaucratic norm, he sues, and he can always cite in court what the going rate is (the cadres at this level are invariably men).

The most wondrous golden handshake was given by General Motors to H. Ross Perot, a mere board member, in 1986, just to get the outspoken Perot, a critic of GM's management, out of its hair. Perot was the founder of Electronic Data Systems (EDS), which GM bought in 1984. The golden handshake involved the purchase of Perot's class E GM shares for almost twice the market price (payment of "contingencies" was the euphemism for providing the extra margin), for a net dispensation to Perot of approximately US$350 million. Of that, $7.5 million was contingent on Perot not saying anything critical of GM after he had gone. "Hushmail," Perot quipped.

Then there are nice settlements to executives who leave under legal clouds. They have to be fired because of their transgressions (from bribery plans to forging a cheque). Corporate cosmetic purposes call for it. The organization, caught out, needs to put on a new face. But the sinning executives, obliged to resign, are gifted in the breach for their troubles.

Lucrative golden parachutes and severance payments have created a bureaucratic subsection of their own made up of consultants specializing in employment contracts, as well as lawyers, accountants, and pension consultants whom the compensation consultants bring in as deemed necessary. These coteries help executives to nail down healthy termination payments in advance, institutionalizing what congenial boards have been doing voluntarily – and taking healthy fees, up to $10,000 in Canada for a major package.

Pensions for executives also exist, therefore they are garnished and enriched by the executives. Annual pensions for CEOs of major U.S. companies average in the US$700,000 range, and sometimes pass the $1 million mark. This is in addition to the lavish compensation collected while on the job, and is 100 per cent paid by the company. Special goodbye payments aren't unknown, if the standard retirement package is not thought munificent enough. Executive pensions in Canada are probably not much different in large organizations; George Albino, fired in 1987 as chairman and CEO of Rio Algom after a lacklustre performance, was scheduled to get C$557,000 annual retirement pay (in pension and annuity combined); he sued for a fat severance package as well. Edgar Kaiser Jr., when the Bank of British Columbia was taken over by the Hongkong Bank of Canada, managed to get a pension which will pay him $100,000 when he reaches age sixty or sixty-five – this after less than two years at the helm, or the equivalent of about $1.75 million a year in pension allowance based on a working life of thirty-five years.

Inflated U.S. CEO pensions are inflated further with high-paying directorships (usually to the age of seventy), consultant retainers (commonly for five years but sometimes extending to ten years) and a supplemental pension from a contributory plan (for major companies, around US$200,000 a year per CEO comes from the company's share of contributions). "The total is pretty damn nice," comments U.S. pension consultant Thomas Paine. The total can be even nicer than damn nice. When the president of Mobil Corporation retired in 1984, he entered into a consulting arrangement whereby he would be paid $800,000 annually for working half time when he had received not much more – $1.1 million – for working full time previously. The late William Paley, chairman of CBS in his late eighties – effectively retired – picked up $250,000 in chairman's pay in 1989, plus another $200,000 as a consultant, plus another $250,000 in supplemental retirement benefits, plus another $300,000 over two years to "defray a portion of the costs incurred by Mr. Paley in chartering helicopters," according to the CBS proxy statement.

If, on the other hand, the CEO happens to die while still on the job, well, there are now "golden coffins" for that, too. The dead CEO continues to collect his salary for several years (payment goes to the estate) while in the grave – in one extraordinary case, for seven years at US$2.3 million per year. At least 15 per cent of Fortune-500 CEOs have such golden-coffin contracts.

Sometimes the extraordinary incomes include bonuses tied to profit levels, but the standard high pay-outs are made regardless of performance. Probably the best-known case of bureaucratic *hauteur* is General Motors, the North American corporate archetype. In 1982, the company signed a contract with the United Auto Workers involving an array of wage and other union concessions. Then, only a few weeks later, it announced a plan to grant management bonuses that would click in at a lower rate of profit. The outcry was such that GM eventually had to scrap the plan. In 1984, however, with workforce concessions still in place, GM announced that its chairman had been awarded a bonus of $1.5 million because profits had gone up, although the improved profits were largely due to restrictions on Japanese imports. The average executive *bonus*, reaching down to middle-management levels – 5,807 executives in all – was more than the average annual *income* of autoworkers. Even President Reagan's trade representative, a friend to such as GM executives, called the bonuses "unbelievable."

In 1986, GM profits declined 26 per cent or more than US$1 billion from the previous year, so there was no profit-sharing with hourly U.S. and Canadian workers. At the same time GM was slashing its salaried white-collar work force by 25 per cent. But GM's executives got hefty, if reduced, bonuses anyway. The chairman's total bonuses were $1 million and his overall compensation $1.8 million; each of its top five executives made more than $1 million. There was such a storm about that one that in 1987 GM switched to all-stock bonuses – management giving to itself with its left hand what it didn't dare do with its right. In 1987, with profits rising again, the chairman's take from bonuses (the new system) and stock options combined was $1.3 million and his total compensation $2.2 million. Other top executives did correspondingly well. Again, however, there was no profit-sharing with hourly workers because the company had earned too little.

In 1989, GM's profits fell off again, after a couple of years of better profitability. Hourly employees saw their profit-sharing bonus cut back 81 per cent, from US$266 the previous year to $50. The bonus of chairman Roger Smith, however, fell only 7 per cent, to a still whopping $1.4 million. He also received an 11 per cent pay raise, pushing his annual salary to $1.1 million. This maintained his compensation at the level of $2.5 million to which he was accustomed, excluding the exercise of stock options which he also had in hand. At the same time, bonuses were added to pensions for 3,350 top GM managers. Smith, who was about to retire, saw his pension almost double from $700,000 to $1.2 million – this at the same time as GM was pushing a cost-cutting program, when merit raises for middle managers had been frozen because of weak sales, and when GM's market share was continuing to decline. Only in 1990, when GM lost $2 billion, did the CEO take a slight cutback.

But GM wasn't the only case of companies boosting executive pay while insisting on employee concessions. Rates of return of companies can decline or companies can suffer a loss; the compensation of the top executives may go up or hold steady rather than go down. Lee Iacocca admitted that he felt embarrassed about making US$17.9 million in 1987, a year when Chrysler's share of the market slipped and earnings fell, although there was no report that he gave any of the money back. In America, the heartland of private enterprise, such perversities are merely commonplace.

Every year the *Business Week* survey highlights the lowest and highest executive pay relative to profitability (where shareholders "got a bargain" as compared to executives who delivered "the least bang for the bucks"). The anomalies between the two are striking. *Fortune* carries a similar analysis, done by Graef Crystal, a professor at the Haas School of Business, University of California at Berkeley, and widely considered the dean of U.S. compensation consultants. It covers the top 200 U.S. CEOs and is based on a sophisticated multi-factor model (company size, industry, long-term performance, business risk, and the CEO's tenure). Actual pay varies wildly from the computer model's pay measure in each case. One CEO in 1990, Time Warner's Steven Ross, even with just part of his huge bonus counted, managed to get 1,363 per cent more than he should have according to the model, and that measure was based on the "standards of the group," which itself was enormously inflated. The second in line, in the same category, exceeded the computer-model figure by 960 per cent.

Crystal's factor analysis explained only 39 to 45 per cent of the variation in CEO remuneration, from one company to another. "Most of the vast difference in CEO pay cannot be logically accounted for," he concluded, and went on to ask, rhetorically, if "the most popular reference work in the compensation committee's meeting room [was] a table of random numbers."

Even where companies are in a similar line of business, large differences may exist. In one earlier case, highlighted by *Fortune*, the CEO of a dismal performer got almost twice as much as his colleague in a company in the same industry that was a top performer.

Deathbed circumstances don't necessarily mean modest pay for corporate cadres, either. Howard Macdonald, brought in as a nurse to watch over Dome Petroleum's death rattle (it lost $2.2 billion in 1986), took home $2 million in 1987 and close to $3 million in 1988, including bonuses. His main function was a diplomatic one, negotiating among creditors and possible buyers. Compare Macdonald's compensation to the pay for much more serious diplomatic functions in the public sector: a range of $116,000 to $137,000 for the deputy minister of external affairs.

The smaller fry sometimes pick up on going practices. After oil prices fell in early 1986, the Independent Petroleum Association of Canada (IPAC) could be found crying poor and lobbying for drilling incentives from government and favourable tax treatment for exploration work. At the same time, the incoming chairman of IPAC, Dick Gusella, in 1987, was making hay as president of Sceptre Resources. In connection with an acquisition – using his company's money to buy another company – Gusella took a bonus of $350,000. Other executives received an additional $370,000 in bonuses. Gusella also got an interest-free loan of $731,000 to buy Sceptre stock. He also arranged a golden parachute for himself of $750,000 (three times his current salary at the time). When an independent oil-industry analyst in Calgary wondered in print how Gusella could cry poor to the government on IPAC's behalf while indulging in fat bonuses himself, Gusella and IPAC complained with indignation. "I'm sure that government officials would rather deal with someone who's successful than someone who's not," he said.

American cases are still more striking. In fiscal 1989, for example, a Miami savings and loan outfit called CenTrust Bank suffered close to US$120 million in operating losses, on the way to going under. The chairman and CEO allegedly pocketed $4.8 million for his year's work. Among his perks: a forty-foot sloop regulators say was bought with bank money (gold nails which studded the chairman's ninety-foot yacht were also allegedly paid for by the bank). "If there was ever a compensation package that proved you could win by losing," *Fortune* remarked, this was the one. Similar cases surface regularly.

Even if an executive gets a little slap on the wrist for bad results, he'll be able to bear the pain (other than the blow to his ego). To cite two examples among many: Because of a falling return on equity in the years 1985-87, the chairman and CEO of American Express took a 20 per cent pay cut. His annual compensation after the cut was US$3 million including stock options. When returns improved substantially the following year, he took in a whopping $10.9 million, including stock options. When returns fell off again in 1989, he was reduced to a mere $3.5 million and, in 1990, to a miserly $3.4 million. In 1990, despite General Motors' huge loss, CEO Robert Stempel, with his emoluments cut back, could still soothe himself with $1.7 million.

These perversities are part of an historical bureaucratic progression. One study, in the 1970s, showed that of 183 companies reporting lower profits in the year surveyed, only 58 executives received pay cuts while 105 actually received raises. Studies covering data in the mid-1970s and early 1980s showed the same pattern – "absolutely no relationship (either positive or negative) between stockholder return and executive pay," and "very little relationship between executive pay and executive performance," as a 1976 analysis concluded.

All this, however, begs the question of why such extraordinary compensation should be paid, even if it did correlate with performance. Motivation is the excuse most often mentioned, even for golden parachutes, but there was already plenty of motivation before executive compensation mushroomed. If $500,000 was considered lucrative compensation a relatively few years ago, why should $1.5 million or the possibility of $15 million now supposedly be necessary? Indeed, if outsized compensation levels are required for executives to do their job, their motivation is on shaky ground.

The most dynamic period of American companies – the post-war years – occurred without the current excesses. Subsequently, in countries like Japan or Sweden, where the gap between top executive salaries and average employee earnings is smaller, industrial performance and innovation have shaken the United States and have sent its trade balance reeling. Towers Perrin (TPF&C) "Worldwide Total Remuneration" surveys in the late 1980s show U.S. CEO compensation far outpacing CEO remuneration in other technically advanced countries, as measured in U.S. dollars, despite the decline in the value of the U.S. dollar (which would increase the relative size of foreign CEO pay) and despite the much greater purchasing power of money in the United States (allowing U.S. CEOs to do with less).

As of 1 April, 1991, the average CEO's total remuneration in the United States, for firms over US$250 million in sales, was 101 per cent greater than in Japan, 105 per cent greater than in West Germany, 151 per cent greater than in the Netherlands, and 123 per cent greater than in Sweden. Excluding perks (relatively large in Japan), U.S. CEO pay levels would be 147 per cent greater than in Japan. Based on after-tax purchasing power, the differences are even more marked in some cases, with U.S. CEO remuneration 222 per cent greater than in Japan, 113 per cent greater than in West Germany, 186 per cent greater than in the Netherlands, and 270 per cent greater than in Sweden. Those are averages. Because of the high incremental tax levels in Japan for extra-large incomes, anybody pulling down the elephantine salaries of some U.S. CEOs would lose much more of it to the public coffer. The spread between top and bottom level salaries in Japan is considerably smaller than in either the United States or Canada.

Japanese executives have expressed amazement over what many of their American counterparts are pulling in, and not just because of the figures. In these days of high technology, where most innovation comes through incremental adaptations to existing processes and where quality of production and cost-saving are so important, the loyalty and motivation of the workforce are crucial. When a corporate administrator is making forty or fifty times, or a hundred times, or now, on occasion, a thousand times what other employees are making, the greed and cynicism caused by the differential risks breaking down the day-to-day loyalty and commitment of employees, on which so much now depends. The "trust gap," *Fortune* calls it. U.S. management guru Peter Drucker has recommended a maximum 20 to 1 multiple, itself extremely high, and has denounced bloated executive compensation and the "greed effect."

How has this stratospheric remuneration come about? There is no particular mystery to the phenomenon, when one thinks about it. A corporation is a bureaucracy by its nature. Executives boost their remuneration by working the bureaucracy. Two American compensation analysts, W. S. Albrecht and Philip Jhin, in a 1978 study, referred simply to the "corporate power structure." In most corporations, "executives play an important role in determining both the board of directors (who establish CEO salaries) and the compensation policy of their respective firms." They are also "good bargainers" and "excellent politicians." They use their political skills to help them rise to the top, and once there they use the same know-how to justify their huge salaries.

CEOs not only select most board candidates and shepherd their nominations through the board and annual-meeting processes, but also outside (non-executive) board members can be dependent on management for business, making them co-operative. Law firms and investment dealers used by a corporation are often represented on its board. They are not likely to cross the management that gives them work and profits, and that has probably brought them to the board in the first place.

In the Steven Ross (Warner) case, the chairman of the board's compensation committee was partner of a law firm that received fees for doing some of Warner's legal work. He personally received US$1 million in a single year in legal fees from Warner. Four other directors were in-house Warner executives whose own compensation was heavily influenced by the CEO and also by what was handed out to the CEO. In the highly controversial 1987 board decision giving Ross his mammoth and seemingly everlasting emoluments, six board members voted against. They described the contract as "outrageous," which, of course, it was. Four friendlier "outside" board members and the votes of the Warner executives on the board, however, carried the day. Subsequent increased stipends to these executives – including $10 to $15 million each from stock options – followed. So did a richer compensation structure for Time executives after the Time-Warner merger; one couldn't very well, in the bureaucracy, pay the Time cadres less than the Warner cadres, now they were one company.

Consultant contracts are another way for the CEO to help his friends on the board and maintain their cosy relationship. Ross Johnson at RJR Nabisco was a master at stroking his board members in this way. He handed out lucrative personal-services contracts (from US$80,000 to $250,000 a year); assigned work to a director's company (shareholder services); provided an office and secretary to another director; made the corporate jets available to them for any reason, at no charge; and handed out money for a university endowment and a wing of a new building in the name of board members. This was in addition to $50,000 each in directors' fees for a reduced schedule of board meetings. Henry Kissinger's consulting firm in 1989 took in $100,000 for advice to the chairman of American Express and another $320,000 in advice and speaking fees from AmEx subsidiary Shearson Lehman Hutton; Kissinger is an AmEx director. Ex-television anchor Walter Cronkite, a CBS director, received from the company an office, secretarial help, and $600,000 as a consultant.

Lucrative board fees themselves, pushed up steadily with the help of the CEO, are nothing to sneeze at. In 1990, the total average compensation for outside directors of major (US$5 billion in revenue) publicly held U.S. industrial corporations was $44,615; the average of the highest paid on each board was $52,555; and the top quarter of those averaged US$80,035, according to Korn/Ferry International's annual survey. Fees for Canadian corporate directors were much lower, but were undergoing their own inflation. The highest group, the upper quartile of directors of banks, service companies and major industrials ($2 billion in revenue) averaged $48,000 to $49,000 in 1990, according to Korn/Ferry. Perks of all kinds, from pensions to accident insurance, are now also being added to directors' compensation, even though directorships are supposed to be positions of honour (representing shareholders) and though most directors get their primary incomes, plus a full range of perks, elsewhere. There are even now, in a growing number of cases, mini-golden parachutes for directors in case they lose their sinecures because of a takeover.

Part of any bureaucratic process is the ability to adapt to challenges while keeping rank and power intact. In the face of criticism about docile directors, corporate fashion now is leaning towards more "independent" directors on the board. Some academic business-school critics, wanting to save the corporate bureaucracy from itself, have recommended that management be represented on the board by only one person, the CEO, and that this person not be chairman. In practice, however, in Canada and also in the United States, the CEO is likely to be the chairman as well. The board chairmen of three-quarters of U.S. publicly listed companies are also CEOs.

Many other board members will be major executives from other corporations; CEOs like to have other CEOs on their boards. The higher the pay of the outside CEOs from their own companies, the more generous they have to be in approving management compensation for companies where they sit as "outside" board members. The best way for a CEO to inflate his take, said a U.S. organizational psychologist, is to "appoint a new compensation committee member who earns . . . more than he does." These other CEOs are only "outside" directors in a formal sense. In bureaucratic terms, they are part of the same extended family. About three-quarters of the members of compensation committees of publicly listed companies in the United States are current or former corporate executives, and often they are the CEO's friends.

Similarly, the higher the compensation that CEOs hand out in their capacity as "outside" board members, the more leverage they have to increase their remuneration at home. Do they balk when the numbers start getting too big? "That would be like belching at a dinner party," says compensation consultant Graef Crystal.

Patronage flourishes in board appointments, particularly for political cronies, and not just in the United States. Ex-Alberta premier Peter Lougheed has been given directorships and advisory committee posts in a couple of dozen major corporations, from which he collects an estimated $200,000 annually, to add to his other income. Jeanne Lougheed, his wife, has been given four directorships. Bill Davis, Bill Bennett, John Turner, and sundry former federal and provincial cabinet ministers, like Pat Carney (ex-Mulroney cabinet) and Lou Hyndman (ex-Alberta cabinet), have ended up with directorships.

Despite much talk of a new breed of boardroom advisers and an end to the days of the "old boy" network, clubbishness and cronyism are still very much with us. New directors who are not friends or fellow corporate honchos of the CEO are still chosen by the CEO and other board members. These newcomers on the board are not likely to be troublemakers and to raise a fuss over a remuneration matter.

One thing many compensation committees do bother with is to find out what comparable companies ("peer companies" in the jargon) are paying their senior administrators, so their own generosity won't be too far out of line. They thereby cover their own backsides, especially from shareholders' suits. Far from this being a check on extravagantly inflated compensation, however, the practice institutionalizes leapfrogging. Each CEO can make a case for being paid a bit more than the guy who, for some reason or other, has been able to push his own remuneration up. "Executives love to cut out articles on how much [the highest-paid CEOs make] and send them to their compensation committees," says the compensation director of Hay Management Consultants in Philadelphia. Executives' pension inflation works the same way.

Compensation consultants are now a regular part of the bureaucracy, supposedly to provide some objectivity. Through their survey-and-comparison method, however – a method that lends itself to creative ingenuity – they just abet the leapfrogging. Besides, compensation consultants aren't called in by senior management in order to cut costs. Generous recommendations help to retain accounts, and any boost in executive compensation that comes from the consultants' advice isn't out of their own pockets. One widely respected Towers Perrin consultant cheerfully told *Fortune*, "There is a fine line between a compensation consultant and a whore." He recalled two instances where he resigned accounts because he couldn't tolerate the greed of the chief executives involved. "Porcine compensation characteristics," was how he described it. Mostly, compensation consultants oblige.

Stock options and bonuses are other bureaucratic adaptations, and they are superb ones, lying behind most of the gigantic emoluments of the 1980s. They are part of a new fad of what is called "pay-for-performance," a label that came into fashion among executives when grumbling arose that their lucrative pay was not based on performance. The adaptation began in the United States in the early 1980s, but only hit full stride in the satellite corporate culture in Canada later in the decade.

With executive bonuses, everything lies in the devising of them. The more complex and elaborate the plans are, the more that executive self-indulgence can hide itself. A feature article in *Fortune* described the "fine print of proxy statements, which are replete with details, sometimes indecipherable," by which incentive plans "typically hint that they are rigorous, then promptly reveal themselves to be squishy." These plans often parade "shareholder protection formulas" but an examination of the formulas equally often shows they provide "about as much protection as a catcher's mask made of gauze." *Fortune* cited one case (NCR) where a bonus clicked in on a return on equity less than half the median for the Fortune 500 and five percentage points *below* the worst return the company had earned in the previous five years. In another case (Sears, Roebuck), the bonus was triggered by a performance "at or above the median of the bottom third of its peer group sample." In plain language, if Sears, Roebuck worked its way up to the top of the bottom sixth of the pack, not as good as 83 per cent of the field, bonuses to its executives would still be paid out.

"Carry over" is another useful bonus device. If executive bonuses aren't earned one year, they are carried over to the next year, and so on. When bonuses are finally distributed sometime down the line – perhaps only because a general economic upswing makes the company look good – the previously unpaid bonuses get paid out, too. If worst comes to worst – if profits don't generate a bonus pool and there is no carryover – the company can always liberalize the rules so it can keep on paying bonuses anyway. This was the caper that General Motors' top executives attempted in 1982.

Another variant allows bonus seekers to pursue "individual objectives" and to have their performance measured against them. It sounds good in proxy statements, but allows management plenty of liberty for rigging the reward. "Super-squish," commented *Fortune*. The long-term bonus plans "are much less a reward for performance these days than an institutionalized variety of salary . . . another layer on top of salary, short-term bonus, stock options, stock appreciation rights, and cooperative-apartment carrying costs." "Base salary in drag," snorted U.S. compensation consultant Graef Crystal.

Nothing quite beats stock options, though. Compensation committees can hand them out freely because they appear not to cost anything, although, by watering the stock, they cost shareholders every bit as much as a cash allocation. Since the big pay-off to executives comes when stock appreciates, and since shareholders' stock appreciates at the same time, the shareholders can be mollified. The result is the huge and widespread annual pay-outs in the millions of dollars, up to that record US$186 million to the chairman of Lin Broadcasting in 1990. Nor is any entrepreneurial risk involved; the options don't have to be exercised. A sag in the stock price isn't critical, either. Executives can simply wait until the price improves before exercising their options and cashing in. In the meantime, they can expect new option grants the next year at a lower price, so that when the stock does eventually go back up, they will make even more. Heads, the CEO and his colleagues win; tails, they don't lose. As if that still weren't enough, a new device was invented called a "reload option," which tops up the original options if they are not exercised to maximum advantage.

While the cadres lap up the gravy in a bull market, from their options, many, depending on their leverage, are not left bereft in a bear market either. After the October 1987 crash, the sympathy in many boardrooms for the plight of top executives was such that stock options issued at the peak of the market were reissued at a new, lower, profit-enhancing price. (When share prices recovered after the crash, the executives who had their stock options reissued at a lower post-crash price were able to pocket a double windfall!) This bailing out of "waterlogged" or "underwater" stock options – options which would cost more to exercise than buying shares on the market – may even happen when the stock market hangs on, but when the individual stock declines. These option swaps, American writers Mark Green and John Berry remarked in their 1985 book on the "corpocracy," are "akin to the house allowing a poker player to change his bet after seeing his opponent's hand."

The bailing out may be of underwater stocks actually owned and not just of underwater options. One compensation gimmick is to grant executives no- or low-interest loans for the purchase of huge blocks of shares below market price. This is a dispensation in itself. When these shares go underwater, however, the executives then find themselves holding a debt larger than the stock's value. Why not have the company, in the name of enlightened compensation policy, make up the shortfall?

Another ploy, used following the 1987 crash, was "Godzilla grants" – giving the executive an option for an immense number of shares at a new, lower price, as compensation for the market collapse. And he could keep the old options at the same time. Graef Crystal, looking at the years 1986-1988, discovered that only about one-seventh of the gains in stock-option compensation could be explained by rising stock prices. Most of the increase came from larger grants, the replacement of underwater options, and other factors. Still another gambit, the extent of which is uncertain, was to comfort executives for stock value lost in the crash by bigger-than-normal cash bonuses.

One excuse bruited about for all this was that executives couldn't really control their company's stock price and, therefore, they should not be penalized for a market downturn. No such reasoning, of course, was heard in the bull market stretching from 1982 to 1987, when stock prices were rising uncontrollably and the same executives as a result were reaping enormous returns.

But the excuse itself for the gravy – that there is a link between stock options and enhanced performance – was itself hollow. Corporate performance is not just the work of a group of executives, much less of the one or two persons at the top of the hierarchy. In advanced manufacturing (which, these days, is almost all manufacturing) and in most service industries, the commitment and creativity of rank-and-file employees often make the difference. The gains of a company, further, may come from external factors like a rise in commodity prices, or a general economic boom, or a bull market, where everybody's stock appreciates. Or the share value of a poorly run company may rise because of a takeover, with the inept managers who allowed the company to founder in the first place making hay with their options.

Common sense says as much about the stock-option gimmick. After all, companies have done superbly well, their stock has appreciated – often rapidly – and executives have been motivated, without this inflated pay-off which corporate bureaucracies have now institutionalized.

Recent studies have confirmed the absence of a performance connection, not just with options but also with the fat executive bonuses. One of the more recent, by California management consultant James H. Carbone, examining 180 companies that were regulars on the Fortune 500 list, and checking ten measures of performance over twenty-five years, found no statistically significant correlation between performance and stock-option compensation. Companies without option plans did as well as companies with them. Another, by Graef Crystal, based on pay-for-performance sensitivity and covering 430 companies over ten years, came up with similar results.

The so-called "incentive compensation," like bonuses and stock options, moreover, has not been accompanied by balancing cuts in salary. It has just been piled on top, and in bigger and bigger dollops, even relative to the base salary, which itself rose faster than inflation. According to a U.S. Towers Perrin vice-president, cited by *Fortune*, option packages not too long ago used to approximate annual base salary, based on total value on the grant date. This already represented a huge extra dispensation. Now the median, as at the beginning of 1990, is almost twice base salary, and many CEOs get "megagrants."

The corporate cadres in the New Bureaucracy are able in this way to pocket anything up to several hundred times the compensation of their counterparts in the much-maligned old bureaucracy (government).

In their dissection of the corpocracy in America, *The Challenge of Hidden Profits: Reducing Corporate Bureaucracy and Waste*, writers Mark Green and John Berry revealed something else – how senior corporate executives have flitted from fashion to fashion in compensation, according to external events, in order to inflate their remuneration regardless of circumstances. In the 1920s, with stock market values gradually spiralling, stock options were in mode. When stocks fell through the floor during the Depression, higher fixed salaries were the latest in corporate compensation. With extraordinary tax rates on high earned incomes in the 1940s and 1950s, deferred and "unearned" compensation (stocks and bonds) came into fashion. With cuts in maximum personal income tax in the 1960s, companies (that is, their top executives) began to emphasize the importance of salaries and perks again. At each stage, undoubtedly, there were high-flown rationalizations for one mode rather than another. What was happening, of course, was bureaucratic adaptation. When, in the late 1970s and early 1980s, the United States suffered two severe recessions – and when foreign competition showed how deficient many U.S. corporations were – the bureaucratic adaptation continued and executive compensation leapt up anyway.

The perks and luxuries of office are something special in their own right, however much annual remuneration of $1 million or $2 million or $20 million might buy for a corporate administrator. They express status every day, physically, in luxury and pleasure – not through money from one's own pocket but as part of the firm and its power to dispense, where some are chosen. The perks gratify a bureaucratic hedonism.

Some of the luxuries hang on the walls and stand on the floors. Osler Inc., the Toronto stockbrokerage firm which closed its doors in December 1987 with a shortfall of $65 million and counting (charges followed), titillated observers with its fittings and accoutrements. "Incredibly opulent," remarked a representative of Maynards, the auctioneer hired by the receiver. In the dining-room, executives were served on Royal Worcester china, drank from crystal champagne and sherry glasses (156 pieces, all told), and were illuminated by brass chandeliers. The style was mostly Regency, although the boardroom table, with its inlaid leather placemats, was surrounded by sixteen Art-Nouveau-style chairs in mahogany and leather, worth about $1,500 each. The seven wing-chairs in the library, of course, were also in leather. One of the finest installations was the CEO's private bathroom – brass fixtures and shower – off the "presidential suite." Osler Inc. had two kitchens, one for the general staff and one for the senior executives. The latter had a special refrigerator with its trays designed to hold only bottles of champagne and wine.

The ostentatious Osler scene was only a sliver of the New Bureaucracy's indulgences. A newspaper report on the auction of Osler's properties commented that, for all the dazzle of the company's fineries, they may have been surpassed in expense by the furnishings of some of the larger firms on Bay Street.

Some U.S. cases show how far the indulgences can go. One of the most revealing involved the debt-ridden energy conglomerate Diamond Shamrock, which suffered large, persistent losses in the mid-1980s and went through corporate restructurings like changes of clothing. It also had a lavish twelve-thousand-acre ranch on the Texas prairie for corporate entertainment, a US$1 million box at the Dallas Cowboys' home stadium, and a fleet of airplanes to whisk the CEO and his directors around the world.

Diamond Shamrock officers received munificent remuneration, too. The CEO in 1985, before taking a pay cut, earned US$892,000 in cash compensation, in a year when the company lost $605 million. Despite lay-offs and asset sales elsewhere in the company, the lavish perks seemed to survive. The ranch, Riverside Farms, was defended as typical of the hunting camps favoured by oil companies (with its extensive acreage, spacious lodge, and two tennis courts, the local tax assessor valued it at $9 million). It was used for corporate meetings and entertainment. Among the visitors was a professional shoot manager, whom the company flew in regularly from Ireland to organize pheasant hunts for customers and Diamond Shamrock executives. During the Republican national convention in 1984, company-chartered helicopters flew guests to the ranch for a media reception honouring a Nevada senator. Wives of directors regularly flew, at company expense, on ostensible business trips to such places as Indonesia, Hong Kong, Europe, Alaska, and Brazil – several such excursions, apparently, being for directors meetings that could have been held at home. Nominations to the Diamond Shamrock board were clubbish matters, sometimes involving reciprocal board seats with other corporations.

Corporate raider T. Boone Pickens humorously described the hunting lodges and other places where the "Good Ol' Boys" at the top of the corporate branch met. "You can usually find their corporate planes on the tarmac at the U.S. Open, the Super Bowl, the Masters, and the Kentucky Derby," he wrote. "The clubhouse is movable, and it moves a lot." There are corporate yachts moored in harbours across the continent. The hunting or fishing lodge might also belong to the company, at the shareholders' expense. Sometimes the CEOs would bring their vice-presidents along and use them like butlers and valets, and the vice-presidents in turn, acting out of fear, scurried accordingly. "Where's his coat? Where's his gun?" they fussed to one another. Size-of-company envy and perk envy occupied the CEOs' egos. Even with the most liberal allowance for how perks were used, some indulgences still went too far. The wife of one executive, Pickens recounted, used a company plane to take her dog to the veterinarian.

(Pickens' delight at tearing a strip off the other guy's corporate bureaucracy also went to show that there is no honour among corporate bureaucrats, for Pickens himself was an adept bureaucratic player. While becoming something of a shareholders' folk hero for roasting large companies, particularly large oil companies, he had manoeuvred his own bureaucracy, Mesa Petroleum, to his advantage. When Mesa cashed in from greenmailing Gulf Oil in 1984 [being bought off by Gulf Oil to avoid a takeover possibility], US$20 million was set aside as a special reward for Mesa employees; Pickens himself collected $18.6 million of that, taken in deferred compensation units. Similar compensation arrangements, and "barbed-wire" protective devices for them, followed suit. Aside from that: In good years, like 1984 and 1985, Pickens' ordinary compensation [base pay and cash bonuses] was roughly three times the figure for the chairman of Exxon, although Mesa's revenues were less than one two-hundreths of Exxon's. At that rate, Pickens could well afford to fly his wife's dog to a veterinarian himself.)

Allegheny International, the conglomerate best known for its Sunbeam and Oster appliances, provides another illustration from the 1980s. Using a dummy corporation, it bought a magnificent Tudor home in one of Pittsburgh's best neighbourhoods, and furnished it to suit, in a year when the company lost a record US$109 million. The excuse was the ostensible lack of a decent hotel in Pittsburgh for entertaining directors and important clients. A condominium on the Rolling Rock estate, a favourite corporate resort location, was acquired. The company's fleet of five jets (wisecrackers called it the "Allegheny Air Force") ferried executives back and forth, and was used to visit vacation homes, take families on trips, and transport guests to the wedding of one of the chairman's daughters; it was unclear how much of these costs, if any, were ever reimbursed to the company.

More than US$30 million in loans at 2 per cent interest was made available to executives. Sons and daughters of senior executives were placed on the payroll. The chairman's son was appointed manager of a Manhattan hotel that Allegheny owned and was allowed to live in the penthouse, which had just been renovated with marble bathrooms and elaborate panelling at a cost of more than $1 million. Annual management meetings were held in places like Boca Raton, Florida, and the Bahamas. Up to a hundred management personnel and spouses were flown in from around the world. At one such get-together, an ice sculpture costing about $10,000 decorated the banquet table. Former executives disclosed they were allowed to take weekend vacations to London and Washington at company expense. Meanwhile, the company was getting burned from a series of poorly thought-out business ventures and going downhill fast.

The board that allowed this to happen had nine blue-chip outside directors, among them former U.S. secretary of state Alexander Haig, the CEO of H. J. Heinz, noted French commentator Jean-Jacques Servan-Schreiber, and sports marketing figure Mark McCormack. Some of them, in their capacity as Allegheny directors, were also onto a good thing in the way of consultant contracts. Haig was given a contract with Allegheny that paid him US$50,000 a year for providing advice "in the area of safety and protection devices" no more than five days a year – or $10,000 a day, plus his director's retainer. Two consulting firms McCormack was associated with did work for Allegheny. Two other outside directors received money from the company beyond their normal directors' fees, and a fifth received large commissions prior to becoming a director. Allegheny subsequently filed for bankruptcy protection under Chapter 11, the well-known U.S. provision for such cases.

RJR Nabisco during the late 1980s, under CEO Ross Johnson, eclipsed even these cases, and then some. The corporate indulgence in Johnson's day has been detailed by reporters Bryan Burrough and John Helyar in their 1990 best-seller *Barbarians at the Gate*. The extravagance, opulence, and throwing around of money on luxury and pleasure mock belief. Merely to read the particulars is exhausting.

Little of the RJR Nabisco story would have become widely known had there not been an extraordinary leveraged buy-out of the company in which Johnson, trying a buy-out of his own, was the loser, and had the two reporters not written their book about it. Similarly, it's not likely *Business Week*, which exposed both the Allegheny and Diamond Shamrock cases, would have latched on to them if the companies hadn't botched deals and otherwise run into trouble. "Such perks are hardly unique," the magazine allowed. And, indeed, the ridiculed Allegheny Air Force with its five jets hardly compared, for example, with the fifty airplanes and helicopters that conglomerate Allied-Signal had at the time, or even with the fleet of twelve to which Allied-Signal reduced itself later in a show of spartan self-restraint, New-Bureaucracy style. Other examples abound. What seemed to bother the magazine most about Allegheny's excesses was that record-keeping was often lax, so that the perks weren't properly accounted for, and that the company was living beyond its means. If there had been the cash flow to spring the means for the indulgences, presumably they wouldn't have been worth mentioning. In fact, in a story on Ross Johnson and RJR Nabisco in mid-1988, *Business Week*, while critical in some other matters, skirted the subject of its lavish spending. Such spending was different in degree, perhaps, but not in kind.

In this fashion, indulgences increase to fill the bureaucratic possibilities. They build up into a *grande bouffe* of perk consumption. "Executive sweets," authors Green and Berry called them. "Bennies" (from benefits) is business-journalism slang for them. "Satisfiers" is what clinically minded executives and consultants sometimes call them, in jargonistic evasion – the perk that satisfies, or is it the satisfier that perks? The term differentiates perks, in turn, from rich cash-compensation arrangements, euphemistically called "motivators."

Stock options and golden parachutes are technically perks. So are other solid dispensations such as supplemental pensions, life insurance, disability insurance (quite expensive), and soft loans (interest-free or at half the market rate). Individual financial counselling is another perk, one provided to most senior executives in major U.S. and Canadian companies (U.S. plans pay from US$5,000 to $10,000 a year per executive, for up to four visits, including help with income-tax forms); cadres, in this way, get inflated compensation and then an inflated perk to help look after it. But those are only the basics, to start with.

The Hay Group's 1990 survey of perks, covering 2,000 individual executives in Canada, found that 85 per cent of them receive a company car or car allowance, 31 per cent get fitness or racquet club memberships, 50 per cent enjoy dispensations for country club memberships (including golf and curling clubs) and 52 per cent have luncheon club memberships looked after ($10,000 in initiation fees and up to $2,000 in annual dues, for top Toronto clubs). More than half the cadres surveyed have "executive medical examinations" laid on (57 per cent); they don't have to put up with just an ordinary visit to a doctor. Top dogs, naturally, do best: 100 per cent snaffle company cars or allowances with, usually, chauffeurs attached, and 82 per cent pick up luncheon club memberships. Sabbaticals with pay, executive vacations, and rides on the company airplane are popular. "Surprise packages," *Canadian Business* magazine called them, in a special "Compensation Planner" supplement. Season hockey tickets, free travel for the wife on executive business trips (no mention of male spouses of women executives), clothing allowances, and even free dry cleaning, and, of course, the proverbial executive washroom also appeal to cadres.

Style counts as well. About a third of respondents in a 1986 survey said it was important that their company car be a luxury import. Corporate bureaucrats become attached to their perks. "In one of my cases," said a lawyer handling a termination dispute, "we wrangled more over the BMW than any other detail." In Canada, a company car is no longer standard issue, because of tax changes; some firms pay mileage and parking instead. In Britain, hours of management time go into deciding which grade of employee should get what car, according to hierarchical niceties and distinctions.

Golf club memberships in Canada, of the kind to which corporate bureaucrats like to become accustomed, range from $16,000 for the Calgary Golf and Country Club to $36,500 for the Shaughnessy Golf and Country Club in Vancouver and $40,000 for the Rosedale Golf Club in Toronto. Some of the newer Toronto-area clubs are even pricier: the National Golf Club at $65,000, Devil's Pulpit at $55,500, and Beacon Hall at $50,000 (it once hit $77,000). Annual dues are on top of that. The corporate memberships and expense accounts for guests (part of which is paid for by the public in lost corporate taxes) come in handy. Some mindful U.S. corporations are urging golf on junior executives as a necessary business skill. Talking business while on the links is taboo, but that's not the point. Costly country club memberships are particularly important to CEOs in Japan, not just for the golf but also for that most important of executive compensations – status. Membership in Tokyo's Koganei Country Club, traded on the stock exchange, costs from US$2 million to $3.5 million depending on the stock price on any particular day.

Executive retreats, for setting onwards-and-upwards common goals and for bonding executives away from the interruptions of the office, also come with golf, Châteaubriand, or *nouvelle cuisine*, tennis (The Inn at Manitou even has a professional tennis program), indoor/outdoor pools, private saunas, Jacuzzis, downhill and cross-country skiing, fishing, windsurfing, antique-furnished rooms, snowmobile safaris, horseback riding, and a landing pad for the company helicopter. (By comparison, the old-style, pre-bureaucratic retreat reputedly featured drunken company presidents humiliating themselves, and executives of all kinds going wild at poker games and losing their cars and houses, plus romantic trysts that broke up marriages. These stories are told to add burnish to the ruthlessly planned, luxury-cushioned modern versions by comparison, and to ease any guilt feelings about the money spent on them.)

Moving expenses? When it comes to top corporate bureaucrats, anything goes. A 1990 survey of 300 corporations by a New York human resources (read "personnel") consulting firm showed companies paid for the move of 30,000 chinchillas (cost: US$250,000), an antique sailboat ($40,000), orchids and other exotic plants ($30,000), 3,000 cases of wine ($15,000), an army halftrack ($12,500), a hook-and-ladder fire engine ($9,000), and a walk-in bank vault (subsequently turned into the foyer of a home, $8,000). "Aw, c'mon guys," *Fortune* complained. The average cost of relocating top managers in the United States was $110,000, up a monumental 175 per cent from $40,000 in 1986.

After that come the low-interest or no-interest loans to help transferred corporate cadres buy the new homes they move into, and sometimes reimbursement for taxes they have to pay because of those loans.

A little bit like in decadent Pompeii, the horizon is open for inventiveness. One new product for corporate communications and in-house use is limited-edition perfumes (at $120 an ounce) blended especially for one's company; minimum order is fifty ounces or $6,000. McDonald's Restaurants of Canada, Labatt Brewing, and Northern Telecom are among past and present customers. Imagine a member of the old bureaucracy – a deputy minister, say – ordering up vials of shiveringly expensive, custom-blended Essence de Public Works Department.

Offices are also bureaucratically important. "Of the trappings of power [in the corporate world] there is an abundance," reports *Forbes*, "chiefly in the form of executive offices the size of drill halls. Drop-dead vistas are effective, too, for conveying a sense of power without anyone's saying a word." A desk in an office has to have the appropriate tools of the trade. Executive fittings now available include everything from a designer tape dispenser ($50) to a Mont Blanc fountain pen ($365), a leather desk agenda ($800), an antique thermal pitcher and tray ($700), an oversized-pocket-watch desk clock ($3,000) and, to work off the tension of a hostile takeover or a proxy battle, an executive yoyo (oak with leather centre sporting a brass Hermes horse logo, $170), sales tax extra.

One of the accoutrements of the corporate office is art work. The New Bureaucracy is the Medicis of the modern world, and the CEOs are the dons of these Medici families. A leader in the United States, where there are an estimated 1,000 corporate collectors, is Pepsico. "We're gonna turn that cow pasture into a new Versailles," the chairman told a protestor when the company moved to an upper-class, horsy section of Westchester County in New York state. "The Sun King of soft drinks," *Fortune* dubbed him. Ten major sculptures decorating the Pepsico grounds are now worth a total of about $14 million.

Epicurean restaurant feeding is another case where indulgence is routinely counted as a business expense. A list of all the high-priced restaurants in Canada, from Winston's down, kept alive by the corporate perk system would fill a catalogue. This minor class of perks alone comes to C$2.6 billion (including convention meals, indulgence by professional partnerships, and so on) – not surprising when a vice-president and a few clients have been known to run up a lunch bill of $1,100. In the dark days of 1981, *Canadian Business* reported the lament of a Halifax *maître d'* that sales of Dom Perignon had fizzled. This was as good a measure as any of bureaucratic fortunes.

Cadres with private dining-rooms, meanwhile, enjoy a level of status of their own. Private dining-rooms are particularly popular with banks, insurance companies, and investment dealers – corporate bureaucrats among corporate bureaucrats. The facilities of the larger banks include spacious anterooms for drinks and several small dining-rooms in addition to the main room. The Royal Bank has a *sommelier* as well as a *maître d'*. Appointments are lavish. The *Financial Post*, recognizing the bureaucratic importance of such finery, once ran a gushing feature on the dining-rooms, mentioning even the table service – transluscent British bone china, Royal Doulton Rochelle ("a white dish with a purple and gold edging"), Coalport bone ("plain white with a royal blue edging"), and so on, to the very Irish linens.

Pampered travel is another perk to which one can become attached. Top-end models in corporate jets – including the Challenger and the Gulfstreams – run from US$19 million to $25 million, plus hefty operating, maintenance, insurance, and hangar costs (a mere medium-size executive jet costs about $2,000 an hour to operate). Some CEOs have less modest tastes; Boeing 727s fit the bill.

Lesser executives who travel by commercial airlines don't do badly, either, in first-class or business-class carriage. The gushy pandering by airlines to the executive traveller, most visible in television commercials and described at length in special reports in the business press, is a chase for these full-fare sales. "A whole new world of services makes every business trip a fantastic voyage . . . pampered luxury" *Canadian Business* exulted. Champagne, snazzy wines, twelve-year old Scotch blends and single-malts, caviar, prawns, dessert tables, amenity kits in leather-bound cases, individually wrapped slippers, baggage check-in and check-out privileges, airport lounges (with free drink thrown in), and five or six times as many flight attendants per passenger as in the back of the plane are some of the touches. At the end of the flight – for those who really count – tarted up "business-class" hotel rooms await, from $200 to $300 a night.

Access to sports events is part of the bureaucratic culture, folded into corporate entertainment and sales promotion. Corporate boxes at National Football League stadiums and season tickets to National Hockey League games are routine bureaucratic extensions. The U.S. Super Bowl is another big bureaucratic occasion. Location is no object. For one game involving the New York Giants, the demand for tickets by New York-based corporations, as reported by ticket resellers, was extraordinarily high, although the game was being held in Pasadena, California. The corporate jet would come in handy. The bureaucratic corporate buyers no doubt played a considerable role in forcing up prices towards the US$1,500 mark for a seat between the 30-yard lines (the face value of the tickets was $75). This was of no consequence to one firm that asked a reseller for fifty tickets no matter the cost.

In Toronto, twenty-five corporations invested C$5 million each in the SkyDome and received exclusive supplier rights, free luxury boxes and parking. They also got places on the board of the Stadium Corporation. (Later, when the stadium ownership was restructured, most dropped their ownership interests.) Other corporations to whose businesses Blue Jay games were important had to be satisfied with a luxury box renting for $100,000-$225,000 a year (ten-year leases only), plus up to $15,000 annually in business taxes. Fittings and accoutrements are extra, and competitive emulation is the rule; $70,000 is the average cost for that bit of show. One sample box, with marble washrooms and exquisite furnishings, came in at $200,000. The 161 luxury boxes have all been taken. About 95 per cent of stadium skyboxes in the U.S. and Canada are corporate-owned. There is even, now, a *Skybox* magazine to help cadres keep track of the latest.

Season tickets, by comparison, hardly count at all – four for $7,200 (in the golds) for the Maple Leafs and $5,670 for four of the best to watch the

Blue Jays. But they're still a perk. About 90 per cent of Blue Jays' season-ticket holders are corporations, professional partnerships (lawyers, accountants, and so on), and other firms. Four VIP season tickets to the forty-three home games of the Los Angeles Lakers cost in the US$62,000 range. For real corporate players, season tickets are essential, not to cover all the games but to ensure that tickets are on hand for play-offs, finals, and tight end-of-season races. Opera and other high-price cultural events are well used, too.

Sports sponsorship is the latest in corporate marketing (US$1.7 billion in the United States, as of 1990). One of the extra perks, for the corporate branch, is hospitality facilities at the events, where cadres can impress clients and employees and do some hobnobbing. Hospitality tents at the U.S. Open golf tournament each cost $100,000 (catering and entertainment packages extra). Four five-year debentures for Wimbledon cost a mere £77,000, or approximately C$30,000 per year; after all, Wimbledon doesn't last that long. Canadian corporate cadres do their best to emulate their American and British peers. "Several companies entertained guests under corporate marquees during the matches," the *Financial Post* reported, so genteelly, of one such event, a Player's Challenge women's professional tennis tournament in Toronto. The paper carries a regular social column noting these and other bureaucratic get-togethers.

The restaurants, hunting and fishing lodges, sports and cultural events, and the hospitality spin-offs of sponsorship fall loosely under the convenient rubric of "entertainment." According to *The Economist* – which once did a detailed guide, in bureaucratic celebration of what was to be had – British firms spend an estimated C$4 billion a year entertaining clients and friends at cultural and sports events and elsewhere. The Japanese spend Y5 trillion ($40 billion) on "business" entertaining, as of 1990, about the gross domestic product of Ireland. The giant Mitsubishi group, the magazine reported, is estimated to spend each year a sum equivalent to the Israeli government's budget. These perks are one of the ways of getting around high taxes on income in Japan.

With the globalization of the bureaucracy, international comparisons are made and competitive emulation flourishes. *The Economist* dutifully rated each event in its "guide" according to business value, exclusivity, ambience, food, and opulence, wasting no details. In Britain, for example, readers learned, the "Season" includes Wimbledon, Ascot week, Derby week on Epsom Downs, the cricket matches at Lord's, and the Henley rowing regatta. Lobster and Krug champagne are downed at Epsom Downs; salmon and strawberries and ice cream are traditional Wimbledon fare. Citicorp, for one international bank gathering, once took over Union Station in Washington for an evening, filled it with thousands of cocktail-imbibing guests, and threw in an assortment of circus acts to keep the guests happy. It's a lifestyle for bureaucratic cadres that, as *The Economist* put it, "was once a preserve of aristocrats and self-made millionaires" – not the impossible "free lunch," but something even better, a very expensive lunch paid for by one's bureaucratic section.

Another perk that comes with sponsorship, and with endorsement contracts, is hanging around with the chic and the famous. It's one of the reasons why Ross Johnson at RJR Nabisco had so many famous athletes and ex-athletes on retainer. These are psychic perks for a corporate bureaucrat who has everything. A round of golf with a Jack Nicklaus, a morning's tennis with a John McEnroe, or trading hockey stories with a Wayne Gretzky isn't to be sneezed at. Sponsorship of opera performances allows one to rub shoulders with scintillating prima donnas and charismatic tenors; a bit of cultural patina and status.

Personal appearances and speeches by the stars – at annual sales conferences, promotional events, or for the production of corporate videos – offer the same shoulder-rubbing possibilities. There are now celebrity brokers who buy and sell star performers and personalities for corporate clients. A-list celebrities on the books of Celebrity Productions, London, start at US$20,000 for a television anchor or top comedian, up to the $100,000 range for an Engelbert Humperdinck. That's for between two hours and a whole day. Ronald Reagan and Margaret Thatcher come in at around $50,000 per appearance. General Norman Schwarzkopf, trading on his Gulf War fame, charges a reported $75,000. One growth area, *The Economist* reports, is "mingling." "A hard night's mingling, being introduced as the company chairman's oldest friend," it noted with a sliver of sarcasm, earns a typical celebrity around $4,000. The maxi-indulgence was Fujisankei Communications' $7 million outlay in 1989 for a week-long visit to Tokyo by Ronald and Nancy Reagan ($2 million to the Reagans for exclusive interviews and a couple of twenty-minute speeches by the former president, and $5 million in expenses, not counting the salaries of two dozen staffers who worked full-time on the visit).

Meeting with peers, politicking, and facing the public – working routines of the corporate bureaucracy – generate another set of bureaucratic costs. The cadres spend freely on arrangements and on themselves.

If corporate bureaucrats want to get away from it all, they can go to policy and strategy conferences and rub elbows with their peers in other organizations. The *Financial Post* is probably the largest bureaucratic subsection providing these conferences in Canada, including an annual "Executive Day: For Corporate Decision Makers" and a luncheon of the "business elite" to toast the Financial Post 500. "Executive Compensation" sessions are also recurrent. The prices are stiff for a layperson but not for the corporate organizations that foot the bill: $325 for a half day, $525 for a day, and $695 for two days, exclusive of hotel accommodation, are sample fees. Other strategy conferences have charged as high as $1,150 for three days, exclusive of travel and hotels. For a corporate bureaucracy that may pay its CEO $4,000 a day, these conference fees are nominal.

Company-paid conferences can also be used to help political friends financially in the same way that they can provide an excuse for expenses-paid fun in Hawaii or Acapulco. One fundraiser in Vancouver, at $1,000 per head, was organized to pay off the debt of defeated Social Credit leadership candidate Bud Smith. Because it featured a discussion on public policy between pollsters Allan Gregg and Martin Goldfarb, it could be officially classified as a conference, and the executives who threw in their corporations' money could have it written off in the company books as a business expense.

To ensure that the CEO or an executive of lesser stripe does not pick up the wrong fork at lunch, particularly while entertaining fellow CEOs and other important personages, etiquette consultants are now on hire for corporate use. "In the boardrooms of the nation," a magazine for executives once explained, "it is understood that the traditional civilities of senior levels of government, of the private schools, of the military, and of what used to be called the upper classes, are observed strictly as a matter of course." Etiquette discussion groups, courses, seminars, and one-on-one consulting sessions for corporate executives are a minor growth industry. The leading guru is American Letitia Baldridge, author of the *Complete Guide to Executive Manners*, whose crash-course one-day seminars cost US$400 per person. Baldridge has even formed a "corporate manners" division in her public relations company. An Ottawa image consultant charges C$1,495 for a corporate seminar for 15 to 150 people and $125 per hour for private counselling (clothes selection and speaking, as well as poise and manners, are covered).

"Power dressing" offered a bit of niche consulting work paid out of corporate coffers – advice on how to dress. This has been succeeded by consulting in "power behaviour" or "charisma training." One Colorado management consultant teaches executives how to develop personal magnetism – for $2,000 a day or $4,500 for a seminar. Such brilliant ideas as firm handshakes, good posture, and putting purposeful pauses into one's walk are part of the curriculum. So is sitting down ("move the chair out one inch to establish territory, slide into the chair from front to back," and, for the ultimate power pose, turn slightly and plant an elbow on the armrest). Her blue-chip business is booming.

Also available to executives are public-speaking lessons, to help enhance the CEO's profile. Media-relations experts are a growing subsection of the corporate branch of the New Bureaucracy as it explains and defends its territory and actions. Firms with names like Executive Speaking, Corporate Communications, and Communications Counsel multiply – full of ex-broadcasters leaving, or laid off from, broadcasting work proper, who see a lucrative opportunity in this bureaucratic subsection. Sample U.S. fee for a one-day senior executive course (including public speaking): US$2,500 per person in a class of six. An individual one-on-one session runs up to $3,200 for a day with hefty increments for extra time. Custom-tailored, multi-day "clinics," with background research into company issues – preparing for any contingency – have a higher, pricey fee range of their own, up to $35,000, all expenses included, for a group of twelve. "Glamour schools," the media-image companies are known in the trade.

Speech-writing is another subsection of this branch, helping to serve up pronouncements on whatever subject is hot, from international competitiveness to the deficit. A speechwriter may even script a formal presentation to a board meeting, to help the uncertain CEO ensure that everything is the way it should be – a hand-holding function. Top freelance speechwriters charge US$6,000 to a rumoured high of $12,000 for a major speech. One well-known cadre has managed up to eight speeches a month. The high speechwriter's fee adds to the CEO's sense of well-being. There is also, now, such a thing as a "corporate humour consultant," not a little unlike the court jester of old. One such, a former stand-up comic in California, realized that the corporate bureaucracy had more money for the trade than the nightclubs and entertainers for whom he used to work, so he switched clientele. He charges $195 for a page of ten to twelve specifically tailored jokes. He also coaches delivery, presumably for a supplemental fee, a kind of "jokesperson training." AT&T, Arthur Andersen and Company, and Xerox have been clients.

No handholding service for CEOs and other executives is quite as important, though, as management consultants – a bureaucratic section that has increased in prestige, individual pay and collective revenue in proportion to the incompetence, bewilderment, insecurity, or lack of imagination of the executive within the corporate bureaucracy.

Canadian CEOs shell out half a billion dollars a year for management consultants who, for all their other skills, have to be bureaucratically agile and stylish. A much-in-demand U.S. consultant sees his work as teaching managers how to manage, notwithstanding that anybody who gets to become CEO or vice-president is supposed to know how to manage already.

Some consulting work is clear enough, like technical assistance, instruction in new technology and management practices, or dealing with specific problems for which there isn't in-house expertise or available executive time.

One popular reason for using consultants is, simply, to get an outside viewpoint. Restructuring and other organizational advice also may be involved, although whether the consultants actually know better than the client is anybody's guess.

But corporate executives – bureaucratic players – also retain management consultants for bureaucratic functions, with the consultant acting as a bureaucrat for hire, to play a role in the game. Writer Jerry White, in an amusing article in the former *Successful Executive* magazine, even gave the functions code names. In "Whitewash," for example, a CEO will hire consultants in advance of an embarrassing annual meeting or disclosure. When the company's poor results are raised, he can point out that consultants are at work and the situation is in hand. Or consultants will be hired by an executive faction to support their case in an internal battle: "Company Politics." The faction taking the initiative has the advantage of hiring the consultant most likely to serve its purpose. The process also allows the sponsors of the work to discuss the consultants' report in draft stage, to challenge what they don't like and to recommend changes. One overly frank executive told White he had been forced to rewrite the consultants' report three times, and even then they hadn't got it right.

In "The Hired Assassin," the real purpose of the consultant is to back up the chief executive's desire to fire somebody, through a performance assessment or, more bureaucratically suave, through a reorganization (Lee Iacocca wrote in his biography that the prestigious consultants McKinsey & Co. were used in this way by Henry Ford II to get rid of him at Ford Motor Company). Some consultants turn this work down because they know, from experience, that the boss and not the subordinate may be the real problem. In the "Cover My Ass" function, the consultants are brought in to do the homework and to recommend a line of attack. If the decisions taken turn out to be less than superb, the CEO and his colleagues can slough the responsibility off on the consultants' report. A CEO need never make a tough or upsetting decision on his own. The more prestigious the consultant firm is – and, by the same token, the higher its fee – the greater its bureaucratic effectiveness as a front. Then there is "Moral Support": With a consultant in his corner, the senior executive feels more secure.

Consulting firms have their own bureaucratic techniques for expansion. One is known as the "self-perpetuating sell" or the "trade-up." The large and most successful corporations are the best client prospects, because once a consulting firm gets in, it has a chance of rolling from study to study indefinitely. A new problem can always be spotted since everybody has problems. Price competition is frowned on. Most of the competitive effort comes in the public activities of the consulting firm – lunches and dinners at which a consultant talks about some aspect of management, executive seminars, articles in business reviews, lectures at business schools. The top company officers, who usually hire the consultants, have huge compensations, so they see nothing untoward in the consulting firms charging a hefty amount. One does not haggle. The pool of money left to consulting firms after costs and quite substantial salaries are paid – to be distributed in bonuses and benefits – may run as high as 40 per cent of billings.

The growth of this bureaucratic section has been enormous. In 1965, general and technical consulting together produced revenues for U.S. management consultants of US$650 million, about twice the total of a decade earlier. By 1990, the take, for domestic U.S. operations alone, according to newsletter *Consultant News*, had hit $13 billion. Worldwide, similarly, management consultants revenue rose from $3 billion in 1980 to $23 billion in 1990. In some years average revenues rose as much as 28 per cent.

The personal take of cadres has followed the same track. A team of four or five consultants from a top-rated firm will charge US$130,000 to $150,000 a month. Veteran senior partners at McKinsey & Co. draw up to $1 million and, in some cases, even more. In the early 1980s, clients were billed an average of 2.5 times what the consultants on the job were paid. Hefty as that mark-up for consulting firms was, by the late 1980s, it wasn't unusual for the multiple to hit 3.6 or 3.7 times base salary.

Management consulting became particularly fashionable in the recession of the early 1980s when many U.S. firms went under and the Japanese upstarts had the U.S. automobile and consumer electronics industries reeling. U.S. corporate executives were befuddled. It gradually became clear how bureaucratized their organizations had become, with enormously wasteful "bureaucratic layering" in the middle management and supervisory ranks. The other side of the phenomenon was the disregard of human values and creativity on the shop floor, hence all those wasteful supervisors to keep employees in line. Management consulting, heralding its teaching of "people skills," became *le dernier cri*. Praise flowed in the business press.

In fact, the management consulting bureaucracy was part of the problem in the first place. Management consulting had become prominent in the late 1950s, a by-product of U.S. post-war industrial success. Then, in the 1960s and 1970s, its growth accelerated. Acting in counterpoint to its clientele, it fed back an increasingly bureaucratic and financially oriented corporate culture – the same which ultimately landed the U.S. economy in such a mess.

Fads of the past litter the management consulting closet. For 1985, MICA Management Centre Inc., a Canadian marketer of management gurus, signed up American quality expert Edwards Deming for their speakers' list. This was noted with approval. The real story is that Deming, who had been around since the 1940s, was treated as a crank by those few, in U.S.

corporate bureaucracies, who even knew his name. Only in Japan, where he became something of a god, was he taken seriously and his books bought.

"Consultants have always had a role in launching fads," reported *Business Week* in 1986, ". . . but [they] have been working overtime to roll out new fads since the 1970s." "Selling new wheezes," *The Economist* once described them. There is the "alphabet list": Theory X (military style, from the 1940s) to Theory Y (*circa* 1950s; let people have a say) to Theory Z (in the 1980s; do what the Japanese are doing). In the 1960s there were the touchy-feely T-Group sessions, where thousands of executives sought self-awareness and sensitivity by, among other things, hurling insults across a room at each other. It wasn't too long before T-Groups gave way to Grid-Groups and before T-grouped managers quickly became G-grouped – rated according to their concern for people versus their concern for production. "Centralization" and "decentralization" were parallel fads co-existing at the same time. "It depended on which consultant you hired," a management professor remembers. "Diversification" of the 1950s became "Conglomeration" of the 1960s became "Restructuring" and then "Asset Redeployment" and "Demassing" in the 1980s. "Demassing" has been hot recently. Translation: laying off workers. "Asset Redeployment": getting rid of what you picked up earlier for no good reason other than conglomerate fashion, and made a mess of.

"Strategic Planning" was all the rage in the 1970s, then went out of fashion, then – when it had recovered its novelty – came back into fashion again. "In . . . an unstable environment, people get anxious," explained one practitioner, a consultant in the Business Futures Program at SRI International in Menlo Park, California. Long-term planning is an antidote to this anxiety – the ultimate in handholding – even if, objectively, it might not do anything since the long term is unpredictable. One variant is called "scenario planning." It looks at "critical uncertainties." Alas, it still leaves the user having to choose which scenario to prepare for. The return of strategic planning does well for "futurists," too, now called "outliers," in the new jargon, viz. an unfettered explorer of the outlying regions of human possibility.

There is also a good market in grids, charts, tests, and quantitative analysis, which help CEOs and other top executives to feel secure. Because of the potential of such methods for theoretical and "scientific" elaboration, there are always some around. Thematic Apperception Tests were in fashion in the 1950s (executives were told to conjure up stories based on series of pictures). "Quantitative management" (trust the numbers; business is a science) was also big. There was PERT (Program Evaluation and Review Technique) – spider-web-like diagrams to chart the progress of a project; it took so much effort to get the charts done, the time would have been better spent just doing the job.

One of the most ingenious and mesmerizing concoctions – not least because it was so simple – was the matrix chart invented by a member of the Boston Consulting Group, a leader in strategic planning. The matrix consisted of a square divided into four sections, for cows (mature companies that could be milked), dogs (marginal performers with poor prospects), stars (the section where positive characteristics crossed), and question marks. Hundreds of executive offices had this Boston Consulting matrix on the wall or in the drawer. The matrix had no section, however, for ways of doing things better. Its hidden premise was that you milked your cows (sometimes until they were dry and became dogs), divested yourself of your dogs, and acquired stars to fill up the favoured quarter of your matrix. In this spirit, the U.S. corporate bureaucracy indulged in acquisition games while others paid attention to productivity and technology. The Boston Consulting Group matrix was the height of management-consulting fashion, in the corporate branch, even if it was fatuous, short-sighted, economically incestuous, and superficial . . . maybe because it was that. Then, all of a sudden, it seemed, but really after the slow process by which a bureaucracy eventually, belatedly becomes tired of an enthusiasm, the Boston Consulting Group was out of fashion.

In the 1980s, the faddish offshoots of management consulting – "patent remedies" in the jargon – proliferated, becoming even more exotic in their subdivision. "The search for instant solutions," *Business Week* commented, "has fueled an industry of instant management gurus, new-idea consultants, and an endless stream of books promising the latest quick fix." Management by best-seller, it was called.

One wrinkle produces another: Somebody inevitably wrote a book called *Beyond the Quick Fix* and a company asked the author to give a seminar on it – to last no longer than fifteen minutes. "Corporate culture" came into fashion (the author of the book did ninety minutes on it for US$5,000). So did "intrapreneurship" and "wellness." The intrapreneuring man joked that "some people . . . think intrapreneuring is the flavour of the month." If "intrapreneuring" does disappear without a trace, he said, "give me a few years off, and I'll come back with something else."

"Organizational therapy" was also in. One such "therapist," Ichak Adizes, was retained by BankAmerica, beginning with a retreat for top management at the posh Silverado Country Club in Napa County, California. As the relationship developed, the bill rose to an estimated US$3 million, as top managers tried, under the Adizes method, to build consensus. "Several senior guys were spending half their time in these meetings for months on end," said one insider. BankAmerica, already shaky, kept going downhill. Too many corporate executives are like compulsive dieters, commented *Business Week*, "trying the latest craze for a few days, then moving restlessly on."

The bookwriters and others give talks and seminars as well. This is a variant of management consulting: pep talks and seminars on "executive creativity" and "unleashing the entrepreneurial spirit," at up to US$25,000 a shot. Fashionable Americans get these high fees. Top Canadians are in the mere C$5,000 to $10,000 range. Motivational speakers are another variant. "Pop preachers" and "profit prophets" are two of the phrases used to describe them. Another is "motitainer" (a combination of motivator and entertainer, get it?). A motitainer does "motitainment." "Chinese food" and "whiskey training" are other, less charitable appellations for it – great for two or three hours, after which the effect has disappeared. Some observers are critical. They say that using motivational speakers is a smoke-screen designed to hide the failure of people running companies and to help them avoid facing up to the real problems. "Pure bullshit," says another. But this does nothing to stop their use.

Revenues for such speakers overall, in the United States, grew at about 20 per cent a year in the 1980s. They gestated as if biologically – spores in a bureaucratic culture. The Chief Executive Officers Club in Chicago enjoys one such speaker for an hour; their companies pay the US$10,000 fee and another $7,000 which the executives put out for packages of motivational books and tapes sold by the speaker. This is the guru and the "super-guru" business. Futurist Alvin Toffler and former U.S. secretary of state Henry Kissinger have also been brought into the act by consulting impresarios who calculate, rightly, that such personalities can garner large fees. Kissinger *circa* 1990 got as high as $35,000 per speech, taking in $875,000 a year from that source alone. (Thirty corporate clients also were paying Kissinger Associates Inc. an annual retainer of $200,000, or $6 million in all, for advice on foreign countries.)

Gurus of another stripe – the priests of the "human potential" movement – adapted their programs for a corporate clientele, in search of a slice of this rich and available market. These programs are variants of management training and "motivational training" as distinct from the strategic-advice subsection of management consulting. *Fortune* writer Jeremy Main, in two articles entitled "Trying to Bend Managers' Minds" and "Merchants of Inspiration," summarized the development. Werner Erhard, ex-Erhard Seminars Training, or "est" to most people, for example, started up a management consulting operation called Transformational Technologies Inc. It got into the act for a few years, licensing its program out to small consulting firms – some with major corporate clients – for a fee of US$20,000 plus 8 per cent of the gross, before fading from the scene.

The est-style school of motivational training is part of what is known, jocularly, as the "woo-woo" factor (as in the sound of a passing train's whistle). Woo-woo instruction, as described by *Training*, a personnel magazine, is New Age philosophy come to corporate culture. Its collected techniques include transcendental meditation, yoga, biofeedback, visualization, neurolinguistic programming, also self-hypnosis, suggestology (sometimes known as "suggestopedia"), guided imagery, alpha waves, out-of-body excursions, rebirthing, flotation tanks, "clearing," triad dialoguing, spinal massages, hot tub encounter sessions, and so on, from the catalogue of "psycho-technologies." On a scale of one to ten, explained *Training's* Jack Gordon, a workshop on filling out time cards might score a one (assuming everyone remains fully dressed) whereas a psychic-travel session with participants lying naked on woven-reed mats and with sitar music reverberating in their headsets would rate a ten.

Even the Church of Scientology has tried establishing a beachhead here through "affiliate" WISE International, which licenses out the "management technology" of Scientology founder Ron Hubbard. A sales-department manager of a small Atlanta company, sent to a Scientology course by her boss, soon found herself immersed in the cult's techniques of obscure language, bullbaiting, and "confront." "They tried to get us to admit guilt because sales were poor," she explained. "They wanted to get us past the analytical brain to clear the inner brain, where the poor sales were caused."

Perhaps the best-known case history of "human potential" training, because employees revolted against the program, involved Pacific Bell, a subsidiary of Pacific Telesis (created by the break-up of AT&T). The company wanted to create a new corporate culture, so it hired two associates of one Charles Krone, a trainer who had done work for Scott Paper and Du Pont. One aspect that crops up in Krone's work is the veiling of ideas in jargon and impenetrable language. Mounting resentment of employees helped launch an inquiry – ordered by the California Public Utilities Commission – and the lid blew off. "Thought police" was how some employees, assured of anonymity, described the "facilitators." The cost of the program also came out: US$40 million.

As *Fortune* writer Main reported, such operations like to style themselves as part of the mainstream, but some go beyond just group dynamics. The old controversies about brainwashing, thought-control, coercion, cultism, and robotization have resurfaced in the context of this new form of management training. The question of coercion – of having to submit to a variant of thought reform – is particularly apt, since employees, for obvious reasons, are under tremendous pressure to participate and to withhold criticism.

"American industry is so desperate to increase productivity, it will do anything," one anti-cult official says. "This is witchcraft in the nuclear age."

Meditation consultants now show up in "respectable" firms. The Ford Motors Executive Program, as of early 1988, had a Philosopher in Residence, whose specialty was "leadership through courage, love and integrity." He had already reached the hearts of many other corporate leaders in such corporations as Amoco, AMI, Volvo, IBM, Xerox, and Rohm & Haas. Another wrinkle is crossing psychotherapy and management consulting. This one is for upwardly mobile executives who find the world too much for them or want to clear obstacles off their career path. "Executive coaching," it's called or, by the sceptics, "Freudians in the corridors." One such executive-coaching firm, in New Rochelle, N.Y., is made up of a Presbyterian minister (turned psychotherapist and management consultant), a psychiatrist, a psychologist, and another psychotherapist. A teacher at the Stanford Graduate School of Business refers to tarot cards.

Rising in fashionability are pricey outdoor programs, with such mainstays as falling backwards off a platform into the arms of others ("trust fall," in the terminology), climbing a high pole, personal confessions, hugging, and acting out corporate concerns in games. In Toronto in the mid-1980s, some executives were paying a tax-deductible $490 to an outfit called Stretch Unlimited, which promised to expand its clients' self-awareness by a series of terrifying challenges over a long weekend. Among the challenges was walking across a bed of hot coals. Stretch Unlimited was part of the "neurolinguistic" (New Age) programming fad. Meanwhile, one of the up-and-coming providers in the lucrative executive management seminar business is Walt Disney Co. – three days in Florida for only US$1,898 per person. As well as some nicely packaged common sense, executives and middle managers get a session at Disney University and a tour behind the scenes at Disney World where, among other things, they can try on parts of Pluto's costume.

If falling off a platform and barking at Pluto fail, there is now Golf University at San Diego and at Lake of the Ozarks in Missouri, with a third campus under construction in Hawaii. Golf University was co-founded by Ken Blanchard, the author of best-selling pop management tract *The One-Minute Manager*. It blends professional instruction in golf's finer points with the precepts laid out in the book. It's a good place for executives to learn teamwork, the guru explains. While the accent is on improving the golf game, "we make people better managers too," he says. "We're big on the reprimanding and praising that we talk about in the book," he adds, although the hugging part of it is downplayed. He would like more companies to send employees to Golf U to have their team spirit built up. Tuition for the four-day program is a mere US$1,250 (room and board at the adjoining luxury resort not included) – not much more, after all, than registration at a typical executive conference.

Lobbying is a mushrooming and proliferating section of the corporate branch of the New Bureaucracy. Like the old bureaucracy (civil servants and ministerial assistants), this section develops policy for political leaders. Indeed, most of the principals of this corporate section in Canada are former civil servants and ministerial assistants. Unlike the old bureaucracy, however, the lobbying can allocate huge resources to any item or objective that it sets its mind to, and can do so, because of ideological cover, without provoking the slightest murmur of complaint.

There are trade associations, such as the Canadian Manufacturers Association and the Canadian Petroleum Association – about five hundred of them with offices in Ottawa (approximately six times the number a couple of decades ago) and upwards of seven hundred overall. The Canadian Petroleum Association (CPA) itself has three offices across the country (until recently it had six). Budgets of the larger ones run into the many millions of dollars. Most of the high-powered trade associations refuse to disclose publicly how much they spend. Well-heeled members can also throw in money for special campaigns. The $11 million the CPA spent on its 1981-1985 media campaign ($16 million in today's terms) was a drop in the bucket for the major oil companies. A 1981 study by the Economic Council of Canada estimated that business and professional lobby groups spent more than $122 million promoting their interests, compared with $2 million a year mustered by public-interest groups. The total expenditures today would be a multiple of that.

Many major corporations have their own in-house lobbyists – the "vice-president, public affairs" or the "director of government relations." They are paid according to the inflated corporate scale, far above what people of the same skills are paid elsewhere or can ever hope to receive, regardless of the relative value and importance of their work.

Then there are the "public affairs consulting" firms, acting for the corporate branch. These firms provide intelligence about government policy and useful contacts in government. They also provide lobbying know-how and increasingly do direct lobbying themselves for clients. They didn't exist at all in Canada before 1968, when the first was established. Now there are about two hundred of them working the Ottawa scene. Ongoing fee packages (retainers plus additional charges) that ranged from $1,500 to $6,500 a month ($18,000 to $78,000 a year) per client in 1980 now range from $5,000 to as high as $20,000 a month ($250,000 a year) at major public-affairs firms like Hill and Knowlton Canada and Executive Consultants (ECL), with some special projects hitting $2 million at the upper end.

Scores of lawyers in Ottawa also act on contract to corporations, as part-time lobbyists or as liaison to government, adding to Ottawa's reputation for having more lawyers per capita than any other city in the country. High-powered Toronto law firms have now joined the act, the appropriate partners flying into Ottawa as required. Some polling firms are a part of this bureaucratic section and contribute to the work for clients. Decima Research belongs to Hill and Knowlton Canada. COMPAS is 50 per cent owned by U.S. megafirm Burson-Marsteller, which acquired the interest when it bought ECL.

There is a special lobby acting for 150 senior corporate administrators: the Business Council on National Issues (BCNI). It declines to disclose how much money it spends. Its members are exclusively CEOs. It purportedly addresses itself to broad public policy issues only – a lobby superior to all other lobbies.

There are intensive lobbying efforts for major defence and other government procurement contracts. Public affairs consulting groups beef up these efforts. Contingency fees have been added to retainers. The lobbying contingency fee on getting the contract for the third terminal at Toronto's Pearson International Airport (paid when the contract was won) was said, by well-placed government sources, to have been between $250,000 and $500,000. A contingency fee for getting a mere fishing licence for a Nova Scotia company was $75,000 (confirmed by the lobbying firm), in addition to the initial fee of $10,000.

A "blooming moneymaker" with "fat fees" is how a special series in the *Globe and Mail* described corporate lobbying. The allocation to public affairs consultants in Canada is up to $200 million annually.

John Sawatsky, in his 1987 book *The Insiders: Government, Business, and the Lobbyists*, detailed the rise of the public affairs consulting groups. He shows how, beginning with ECL, the trade was created and built up by former executive assistants to cabinet ministers and former civil servants. This was typical of the whole lobbying section. Tom d'Aquino, president of the Business Council on National Issues, had been executive assistant to a Liberal cabinet minister and then special assistant to Prime Minister Trudeau. Simon Reisman and Jim Grandy, former deputy ministers, established a firm of their own catering to high-paying corporate clients. Gordon Ritchie, deputy chief negotiator for the Canada-United States trade talks, set up a free-trade consulting firm, Strategicon. Some of the public-affairs consultants were political junkies, taking leaves of absence to work on federal election campaigns.

Regulatory officials also cross over after soaking up know-how – going to work for the very same corporations they were "regulating," but at a much more lucrative rate of pay. Marshall Crowe, the one-time chairman of the

National Energy Board, for example, became an energy lobbyist for such clients as Dome Petroleum and Mobil Oil. Several prominent communications lawyers helping broadcast and cable companies to deal with the Canadian Radio-Television and Telecommunications Commission (CRTC) have come up through the CRTC itself. Government procurement officers – defence department officials, for example – cross over.

According to the mythology, only the crass and morally corrupt United States was supposed to have a revolving door between government and corporate bureaucracies, through which ambitious civil servants passed into the corporate hierarchy. In fact, well before Sawatsky's book came out, the revolving door had been spinning in Canada, with deputy ministers and executive assistants going not just to public-affairs consulting companies but also to corporate trade associations. The lobbying section of the New Bureaucracy, corporate branch, is almost entirely transplanted old bureaucracy.

The lobbyist section's sheer payroll power, by which it pulls civil servants through the revolving door, undermines the independence of the old bureaucracy in turn. Ministerial assistants, deputy ministers, regulatory officials, and procurement officers are not likely to take a strong critical position regarding corporate special interests when one of the possible destinations of their career path is lucrative corporate lobbying. It's an old story.

The New Bureaucracy's lobbying section also makes use of personal relationships. The creator of Government Consultants International (GCI), and one of the more flamboyant of the public-affairs practitioners, was Frank Moores, former premier of Newfoundland and a close friend of Prime Minister Brian Mulroney. Other GCI principals had close and long-standing connections to the holders of political power. It's one of the reasons that GCI became such an astonishing success; those connections sell. GCI, wrote journalist Stevie Cameron in the late 1980s, was viewed in many quarters as almost a parallel Prime Minister's Office. The Conservative and Liberal connections of other firms are different only in degree.

One sign of bureaucracies gone bad are their political hangers-on. The lobbying section is one of the few places that executive assistants can go to when they leave the employ of cabinet ministers and other MPs – that is, where they can go to and make the large incomes to which they would like to become accustomed. "Government relations" firms are a New-Bureaucracy patronage trough for them.

Outgoing executive assistants are not the only ones who have been helped out by hanging on. Gerry Doucet, an ex-Conservative cabinet minister in Nova Scotia and one of the co-founders of GCI, got into government relations in Halifax when he was insolvent and when he didn't have the confidence to practise law any more. Frank Moores, the other GCI founder, found his calling in the high-fee, high-level lobbyist's world after a long black period during which three prominent businessmen paid him a salary just to sit and think so he could get back on his feet. His business ventures in Newfoundland had turned sour and eaten up money. Brian Peckford, Moores' successor as premier of Newfoundland, on leaving that post, found a warm place as part-time lobbyist for rival firm Public Affairs International (PAI, now Hill and Knowlton Canada). He had complained of being financially strapped despite his $76,000 annual salary as premier. The lucrative lobbying stipend would help supplement Peckford's mere $60,000 annual legislative pension and the $100,000 lump sum generated at a fund-raising dinner so he could buy a house and car.

The interconnections in this debased bureaucracy are myriad and political. Francis Fox, an ex-federal cabinet minister, is vice-chairman of GCI. Judy Erola, also an ex-federal cabinet minister, acts for the Pharmaceutical Manufacturers Association of Canada (which also retained GCI and Gerry Doucet to steer through highly controversial 1987 drug-patent legislation). Jean Chrétien, between parliamentary sojourns, held down a corporate job with the Ottawa branch of Lang, Michener, Cranston, Farquharson and Wright, a top-drawer Bay Street law firm. There, for the usual top-drawer fees, he helped the firm's clients deal with the federal government. Peter Lougheed established an Ottawa branch of his Calgary law firm, Bennett Jones, to cash in on lobbying business pursuant to the free trade agreement. Many of Bennett Jones' clients are American.

The good life offered by a rampant bureaucracy doesn't hurt its growth, either. GCI became known for throwing Ottawa's splashiest parties, inviting five hundred of the city's top civil servants, politicians, and journalists. Tom d'Aquino of BCNI has a reputation for giving the best "power parties" in the city, with cabinet ministers and deputy ministers mingling with captains of industry in his Rockliffe home. If Ottawa is Fat City, the lobbyists' section is the fattest of the lot.

The lobbyist section has its own internal bureaucratic dynamic whereby it expands simply because it exists. The *Financial Post* described it as the "snowball effect." Once one company has established a full-time lobbyist or retained a consultant in Ottawa, others, afraid of what they may be missing, quickly follow suit. Then they raise the bureaucratic ante on each other. Some companies use lobbying firms in addition to their own in-house lobbyists. Others use several lobby firms according to the project (but presumably pay retainers to them all). The construction company which got the contract for the third terminal at Pearson Airport in Toronto covered the bases by hiring not one, not two, but four lobbying firms (total fees to the four firms were estimated in the $1 million range). American Express had at least five firms working for it to help obtain a banking licence and government contracts (as of early 1990, it retained nine lobbyists from three firms). The lesson hasn't been lost on others; lobbyists now predict that when a big battle heats up, there will be multiple retainers on each side. Some companies have retained particular lobbyists merely to prevent them from working for a potential competitor.

Foreign multinational companies are free-spending and hence powerful bureaucratic players. Seventy per cent of the revenue of Hill and Knowlton Canada (formerly PAI) comes from foreign-owned firms. GCI clients also include many large multinational groups. For combatting opposition to the patent protection legislation on behalf of the Pharmaceutical Manufacturers Association of Canada (almost exclusively foreign-based firms), GCI was reported to have pocketed $15 million in a multi-year retainer and contingency-fee package. GCI heatedly denied this figure, but it's safe to say the take was substantial. New players flock to the game. Extension to provincial centres was inevitable. A service subsection has sprung up, producing handbooks (costing up to $387) and newsletters (up to $900 per year). There is even, in Canada, a biweekly newsletter, monthly digest, and consolidated monthly register on lobbying activity itself ($790 per year for the package), so the cadres can keep track of each other.

Because the corporate clients can and do pay almost anything, a certain swashbuckling image has attached to the new lobbyists, but they are the most bureaucratic of peoples – more bureaucratic, in some ways, than they were in their days as civil servants or ministerial assistants. Civil servants are often caricatured as having an obsession with the intricacies of the bureaucratic order and its personalities and with the political winds swirling in government. According to the caricature, they use this knowledge to pilot recommendations and policies through to the deputy minister and then the minister, and do so in such a way that the recommendations get through cabinet, too. This is exactly what the the corporate branch's lobbyist section does – getting its clients' objectives on the bureaucratic and ministerial "priority pile" – and it does so through intimate knowledge of government departments and their players.

"The unofficial arm of government," the *Financial Post Magazine* described this bureaucratic section – like the old bureaucracy but with better remuneration, fancier parties, and special-interest objectives added. What this means, as well, is that foreign multinationals, through their public affairs consultants, are a part of Canadian governments much as if they were paying for, and giving orders to, an assortment of civil servants in actual government departments.

In-house lobbyists and public affairs consultants aren't the only subsections of the lobbyists' section. Political contributions are a form of indirect lobbying – a pre-emptive bureaucratic ploy to help elect parties and candidates favourable to one's interests and make direct lobbying more successful after elections. It is accomplished with nothing more complicated than money. If the old bureaucracy allocated departmental money to chosen political parties, on the other hand, there would be furious denunciation.

Another subsection is media propaganda campaigns, also forbidden to the old bureaucracy. Cost is no object. The $11 million outlay by the Canadian Petroleum Association for its media campaign in the early 1980s was almost twice as much as the money spent by any of the major political parties (national non-candidate spending) in federal elections (Liberals $6.3 million, Conservatives $6.4 million, and NDP $4.7 million in 1984). The CPA propaganda campaign also made use of polling firm Decima Research for which, subsequently, surveying public opinion for the corporate branch became a major revenue-earner – indeed, kept Decima Research alive.

There is no limit to the bureaucratic allocations that can be made in this way. When the tobacco industry geared up to fight legislation prohibiting cigarette advertising and promotion, it hired Bill Neville, then president of PAI and one of the pioneers in Canada of public affairs consulting, and a close friend of the prime minister and other cabinet ministers. His reported pay: $500,000 a year. The industry also ran a series of expensive full-page newspaper advertisements ($800,000 worth). Total expenses hit upwards of $2.5 million (whether that included auxiliary expenditures, like $650,000 in grants to psychologists for selected studies, wasn't reported).

The aggregate spending by the corporate coalition backing the U.S.-Canada free trade agreement came to an estimated $13 million (of which $5.24 million was in direct cash contributions). Alcan, Canadian Pacific, and Shell Canada led the way with $250,000 each in cash. Contributions to political parties were on top of that. This outstripped by far the cost of the 1988 national election campaigns on the issue of each of the opposition parties (Liberals $6.8 million, NDP $7 million) and easily surpassed, also, the ceiling on national-party election spending (just over $8 million, exclusive of individual candidates' spending).

Another lobbying subsection is "research" organizations, underwritten largely by the corporate branch and governed through corporate membership – the Conference Board of Canada, the C. D. Howe Institute, and the Fraser Institute. Their expenditures in 1990 were $12.1 million, $1.7 million, and $1.4 million respectively, mostly financed by corporate contributions. Although they attempt a pretence of independent scholarship and research, they are bureaucratic extensions of the corporate branch, like public-affairs apparatchiks. "Flak merchants," Jim Winter, a University of Windsor communications expert, calls them. They also act as ideology merchants. The volume of their publications and the statements of their spokespeople add to the corporate branch's bureaucratic weight.

Another bureaucratic extension is the university connection. The corporate branch's financial contributions, earmarked for some kinds of programs rather than others, and their funding of research programs, change the composition and balance of universities. The connection works indirectly as well, by influencing university administrations. Program and research grants also have a pre-emptive side-effect: Scientists, ecologists, and social scientists receiving grants from companies are not likely to put at risk the continuation of their grants by criticizing those companies on matters of public concern. Yet academics are supposed to be a key source of independent knowledge and criticism for society. The endowment of "chairs," common in the United States but also occurring in Canada, promotes and adds cachet to certain activities or points of view – a kind of indirect, long-term lobbying, which continues on auto-pilot indefinitely.

Inflated as the lobbyist bureaucracy is in Canada, it trails its counterpart in the United States, which it merely imitates. Nothing in the field beats American lobbyists for bureaucratic sprawl, inflation, and waste, for bogging down decision-making, for generating corruption, and for cost to the public. It shows all too graphically how far the bureaucratic progression can go, and where the same bureaucracy is heading in this country.

"Lobbying . . . has become . . . established, highly paid, big-league stuff," *Fortune* reported with awe, in 1987. As public relations firms and lawyers scrambled to capture the ever-increasing bureaucratic loot, the lobbying "megafirm" was created. "One-stop shop," "lobbying supermarket," and "super lobbyist" are other appellations. The megafirm does it all, from verbally massaging a legislator at the top to organizing a "grass-roots" campaign at the bottom. One megafirm now has a management consulting division, all the better to synchronize a business plan and the lobbying effort into one. Lawyers (particularly tax and environmental lawyers), scholars, video production experts, people with technological know-how, and corporate and academic researchers may be found in lobbying teams.

Advertising agencies have moved into the lobbying section. Giant international agencies JWT (through Hill and Knowlton, which it already owned) and Ogilvy & Mather acquired a 100 per cent and 30 per cent interest respectively in fashionable lobbying firms. The London-based WPP Group then bought JWT itself, subsequently added three lobbyist and two related research (polling) organizations, among them PAI and Decima Research in Canada, and then acquired the Ogilvy Group, too.

The U.S. lobbyist section has its own several subsections. There are lobbyists who specialize in forming lobbying alliances with others. There are direct-mail specialists and advertising specialists. All of these are now needed in Washington for a major campaign. Gathered together in a megafirm, they eat up considerable overhead. Then there are the smaller, more specialized outfits – the "boutiques" or "designer lobbyists."

A typical megafirm "full-service" retainer fee runs at about US$16,000 a month ($192,000 a year). Low end is $10,000 a month ($120,000 a year). Global representation ranges up to seven figures annually. A sample boutique charge comes in at $8,000 a month ($96,000 a year). That's considered cheap. Expenses are added to that. A "superstar" lobbyist can command upwards of $350 an hour with lesser luminaries charging around the $300 per hour mark. American lawyers in the lobbying game making $250,000 to $400,000 are commonplace. The bosses of the larger trade associations have incomes in the same range.

Former White House aides, cabinet ministers, senators, and political apparatchiks (with their IOUs) can charge even more, for undisguised influence peddling. The gross billings of former deputy White House chief of staff Michael Deaver, a friend of Ronald Reagan, were heading for the US$4.5 million mark annually when his business came unglued in 1986, hit by scandal. Deaver acted for Canada on acid rain – a minor contract for $105,000. His biggest retainers were from a South Korean government front organization at $475,000 per year and from the Saudi Arabian government at about $400,000 per year (originally part of a $1.5 million multi-year deal). Among his corporate retainers, Rockwell came in at $259,000 annually, and CBS and Boeing at $350,000 each. One ex-departmental housing official took in $1.2 million in "consulting" fees helping to push federal housing subsidies towards developer clients.

"Pricey," says *Fortune* of the fees. "Hitting the ozone." The corporate branch pays the shot anyway. By going with the most expensive firms, that is the ones with the best reputations, *Fortune* explained, the corporate underling concerned provides himself with "megaprotection by which to cover his you-know-what."

Lobbying for U.S. defence procurement is particularly rich in rake-offs, with its pay-outs included in contract overheads, which sometimes amount to one-third of total production costs. Everything gets thrown in, from the large stables of former military officers on defence company payrolls down to golf outings, country-club memberships, goose hunts, rides on corporate yachts, and football tickets. The system is known as "rent-a-general." Public-affairs consulting middlemen are known as the "Beltway bandits" after the Washington Beltway area where they operate. The 1988 Pentagon scandal, involving charges of bribery (for inside information) and fraud, raised an enormous stir, but criminal acts are just a sliver of the lobbyist and government-relations activity overall in defence procurement. Topping this activity, like a very sweet icing on the cake, is bountiful, slick advertising by defence-production companies, in industry and business magazines, pitched to the generals, admirals and the denizens of the Pentagon who might read them. Meanwhile, the funnelling of illegal information to companies and the fraud in billing the government requires the beefing up of Justice Department investigatory staff and of Pentagon monitoring staff – more ranks and more complexity. There are 22,400 auditors, reviewers and investigators in the U.S. Defence Department, of which almost 5,000 are investigators alone.

The bureaucratic overlay by foreign governments and corporations similarly can be staggering. Some one hundred and forty Japanese companies and government agencies spend a loosely estimated US$400 million annually on lobbyists. Among the consultants are former cabinet officers, White House aides, U.S. senators, and top Democratic and Republican party officials. Multinational companies and foreign governments, principally the Japanese, have retained some two hundred one-time top officials of the administration and Congress. Some of the characters walking through the revolving door are particularly suited. Four of the last eight U.S. Trade Representatives – the top U.S. trade negotiators – have become lobbyists for foreign concerns, three of them Japanese. The scandal-ridden Bank of Credit and Commerce International (BCCI), Pakistani-controlled, by itself had half a dozen top lobbyists and lawyers on the Washington scene.

One of the most arcane subdivisions of the lobbying section is the "grass-roots campaign" subsection. It bureaucratically produces "grass roots" the way an astroturf company produces grass – synthetically, except with paper instead of plastics. A lawmaker may be willing to accede to a corporation's importunities but wants a grass-roots campaign to cover for it. Or the lawmaker may be resistant to the corporation's representations and needs softening up. So the corporation, with its bureaucratic power to allocate resources, orders grass-roots from this lobbyist subsection – public relations firms or branches of lobbyist megafirms that use direct mail and sophisticated phone banks to mount grass-roots campaigns.

A typical example was the Citizens for Sensible Control of Acid Rain (CSCAR) – a "grass-roots" group. It was actually a sophisticated lobbying campaign operating from the offices of a Washington public relations firm and underwritten by giant electric utilities and coal companies trying to kill acid-rain legislation. So slick was the bureaucratic manipulation that some people who were against acid rain were taken in and wrote their representatives opposing the legislation.

This bureaucratic overlay can smother most genuinely popular expression with a paper "grass-roots movement" of its own. In a sample referendum campaign, on nuclear power in the small state of Maine in 1987, a utility consortium spent $6.6 million. This allocation was made, simply, by the decision of a handful of corporate officers. Costs are pushed upwards inexorably. The other side, which did not have access to corporate cash flow, had to make do with $800,000, or less than one-eighth the bureaucratic allocation.

The number of lobbyists in Washington increased by four or five times to an estimated twenty-five thousand in the years of the Reagan administration, and keeps rising. Current estimates put the number at as high as forty thousand (thirteen thousand registered) – a huge bureaucratic cadre. When people talk about the city being "filled with bureaucrats," as often as not they point to the lobbyists as an example. Lawyers in the trade, and also those working the regulatory arena, match lobbyists. Membership in the District of Columbia Bar Association more than doubled between 1975 and 1986, from twenty thousand to forty-four thousand, despite deregulation, which should have meant fewer lawyers. There are now about fifty thousand lawyers working in the city, of which an increasing number do lobbying.

Similarly, so many trade associations have moved to Washington or set up operations there that associations are sometimes touted as the city's third largest industry, after the government and tourism.

New Republic journalist Fred Barnes, in a perceptive piece of social reporting in 1986, referred simply to the "parasite culture of Washington." He described people he personally knew, not composites, who had left the government side for government relations work and lobbying. Exactly what they did was a little vague, he explained. They didn't necessarily do much lobbying themselves, even when on a company's payroll (the company in one case had retained law firms for that). One of them went to a lot of meetings, lunches and receptions. Another arranged a few deals and massaged major clients. Another offered "inside" advice. A fourth rode around town in a limousine as she did her rounds. All were lucratively paid; the money poured in. One time-consuming pursuit was chasing after "visibility" – mentions in the papers and newsmagazines and, best of all, appearances on television. A mention constituted proof to their clients that they mattered in Washington. It was also good for egos.

"There are thousands like [these people] in Washington," Barnes wrote. "They do Washington work, which means you can't put your finger on it. One thing's clear: they don't produce anything tangible." But these people weren't wholly to blame. "All they did was respond to the seductive cues that Washington offers these days. The message is: take the money and stay." The work they did was "more and more superfluous, but they are paid better and better." And the pace of this subtle "corruption" had so quickened that it was getting out of control.

It put its stamp on the city in turn. An entire luxury industry – restaurants, limos, caterers, hotels, specialty shops, wine consultants – emerged in Washington to cater to the lobbying subsection. On any given day, in Washington, there are a thousand limousines leased by itinerant CEOs, lawyers, and sundry lobbyists aiming to make an impression. "Washington is bloated, wasteful, pretentious, myopic, decadent, and sybaritic," Barnes wrote. "It is the paradise of the overpaid hangers-on."

Ironically, this holds true not least for "conservative" groups and their proliferating foundations and "research institutes." "We've created a new gravy train," complained one foundation official. The conservative groups fervently oppose dominance of the country by Washington, but their own bureaucratic growth in Washington explodes. They have an "edifice complex," Barnes wisecracked. A lot of the free-flowing wherewithal for building this bureaucratic edifice comes from the corporate branch; companies stepped up their contributions to these groups in their attempt to influence the public-policy agenda. There was another irony Barnes didn't mention: These conservative groups most furiously espouse anti-bureaucratic private-enterprise ideology behind which the New Bureaucracy, both inside and outside Washington, has mushroomed. The upshot of all this in Washington is that it becomes increasingly burdensome, time-consuming, expensive and difficult to do business.

Many U.S. companies also have in-house lobbying offices of their own in the capital. Of 300 major companies surveyed in early 1988, more than half had Washington offices. A fifth of those offices were opened in the Reagan years alone. In the same period, twice as many companies increased their "federal affairs" staffs as reduced them.

Going through the revolving door from government to corporate lobbying is not only endemic, it is also virtually mandatory for newcomers wanting to establish a career in lobbying. They need experience as Congressional staff members before moving "from the Hill to downtown," said an Allied-Signal man. The process is actually three-step: first, a Congressional job or work on a presidential campaign, then into government administration, then onto the corporate branch's bureaucratic gravy train. Because more and more of these riders start out in the progression young, sometimes right out of college, they never experience real life outside the political capital. They become living caricatures of the bureaucratic type.

CEOs themselves also lobby. A *Business Week* survey in the early 1980s found that 65 per cent of the CEOs of the 200 largest American corporations went to Washington at least once every two weeks, compared to only 15 per cent a decade earlier. Even if some CEOs don't like the idea of going to Washington, the lobbying process more or less forces them to do so. "It's much more persuasive for the business people themselves to come and make the presentation," explains a Washington lawyer in the trade. If they don't show up against competing CEO lobbyists, in this leapfrogging, they lose points. The public affairs consultants, meanwhile, add to their retainers by tutoring the executives on how to play the game. (Lesser minions can turn to such how-to books as *How to Win in Washington*.) The CEOs of the major companies put in extra lobbying time as members of The Roundtable, their high-powered collective lobby.

Aside from flying in to Washington on their corporate jets, the CEOs also have their entertainment budgets. Not much, except style, appears to have changed from the 1970s when, a veteran lobbyist recalls, "there was always plenty of booze, women, and parties on someone's boat or in a hotel suite" for leading lawmakers who were so inclined. Another hospitality caper: letting politicians and government officials travel on the corporate plane.

The political subsection has also swollen dramatically in the United States, with "political action committees" (PACs). PACs collect and disburse "voluntary" political contributions. They came into common corporate use when prior ways of abusing the system were checked by reform. PACs quickly became a bureaucratic world of their own. Corporate PACs rose in number from 89 in 1974 to 1,800 in 1988, plus related association and umbrella PACs, and other PACs that surface and disappear during an election cycle. "Money spigots," they have been called. Corporate PACs make up almost half of all PACs put together. PAC contributions also serve as adjuncts to lobbying – to gain access to grateful legislators and to help push through or derail legislation. "We're headed for a government of, by, and for the corporate PACs of America," commented Common Cause, a U.S. public-interest organization. At the same time, both PACs and corporate executives working outside PACs have become skilled at getting around the intent of political financing rules. They have been able to put much more money into election campaigns, and into influencing legislation with such contributions, than was ever envisioned when PACs were originally allowed.

The corporate PACs and other political allocations have helped to create, in turn, a huge election-campaign bureaucracy of pollsters, consultants, public relations firms, and assorted other apparatchiks. Expenditures have risen to as high as US$26 million for a Senate race. Congressional campaign expenditures more than doubled in the fourteen years 1974-1988 in constant dollars. Incumbents, who collect most of the PAC funds, have the wherewithal to keep getting elected almost regardless of their performance and events. Drowning their opposition with television propaganda is the main device. Television-station owners now have an entrenched interest in this bureaucratic subsection and a special lobbying lever of their own to protect it against reform: Legislators are loathe to take the chance of offending broadcasters.

This bureaucratic overlay has come to defeat all but the crudest political debate. Cynicism about the process has produced low voter turnouts, defeating democracy. "Money politics," it's called. It should, more properly, be called "bureaucratic politics fed by money." Meanwhile, many "non-connected" PACs founded to promote free-enterprise ideology, and gathering money from the public at large, have become bureaucratic comedies themselves, spending more and more money raising funds, keeping their apparatchiks in pocket and otherwise feeding their bureaucratic machinery. One such high-powered PAC – high-powered bureaucratically, that is – spent 91 per cent of contributions received in 1989 on its own operating expenses, and only 1 to 2 per cent on political candidates.

PACs may eventually be banned and more obvious loopholes closed, but without tackling the New Bureaucracy, even apparently sweeping reforms fail. Voter initiatives (referendums) in California are an illustration. They were introduced, in 1911, to foil lobbyists. A new section of lobbyists underwritten by the corporate branch – "initiative lobbyists," they're called – now manipulate the initiative process instead, with huge funds at their command. One initiative lobbyist firm, Woodward and McDowell, for example, earned between US$3 million and $5 million in commissions from corporate clients for the 1990 California initiatives alone. Even when initiatives do get passed, they likely as not end up in the state Supreme Court where armies of high-priced lawyers battle over the details: more bureaucracy.

One bureaucratic subsection leads to another, which leads to another, which leads to another.

The "tax community," of tax lawyers, accountants, and financial officers, makes up another subsection of the corporate branch. It is not only a section of the corporate bureaucracy on its own but is also a part of the lobbyist section. The loopholes and complications that the tax community exploits in favour of its corporate clientele were created in the first place by its lobbying of the government on tax matters on behalf of corporations.

Linda McQuaig, in her 1987 book *Behind Closed Doors*, gave a chilling account of how this happens in Canada. "The cosy world of tax," she described it – a world in which tax practitioners (lawyers and accountants), who work mostly for corporations and investors, also act as advisers and consultants to the federal Finance Department. The most prominent and influential practitioners – the ones most heeded by the old bureaucracy – spend much of their time on large corporate accounts and are closely tied to those corporations.

There is also considerable movement of people between private practice, corporations, and government. Here, the corporate bureaucracy and the old (government) bureaucracy are virtually fused. The process of fusing goes back to the 1950s. The enormous cumulative tax exemptions for corporations and the tax advantages to high-income corporate executives and other high-income recipients – and the crippling public debt that Canada has been burdened with as a result – followed with a vengeance.

Another negative bureaucratic characteristic of these tax practitioners is the hiding of bias in a sea of technical arguments that pretend to be neutral. This is the bureaucratic mystique *par excellence* – Parliament can't understand, and some things Parliament should not find out about. The language of argument is made more and more prolix and technical, which protects the practitioners' bureaucratic power. To make matters worse: Because of the sheer bureaucratic weight of corporations – that is, their ability to allocate large resources to tax matters – almost all the expert tax practitioners are part of their branch. There isn't any public-interest counterweight to speak of.

The minutely codified system of laws the tax practitioners brought about also opened up endless opportunities to take action in the courts on behalf of their clients. This, naturally, added again to their fees and incomes and added, in turn, to the costs of the public courts, which hear these cases, and to the government's own legal bill – additional charges to the economy. The tax community "lobbyist" subsection generates expansion of the New Bureaucracy and of the old (government) bureaucracy at the same time.

So great is the bureaucratic power of the corporate branch and its "tax community" subsection that not only have they escaped blame for the devastating debt consequences which their bureaucratic fiddling produced, they can also sweepingly attack the size of the old bureaucracy – an everlasting scapegoat, it seems – in the name of anti-debt righteousness.

Much the same bureaucratization happens in the regulatory arena – in cable and telephone rate regulation, for example, or in broadcasting and cable takeover hearings. The new cadres have discovered the value of a time-honoured bureaucratic device: flood the proceedings with paper. High-priced communications lawyers have been used freely, in some cases frivolously. Consultants and their reports have been thrown in (the consultants and their topics chosen to serve the company). A small bureaucratic army of executives, financial officers, and lawyers, backed up by paper instead of tanks, might invade a proceeding. This process can do wonders for a corporation's financial statement, its expansion, and for the status, and hence remuneration, of its top executives.

The bureaucratic inflation in regulatory pleading in the United States is not much different and hides behind ideology in the same way. Private-enterprise ideology attacks the increasingly burdensome regulatory process as the product of a civil servants' conspiracy. Anti-business government bureaucrats, goes the criticism, take delight in harassing business with endless trivial demands and with requirements for reams of detail. But, as American business analyst Robert Reich has pointed out, the vast majority of regulatory-agency lawyers and middle-managers, far from being anti-corporate, have no other ambition than to move on to the private sector themselves. There, as corporate lawyers or with consulting firms, accounting firms, research institutes and public relations firms, they become corporate bureaucrats of the first water – far and away better paid and coddled, of course, than if they had remained in low-salary spartan government. And, mysteriously, although the Reagan administration abandoned some regulation, the regulatory process became even more inflated with new interpretations, elaborations, and directives during the Reagan years.

What actually happens is that corporations, in search of loopholes and advantage, test the limits of regulatory laws and rulings. To plug the loopholes, the old (government) bureaucracy has no other choice than to add specifics. The corporate lawyers then find other dodges. They launch court actions, working their way up from the trial division to the appellate divisions. Congress has to get involved to shore up the regulatory purpose with a new law or series of laws spelling out in excruciating detail what is required. Ultimately there accumulates a whole body of statutes, regulations, rulings, advisory opinions, interpretations, court opinions, and appellate decisions clogging up the regulatory process.

If the corporate bureaucracy is willing to pay out handsome sums to lawyers to exploit the process, the lawyers are only too willing to oblige. As Reich put it, "they cultivate reputations for their elegant pirouettes around statutes . . . talented people have been known to spend entire careers circumventing a single, arcane area of regulation for the benefit of a few corporations." The increasing technical complexity keeps them in business and makes them rich. Only they have developed the esoteric expertise to deal with the complexity. Meanwhile, any corporation that willingly accepted the original, simple regulatory purpose is now obliged, also, to hire lawyers and send executives to Washington to manoeuvre through the complexity. Naturally it complains about bureaucracy.

The public pays one way or another for this lobbyist inflation. Since the cost of the lobbyist activity can be counted as a "business" expense, it is deducted from taxable income. The public, as taxpayer, has to make up the margin lost in taxes – in effect, an unlegislated "corporate tax" on the citizenry. For defence and other government procurement arrangements, the corporate branch adds the costs of its lobbying to its contracts, hence to the tax bill. In regulated activities, such as telephone and cable, the cost is added to subscriber rates. But the public suffers the cost of lobbying no less when it pays for it indirectly – which it does – through the burden of waste on the economy as a whole.

Nobody, however, checks the mushrooming lobbyist bureaucracy and its costs because nominally they are in the private sector. If anybody did attempt to check it with rules limiting expenditures, they would be pelted with a storm of private-enterprise ideological invective. (Bureaucracies everywhere entrench themselves by exploiting and hiding behind ideology.) It is no coincidence, either, that the most rapid expansion of the U.S. lobbyist bureaucracy should have taken place during the Reagan years. The Reagan government most ardently subscribed to the ideology that gives the lobbying bureaucracy its cover.

So strong is this ideological cover that it can hide from the bureaucrats themselves what they are. When British Columbia Telephone lobbyist Jocelyne Côté-O'Hara left the Prime Minister's Office, she reflected that "the private sector [was] the engine of wealth" and she would find more challenges there. However, she didn't leave the old bureaucracy to become, say, a manufacturing supervisor in a plant producing goods for an open market. Her job with BC Tel was "vice-president of government relations." The function of the job, in her own words, was "to work this town [Ottawa]." Supported by a staff and walking the corridors, that's what she did – as bureaucratic as ever.

In addition to waste and indulgence, an uncontrolled bureaucracy inevitably degenerates into sleaze around the edges, with the sleaze creeping slowly towards the centre. A fully expanded lobbyist bureaucracy, like the American one, is rich in debasement. "Giving sleaze a bad name," was how one American columnist described the Michael Deaver affair. "Grubby venality" and "snakepit" were other descriptions. Deaver's indictment was for perjury, having to do with a time-lapse rule between dealing with issues as a White House staffer and later acting as a lobbyist on the same issues. In the main, though, his activities were no different than those of other firms, except – as with Frank Moores and GCI in Canada – he pursued them with more brazenness and gall. This upset other lobbyists, on both sides of the border, who wanted to be seen as different because they were more discreet.

If moonlighting members of the old bureaucracy sold special access to lawmakers, they would be automatically indicted. The same practice by the lobbyist section of the New Bureaucracy passes as routine business. There is no practical difference between trading on one's closeness to lawmakers through a government department, on the one hand, and trading on one's closeness to lawmakers from having run their political campaigns or having worked in their offices, on the other. The difference is only of form and of ideological protection.

In Canada, tax favours engineered by the corporate branch have aided and abetted the building up of huge corporate empires controlled either by a relatively few corporate managers or by family holdings, and have fattened up balance sheets. The large size of the federal public debt can in good part be traced back to those favours. The lobbying for relief in one form or another (lower stumpage rates, lower resource royalties, accelerated depreciation, and import restrictions, for example) is a standard management device. Lobbying is an integral part of corporate operations like administration and sales.

The bureaucratic rewards generated by the lobbyist section filter down to senior executives personally. The section's tax lobbying, for example, militates for lower income taxes for high-income earners, that is, for the executives. Other lobbying which helps indirectly to fatten up operating statements and balance sheets adds to executives' take in inflated salaries, bonuses and stock-option pay-outs. Lee Iacocca's huge remuneration, largely through stock options, was the product of Japanese export restraints in the early 1980s, resulting from U.S. industry pressure, and from higher price levels which followed; in effect, it came out of the extra US$4-6 billion or more which North Americans paid out every year for their cars in the restriction years and an unquantified margin later. The greatest achievement of Iacocca and other U.S. automobile executives was this bureaucratic one. In the critical years leading up to the restraints, Iacocca was constantly in Washington, lobbying.

What goes for the lobbyist section goes for the corporate branch as a whole: its executives' inflated compensation and perks, its puffed-up pay-outs despite mediocrity or failure, its pampering and luxury, its golden parachutes, the cozy relationships at the top, its hand-holding consultants and its exotic and expensive management fads. Its bureaucratic progress almost makes one grow nostalgic for the robber barons of old who fixed markets, bribed lawmakers, and bought journalists, but who weren't part of a large and self-feeding bureaucracy. Organizationally speaking, they were clean by comparison.

3

The Paper-Entrepreneurialism Branch

In September 1980, Robert Reich, at the time an official at the U.S. Federal Trade Commission, wrote a piece in the upscale *Washington Monthly* magazine called "Pie-Slicers vs. Pie Enlargers." In it he catalogued all the people who, rather than increasing the size of the economic pie, were just reassigning the slices. They weren't doing anything productive; they were just a burden on the economy. There were the accountants manipulating the tax laws and depreciation rules to produce glowing annual reports. There were the financiers dreaming up new varieties of debentures and mutual funds. There were the consultants planning acquisition campaigns, and the lobbyists busy cornering subsidies in Washington. There were the corporate executives who hired all of the above and their lawyers, with bulging briefcases, whose elaborate devices were necessary to carry out the executives' strategies.

Reich calculated that the ratio of asset-rearrangers to asset-enlargers in the U.S. economy was running at about two to one, while the productive part of the economy was languishing and the Rust Bowl was decaying in splendour. Reich called this re-arranging of assets "paper entrepreneurialism." The expression brilliantly caught the wastefulness and vacuity of the game and its players. Now "paper entrepreneurship" and "paper entrepreneur" are part of common parlance.

In fact, Reich wasn't the first observer to notice the waste. Financial and stock speculators have long been considered parasites, battening on to the real work of enterprise and sometimes bleeding or destroying it. The more notorious of the stock players in the United States in the nineteenth century were known as "wreckers" and "hyenas." Even the *New York Times* deplored them. But they were marginal in the economy overall. It was maverick American sociologist Thorstein Veblen, in 1899, in his book *The Theory of the Leisure Class*, who perhaps first understood the scale that paper enterprise could take. He wrote about people in "pecuniary" employment as different from "industrial" employment (actually making goods). In the "pecuniary" category, financiering operations led the way. Its main aptitude: acquisition. Its style: predatory. It was served, in turn, by bankers and lawyers. The lawyers, Veblen wrote, had "no taint of usefulness," other than helping to play the acquisition game. His tart description of their activities – "exclusively occupied with the details of predatory fraud, either in achieving or in checkmating chicanery" – could serve today as a description of corporate lawyers achieving or checkmating hostile takeovers.

Little did Veblen know, however, how bureaucratically elaborate the paper entrepreneurship of his time would eventually become. He saw it more in terms of animal combativeness. For that matter, little did the Robert Reich of 1980, a decade ago, realize how bureaucratically inflatable paper entrepreneurship was, particularly mergers and acquisitions.

Of all paper enterprise activities, mergers and acquisitions (now known simply as M&A) were the most astonishing, for Reich. He could hardly believe that acquisition deals in 1979 in the United States totalled US$43.5 billion. This was 28 per cent greater than the year before and almost twice the level reached just two years earlier in 1977 when they totalled $22 billion, itself a remarkable figure. But these figures look puny next to what was yet to come. In 1986, the M&A re-arranging of slices hit a record $220 billion, according to IDD Information Services, New York. In 1987, despite the dampening effects of Black Monday in mid-October, the partial total still reached $195 billion (the fifty biggest deals by themselves amounted to $92 billion). In 1988 it was up to a record $265 billion. The paper-entrepreneurialism branch of the New Bureaucracy just kept growing – growing beyond imagination.

Even in 1989, when the junk-bond market (one of the financing mechanisms) ultimately fizzled, U.S. M&A reached $254 billion, before dropping off, finally, in 1990. The total for the decade 1980-1989 (all after Reich's article): upwards of $1.45 trillion.

The size of the deals also also grew astonishingly, so that only the very largest companies appeared immune from takeover. In the mid-1970s, the largest contested takeover had come in at $350 million. This would be dwarfed by subsequent takeovers as the syndrome grew more intense. The swallowing up of oil companies led the way: Conoco at US$6.9 billion, Marathon Oil at $6.1 billion, Getty Oil at $10.1 billion, and the grand-daddy of them all, Gulf Oil, taken over by Standard Oil of California (Socal) for upwards of $13 billion.

The already huge General Electric snaffled the already huge RCA Corp.

for US$6.1 billion. Later in the decade, Philip Morris picked up Kraft for $12.9 billion. Campeau Corp. (Robert Campeau) put out $6.5 billion for a mere department store chain, Federated Department Stores. (Not much more than a year earlier, Campeau had acquired Allied Stores for $3.5 billion.) Pharmaceutical deals, too, hit the roof at the end of the decade, with Bristol-Myers picking up Squibb for $12.7 billion.

Kohlberg Kravis Roberts, the leveraged buy-out operators, acquired conglomerate Beatrice Cos. for US$6.25 billion. Then it outdid everything that had been done before with the mammoth 1989 buy-out of RJR Nabisco for $25 billion, the largest takeover of all time. In the record M&A year 1988, even the last in the *Fortune* list of the fifty largest deals came in at over $1 billion.

Merger and acquisition activity also caught up corporate bureaucracies in Canada. Major mergers and takeovers in Canada in 1984 involved seven transactions valued at C$900 million. Half way through 1985 – with Canadian corporate bureaucracies belatedly getting the hang of things – fourteen large transactions had already taken place with a total value of $4.7 billion. Several blockbusters were yet to come. Leading the way was the Olympia & York acquisition of Gulf Canada ($2.8 billion taken alone). Foreign-owned Montreal conglomerate Imasco bid $2.4 billion for Genstar (which had just swallowed Canada Trust, and Permanent Trust before that). In 1988, Dome Petroleum went for $5.5 billion to U.S.-owned Amoco. The loss-making Dome had ended up in the soup because of earlier takeovers of its own.

These were only the largest of a whole host of merger and acquisition cases in the country which, further, in the smaller Canadian economy, also brought with it increasing concentration of economic power. One study found that the transaction value of the largest twenty mergers in Canada between 1980 and 1985 was 2.5 times the size of the largest twenty in the United States, compared to the relative size of each nation's gross national product. "The gathering takeover frenzy," as it was described in 1985, became "The new takeover frenzy" in 1986 and, by 1988, the *Financial Post* could announce "takeover speculation runs rampant," as acquisitors continued to stalk takeover targets.

By 1987 M&A deals in Canada reached $28.7 billion – as whipped-up a pace of activity, relatively, as in the United States. In 1988, despite the after-effects of the 1987 stock market crash, they still got as high as C$23.7 billion and in 1989 they rose to $30 billion.

Strange as it may sound, it wasn't too long ago that hostile takeovers were actually taboo in some quarters, particularly among major corporations. Until Inco made a tender offer for ESB (a U.S. battery company) in 1974, no hostile takeover had ever been attempted by a full-fledged member of the corporate élite. Once the barrier was broken, one large company after another indulged. Their senior executives were soon joined in the game by another kind of player, called "raiders" or "sharks." These were individuals who, with financial backing, went after the shares of undervalued companies and then, by breaking them up or selling off some of their assets, paid off the debt incurred to launch the raid and still had a prize left over. This was the "leveraged buy-out" (LBO) – using the assets of the target company as collateral (the "lever" for the financing) to raise the debt in order to take over the company with little money of one's own. No longer were large corporations the only ones that could undertake large takeovers.

Many of the raiders were also known as "greenmailers." After picking up a block of shares and threatening a takeover push, they would desist if the target company (through the decision of its management) would buy back the share block, at a premium. The raiders would pocket the difference. "You don't have to win to win at the takeover game," commented *Forbes* magazine, "you can be so pushy that people will pay you to go away."

The names of these raiders, in the United States, became notorious and celebrated: T. Boone Pickens, Carl Icahn, Jimmy Goldsmith (an Anglo-European), Ronald Perelman (who went after and got Revlon), and countless others, big and small, each with their own stratagems. Canada produced its own raiders riding south across the border: the Belzberg brothers and Robert Campeau in particular.

Greenmailing profits by themselves could be sizeable, with no takeover taking place. Mesa Petroleum (Pickens), for example, picked up US$40 million from a run at Cities Service (another oil company). Mesa and the Icahn group turned profits of $89 million and $40 million respectively from greenmailing Phillips Petroleum. Revlon (Ronald Perelman) netted $39 million from a feint at Gillette. Jimmy Goldsmith and his partners took home $90 million from a run at Goodyear Tire and Rubber.

They were making these lucrative sums of money from thin air, or so it appeared. In fact, they were making it from preying on corporate bureaucracies who did not want to give up control and who otherwise wanted to get the greenmailers out of their hair. One section of the New Bureaucracy (the raiders) manipulated another section (the corporate branch) at shareholders' expense.

As the takeover machinery evolved, it soon became clear in turn that if the raider was intent on taking over the target rather than just collecting greenmail, and was properly financed, then the existing management would find it very difficult, if not impossible, to retain its independence. Their ultimate recourse was to find a "white knight" to take them over instead, rescuing them from the "black knight" – the raider. The bidding would start. The tender offer, or simply intention to bid, or sometimes even rumour of intention, which initiated the process, was called putting the target "in play."

The raider then won whether he won or lost. If the hostile takeover attempt succeeded, he snaffled the prize. If it failed, the raider, having armed himself beforehand with a block of shares, would surrender those shares to the "white knight" at the higher, bid-up premium price and pocket the difference. This was vastly more profitable than greenmailing alone. Mesa Petroleum (Pickens), for example, netted an estimated US$400-500 million from putting Gulf Oil (taken over by Socal) into play ($750 million for the raiding syndicate overall). The Belzberg brothers picked up a reported $70 million for their participation. Mesa wasn't even among the main contenders when the bidding ended.

This making hay either way – "heads I win, tails I win" – for doing nothing productive at all, had a predictable effect. It drew new raiders into the game like moths to a light. The more raiders on the scene, the more companies that would be put into play, and *ad infinitum*. It seemed, too, from some of the players, that anybody could get into the act.

The management of target companies soon realized that if a victorious raider could strip the assets of his conquest to pay for the takeover, the target company could use the same device in its defence – sell off assets at their higher break-up value, strengthen the numbers thereby, and, in the process, increase the share price, previously discounted. This procedure made the company a less attractive buy (it used up some of the asset-stripping possibilities) or raised the cost of the company's shares beyond what the raider was willing to pay. Improving the productivity of the actual enterprise didn't come into it. This is what Texaco did – sold off some important assets – when Carl Icahn bought a "strategic block" of shares in the company and made a hostile offer for the rest.

But the raider, from the capital gain on his own share block, made a fortune anyway. Icahn's ultimate profit from his unsuccessful run at Texaco was in the US$650 million range. At one stage, in 1988, his profit from twenty raids in less than a decade beginning in 1979 was put at $1.66 billion. Even when two major unrealized gains in the total later turned flat, he didn't need to go begging.

The rake-offs for raiders came so easily that they had no trouble raising larger and larger sums of money in the form of "junk bonds" – subordinated debt at high interest rates – to swing their deals. "Subordinated" meant that prior lenders, like banks, who offered "senior" debt, would get paid first in case of default, or that senior debt wasn't available in the first place because of risk. From the extra risk of the loan came the higher interest charges. This was the short-term financing raiders needed to get their hands on the target companies.

Fortune magazine in 1987 published a scorecard rating the top corporate raiders. The measure was done in "fin" ratings on the "Shark Scale."

Four fins for swallowing companies, three for taking big bites, two for drawing first blood, and one for nibbling and running.

The rise of hostile takeovers and all their paper devices brought with them, almost like a Newtonian law of physics, the rise of defensive manoeuvres and their own paper devices – paper against paper, in an increasingly complicated, ornate, bizarre, and costly bureaucratic proliferation. Most of these devices had their own code names. In a "poison pill" defence, the target company issued rights to shareholders that allowed them to buy additional stock at a huge, say, 50 per cent, discount, once a raider acquired a certain percentage of shares (20 per cent was a common trigger level). This automatically watered down the percentage of the raider's holdings and the value of his investment, making it ruinously expensive for the hostile bidder to follow through. Poison pills could be rigged whereby, once the threshold was reached, the rights would "flip over" and shareholders could get stock at a discount in the *acquiring* company. The increasingly complicated ins and outs, devised by lawyers, became known, collectively, as "poison pill technology."

"Poison debt" was a cousin of the "poison pill." If a hostile raider achieved a certain grip on the target company's shares, a "poison debt" provision would trigger the taking on of a vast amount of debt by the target company in terms that made the target rancid to the swallower. The proceeds from the debt would usually be distributed to the shareholders in the form, say, of a special dividend. Often this was done pre-emptively, to keep potential raiders at a distance. The poison-debt manoeuvre was particularly aimed at LBOs. The more that the assets of the target company were already tied to debt, because of the poison-debt caper, the less leverage there was for an LBO. This particular defensive refinancing device became known as a "leveraged recap" or, as the *Institutional Investor* put it, "companies doing LBOs of themselves."

Cash-rich companies or companies with little debt, and hence considerable borrowing power, were particularly attractive targets. Such companies, consequently, might indulge in takeovers themselves, using up their cash and their borrowing power for the purpose, and adding to the takeover syndrome and to corporate debt while they were at it. Use up – cynics would say "dissipate" – your capital and debt capacity before they were used up against you, was the strategy. Whether or not the defensive takeovers made economic sense was irrelevant.

Or the target company could respond by selling off its best assets. These were "scorched earth" strategies. Scorched earth, poison debt, and buybacks could be used in combination. *Fortune* referred to "the host of company-bruising contortions chief executives have used to evade raiders and save their jobs." In this bureaucratically bizarre world, companies looked after themselves by mutilating themselves.

The most sensational defensive manoeuvre, however, was the "PacMan defence:" a hostile tender offer for the company attempting to take over one's own company. The PacMan defence was made famous by an attempt by Bendix Corp. (an autoparts and aviation products manufacturer) to snaffle Martin Marietta (an aerospace company) in 1982.

The Bendix takeover attempt, and Marietta's PacMan response, reached high farce. Each company had the other on its takeover list and was also on the takeover lists of other companies. Marietta, as well as tendering for Bendix shares itself, arranged for a white knight to make a separate offer for Bendix and to sell some of Bendix's assets to Marietta if it, the white knight, were successful. Another knight showed up on the other side, offering to buy all or part of Bendix, complete with Bendix's Marietta shares. It looked, for a while, in the PacMan game, as if Bendix and Marietta were going to swallow each other. Ultimately, the white knight on Bendix's side, Allied-Signal, bought Bendix and arranged for Bendix and Marietta to give their respective shares back to each other, with a "standstill" agreement to forestall renewed cannibalism. Allied-Signal itself was a creation of paper entrepreneurship – the product of "a dazzling, sometimes bewildering, series of mergers, acquisitions, spinoffs, shutterings and restructurings . . . a born-again amalgam," as *Chemical Week* put it.

One of the most frequent defensive manoeuvres against hostile takeovers was legal action. It was used almost automatically, if only to slow down the takeover process and allow more time for beseiged management to find a white knight. Raiders responded in kind, citing the right of shareholders to profit by takeover offers. These legal actions had some effect: The use of poison pills was constrained by court actions. Lawyers for existing management, in turn, however, responding to the raiders' response, came up with new poison pill variants, much like a new antibiotic is developed when immunity builds up to an old one. Companies would be reincorporated in states where the courts were more tolerant of poison pills. Lobbyists went to work pushing for protective state legislation, succeeding most notably in Pennsylvania where a Belzberg raid on Armstrong World Industries (the tile-and-flooring maker) was foiled with the help of tough new anti-takeover laws. Other state measures, in Delaware, Massachussetts, and elsewhere, boosted defences.

"The battle has clearly swung from offense to defense, like a football game," one observer, quoted in *Business Week*, commented in 1986. And then it swung back to offence, just as surely, and then to defence again.

Some of the more arcane battles occurred in Canada. One was the attempt by Olympia & York (the Reichmann family) to take over Hiram Walker Resources in 1986. Hiram Walker management, expecting to be put out on the street, spent $35 million of the company's money trying to fight off the intruders, even if it meant self-destructing, as management of the company, in the process. A compliant Hiram Walker board armed its top eight executives with golden parachutes equal to three years' salary if they were laid off. Then the Hiram Walker directors set out to scorch some earth. If Olympia & York was going to break up the company, as seemed likely, they would do so first. They sold off the key business, the distillery, responsible for 40 per cent of the company's profits, to British conglomerate Allied-Lyons. The strategy was to use the proceeds of the sale to bid against Olympia & York for the remainder of the company.

Hiram Walker also got conglomerate Bell Canada Enterprises, through TransCanada PipeLines Ltd. (TCPL), to make a bid, raising the ante. When, as expected, the TCPL bid was exceeded by a higher Olympia & York offer, TCPL, instead of bidding back, stood on the sidelines . . . and collected a pre-arranged fee of $7.5 million for its troubles. Olympia & York eventually prevailed over Hiram Walker but there was still the matter of the distillery, whose cash flow was one of the objects of the takeover attempt in the first place. Olympia & York went to court to reverse the sale of the distillery to Allied-Lyons. The legal action failed. The takeover victim in all this, Hiram Walker Resources, was itself the product of a merger and sundry takeovers.

Once locked in their bureaucratic wrestling match, the contenders in a hostile takeover attempt could usually be counted on to try any number of holds, on any number of parts, and continue running up the legal and adviser bills – often with peevishness and silliness growing – until some manoeuvre or sheer financial power on one side finally put an end to it. One relatively minor bout, the reverse takeover of Trans Mountain Pipe Line by Inland Natural Gas in 1982, had at one point twenty-two separate legal actions going, and altogether lasted fifteen months or, as *Canadian Business* remarked sardonically, "about twice as long as the Battle of Britain."

If a raider could use the target company's assets to borrow junk money for the takeover, burdening the company with debt, and then sell off parts of the target to reduce the debt, why couldn't management and collaborators do the same, with little equity capital? This was a "management buy-out" (MBO) – taking the company "private" under management's direct owner-ship. It eliminated the threat of hostile takeovers and also eliminated the pesky nuisance of outside shareholders in general, not to mention the nui-sance of financial disclosure required of publicly traded companies. MBOs came on stream. Or, particularly in the case of larger takeovers, a firm specializing in LBOs would be invited in by management as a white knight. The LBO firm would engineer and control the rescue takeover deal but would at the same time offer senior management a significant minority share and with it a share of the pay-off that came with the manoeuvre.

MBOs, and LBOs with a management component, raised questions of their own. One of the purported advantages of senior management being a significant, if often a minority, shareholder was that they would work harder and better, having such a stake in the company. This led to the invidious inference that under the old, general shareholders' ownership, the executives hadn't been exerting themselves enough, in which case the management group didn't deserve to end up on top, and especially not by using other people's money.

Sometimes the sell-off of parts to offset the debt of a takeover was so extensive that the remainder seemed insignificant. By the time Campeau Corp., for example, finished peddling different holdings of its retail store takeovers in order to reduce debt, eighteen of twenty-one divisions of Allied Stores (taken over in 1986) had gone, and eight of fourteen divisions of Federated Department Stores (acquired in 1988) had been sold – all to no avail, as it turned out, as the Campeau financial superstructure soon crumbled. A company, led by its corporate chief, might go through a whole series of complicated mergers, acquisitions and divestitures, changing its character altogether as it sidestepped across the corporate landscape.

One particular U.S. CEO, Donald Kelly of holding company Esmark Inc., made fifty acquisitions and divestitures in a short eight-year period. Among the acquisitions were companies which had themselves acquired other companies along the line. The CEO ended up surrendering the takeover vehicle to another takeover company – his fifty-first deal. Then that takeover company was taken over. One of the subsidiary companies, car-rental company Avis, after having originally lost its independence at the beginning of the merry-go-round, had its corporate parent changed four times in six years.

There were circles within circles, and smaller circles within them. A company could go from incurring huge debt, buying back its shares, and selling off assets, in a defensive manoeuvre, to issuing new shares, retiring debt and taking over other people's assets, all in the same cycle.

As American business writer Jeff Madrick remarked, the "takeover movement increasingly looked like a board game, with its participants about as remote from the reality of business as children sitting around playing Monopoly."

With upwards of US$200 billion in deals being done each year in the United States, as the decade ended, the paper-entrepreneurialism branch had come to indulge in a dizzying – some described it as "frenzied" – shuffle of companies back and forth. The business press played up the practitioners (in

Canada, the likes of Robert Campeau and Paul Reichmann down to the medium fry like Jim Pattison) as if they were economic heroes. On occasion, pages of the *Globe and Mail*'s "Report on Business" or of the *Financial Post* would give the impression that takeover action constituted business, period, so omnipresent and elaborate were the M&A stories. The coverage of Robert Campeau's takeover of Federated Department Stores would have done justice to the parting of the Red Sea. Corporate executives snaffling other companies carried with them the imagery of masterful industrial titans, of leaders, of movers and shakers. "Raiders" and "sharks" had an even more swashbuckling imagery. Junk-bond dealer Michael Milken's huge 1987 income (an estimated US$600 million plus, including income from his own participation in deals) seemed fantastic.

People could even catch a slice of the game on the big screen, in *Wall Street*, starring Michael Douglas. The movie borrowed, for its inspiration, from several notable corporate raiders, an airline grab (in real life, Carl Icahn snaffled TWA), the "greed is good" philosophy of indicted arbitrageur Ivan Boesky, and the passing of inside information by Boesky collaborator Dennis Levine. In real life, Boesky ended up surrendering a large piece, US$50 million, of ill-gotten gains and paying another $50 million in fines, and went to jail. The case created a sensation. Then, in 1988, came a ninety-eight-count indictment for fraud and racketeering against an even larger figure in the paper-entrepreneurialism branch – indeed, a bureaucratic god-head – Michael Milken himself, of investment bankers Drexel Burnham Lambert. Drexel was also indicted, but caved in, paying fines and restitution of US$650 million, and abandoning Milken to his fate in the process.

Colourful and, in their way, damning books had begun to chronicle these happenings. One of the best known was *The Predators' Ball* – the title taken from the unofficial name for Milken's annual junk-bond conference in Beverly Hills. It was written by a reporter for the *American Lawyer*, Connie Bruck. Milken was a "charismatic and messianic leader" prepared to do "whatever it took to win," and putting together partnerships "custom-made for patronage [and] manipulation." His staff, cult-like, saw him larger than life. Drexel, the firm, with Milken in the lead, was "the brass-knuckles, threatening, market-manipulating Cosa Nostra of the securities world."

A play about a takeover shark, *Other People's Money*, appeared off-Broadway and became a hit. A touring production even went to Toronto. It was wheeler-dealer as villain. Then there was *Barbarians At The Gate: The Fall of RJR Nabisco*, the book by Wall Street reporters Bryan Burrough and John Helyar. It quickly rose to the top of the best-seller list. This account of the Kohlberg Kravis takeover of RJR Nabisco, outbidding the management buy-out offer, savages the players. It's a catalogue of greed, ego, ineptitude, and conniving that even, by its excesses, surprised the authors, who thought they were already quite cynical.

Then the department store companies that Robert Campeau had taken over amid so much publicity couldn't handle the leveraged debt and went under, with a Chapter 11 bankruptcy filing. Without Michael Milken, meanwhile, Drexel also went under, spectacularly. Then Milken paid a fine of US$600 million. He was banned from the securities industry for life. Later he would be sentenced to ten years in prison. The junk-bond market tumbled and was declared dead. Without gobs of junk-bond money on hand, the LBO break-up artists – the so-called "financial buyers" – were largely sidelined.

All manner of expressions of shock and righteous denunciations followed these events. Writing of Boesky, Milken, and Drexel in *Maclean's*, Peter Newman talked about sleaze, corruption, felony, thuggery, and related attributes such as fear and greed. When Campeau bit the dust, leaving Bloomingdale's in New York an orphan under the care of the receivers, an offended columnist from the *New York News* denounced him as a "greed-driven barracuda" and the *New York Times* sniffed at his "overreaching grasp and oversized ego."

The language in all this was either martial or of crime and gluttony: "predators," "warriors," "barbarians," "fraud," "felony," "greed," "corruption," and, of course, "feeding frenzy." Because so much money was involved, beyond the world of common sense, the events were seen as extraordinary and dramatic. When the cracks began to show, business reporters began talking of the end of an era. Forgotten in the shouting was that there had been takeover waves in the 1960s and 1970s not much different in kind, and that, behind the imagery, was the encroachment and inflation of bureaucracy. The most appropriate word for it wasn't "felony" or "barbarian," but "waste."

Bureaucracy generated the cycle on the way up, worked the cycle on the way down, and would try to keep the make-work going – and generate another wave if it could – after that. At each successive cycle, it became more elaborate and entrenched than before.

The bureaucracy starts with the corporate branch – its cadres' territorial ambitions, vanity, and bureaucratic cast of mind. Take, for example, the first stage of the takeover movement after World War II, the conglomeration rage of the 1960s. The impulse of a bureaucratic organization like a corporation to grow, and to grow at all costs if the organization can get away with it, was at the forefront. The star and archetype of the movement was Harold Geneen of ITT. Geneen, looking back on his days at ITT, was frank about the bureaucratic impulse, although he didn't call it that. "A company has a momentum of its own," he told author Jeff Madrick. "When you have an organization, you need room for people to expand, to grow into new jobs. I always say there is one word for happiness in a business organization: growth." Not mentioned as feeding this impulse, but also impelling it, was the vanity of power – the sheer bureaucratic power and status of having more territory than the next guy. The easiest way to grow in the 1960s was diversification through acquisition and the astute use of accountants – bureaucratically-devised expansion.

Geneen was a compleat bureaucratic type. He himself trained as an accountant. His administrative method was bureaucratic: tracking detailed financial reports which his corporate managers had to submit to him. His administrative culture was bureaucratic: abstraction from the real world of producing and marketing goods and services. This was the era of conglomerates like ITT, Gulf & Western, LTV, Litton, Northwest Industries, and Teledyne – huge organizations which, it appeared, had been created out of nothing.

One of the characteristics of an inflating bureaucracy is that it has enough power and allies to cover for what it is doing. This was no exception. When the leading conglomerators claimed that professional managers like themselves could manage all kinds of businesses, and that what was required above all was their financial skills – their abstract, bureaucratic skills – they prevailed. There were plenty of willing academics to help out with the rationalizing, too. "Synergy" – the idea that adding new parts would, in combination, produce more than the sum of the parts – entered the business jargon of the time.

In the real world, the synergy turned out to be mostly in the stock market, where conglomerate stocks rode the wave of takeover excitement. When the bottom fell out at the end of the 1960s, the conglomerates' share prices tumbled. ITT itself became a shambles. However, a new wave of takeovers began in the 1970s, pushed by the same bureaucratic impulses, as if the deception and disillusion of the 1960's wave had never happened.

Game-playing is another bureaucratic trait, and the paper entrepreneurialism of M&A is almost entirely game-playing. As long as the game goes on, and the players rank themselves against each other, there is no end to it. The game inflates by its own impulses. "There is a sense of challenge, the challenge of doing something meaningful," Paul Reichmann once confessed. "In the end, though, it is an addiction."

For a CEO of a publicly traded company with wide share distribution, more territory generally means more pay and hence more sheen, giving the CEO extra standing in both the business and social worlds. It's the bureaucratic equivalent of displaying feathers. "Statement acquisition" entered the lexicon. A "statement acquisition" is an acquisition made by a newcomer to a scene – usually to the United States – to show that he has arrived and is a force, or at least a phenomenon of some sort, to be reckoned with. It's a case of acquisition as bureaucratic calling card.

All this vanity is egged on by the veneration and glorification in the business press and the mass media. Imagine deputy ministers in the old bureaucracy (government) playing tiresome and boring, but exceedingly clever and elaborate, games, to merge departments and increase their territory, for no other reason than an addiction to the game-playing. Imagine, also, that in moments of weakness, they admitted as much. They would be ridiculed and castigated by the media. The same people in the New Bureaucracy, like Paul Reichmann, who admits the addiction, are revered instead – are treated with awe instead of satire even when they are criticized.

Bureaucracy, in its pejorative sense, is unproductive make-work generated by its denizens to preserve their income and status and to cover for their productive limitations. Paper entrepreneurialism – no exception to the rule – hides entrepreneurial failure and lack of ability.

The first element of this failure is the inability to develop and market new products, to improve old ones, or to increase productivity and technological inputs. Take the case of William Agee, who led Bendix Corporation into its takeover battle against Marietta. Agee came up quickly through the corporate world as a financial officer, heavily involved in buying and selling subsidiary companies. He became chairman of Bendix without having had much experience in actually running a company. Acquisitions and divestitures were the only thing he really knew. This wasn't untypical.

Similarly, when builder Robert Campeau began buying and stripping retail-store properties in the United States, rather than developing new building technology or other new industry, he *de facto* admitted he had reached his level of entrepreneurial incapacity and was getting into bureaucracy instead. T. Boone Pickens joined the paper bureaucracy in a big way to cover for his failing business. His Mesa Petroleum was spending $500,000 a day drilling in the Gulf of Mexico, was losing money, had failed to reduce its exploration budget fast enough, and was heading for the last round-up. His paper raid on Gulf was aimed at refloating the failing Mesa. Some of the companies that indulged in takeovers defensively, in order to use up their visible supply of cash and prevent themselves from being taken over, were poorly managed in the first place. The end result was that the mediocre management had two or three businesses to look after instead of one: mediocrity extending itself, bureaucratically, to protect itself.

The sidestepping by companies from one sector to another through acquisitions and divestitures, changing their assets and identity, hides the failure of those companies to retain their traditional markets by increasing productivity and by introducing new technology and products. It's a running away from the real job of entrepreneurship.

The resort to takeovers reflects a general entrepreneurial failure: the inability of enterprise to generate enough interesting new projects to absorb available capital. A "lack of alternative investment opportunities" is how corporate analysts put it, to explain the corporate indulgence in takeover games. Translation: The corporations don't have the entrepreneurial imagination and know-how to put their available cash to work productively, and they are too bureaucratically self-interested to distribute the cash to shareholders in the form of dividends. The ill-fated conglomeration wave of the 1960s was no different. U.S. businesses at the time began losing export markets and had no new ideas for expanding at home, so they reverted to takeover activity.

The capital markets reflected the same pattern, from the financial side. New players flocked to the junk-bond market, which underwrote most of the leveraged buyouts, because there was "a dearth of tempting investment opportunities," as *Business Week* put it. Translation: Entrepreneurship isn't generating enough new, good ideas, and even if it were, the capital markets, so eager for short-term high returns, wouldn't recognize good new ideas anyway.

All this, however, doesn't by itself explain the spore-like growth of takeover activity leading to its explosion in the 1980s. It happened by the growth of a takeover bureaucracy itself.

In his probing and endlessly revealing 1987 book *Taking America*, business writer Jeff Madrick traced the progression in all its myriad interconnections. Two of the leading corporate takeover practitioners of the 1970, for example, had been with Litton and ITT respectively, the conglomerators of the 1960s. Having acquired the necessary M&A skills in the 1960s, it was only natural that they exploited those skills in the next decade.

But more important was the takeover bureaucracy properly speaking – the lawyers, investment bankers, and ancillary functionaries like accountants, who drew increasingly large fees from selling, advising on, financing, and processing takeover deals. The increasingly intense takeover activity was their creation – sustained and inflated to keep them rich and growing. Corporate chieftains appeared to be leading the takeover march, but more and more they became figureheads or agents of the takeover phenomenon, lending their vanity and ambition to the takeover machinery. The real takeover practitioners were the investment bankers and the lawyers – the back-stage bureaucrats.

The investment bankers turned to takeovers in a big way when the U.S. Securities and Exchange Commission (SEC) ruled to eliminate fixed brokerage and underwriting commissions in 1975. The competition in brokerage dealings that followed cut margins for the investment banking firms. They were hungry for new business. Pumping up takeover activity filled the gap.

Morgan Stanley, the leading investment banker at the time, established a large mergers and acquisitions department. It agreed to manage hostile takeovers (starting with the Inco raid on battery company ESB in 1974) and was soon launched on a whole campaign of them. In the "bear-market days on Wall Street," Madrick observed, "Morgan needed the money." Other investment bankers began to build merger and acquisition teams. The net profit from such work was extremely high, although it would be dwarfed by the huge advisory fees of subsequent years.

The more lucrative that fees became, the more that investment bankers shopped deals and generated takeover activity. Takeovers promised to become the main profit centre of several investment-banking firms. By the early 1980s the M&A bureaucracy, with its accumulated tactical experience and its size, had reached critical mass. "Virtual armies of takeover specialists were now available on Wall Street," Madrick wrote. "... The machinery proved far too developed, the process far too lucrative," to be stopped by recession or common sense. The maximum size of possible takeovers escalated, making the fees even grander.

A CEO of a substantial company, or even a freelance raider, could now "press a button and put a vast and efficient machinery in process." Investment bankers, scouring the corporate countryside for possible targets, formulating and shopping deals, flogged the temptation wherever there was a likely acquisitor candidate or where they crossed paths with somebody with enough vanity and ambition. "Deals are not bought, they are sold by investment bankers," U.S. takeover lawyer Martin Lipton described it.

Once the idea of a hostile takeover was sold to one party, the chase would be on by another investment banker to find a friendly "white knight" to foil the raiders, usually by outbidding them and taking over themselves. If the white knight won in the end, that other investment banker would pocket the large fee. American economics writer Robert Reich once described, satirically, how the investment banks advised all the parties – corporations on the look-out, targets, raiders, and white knights – and how their fancy analysis always seemed to boil down to the same advice: "Move your money! Quick!" – with the investment banks taking a little piece of every dollar that was moved. "No deal maker advises his corporate client not to deal," Reich quipped.

It made little difference whether there was an economic rationale to the takeover or whether prices paid were out of line. Once the machinery was engaged, it turned over in a predictable, complicated, and ever-more-costly pattern. The process (the "game") took on a life of its own.

The ultimate skill for investment-bank advisers was in demonstrating, through working the computer, that a high enough price could be paid to carry the deal. Each side would work its computer against the other, because the highest price that could be justified on paper won the game and the M&A advisers who had worked out the justification would go home with the big fee. "Pushing the numbers" was the jargon for it. Madrick compared the role of investment bankers to Iago pushing and manipulating Othello into counterproductive acts. (As these calculations and their assumptions became increasingly complex, it was almost inevitable that too much would be paid. By the law of averages, somebody would calculate too high, somebody too low and others in between. In competitive takeovers, the calculation that was too high *ipso facto* won the day and was used, barring exceptional circumstances.)

Madrick's account ended in 1986. Unlike others who that year were expecting a drop-off in deals, he had no illusions that the paper takeover activity would end. Earlier confident predictions that such happenings couldn't repeat themselves, because of their foolishness and excesses – after the conglomeration wave of the 1960s, for example – had proven false. The pundits had overlooked that the takeover activity was essentially a bureaucratic phenomenon and that the growing bureaucracy that undertook it, unchecked, would inflate by its own momentum. What *Fortune* described with a hint of drama as "unprecedented steps to win merger fees" was just a playing out of this momentum.

The more esoteric and complex the investment bank's bureaucratic tactics – one adviser versus another – the more they could ante up fees and leapfrog over each other into the higher realms of luxury. In 1975, a fee of US$750,000 was considered very high, particularly since it involved just a handful of professionals, some miscellaneous expenses and, usually, no capital. By the early 1980s, fees to individual investment banks for single deals, worked out as a percentage of the size of the deal, would reach $20 million and more. The Gulf takeover of Chevron in 1984 generated $62.5 million in fees (the two advisers to the buyer alone getting a $45 million fee between them). By 1988, advisory and legal fees amounting to $100 million were commonplace in major deals.

Forfeiture penalties, financial fees (for arranging or putting up bridge loans and financing), legal fees, and golden parachutes added to totals. The aggregate fees and related costs for the takeover of Revlon in 1985 was in the US$200 million range, or more than 10 per cent of the transaction. By 1988, Campeau Corp.'s takeover of Federated Department Stores cost more than $517 million in golden parachutes, advisory, legal, and other fees, and bridge-loan fees and interest. For the takeover of RJR Nabisco, later in the year, all fees inclusive hit an estimated $1 billion, including commercial banking fees of $325 million and $75 million to LBO firm Kohlberg Kravis, the head of the takeover syndicate itself.

"Merger fees that bend the mind," *Fortune* observed with not a little awe in early 1986. "Wall Street dealmakers stuffed their pockets with record advisory fees," it marvelled again, a year later. *Fortune* runs an annual scorecard of the fifty biggest investment-banker deals of the year, which generate leading megafees. Of the 200 deals covered in the years 1987-1990 inclusive, 177 were takeovers, defensive recapitalizations, or their byproducts. Columbia University law professor Louis Lowenstein estimated M&A fees and separation agreements, including legal and financial fees, at roughly 4 per cent of transaction values in this period. A later study, of large management buyouts, by Steven Kaplan of the University of Chicago and Jeremy Stein of MIT, found that median fees for the MBOs in their sample had risen to 6 per cent. The aggregate M&A fees for the decade, according to *Fortune*, were $60 billion.

Unless they are helping a besieged client fend off a raider, investment bankers usually accept a lower fee if the deal doesn't go through. The lower fee appears to reflect the actual hours worked on the deal, as estimated beforehand. These lower fees, still high in absolute terms, may be as little as one-seventh to one-fifteenth of the fee if the takeover, merger, or divestiture goes through. The difference, in the higher fee – up to fourteen-fifteenths of it – is the extra fat on top of the ordinary fat.

These fees meant extraordinary bureaucratic incomes. The LBO and junk-bond specialists led the pack in the late 1980s, because of the step-up advisory fees, the financial fees, and for LBO shops, their slice of the turn-around capital gains. The more than US$600 million Milken was estimated to have pulled in from all sources in 1987, and which generated so much indignation, was unusual, but extraordinarily inflated incomes had long been the rule. Michael David-Weill took home $125 million in 1986 from his stake in investment bank Lazard Freres, no less bizarre. Nobody in the New Bureaucracy uttered a peep other than of admiration and envy. The two senior and active partners in Kohlberg Kravis, Henry Kravis and George Roberts, picked up at least $70 million each in 1987, $110 million in 1988, $45 million in 1989 (a tough year because RJR Nabisco was such a lot to swallow), and $90 million in 1990.

Indeed, in peak year 1988, the top forty in *Financial World's* rankings of the Wall Street 100 – most of which were involved in M&A, LBOs, strategic-block investing and other variations of the game – all made at least US$20 million. The last, and 100th, on the list made $6 million, itself astonishing. Milken led the way with about $200 million (withheld by Drexel because of court order), having only worked for part of the year.

Almost as impressive, in their more modest way, were the situations where the revenue had to be shared with a large number of people. For example, the leading handler of mergers, acquisitions, and divestitures in 1987 in the United States was Goldman, Sachs. It was a banner year for the firm. Of the top forty-eight partners, twenty-two took home US$4 to $8 million each, sixteen managed to pocket an estimated $9.6 to $12.7 million, nine were in the $15 million range, and the senior partner took home at least $32 million. (Some of that income would have come from other investment-bank functions.)

J.P. Morgan's advice was to pay the lowest-paid employees at least one twenty-fifth of the highest. Had investment banks and LBO boutiques followed that advice, secretaries in a few chosen firms would have been earning millions and even janitors in firms at the bottom of the list would have pulled in a couple of hundred thousand per year.

The bureaucratic machinery of a major takeover, once in motion, churned out no end of tactical variations, nuances, and complexities, requiring an ever-larger bureaucracy to deal with them – especially so for auction-style and hostile takeovers. On hand, in a typical, large dealmaking process, were, first of all, some top takeover bureaucrats (the "virtuosi" or "stars") from leading investment banks (or M&A boutiques) and from law firms in the field. Behind the virtuosi were merger departments – in some cases, deal factories employing scores of professionals and their back-up staff. These rank-and-filers didn't do too badly either. In the 1960s, an investment banker started at US$9,000. By the late 1980s, starting pay was as high as $100,000, and sometimes reached $150,000 with bonuses. A few years' experience brought cadres into the mid-six figures, and even $1 million and a chauffered limousine to take one to work were possible.

The M&A factories had by this time standardized the basic dealmaking techniques and could recycle information developed in earlier deals. Far from simplifying the process, this allowed the senior dealmaking bureaucrats to devise new stratagems and think up new kinds of transactions. Meetings with potential allies, bankers, corporate finance experts, securities analysts, and publicists ate up more time and money. Devising securities to finance deals also ate up the days. The takeover teams put themselves through endless "analytic drills." In one sizeable, but not gargantuan, takeover, the raider's investment bankers developed twenty "strategic alternatives" and kept developing more. "Deals incubate and hatch in nests of printouts," *Fortune* described it.

And all the hands needed to be fed. Well before the Milken and Drexel prosecutions and the RJR Nabisco affair, the M&A departments were called "instigators" and "Samurais" and accused of doing anything for money. Their ethics were questioned in corporate dining rooms and in grave articles in business publications bearing titles like "The Decline & Fall of Business Ethics." Executives, business school professors, and psychoanalysts were quoted decrying the takeover mania. "Ethics consultants" and "ethical institutes" sprang up in the wake of this belated righteousness – another bureaucratic offshoot.

The M&A departments kept growing in Canada, too, like wheelers and dealers from a small town trying to get at least a little share of big-city-style patronage. First in line were the major brokerage (investment-dealer) firms which created M&A departments – RBC Dominion Securities, Scotia-McLeod, Nesbitt Thomson, Burns Fry, and others. Then there were the many lesser M&A companies – up to fifty of them at one point – working mostly niches and smaller deals. Then came the U.S. investment bankers doing deals in Canada, either through subsidiaries (like Morgan Stanley Canada) or through their U.S. offices (like Wasserstein Perella).

The fees in Canada were cranked up. In a 1987 merger creating Placer Dome Inc., a gold mining company, $23.5 million plus expenses was paid to the four investment-dealer firms that acted as bureaucratic midwives, for what was a routine, non-hostile transaction. This is the same kind of re-arranging, paper-shuffling work that senior civil servants and lawyers in government get done, say, for $250,000 (one hundredth of the cost), all overheads folded in – a bureaucracy that, in private-enterprise legend, is supposed to be horribly bloated.

When these fat M&A fees first were paid out in Canada, there was the odd gasp and then the odd complaint, but there was always the American example to point to, as an excuse. Another excuse, offered in the Placer Dome deal, was that the high fees were needed to offset the "opportunity cost" of advising on the transaction. Not only were the advisory firms forbidden to trade in the stock concerned, the argument went, but also the people required for working on the deal weren't free to handle other business. Translation: The fat fee was both for the work done and for the work that couldn't be done. No member of the old bureaucracy (government) would so baldly suggest that one should be paid twice for the same time.

As in the United States, nobody bothered, anymore, to hide the make-work character of the activity. "Action moving to merger front," said a headline in the *Financial Post* at the end of 1988. "Brokers turn to deal-making as stock sales struggle," said the sub-head. "Investment dealers – both big and small – are building their M&A departments as profits from stock trading and underwriting dwindle," explained the text. "The job of brokerage firms' M&A specialists is to pitch deals all day – every day, in every sector of business," an anonymous industry expert intoned. How best to mimic their American M&A counterparts and get what they had going was discussed.

The "finding and soliciting" subsection is also worked in Canada for extraordinary fees. In 1986, eight officers of the Continental Bank received an estimated $4.6 million for finding a buyer for their bank (a $2 million flat fee and approximately $2.6 million in a share-price bonus). Eyebrows were raised because these officers were already highly paid and it was their duty as such to find a good buyer. But soon all that would be forgotten, because much higher fees were being posted. Bill Richards, who as president of Dome Petroleum did so much to give takeovers a bad name, received a rumoured seven-figure fee (that's $1 million or so) for acting as a marriage-broker in the takeover of Husky Oil (52 per cent) by Hong Kong financier Li Ka-shing. Investment dealers are routinely hired to find buyers, for lucrative fees. The finders' fee in the 1989 sale of Consolidated-Bathurst Inc. to Stone Container Corp. was $26 million. The main finder was an individual "business consultant" (former cabinet minister Maurice Sauvé) who was a former executive of Consolidated-Bathurst and a friend of the CEOs of both the seller and buyer. The action reportedly got going when the seller put a bug in the finder's ear at a party. But the working of personal and social connections is part of all bureaucracies.

Sitting beside the investment bankers are the lawyers and their law firms. Two lawyers in particular, Joe Flom and Martin Lipton, led the way in M&A in the United States. Flom had been retained by Morgan Stanley to help Inco in its hostile takeover of that small battery company in 1974. He was already well-established in the takeover field and quickly became the top takeover lawyer in the country. Securities lawyer Martin Lipton began working for companies defending against takeovers, and faced Flom head to head in many battles. He deliberately chose to be on the other side. It reminded one of the aphorism: A lawyer can't make a living in a small town unless there are two lawyers in the small town. Lipton once referred to Flom as "the genius who started it all." The equal matching of the two lawyers encouraged their clients to battle to the end in their M&A confrontations. The lawyers' creativity generated a catalogue of complex and costly stratagems. Lipton devised the poison pill. Other lawyers followed in their train.

Lipton's "small" legal firm – considered a "boutique" because it had fewer than 100 lawyers – led all law firms in profits per lawyer by the mid-1980s, with average profits per partner in 1986, 1987, and 1988 of US$1.4 million annually. Lipton's favourite protagonist, Flom, had joined a small firm when he left law school so he would have more opportunity. The takeover shuffling gave him more opportunity than he imagined. In the first six months of 1988 – the record M&A year – Flom's firm handled thirty-nine of the U.S.'s ninety-nine largest takeover fights. Each of the firm's 177 partners that year earned US$1.2 million. Flom himself took home around

$5 million, the leading U.S. corporate lawyer. Lipton, with $3 million plus, trailed in fifth place. Flom's firm, 850-lawyers strong at the time, grossed close to half a billion dollars in 1988. About three hundred client corporations were paying it an annual retainer of from $20,000 to $50,000 to ensure that Flom and his colleagues didn't work for an opponent. The firm easily managed the £1 million to buy a London house for one partner, who split his time between New York and London. The firm also managed, without blinking, to install at home in New York its own gym with a staff of seven professional trainers.

There was no problem in setting fees high. As one legal consultant in a management consulting firm remarked, lawyers' clients throw out all cost inhibitions when they're involved in mergers and acquisitions. A lot of billing days can be piled up in M&A work, too. In a takeover raid on an insurance company, licensed individually in different states, Flom's firm, which played the defence, tied up the raider in legal actions in twelve states. Umpteen depositions were asked for. Miles of paper are printed out on countless laser printers for such actions, in a version of Parkinson's Law: The legal work expands to fill the capacity of installed computers. Flom's firm also acted for RJR Nabisco in the 1988 takeover auction; at times the team swelled to over thirty lawyers, exclusive of the lawyers acting for the two takeover protagonists. In the takeover of Federated Department Stores by Campeau Corp., there was the usual suit, countersuit, and the rest of the predictable bureaucratic progression. The six law firms involved billed a total of about US$40 million, of which Flom's firm, acting for Federated, reportedly collected $10 million. Just ten or fifteen years earlier, $100,000 was considered a large legal fee!

Flom's firm isn't shy about how it plays the game. It markets its services by sending out weekly mailings on new developments and recent court decisions to three to four thousand clients. "Business development," it's called, in U.S. legal circles. The takeover lawyers are more than mere litigators, the editor of *American Lawyer* observed. "They drive deals, they create deals." At a certain stage in dealmaking, lawyers become investment bankers and investment bankers become lawyers.

Some rogue actions also take place after takeovers are completed, in the best tradition of U.S. negligence suits. In the celebrated Pennzoil-Texaco case, Texaco was assessed US$10.5 billion in damages for alienating Getty Oil from Pennzoil's affections, in a takeover skirmish (Pennzoil later settled for $3 billion). That one was a shocker, but there were others. Unocal Corp. (Chevron) sued its own investment banker, Goldman, Sachs, and another investment banker for $2.4 billion, in part for alleged bad advice in a takeover. *Forbes* magazine, never fond of lawyers, called such cases "megatort mania" and pictured lawyers as grinning vultures, briefcases in claws, stooped on lampposts in the urban landscape, waiting to pounce on the next corporate candidate for corpse. With the American predilection for litigation, about 12 per cent of U.S. mergers, acquisitions, and leveraged buy-outs lead to lawsuits against directors and officers of the firms, over and above the major company-against-company actions. All this adds to the paper entrepreneurialism branch's legal section. The fattest of the fat: Houston-based Joseph Dahr Jamail who took home an estimated $420 million for the Pennzoil strike against Texaco, through a contingency-fee arrangement, and anything from $450 million to a high-end estimate of $600 million for the year 1988 as a whole.

Takeover lawyers in Canada also do well, if not quite as well, the Canadian takeover bureaucracy being a mite less developed than the American one. For Olympia & York's (Reichmanns') 1986 takeover of Hiram Walker Resources, lawyers proliferated. One insider on the Reichmann side complained that the involvement of so many lawyers turned the altercation into a battlefield. "Lawyers have been making business decisions, doing things that don't make sense," he said. "Both sides end up in court and everybody's mad at each other." Nobody, however, leaves out the lawyers.

The hostile takeover of Union Enterprises by Unicorp Canada in 1985 provided another gossipy illustration. The raider's legal counsel included a lead lawyer, a second in command, a well-connected senior partner for additional strategic advice and for Queen's Park (political) dealings, another for cross-examinations before the Ontario Securities Commission (where a skirmish occurred), a couple of others for Ontario Energy Board appearances, two more making submissions for a Revenue Canada ruling, and many bit players. In all, two dozen lawyers ran up more than three thousand hours, at rates perhaps as high as $400 an hour. The defender's legal firm fielded an even larger legal battalion: about forty lawyers committed over two months at unquantified hours, plus lawyers from another firm for a second opinion on a tactical matter. Each side also had its investment dealers, who retained their own lawyers. In the 1990 Bayer acquisition of Nova Corp.'s rubber division (ex-Polysar), the legal team on the winning side at one time was up to fifty lawyers, and pocketed $5 million.

Add to that the public court system and the regulatory system – the judges, also juries (in the U.S.), court clerks, regulatory personnel, and the infrastructure – which get dragged into hostile takeovers by the M&A lawyers' strategic games and tactical ploys. Nobody counts the costs of this inflation of the old bureaucracy (the court system) generated by the New Bureaucracy's legal section, paper-entrepreneurialism branch.

Another section is the "risk arbitrageurs." They buy stock in companies being put into play and then sell the holdings after the takeover offer or the bidding between raider and white knight has pushed up the value of the shares. The high, sometimes enormous, premiums paid in takeovers gives the impression that traditional shareholders are blessed with windfalls but, more likely, they have sold out early in the sequence of events to the arbitrageurs, who capture the rest of the margin. Sometimes, in the middle of a deal, the arbitrageurs together may own as much as 90 per cent of the stock. Effectively, in a tender-offer or auction-style takeover process, they will decide when a bid is high enough and will settle the deal by tendering their shares – determining the outcome of takeover battles.

The arbitrageurs discovered what Jeff Madrick called, simply, a "money machine." "It's no-brainer time," said one "arb" in early 1988, of the process. "Just buy, hold, and go on to the next deal." The "folks who feed off merger mania," *Fortune* put it. In 1985, in a book titled *Merger Mania*, Ivan Boesky described arbitrage as "Wall Street's best-kept money-making secret." Everything depends on whether or not the takeover action is hot. If there are bidders fighting each other or raiders trying to overcome resistance – and raising the ante in the process – all the better.

The arbitrageurs' take can be enormous because it combines the short-term holding of shares with the high premiums of takeover action. This compounds the return on investment. That leverage, in turn, can be boosted with borrowed capital. In a good takeover year, like 1985, three of the top ten money-earners on Wall Street were arbitrageurs, and a fourth also did some arbitrage. Top of the pack was Ivan Boesky, who netted US$100 million, and that was just his share, exclusive of the take of others in his limited partnership.

Boesky, it turned out, cheated by getting inside information. But the runners-up in arbitrage that year did not do too badly either, at an estimated US$30 million and $25 million respectively. Rising takeover bids give another indication of the fat financial layer the U.S. arbitrageurs draw on. In just less than three months into 1988, the combined market value of only nine takeover stocks had advanced by more than $12 billion. The arbitrageurs didn't capture all of that gain, but they would have taken a big bite out of it. The arbitrage share from the April 1988 Campeau Corp. takeover of Federated Department Stores was an estimated US$300 million, or an annualized return of 109 per cent. "The streets of Manhattan are again paved with gold," *The Economist* quipped.

Cheating with inside information about an imminent takeover offer is taboo. An investment-banking department working on such an offer for a client is supposed to keep its activity secret behind a "Chinese wall." But somehow the word gets around, or at least enough of an inkling filters out to get things going. In an SEC study of 172 successful tender (takeover) offers from 1981 to 1985, shares *in every case* rose abnormally more than three weeks before takeover bids were announced. A similar 1984 study by investment bank Dean Witter Reynolds found that in eighty-nine large takeovers that year, stocks of the targets advanced 12 per cent on average in the month *before* the announcement. Arbitraged, that would be an annual return on investment of 144 per cent and, leveraged with borrowed money, an even higher return.

When deals unexpectedly fall through or are blocked, and the stock price falls away, arbitrageurs get stung, sometimes badly. This and the name "*risk* arbitrage" – and the parallel imagery of arbitrageurs as freelance outriders – suggest terrible risk and speculative adventure. But risk arbitrage is just bureaucratic work, like the rest of the paper-entrepreneurialism branch. Arbitrageurs spend their days filtering information from documents, rumours, odd contacts, and from their "networks" of executives, investment bankers, and lawyers. Most major investment banks have arbitrage departments – a regular part of their bureaucratic machinery. U.S. corporate treasurers have been known to invest spare corporate cash in risk-arbitrage funds (there are such things, for institutional investors). Losses from time to time are expected and absorbed as part of the routine, the way insurance companies pay out for claims. As long as the takeover machinery keeps turning over, the risk gets cancelled out if the arbitrage is sufficiently financed to get over individual setbacks. Conversely, when the shuffling of the M&A bureaucracy declines, arbitrage has less to go on and arbitrageurs, like discarded clerks, begin grumbling.

A seemingly minor variant of the investment bank, the leveraged buy-out (LBO) specialists, hardly existed until the mid-1970s. At that, they were "boutiques" – bit players playing the fringe. By the late 1980s, through bureaucratic evolution, they had risen up the hierarchy. The most clever of them – Kohlberg Kravis Roberts – stood atop the heap. So did investment bank Drexel Burnham Lambert, coming out of nowhere with junk-bond financing. Originally, junk-bond financing was to help venture companies too small and risky for more conventional debt financing. Then Michael Milken, Drexel's junk-bond pioneer, began using them to orchestrate assaults on asset-rich established companies. Once started, there was no stopping it. "A large cross section of corporate America," *Institutional Investor* magazine remarked in a 1986 feature on LBOs, "has become a collection of properties to be bought and sold and flipped like high rises, office buildings and shopping malls." The way that LBOs are put together, LBO shops rake off extraordinary bureaucratic margins.

The LBO is based on leverage – using a small amount of equity to take over a large company. The rest is financed with debt. An investor in this way can get control of a large company with minimal capital – purchasing a company with somebody else's money. During the 1980s' M&A wave, buyout leverage was typically 10 to 1 and sometimes got as high as 20 to 1, which was the original leverage in the RJR Nabisco takeover. That doesn't end the leverage, though. When an LBO boutique puts together an LBO fund, made up of equity, it need provide only a small part of the equity capital itself. In effect, it levers the lever.

In the summer of 1987, for example, LBO boutique Kohlberg Kravis put together an LBO fund (equity) of US$5.6 billion, mostly with other people's money. With debt-financing, such as bank loans and junk bonds, this war chest could have been expanded to the US$40 or $50 billion mark. This was the fund Kohlberg Kravis used to buy RJR Nabisco. For the $25 billion for the takeover, Kohlberg Kravis reportedly contributed about US$95 million of its own money, which represented levered leverage of 262 to 1.

Because of the leverage, a relatively small capital gain from the buyout and selling off of parts, or alternatively a modest improvement in performance of the acquired company, can bring a high rate of return on the equity portion. The LBO operation is also "subsidized" by tax laws, since the interest on the debt is tax-deductible, unlike the profits and dividends which are the "cost" of equity capital, which the LBO debt replaces. (The U.S. Congress, agitated by the sheer magnitude of the RJR Nabisco mega-LBO, recently limited this tax break, but only on the riskiest kind of junk securities). In the early 1980s in the United States, before the law was changed, special asset "write-up" and accelerated depreciation provisions also brought tax advantages to LBOs. These tax advantages levered the levered lever. It's one of the reasons why LBO players in the 1980s were able to offer such large premiums over a target company's prior stock-market price and, if all went well, still make a killing from downstream sell-offs. (Estimates of the average premium offered vary from 30 per cent to 80 per cent, depending on the study and the time period covered.) Also, because an LBO vastly increases the debt-equity ratio of the company, hence increasing the risk, the company's ordinary corporate bonds, already issued, are downgraded by the bond market and decline in value. Indirectly the LBO is paid for, in part, by these bondholders' losses. They provide more fodder. (Bondholders, in turn, were "mad as hell," as *Business Week* put it, and started filing suits and demanding protection.)

The bureaucratic cleverness of LBO boutiques lies in the fees and capital gains they take in the LBO's different stages. First is a 1.5 per cent annual management fee, producing a hefty sum on a fund in the billions of dollars ($15 million for every $1 billion), although if the fund isn't making deals, the partners may complain about the fee and get it reduced. Then there's a "transaction" fee for putting deals together, rising to as high as US$75 million in the RJR Nabisco case. Then the LBO shop takes a fee of 20 per cent of any profits (including capital gains) earned downstream. This is a slice of the profits of the other partners in the syndicate, over and above what flows to the shop from its own equity participation. Then it gets the return on its own equity. In other words, it pockets its own profits and some of the profits of everybody else, too. Kohlberg Kravis also instituted divestiture fees (a fee for selling off parts, post-takeover) and directors' fees, on top of that. "The game now is not being an investor but servicing investors as a middleman," *Business Week* quoted one dealmaker as saying, in 1986. Any fool could get money for a takeover in those days, he explained (Robert Campeau comes to mind); the trick was to occupy the vital bureaucratic bridge. And, naturally, the bigger any single deal that can be put through this engineering, the larger the pay-off at the anchor of the cantilever, namely the LBO shop. Kohlberg Kravis fed itself RJR Nabisco for just that reason.

The investment-bank middlemen also operate in several layers of an LBO. They garner fees as advisers (for helping out or doing the initial deal). Where long-term debt financing isn't already in place – which was often the case for large LBOs in the 1980s – the investment banks also get fees for temporary "bridge loans" provided with their own capital. Another reason for providing the bridge loans is to keep alive dubious deals that otherwise would founder, in order to collect all the other fees attached to them. The bridge-loan fees in the RJR Nabisco deal hit the US$100 million mark. These fees, however, don't include the interest on the loans, which the investment banks also collect – extraordinarily lucrative interest, at about five percentage points above the prime rate. A bridge loan in the billions can earn a lot of interest, even if it's loaned for only a short period of time.

Then the investment bankers get fees for refinancing the temporary bridge loans with long-term debt (like junk bonds or other "subordinated" debt) or for putting the bond financing together for the making of the deal in the first place. In 1986, when Kohlberg Kravis took over conglomerate Beatrice Cos. in a US$6.2 billion LBO, Drexel collected a then unprecedented $86 million fee for selling the necessary junk bonds. This financing fee made the huge advisory fees of the investment bankers look like small change, *Business Week* remarked. It wasn't any wonder, given these rake-offs, that Michael Milken and Drexel aggressively and persistently developed connections with LBO boutiques, urging them to come up with deals. One investment bank, Merrill Lynch, hungry for the business, at one stage presented a new LBO idea to its junk-bond department every forty-eight hours. LBO and MBO possibilities were also flogged to managements of companies, like RJR Nabisco – building in sweet equity deals for management, in the proposals, to get them to bite. "Managements of companies," *Institutional Investor* observed wryly, " . . . have also begun to discover the LBO jackpot."

Then come the commercial banking fees, or "origination" fees, paid out to ordinary banks for organizing loan syndicates and committing themselves to the "senior" debt in LBOs. Given the large sums involved, and a charge of up to 2.5 to 3 per cent of the total loan, these fees are rich gravy. In the RJR Nabisco deal, they came to US$325 million. A negotiated portion of the fees is typically collected even if the deal doesn't go through. "Drop-dead" fees, they're called. The interest earned on the actual loan for a successful deal is a separate layer. Notwithstanding that the loans are "senior" debt, protected ahead of junk bonds and LBO equity, the banks collect a spread of 1 to 2.5 per cent over prime rate (a spread of up to 5 per cent over their own cost of money) on these loans. This is rich gravy spread on the rich gravy.

The lead bank that organizes the loan usually lays off, or "syndicates," most of the loan with other, smaller banks and investors. It then collects a spread (typically about half a percentage point) between what the LBO client pays and what the secondary banks and other downstream buyers of the loan agree to. This is called a "syndication fee." More gravy. Also, by laying off most of the loans (on which it nevertheless collects a spread), the lead bank reduces its risk and keeps cash for other transactions. So ardent are the resellers that, at the height of the LBO activity in 1988, one local U.S. bank was pressed by five or six banks to buy into the same deal. At one point, Citibank had more than three hundred "customers" sharing in its LBO loans, and managed one LBO deal a week.

There can also be "administrative agent's fees," boosting the total fee remuneration to as much as 6 per cent, and doubling or tripling a bank's normal returns. "Fees are only limited by imagination and an ability to use the English language," one banker joked at the height of the LBO wave. Occasionally, in an MBO, fees amounted to more than the equity contribution of the management takeover group.

That's not the end, either. The leveraged company that has made the acquisition usually needs to sell off some of the acquired assets to pay interest and to reduce its now-huge debt. The investment banks and commercial banks earn more fees for that – advisory fees to both sides in the transaction and financial fees if financing is required by the buyers of the parts. Nor is that the end. The LBO syndicate may take the core company remaining "public" again, by issuing shares. This is known in the bureaucracy as a "round trip." The buyer of any cast-offs may similarly issue shares to the public for the properties it has picked up, taking them "public." More fees – "underwriting" fees, in this case – for the investment bankers. Investment bankers, toting up these downstream fees, jokingly call these latter underwriting fees the "son of son of son of phenomenon."

Nor does the take end there. The investment banks couldn't help noticing the gains taken downstream by the LBO syndicates they helped finance, sometimes reaching 50 per cent or more annually. So they began taking equity positions in the syndicates themselves, becoming investment partners. Drexel at one point held minority interests in close to 150 companies.

Inevitably the investment bankers began asking why they shouldn't lead-manage LBOs themselves, and collect the fees and the fat slice of profits earmarked for the syndicate organizer. Many investment banks, consequently, began putting together LBO funds of their own and working the various fee layers. An investment bank leading a syndicate usually, as well, won the contract for the ordinary corporate-finance business of the company bought out.

That's still not the end. With such great gobs of money to be had, everybody, as *Fortune* put it, wanted "to hold their buckets under the golden shower." Large U.S. commercial banks, suffering from waning fortunes, stampeded to join the M&A bureaucracy and fatten their balance sheets with investment banking fees, financial fees, bridge loans, junk-bond dealings, and equity stakes, over and above their senior-debt LBO loans. Lesser banks also joined the rush. *Business Week* in 1987 ran a story of a "boot camp" held by Marine Midland, the nineteenth largest bank in the country, to train its bankers in M&A and other investment bank deal-pushing arts. The consultant put before them a fictional case of a client (a printer, in this instance) wanting to double its business by an acquisition. The bankers, looking at the printer's already leveraged balance sheet, wanted to call in their existing loans instead. "They're still real bankers," *Business Week* commented wryly. The consultant had to remind the bankers that they were supposed to sell the client their M&A service, not worry about the client's credit exposure. "This is the cultural leap you've got to make," he said.

Insurance companies, pension funds, foreign investors, limited partnerships (private syndicates), mutual funds, and thrifts (savings and loan institutions) also got deeply involved, to varying degrees, right down to creating their own LBO funds. "Each LBO is a three-layered parfait," *Institutional Investor* quipped, "senior debt, subordinated debt [junk bonds] and equity [the whipped cream] – and the players no longer seem content to feast on just one tier. Nowadays some big institutions want to hog the whole dessert." The junk-bond losses of the thrifts became part of the US$500 billion thrift scandal (the estimated cost of the cleanup, including interest on the debt incurred). There was even such a creature as a specialized "LBO mutual fund" (a mutual fund that invests in LBO syndicates themselves, and not just in junk bonds). Deals and the inflated prices paid became driven not just by fees but also by the amount of money available, which was plenty, given the huge pools of M&A capital that had been pulled together, chasing the hefty take from this paper activity. Cases were common of lenders putting pressure on takeover syndicates to take more money for a deal than the syndicates themselves wanted to pay for the target, to encourage the deal to go through.

Foreign banks became increasingly involved in U.S. M&A, first the major Canadian banks and later offshore ones, especially Japanese. The total LBO outlay in the United States of Japanese banks wasn't much less than the outlay of American banks themselves. Among many other deals, some of the Canadian big six banks participated in the bank syndicate which financed Robert Campeau's 1988 takeover of Federated Department Stores. The Canadian banks also tried worming their way into the advisory-fee honeypot on the more lucrative American side of the border and also, in one case at least, Toronto-Dominion, took an equity interest in a U.S. LBO syndicate, and hence in companies acquired by the takeovers.

The large Canadian chartered banks, in fact, had long grown fat on paper entrepreneurialism. They eagerly financed the takeover of Canadian companies by U.S. multinationals in the post-war period, and just as eagerly financed the paper-shuffling takeover rush of the late 1970s and the 1980s, including Dome Petroleum's ill-fated acquisition flurry.

The corporate cash, the investment banks (investment dealers), the commercial banks, and the banks' syndication networks, the insurance-company "mezzanine" financing, and later the junk-bond financial machinery; the LBO shops and LBO funds, and the pension funds, and the mutual funds; the savings and loan outfits, the limited partnerships, and the foreign banks, and their syndication networks pushed takeovers right along.

Proxy solicitors and their subsection, "shark watchers," make up another section of the paper-entrepreneurialism branch. Another subsection: detectives.

Shark watchers ("stock-watch" services), of which there are more than half a dozen firms in the United States (either proxy solicitors or breakaways), are retained to track down who is behind unusual activity in a company's shares. The object is to identify a potential shark or raider early, before it has acquired 5 per cent of the company's shares and is forced to disclose its interest. The purpose, for the company's management, is to head off the raider at an early stage with defensive tactics. The shark watchers did particularly well in the 1980s when there were plenty of active sharks around. As the takeover action heated up, so did fees, some rising to over US$100,000 per year. Shark-watching became a "profit centre" – another new and lucrative bureaucratic offshoot.

Shark watching, contrary to its moniker, is pure bureaucracy. It involves the use of electronic data bases to track stock positions, build-ups and trading patterns; to set off alarms, and to separate false-alarm trading from the machinations and camouflaging of a lurking shark. Then, to identify who the shark actually is, comes extra tracking through various data and news services, reading of research reports, confirming hunches with Wall Street contacts, building up guesswork hit lists depending on which broker acted on the trade and who the broker's major clients are, and tracing connections upwards from low-level brokers who have made some of the trades until finally reaching the customer's name. Between the shark and the shark watchers, paper obfuscation techniques versus detection techniques, a bureaucratic game is created, becomes more complex, inflates – with its apparatus, data bases, personnel, and rising cost attached.

"We're a lot like private investigators," says one practitioner. In fact, there are private investigators in this bureaucratic section, although not for identifying sharks. Their job is to find out anything that might prove damaging to a raider. "Specialists in corporate intelligence" is the euphemism. "Private dick" is the jargon version. But, again, the moniker overromanticizes the nature of the work. These cadres form a bureaucracy of their own.

The best known of the Wall Street private eyes, Kroll Associates, has a team of two hundred full-time professionals – for M&A work, when available, and other tasks. The cadres include business executives, lawyers and PhDs skilled in research, as well as a complement of former FBI and other law-enforcement officers and investigative reporters. It has a business library of its own and uses the usual electronic data services. It also has on call more than five hundred detective agencies, specialized industry consultants, accountants and lawyers in the U.S. and around the world. The fees for checking on a corporate raider are a nice bit of cream, averaging about US$250,000 and sometimes reaching $450,000. Kroll Associates was the firm hired by Armstrong World Industries to dig up dirt on the Belzbergs, in order to discredit them and help foil their raid.

The proxy-solicitor branch proper also grew with the increase in takeover activity, changing from an esoteric specialty into a prosperous bureaucracy in its own right, with its own notable bureaucratic "stars." Proxy solicitors track down shareholders and try to get shareholder support either for the attacking raider or the defending management, depending on who their client is. Like investment banks and lawyers, they will work either side of the fence. The more ornate that takeover manoeuvres became, the more the proxy-solicitor branch expanded. A new wave of proxy-solicitor work on the raiders' side, for example, was generated by the introduction of poison pills, protective state laws, and other defensive measures on the side of existing management.

Proxy solicitors, of course, need to persuade shareholders. This is done through teams of telephone callers – well-turned-out junior bureaucrats described, in the appropriate style, as "solicitation managers." A full-blown proxy battle will include newspaper ads and mass mailings. The cost of such a battle in the United States (with tons of paper going out by hand, truck, air freight, mail, "mailgrams" and "datagrams," plus full-page newspaper ads, "mechanical expenses" and fees) can range from US$1 million to $10 million. Corporate management, having all of their corporation's resources at their disposal, can do as many mailings as they want. This raises expenses all around.

The proxy-solicitor firms and the lawyers take the biggest chunk out of the allocations – this, for providing what was once a fringe service. Proxy solicitation constitutes a bureaucratic layer, if a lesser one, in Canada, too. Dome Petroleum handed out an estimated C$5 million to brokers for delivering shareholder support for its sales to Amoco in 1988, at a maximum rate of $2,500 for a block of 125,000 shares or more (not bad for a phone call and a bit of routine paperwork).

Proxy solicitors aren't the only people who do M&A public relations work. Corporate in-house "investor relations" executives and outside public-relations firms have long occupied the territory. M&A activity has fattened them up as well. Armstrong hired Hill and Knowlton, the world's largest public relations firm, in its battle against the Belzbergs. PR firms like to talk about the need for pre-emptive strategies – all the better to hook clients on annual retainers.

The paper-entrepreneurialism branch itself helps feed the growth of other branches of the New Bureaucracy. M&A activity, with its huge blocks of shares moving back and forth, props up stock market activity, feeding the stock-market branch. At its high point, 1988, it accounted for as much as 25 per cent of trading on the New York Stock Exchange, according to one estimate. Tracking merger and divestiture activity adds to the amplitude of institutional investors and other money managers (the money-manager branch). Wealth Monitors, a Kansas City, Missouri, money-management firm, developed a niche for itself by tracking the profits of top corporate raiders, among other major investors, for the purpose of "piggy-backing" a fund it manages on the backs of the most successful players.

The paper-entrepreneurialism branch also has its conference and publications sections, promoting its own expansion. In Canada, the *Financial Post* has an annual conference on mergers, acquisitions, divestitures and restructuring, altering the focus slightly to whatever is fashionable at the time. Magazines have sprung up, as a bureaucratic offshoot. *Mergers & Acquisitions* in the United States and *Acquisitions Monthly* in the U.K., at $40 to $50 per issue, are the biggies. These magazines, along with computer-information banks and even-more-specialized magazines, newsletters, and handbooks, are the finishing blocks in a myriad bureaucratic edifice.

And as for the dashing raider – the swashbuckling "entrepreneur" – like Robert Campeau? In reality, Campeau was much like a mannikin in a

Bloomingdale's show window, propped up in his case by the bureaucracy. They used his ego and ambition to help their bureaucracy keep churning. If not Campeau, anybody else with the same grubstake and vanity would have done as well.

An essential part of the bureaucratic process is generating a cover, or rationalization, for what it is doing as it goes along, and glamorizing the process with fashionable jargon. This M&A shuffling was no different. In the 1960s (the conglomeration wave), the magic word had been "synergy." In the 1970s, when the conglomeration wave had been discredited, a new word was found, "diversification." In the 1980s, when the diversification takeovers had become discredited, but other diversification takeovers were simultaneously being engineered, the jargon proliferated to take care of all contingencies. In mid-decade, American author and political economist Robert Reich commented acerbically about how CEOs "speak wondrously of 'synergy' as their companies merge, of 'trimming the fat' as they divest prior acquisitions, of 'aggressive growth' as they diversify into new businesses, of 'integrity' and 'independence' as they fight off unwanted suitors or buy out shareholders." There was no particular pattern to it. Since then it's been "restructuring," "unbundling," "focused companies," plain, old "deconglomeration" for divesting of acquisitions, and plain, old "strategic acquisitions" for making them. "Restructuring" is a particularly useful word because it sounds good, purposeful, and can be applied to almost any manoeuvre. It began showing up as the title of M&A conferences. There is now a catalogue of accumulated jargon and rationalizations to explain whatever action suits the bureaucracy at the moment.

The ascendant LBO firms, the leading junk-bond financiers, the raiders, and their hustling investment-banking advisers – enough of them anyway – had their own rationalization. They began talking of their role as saviours of American capitalism. In this scenario, they or their clients were acquiring badly managed and inefficient companies, kicking out the entrenched and mediocre management, selling off holdings that weren't in synergy, cutting unnecessary management and employees, raising stock-market value, giving top management a more direct ownership incentive, and generally bringing discipline and efficiency to what had become bloated corpocracy. The extra debt load that a leveraged firm had to carry was trumpeted as a virtue: The carrying cost of the debt forced even more cost-cutting discipline on operations, went the argument.

True, some LBO operators made no pretence about economic purpose. They freely admitted they were doing it just for the money (and, it went unsaid, for the status and the attached power that went with it). But this served economic purpose anyway, or so went the rationalization. And there were enough cases of successful restructuring, some spectacularly profitable, that the rationalization could be offered.

Reality wasn't so glorious, though. In the first place, acquisitions by corporations, rather than LBOs by raiders, dominated the M&A scene – the same, old-fashioned bureaucratic expansionism of the past. LBOs weren't so beautiful, either. Selling off parts of the target company to help pay off the cost of the LBO was routine paper entrepreneurialism. "Synergism-in-reverse," it was called. Mind you, the breaking up and splitting off of parts could have a rationale – the unbundling of unwieldy conglomerates, which were the creation of acquisition manoeuvres and the takeover bureaucracy in the first place. The two bureaucratic cycles fed each other.

Most large corporations, moreover, had stock-option plans and other bonuses for management, so theoretically one didn't need an LBO, with a management slice, to establish that incentive. Indeed, as the decade progressed, managers of post-LBO companies were found to be cashing out percentages of their stake at an accelerating rate. "So much for a more committed management," *Fortune* remarked.

As for saving American capitalism from bad management, it was better to buy out a company that was basically healthy to begin with. This went for LBOs as well as for more conventional corporate deals – maybe more so, because the "financial buyers" (LBO syndicates, raiders, and so on), as distinct from corporate buyers, would be less likely to have the industrial background for real rescue work. "The LBO format is useful only for companies that meet the classic requirements of adequate cash flow, stability and lack of serious problems," a Shearson Lehman M&A specialist pointed out.

That was why so much LBO activity gravitated to food companies and retail groups – stable cash flows, limited capital requirements, and low technology. These aren't areas of great entrepreneurial and technical doings which move economic development forward, but they are just right for LBO bureaucracies. Natural-resource companies, particularly oil companies, have also been a hot M&A target in the last fifteen years. There was no real entrepreneurship there, just takeovers based on the premise that prices would rise and that it was cheaper to buy oil and gas reserves than to find new oil and gas – a turning one's back on the real work of enterprise.

Jeff Madrick, in his book *Taking America*, found that, counter to the prevailing rationalizations, "a close look reveals little improvement in management. Quite the contrary. For the most part, companies were bought because they were well-managed." Plus, they happened to be bargains. Earlier studies had uncovered just that. One survey of hostile takeovers for the years 1975-1983, by Edward Herman of the Wharton School and Louis Lowenstein at Columbia University, found that the target companies taken together were more profitable than the takeover companies, were in more profitable industries, and had grown more profitable, not less, as the date of the takeover bid approached. It also found that in the latter years of the period, as the best opportunities for snagging underperforming companies were used up, the bidders did worse than before in terms of return on equity, and worse than the targets had done previously, even accounting for changed economic circumstances. In cases like the U.S. Steel bid for Marathon Oil in 1981, a company that wasn't succeeding in its own business simply sought to take over a better-run company.

Other, more sweeping criticisms were made of takeovers in general. They were destructive of creativity. They forced managements into short-term attitudes to defend against takeovers, robbing the future through deferring capital investment, research and development (R&D), and long-term projects, and hurting communities. "Investment bankers are seeking – and getting – astronomical fees for teaching managers how to run their companies less soundly," complained prominent business columnist Louis Rukeyser. Or, alternatively, if the hostile takeover succeeded instead, the new masters did the slashing of long-term allocations, to reduce the debt incurred for the takeover.

The U.S. National Science Foundation, trying to find out why industrial R&D had levelled off in 1985 after ten years of substantial growth, ended up looking into mergers, acquisitions, and restructuring. It discovered that companies involved in such deals in the surrounding years (1984-1986) had reduced R&D spending, and these reductions had offset R&D increases by other firms. It also found that the percentage cutbacks by restructured and LBO companies were more than double the reductions by conventionally merged firms. Two other studies on this point, however, of mergers and LBOs respectively through to the mid-1980s, found no appreciable fall-off in R&D. LBOs, yet another study showed, cut back on capital expenditures.

The takeovers also broke up loyalties and were demoralizing. They played havoc with the cohesive community character of enterprise, the commitment of employees and the strength of continuity.

Hostile takeover attempts could also lead to a kind of economically perverse "debt competition." Between a company defending itself by buying up shares and going into debt, and a leveraged predator trying to take over a company by putting the company into debt, the prize went to whomever dared assume the most debt. One bitter executive likened the more aggressive defensive tactics to a pretty girl scarring her face and making herself ugly to get safely through a tough neighbourhood. Another asked rhetorically: "Is ripping your company apart so it isn't done by somebody else the same as winning?" *The Economist* charged that leveraged buy-outs were "eating at the foundations of America's stockmarket economy" and were a technique "exploited to the point of folly."

Worse, hostile takeovers in general took up vast amounts of executives' time and attention, which should have been focussed on productive tasks. Somehow, although hostile takeovers had been a major phenomenon since the mid-1970s, productivity growth in the United States was stagnant. Meanwhile, companies in countries like Japan, West Germany, and Sweden, unblessed by hostile takeovers, were steadily raising productivity and giving Americans economic heartburn.

An LBO or MBO, or simply a change of ownership, might fire up a discarded subsidiary, but there were also failures and long-term weaknesses. Different studies showed different things. "The LBO shouldn't be confused with corporate alchemy," *Business Week* observed. People then began realizing that while, in the beginning of the LBO cycle, there had been some good buys and improvement possibilities – analysis of the earlier, generally smaller and friendly, LBOs showed as much – these possibilities had become scarcer and scarcer as the cycle progressed. The takeover bureaucracy, however, with pools of money flowing into it, had kept expanding by its own momentum – raising prices out of all proportion and pushing deals anyway. The Campeau debacle and the junk-bond collapse brought this home.

The fallout grew. Several prominent raiders who had ended up actually owning and managing companies were making a mess of things. This could have been predicted. Their engineering skills were "financial engineering" – playing on tax advantages, sale/leaseback arrangements, pension-plan stripping and other such manoeuvres – essence of paper-entrepreneurialism. Their quick financial solutions didn't work. Besides, as *Fortune* put it, "a raider buys companies to take money *out*, not to put it in."

Other high-profile LBOs, besides Campeau's, came apart and either went into bankruptcy or forced creditors to accept debt renegotation. Among them were two LBOs engineered by Kohlberg Kravis. Another, which defaulted on US$1.5 billion of bonds and commercial paper, had been featured just a couple of months earlier at Drexel Burnham's annual junk-bond conference, the Predators' Ball. A Dallas-based supermarket chain, which had been financed by junk bonds underwritten by Drexel, filed for bankruptcy. Then the Trump superstructure hit the wall. There were many others. Formerly profitable companies with large revenues were on the ropes or worse – as often as not companies that had taken on debt in a defensive recapitalization to ward off a hostile takeover. "The wreckage of the '80s," it was dubbed.

Many mid-sized U.S. companies which had expanded by conventional, but still debt-financed, acquisitions, in the takeover binge, were gasping for financial air and undoing their acquisitions, if they didn't default first. Many large corporations were also getting rid of acquisitions. The bureaucratic cycle had become so shortened, in cases, that the takeover and the subsequent divestiture almost bumped into each other. In Canada, Nova Corp. had hardly managed to swallow rubber and plastics producer Polysar, after a much-trumpeted takeover battle, when it disgorged the rubber division to Bayer AG in West Germany. BCE spun off oil and gas company Encor from its TransCanada PipeLines, after an embarrassingly short embrace. (Its takeover of majority ownership of development company BCED, ending in a write-down of $440 million in BCE's share alone, was even more disastrous). Then it got rid of its controlling interest in TransCanada PipeLines itself. Unicorp Canada, the conglomeration darling of just a few years earlier, went on a restructuring diet. The same "deconglomeration," "rationalization," "streamlining," was taking place with U.S. conglomerates like W. R. Grace and Tenneco, Australian conglomerates like Elders IXL, and countless other U.S., Canadian, and offshore companies – shades of the previous deconglomeration after the previous diversification.

All this contention and change-about just bounced off the takeover bureaucracy which had been behind it all from the beginning. The cadres worried only about their own layoffs and reduced take – which hit as the M&A wave descended – and how to keep their bureaucracy going. Having progressed by their own bureaucratic impulses from woeful conglomerization to hapless diversification to restructuring – putting parts together and taking them apart and putting them together again, in a circle – they now began to take their rake-off from the debacle as well. This wasn't as lucrative as heated M&A activity, but it provided some good bureaucratic feeding nevertheless.

Every time there is a divestiture (dressed up by a fashionable announcement of a company "returning to its core operations" or whatever else), fees are generated, just as they were when the divested operation was acquired in the first place. "Booming market for sell-offs," trumpeted *Mergers & Acquisitions* magazine in 1989. Three of every ten completed M&A transactions in the United States in both 1988 and 1989 were for sell-offs. In Canada, in 1989, more than half of the M&A "market" was accounted for by divestitures.

LBOs whose debt proves too much for them make vulnerable takeover targets for others. A new LBO buys pieces of a prior LBO having troubles, or an established corporation buys up a company whose M&A or defensive leverage put it in a bind. More M&A advisory and financial fees are collected in the process. "Some power investors are already eyeing as perfect targets the very companies that their peers helped saddle with unmanageable debt in earlier LBOs," reported *Business Week* in 1988, envisioning the prospects. The larger investment bankers, who had got many of the companies to lever up in the first place and now looked on fall-out fees as a way of taking up the M&A slack, brushed the irony aside. "If we go into a massive downturn," said one of its executives, as if hoping for a recession, "workout activity could become a major business." "An enormous opportunity," exclaimed a boutique general partner. "You are going to see a lot of interesting ways of playing on those restructurings."

"Financial necrophilia," commentator Donald Coxe called it in *Canadian Business*. By 1990, the Canadian possibilities were also apparent. "Corporate 'doctors' specialize in right Rx for LBO sufferers," read a headline over an article in the *Financial Post* about capitalizing on the "failure boom" and the players in "Canada's burgeoning turnaround acquisition market." Business school graduates who, just before, had been anxious to get into the M&A bureaucracy and snag their share of millions in fees, were now clamouring for starting positions in turnaround organizations – the latest of M&A's bureaucratic spin-offs.

U.S. investment banks launched new mutual funds that specialized in investing in troubled companies. Chemical Bank (a commercial bank) opened a department that used the bank's capital to do the same. Some LBO funds got involved, looking for new ways to use their money. "LBO funds make particularly plump targets for bankruptcy pitches," the *Institutional Investor* commented. Bureaucratic history began to repeat itself in reverse.

"Somebody will invent some new definition of bankruptcy reorganization and say it's the 'new look' in merchant banking," quipped noted U.S. investment banker Felix Rohatyn. No sooner said than done. "Bankruptcy M&A," the new look was called. As if to hammer home the irony, old Drexel hands began showing up everywhere in bankruptcy work.

Where the investment banks and merchant banks go, the rest of the branch's bureaucracy follows. The billings of bankruptcy sections of New York law firms couldn't be better, the *Financial Post* reported in 1989, in a feature on companies faltering because of LBO debt. This was even before the Campeau, Drexel, and other subsequent defaults. "LBO's carrion crows," *The Economist* described this subsection of lawyers. Bankruptcy lawyers' fees rose to match the inflated fees for M&A and other paper-entrepreneurial work. Lawyers working for junk-bond holders on credit committees, in bankruptcy proceedings, drew up to US$500,000 a month ($6 million annualized). Skadden, Arps, Slate, Meagher & Flom, Joe Flom's firm of M&A fame, set up a seventy-five-lawyer restructuring unit.

The undertaker work on Dallas-based Southland Corporation (7-Eleven stores) shows the bureaucratic rake-off to be had. Southland went under when the debt from a defensive LBO, to ward off an outside takeover, proved too much for it. Total fees for the bankruptcy workout and the subsequent acquisition by Japanese retailer Ito-Yokado Co. came to more than US$135 million, including $85 million in bankruptcy trustee fees (the trustee, in turn, spins off fees to lawyers, investment bankers, accountants, and brokers). The fall-out generated more than twice as much in fees, for the cadres, as the original, juicy LBO! LTV Corp.'s bankruptcy reorganization fees had hit $150 million by mid-1991 and the clock was still ticking. Drexel Burnham Lambert and Federated Department Stores proceedings weren't far behind, passing the $100 million mark. Up to twenty-six firms, including a dozen law firms and a dozen investment advisers, might be involved in a proceeding. "There's plenty for all at the bankruptcy banquet," a *Business Week* headline put it. It's "a veritable gold mine," the magazine reported.

The shuffling of Dome Petroleum to Amoco, after Dome's ill-fated takeover gambits, illustrates the lucrative fall-out in another way. When, after drawn-out skirmishing and legal finagling, the deal was finally closed, 150 bankers and lawyers from Toronto, Chicago, London, Geneva, and Frankfurt filled two floors of Dome's office tower simply to sign the necessary documents, the *Toronto Star* reported. The legalese created 850,000 pieces of paper which, if stacked, would have climbed almost as high as the skyscraper's thirty-three floors.

The investment banks also get into the act, in default cases, as representatives of creditors. They court bankruptcy lawyers assiduously, because the lawyers' advice to creditors is often decisive in their choice of investment bank. Before, the investment banks kept lists of possible takeover targets with which to feed empire-building corporate executives and raiders and to generate fees. After, along with law firms doing corporate bankruptcy work, they also kept lists of over-leveraged LBOs gasping with financial emphyzema. Given that corporate debt in the United States doubled from 1983 to the end of the decade, the law of averages was on the bureaucracy's side. As of mid-1990, one law firm was said to have 150 companies on its "deathwatch" list.

Even the junk-bond graveyard, dubbed the "junkyard," provides bureaucratic possibilities. Some of the 1980s' most opportunistic raiders in the United States, who helped propel the frenzy that launched the junk, began picking over the distressed junk for bargains. Syndicates began to buy up distressed junk in a company, rather than its common stock, as a way of taking over control or making a favourable deal with its managers – a new fashion in takeover raids feeding off the carcass of the last fashion in takeover raids. The final irony: Arbitrageurs have migrated to the junkyard, too. Arbitrageurs invest in the stocks of takeover targets, but with hot and heavy takeovers in decline and some deals falling through, they were taking a beating. They turned to junk instead. When a distressed LBO company announces it will restructure by adding new equity and shoring up the balance sheet, the arbitrageurs rush in to buy the junk which is expected to rise in value at the same time.

Financial restructuring, which mostly doesn't show up in the M&A statistics, wasn't the only activity being touted into fashionability when the huge M&A wave of the 1980s crested. Behind the headlines about the end of an era, the cadres began pushing the idea of "strategic" M&A – M&A by established corporations. They chatted up the notion that with the freelance raiders and highly-leveraged deals – and the huge premiums they paid – largely departed from the scene, there were bargains to be had.

This was mainstream M&A recycled, with all the pretension of the conglomeration cycle of the 1960s and the "tactical" cycle of the late 1970s. "Back to the future," *Mergers & Acquisitions* described it. *Business Week*, in full metaphorical flow, referred to the change in style as "the less threatening but still potent, strains of the New York Philharmonic," as compared to "the hard-pounding, impossible-to-ignore heavy metal of Motley Crue" (namely the unvarnished LBO, greenmail, and junk-bond crowd).

Simultaneously, "cross-border" deals – the jargon for international deals – were touted as the great new field of deal-making for the 1990s. If one way of activating those deals was to push the acquisition of U.S. companies by, say, the Japanese and Europeans, whose currency was stronger than the U.S. dollar, and if that meant a loss of Americans' ownership and control over their own economy, it was of no concern to the bureaucracy's cadres. The "middle market" – medium-sized deals – was also touted as a comer. This field, too, wasn't anything new, but it was seen that more could be made of it, in proper M&A-bureaucracy fashion. And, indeed, U.S. M&A in 1990, which the now-entrenched cadres considered a terrible year, was comparable in both value and number of transactions to the mid-1980s, hailed at the time as an age of deal mania.

Raiders, faced with the demise of junk-bond financing for their forays and with state anti-takeover legislation, also moved sideways. They began using proxy fights in attempts to grab control of companies. This became fashionable for hostile takeovers, and fed the proxy-solicitor bureaucratic section and the shareholder identification subsection. Proxy-solicitor work was also inflated by restructuring from M&A debt excesses. Such restructuring usually requires bondholder approval. The proxy solicitors are hired to chase after it (and, first of all, to identify bondholders in order to engage in the chase). One proxy-solicitor outfit even established a debt-services division.

As for another wave of hostile takeovers, one could always hope. "Soon enough, they will be [two a penny] again," *The Economist* intoned encouragingly. The M&A cadres themselves realized how important their sheer entrenchment was, despite the fall-off from 1988. "Establishment of the M&A market may be the most enduring outcome of the 1980s M&A wave," wrote the editor of *Mergers & Acquisitions.* "The very fact that dealmakers of the 1990s have a functioning market in which to operate gives them a great headstart over their predecessors of 10 years ago and a well-entrenched foundation for continuing to fuel M&A activity in the next decade."

The paper-entrepreneurialism branch shuffles its paper forever.

4

The Stock-Market Branch

The corporate branch and the paper-entrepreneurialism branch of the New Bureaucracy meet in the stock-market branch, a world of paper bureaucracy unto itself.

As if chicanery weren't enough! Not too long ago, that's what struck one, about stock exchanges. American financial adviser Richard Ney, for example, in his 1970 best-seller, *The Wall Street Jungle*, described the stock market as nothing more than a legalized crap game bilking small investors. "Hidden behind a façade of pompous jargon and noble affectations," he wrote, "there is more sheer larceny per square foot on the floor of the New York Stock Exchange than any place else in the world."

Ney told the story of old-time gangster Lucky Luciano, visiting the floor of the exchange before he was deported to Italy. When the operations of floor specialists had been explained to him, Luciano recounted, "A terrible thing happened. I realized I'd joined the wrong mob." Ney called the "larceny" of the exchange "lunatic economics." Marshalling case history after case history, detail after detail, he inveighed against the stock exchange's self-serving manipulative ways, its protection of its own status and power, and its pomposity.

He also was sardonic about the talents of stockbrokers as a club. "Most of us enter the investment business for the same sanity-destroying reasons a woman becomes a prostitute," he wrote. "It avoids the menace of hard work, is a group activity that requires little in the way of intellect, and is a practical means of making money for those with no special talent for anything else."

These days, stockbrokers – or at least some of them – do work harder and, particularly in bull markets, get paid immensely more than ever before. There is more room for cleverness and intellect. True, infamy is still around.

Fines, suspensions, and sometimes criminal indictments punctuate their activities. But now what strikes one is the growing volume of activity, the paper and electronic flows of information, the ever-increasing convolutions and refinements, the technical aura, the repetition, the esoteric and the bizarre, the cowed reverence by lay people – the signs of a wasteful bureaucracy so well-established that it can no longer be challenged.

The stock-market branch is a vast and ever-more ingenious make-work project in the finest (that is, the worst) of bureaucratic traditions. Lucky Luciano, who only knew about rackets and robbery, would have been flummoxed. Franz Kafka, on the other hand, would have understood.

The usual picture of a brokerage office is rank upon rank of cubicles with computer monitors flashing the latest share prices. These share prices reflect the strategic action of umpteen players located along unseen perimeters. The gamesmanship of the action gives it a warlike, dramatic quality. There are winners and losers. Money is involved, sometimes a lot of money – sometimes billions of dollars in value of shares traded. A movie like *Wall Street*, expanding on this imagery, has takeover raids swirling mistily around the share trading, weird alpha-numeric apparitions appearing late at night on home-computer terminals in the urban jungle, as well as exotic living, the obligatory limousine, spying, and colourful fauna, prostitutes included.

The floor of stock exchanges like the Toronto Stock Exchange (TSE) or the New York Stock Exchange (NYSE) has the appearance of portentous excitement, on busy days. There is a constant hubbub of activity, noise, shouting, gestures, signals, discarded slips of paper on the floor, and people moving. "Something important is happening," this hubbub murmurs. A frenzied day is particularly impressive. Even on slow days, the pretension of importance is there. This is no less the case for remote and often torpid outposts like the Winnipeg Commodity Exchange, for example, where absolutely nothing might be happening at any given moment. Exchange floors are arenas that one looks down upon from public galleries, as if into a ring. Combat, or at least financial and mercantile significance, is assumed, if only because it looks complicated and mysterious. If all those people are hanging around, it must signify something extraordinary. Television routinely turns to this imagery when it wants a visual symbol of business activity or the business community. This is more confirmation. "Business" papers and the "business" pages of daily newspapers assiduously report on the doings of stock markets and run pages of share-price listings. Again, some important economic activity is inferred. Behind the imagery, however, is bureaucratic make-work, but on such a vast scale and with such powerful mythology behind it that nothing can stop it.

Take the ordinary stockbroker. The basic idea is first to catch customers and then to keep them buying and selling. Get them to take money out of one stock and put it into another. Keep them moving, and collect a commission each time. "We don't care what they buy as long as they buy," a vice-president of a large brokerage firm once confessed. "Wall Street," Harvard finance professor Jay Light put it, "is a multibillion-dollar business dedicated to getting people to change their minds and ringing the cash register each time they do." It's a conflict of interest (between giving advice and making money from the action recommended) that, if it involved a member of the old bureaucracy (government), would raise a storm of denunciation. "Shearing sheep," it's known in the business.

For novice brokers and others trying to drum up work, there are "cold calls" – calling unknown names to build up a client base. The more telephone calls one makes, the more chance of snagging the odd customer. A sharp beginner might get one client for every forty contacts – people on a list whom he or she actually reached. This is aside from secondary telephone calls trying to track down possible new players. The average novice would do even worse. A typical routine, as described by *Forbes*, is forty to fifty calls an hour, or more than three hundred calls a day. That's a lot of calling. "Dialling for Dollars," it's called, cynically, in the trade. It's "pick and shovel" work – totally unglamorous, routine, bureaucratically organized in the most prosaic fashion, and unpleasant. "Let's face it," said a young Vancouver broker with three years of experience but still cold-calling, "nobody likes to be rejected, but this is something I have to do."

The call lists consist of piles of cards purchased from Dun & Bradstreet, from similar namelist publishers, or from specialized telephone directories covering upper middle-class professional and business categories. Other brokers buy the same cards, so there is a lot of overlapping in the cold calling. One Wall Street veteran estimated having made over one million cold calls in his career. He still spent several hours a day on them and, as well, had a three-person calling corps to help him out. At the training school for brokers at Merrill Lynch, hopefuls rehearse cold calls "in the time-honored fashion of vinyl-siding salespeople," as one wit put it. These training schools, or "boot camps," drill the trainees in pre-scripted responses in order, first, to establish communication with potential clients and then to disarm them. Script cards are used to help awkward trainees.

Because selling is involved, business enterprise is imputed to the activity. By association of ideas, some productive function is assumed. *Business Week*, for example, once called stock brokerage "intrinsically entrepreneurial." It is no more entrepreneurial, however, than some ambitious but crazed civil servant going through the routine of memos, lists, meetings, and endless telephone calls to "sell" a meaningless administrative change, and then doing it again, and again, and not much else, day after day.

With a client base established, the broker's challenge is then to keep the clients trading. The trick is to bone up on a few chosen stocks in order to talk knowledgeably about them, or with the appearance of knowledgeability, in order to move clients into buying the stocks. It makes little difference whether the talk is actually knowledgeable, that is, whether the intelligence is actually intelligent. How in any case does one broker get an edge of information on another, and if he or she could get such an edge, why bother with brokerage anyway? Why not invest on one's own personal account and become enormously rich in a short time? The talk's the thing.

Here is where the in-house "research" department of a brokerage firm comes in handy. It prepares analyses that brokers can use in talk to clients. The best analyses are kept simple. They provide just enough numbers to give the brokers ammunition – a selling point – as they telephone through the client list, talking to each client for as little as a minute or sometimes, even, just thirty seconds. Or the broker will work out a formula that has a cachet of special objective "truth" to it. One formula is the return on equity of a company, but that's such an obvious one, followed by so many analysts – with the company's share price reflecting the fact – that there may be no special advantage to investing in that company's shares. So a more esoteric formula has to be developed: high capital assets, or low capital assets, or something else. It hardly makes a difference.

The talk is packaged and presented to promote the huge daily volume of share trading. The in-house analysts – copywriters, in effect – who produce the window dressing are the "research department," an upscale expansion of the old "statistician." They don't have any arcane knowledge behind their recommendations, which are bad as often as they are good, but stock platitudes have been developed to generate an aura of wise counsel. "Gilt-edged situations, blue chips, diversified portfolios for safety and growth, long-term capital appreciation, sound investments in solid companies . . ." one ex-stockbroker listed them off. A "confidence game," he called it, meaning it literally, for the broker's and analyst's use of words, without any objective advantage in the counsel, is meant for precisely the purpose of establishing confidence – to the brokerage firm's advantage. The use of the phrase "We feel" by a "research department," suggests that serious and superior minds are behind a recommendation. When the analysts botch it altogether, they have an arsenal of doubletalk and jargon to help cover their tracks.

Individual client investors, however, are a declining presence in the major stock markets. Institutional investors have become the dominant force. They compete against each other in trying to beat the market, moving in and out of stocks accordingly. Large blocks of shares change hands. This contributes to the churning. By 1984, large block transactions accounted for 50 per cent of shares traded on the New York Stock Exchange. In 1965, it had only been 3 per cent. Including trades in smaller blocks and the professional trading by investment banks (which are also brokerage firms) for their own accounts, institutions are responsible for an estimated 75 per cent of all activity. Figures for Canadian stock trading are similar. If institutional investors are ready to shift big chunks of stock at the slightest provocation, the brokers who handle their orders are not about to discourage them. The brokers get a little piece of everything that moves.

Add the trading by speculators big and small who actively play the market. They are churners by definition. Then add bureaucratic subsections, such as the processing of trades, which inflate with the churning. During a bull market, the activity increases as share prices go up and people and institutions chase each other to invest and capture share-price increases, pushing the market ahead even further. The stock-market branch collects its fees. Then, when the bull breaks, large numbers of shareholders sell in a hurry to save themselves. The stock-market branch collects its fees.

If the market is slow, stock-market bureaucrats have to try all the harder to get their clients (individual and institutional) to keep shifting their paper around or, failing that, to substitute something equally lucrative for themselves. When retail clients proved difficult, following the 1987 crash, and with growing disillusionment over churning, brokerages began to introduce optional fee-based accounts for large-portfolio retail customers. This would give the brokerages an annual slice of those big accounts regardless, equivalent to a hefty 160 to 240 per cent churn on every dollar in the accounts, year in and year out, were the clients still paying by commission. "A hidden revenue grab," some observers described it.

All this is yet another part of the "paper economy" or the "symbolic economy." The stock exchange bureaucracies work assiduously shifting their "paper," piling up commissions and fees as the players manoeuvre against each other, detached from the real world of producing goods and services.

The New York Stock Exchange is, or at least was, the bureaucratic ideal – no more so than during the record-breaking 1980s' bull market which pumped up the make-work. The *annual* volume of trading by *share value* in 1987, the last year of the bull market, amounted to an astonishing 86 per cent of the total market value of companies on the exchange. That is, the equivalent of almost all those huge and middle-sized companies on the exchange moved in and out in trading on the NYSE in that year, or US$1.9 trillion worth. In 1977 the figure was only 19 per cent, in 1967 23 per cent, and in 1957 only 13 per cent. The same bureaucratic inflation occurred in the *number* of shares traded. In 1987, the turnover rate (percentage of total shares listed) was 73 per cent, whereas in 1977 it was only 21 per cent and in 1957 only 12 per cent.

Similarly, in the decade 1977-1987, which ended with the collapse of the bull market, the U.S. gross domestic product rose 126 per cent (unadjusted for inflation), but the value of shares churned through the New York Stock Exchange increased from US$155 billion to $1,889 billion, or a whopping 1,116 per cent. The volume of shares traded showed the same bureaucratic inflation, increasing from 5.4 billion to 48.1 billion in the ten-year period, or almost 800 per cent, while the U.S. gross domestic product, discounted for inflation, increased only 21 per cent and the U.S. population increased only 11 per cent.

Institutional investors such as pension funds and mutual funds contributed freely to this churning, their portfolio turnover hitting an estimated 60 to 65 per cent in 1987, and in some individual cases many times that.

Not even these comparisons indicate the true scale of bureaucratic inflation, however, since they don't take into account the increased trading in NYSE-listed stocks on regional U.S. exchanges and foreign exchanges, where many of the stocks are interlisted. Nor do they take into account the extra trading in stock-index futures, stock-index options, and options on individually listed NYSE stocks. With just the stock-index futures factored in, the 1987 turnover rate for NYSE shares was well over 200 per cent by value. Trading in stock-index options (calculated by the contracts' underlying value) brings the turnover rate to 330 per cent. With options on individual stocks added, it would be anybody's guess. The relationship of such bureaucratic inflation to the increase in GDP becomes even more attenuated.

It made no difference whether the real economy was rising or falling. In 1979-1980, as the U.S. economy began to founder (no increase in the gross domestic product, in real terms), the volume of shares traded on the NYSE increased 39 per cent. In 1981-1982, as the economy headed into a deep recession (a 2.3 per cent real decline in GDP), the volume of shares traded still increased 38 per cent. When the economy pulled out of recession the following year, the volume of shares traded again increased out of line, by 31 per cent. In the sample year 1985-1986, a good year economically between two other good years (in other words, a regular and stable progression, with incremental GDP increases), the volume of shares traded continued to show extraordinary inflation, with an increase of 30 per cent on an already inflated base figure.

NASDAQ (short for the National Association of Securities Dealers Automated Quotation System), an electronic stock market for over-the-counter securities not listed on older American exchanges, is the second-largest stock market in the United States. Its turnover by number of shares tripled to 90.1 per cent annually from 1977 to 1987 and its turnover by value of shares rose from 33 per cent to an astonishing 150 per cent annually in the same decade – measures of how churning paper back and forth and around had been stepped up.

Similarly, the number of people directly employed in the stock-market branch in the United States (the "securities industry" including futures trading and investment-bank functions) grew from 181,800 in 1977 to 457,300 at the peak in 1987, according to Bureau of Labor statistics. This was an increase of 152 per cent compared to a population increase of 11 per cent and an increase in government personnel (federal, state, and local) of only 12 per cent.

Stock exchanges in Canada followed the same pattern although, not being as well established bureaucratically as the NYSE, they actually suffered some annual declines in the 1970s and the early 1980s. Dollar value traded on the Toronto Stock Exchange increased from C$6 billion in 1977 to $100 billion in 1987, or almost 1,660 per cent compared to a 153 per cent increase in the Canadian gross domestic product. In the period 1984 to 1987 inclusive, annual increases in dollar value traded measured 66, 44, and 57 per cent respectively, or 276 per cent for the three years taken together, compared to a GDP increase of only 24 per cent. The number (volume) of shares traded on the Toronto, Montreal, and Vancouver exchanges showed the same phenomenal inflation in that period, in a different world from the small, incremental changes in GDP.

No new money goes into company treasuries from this activity. The original issue of the stock by companies, to raise capital, has already happened, in the past. Trading of the stock after that, through stock exchanges, just moves it around between parties, like trading in baseball cards.

After the October 1987 market crash, the volume of trading declined in stock exchanges around the world, and the bureaucracy slowly declined with it. There were well-publicized lay-offs in New York, Toronto, and elsewhere. Pay packages, bonuses, and commission fees were reportedly cut back. "A sad time for brokers," *Maclean's* cried in a headline a couple of years later. The copy referred to "shell-shocked stockbrokers" as if the cutbacks were equivalent to the Iran-Iraq war. There was wailing at the New York Stock Exchange, following the crash, about the decline in trading volumes as small shareholders fled the market and institutional investors hung shy. Most trading was crowded into the opening and closing hours of the day, leaving floor traders with not much to do in the middle hours.

But the cutbacks, when looked at objectively, were a relatively minor adjustment to a long and self-feeding bureaucratic growth. As of the end of 1990, post-crash net layoffs of U.S. securities personnel, including commodities brokers (futures) and related services, came to approximately thirty-seven thousand, according to Bureau of Labor statistics, or a reduction of only 8 per cent, not even getting back to the massively inflated 1986 levels. Securities Industry Association figures, excluding futures traders and some other Bureau of Labor categories, showed a net loss of fifty-two thousand jobs on a smaller base (NYSE member firms), or a decline of 20 per cent. Brokerage houses in Toronto mournfully intoned about the slashing of jobs. The cuts for TSE member firms, as of the end of 1990, came to 28 per cent of the 1987 high. This was more severe than in New York, but only brought the total employment figure down to roughly the 1985 level. To slim down to 1950 levels, cutbacks in the securities industry in the U.S. would have had to be in the 80 per cent range.

Similarly, although the average daily share trading volume at the NYSE had gradually declined from 189 million shares in 1987 to 157 million shares in 1990 (or 17 per cent), it was still three-and-a-half times its level just ten years earlier in 1980 and almost fourteen times what it had been in 1970. True, the number of shares represented by listed companies had increased in the same period, but that accounted for only a fraction (about four-tenths) of the overall rise in daily trading for the period 1970-1990. Turnover rates (by volume) were a mirror reflection of this, falling off considerably from 1987 but still two or three times as high as in earlier decades. Declining post-crash TSE trading volume, over which the bureaucratic ranks despaired – "recession," they called it – actually remained higher through to the end of 1990 than in any year except the wild churning of 1987.

The stock-market branch also established for itself hugely inflated compensation, pushed to extraordinary levels during the unchecked expansion of the 1980s. In 1986, towards the end of the extended bull market, "professionals" on Wall Street with just three years' experience were typically earning as much as US$300,000 with bonuses. Many thirty-year-olds, and the occasional person with even less experience, were making $1 million a year. These "professionals" (equity and bond salespeople), who were earning such inflated incomes were, in reality, little more than glorified order-takers. (The stock-market branch, with typical bureaucratic pomposity, called them "account executives"; more recently they have been redubbed "financial consultants.")

Managing directors, meanwhile, were earning in the US$1 million range. The highest paid brokers (below top-level bureaucrats) in the large retail firm Merrill Lynch made the $2 million range. One legendary Shearson Lehman trader, who generated over $10 million in commissions single-handedly, was taking home $4 million a year. Charles Schwab, the head of Charles Schwab discount brokers, pocketed $6.1 million in 1987.

The Canadian sub-branch wasn't far behind. Middling but proficient stockbrokers hit the C$250,000-$300,000 mark in the bull market. "High performers" (some in their early thirties) were getting $500,000. The dozen at the top were reported to be pulling in as much as $1.5 million take-home, after taxes. Junior institutional block traders, without even the cover of being "salespeople" as an excuse – clerks simply executing orders – were in the $200,000-$250,000 range. Senior institutional traders earned double that, with the top man taking in close to $1 million. Senior partners pulled in $1 million bonuses.

Larry Grossman, the former Ontario Conservative leader, moved through the revolving door to Richardson Greenshields in late 1987 and was handed a salary in the "mid-six figures." The $50,000 Porsche 944 was declared out of fashion in brokerage circles, giving way in status to the Porsche 928 at over $100,000. Jokes about the money and extravagant expenditures (a $10,000 sofa for a $1 million apartment) were bandied around at Butterfields, a bond traders' bar in Toronto's First Canadian Place.

Indulgence in luxurious outfittings and amenities was also part of the scene, even when a firm was financially shaky. The spending was part of the bureaucracy's image of itself. The Osler case has already been mentioned. In the United States, the CEO of E. F. Hutton, another venerable brokerage firm that came a cropper, signed a long-term lease in New York, at an appreciable premium, for an elaborate, pink marble office tower with Egyptian overtones, then spent an additional US$95 million on improvements, which he supervised right down to the the urinals off the trading floor. Other E. F. Hutton spending, such as lavish company trips to exotic places and offices near brokers' homes rather than in strategic locations, was equally profligate.

Towards the height of the 1980s' bull market, Canada's chartered banks clamoured to be let in on the bonanza. One prominent bank chairman sniped at the protection given brokerage firms, whose senior partners were getting $1 million bonuses. A leading broker, while not denying the extravagant rakeoffs on his side, sneered in turn at the banks' executive dining rooms, chauffeur-driven cars, and big fat salaries for executives who had made huge lending errors, like the Dome Petroleum loans fiasco. As it happened, the banks soon took over many of the brokerage (investment-dealer) firms, willingly indulging the extravagance even further. Five senior partners of Dominion Securities collected $42 million in cash and shares when the Royal Bank of Canada bought out the firm in 1988.

Despite the post-October 1987 cutbacks and losses, Wall Street firms were still making lucrative offers to lure away top brokers from other firms – those brokers, that is, able most successfully to generate commissions. Sign-on bonuses, either to the switcher or to the broker who recruited the switcher, were handed out in Canada, too. In Canada, as well as in the United States, most of the stock-market branch's high-flyers, who account for the largest slice of brokerage overhead costs, faced only modest retrenchment in their salaries during the cutbacks. In fact, the average total pay per employee in U.S. securities firms (all employees) rose slightly from 1987 to 1989. The lay-offs also hit few executive offices. Despite the bad times, the stock-market branch was still much larger than it had been only a decade or a generation earlier.

The brokers who promote the buying and selling of shares, and the stock exchanges which process the churning, are only two sections of the stock-market branch, with its prolifically subdividing and diffuse bureaucratic cell structure. Another is the analysts, one of the most expansive and bureaucratically far-fetched sections of the branch.

There are the rank-and-file brokerage-firm analysts, mentioned above, churning out their investment advisory sheets (tip sheets, in effect) for use by brokers. Although called "research," it is increasingly tied into "sales," that is, into the make-work function of churning shares. The analysts are the equivalent of the memo writers and brief writers in the old bureaucracy (government) except that they produce their advisory sheets whether there is something worth writing about or not. People with literary skills are good at this story-writing work, just as they would be good in writing bumf for a department of immigration or of public works. Every morning in large brokerage firms in the United States and Canada analysts also go on the "squawk box" – loudspeakers in local offices, tied to home office through conference telephone calls – to get their fodder out to all points. They have to keep generating ideas.

The higher category of these rank-and-file analysts are the industry "specialists," usually in large firms. They may, for example, be specialists in the oil industry, or high-tech, or communications companies. These are the people who are often interviewed by business papers or on television to comment on some company or development in a particular industry. Industry analysts regularly call companies to get the inside track, sometimes several times per week. The corporate official looking after them in each case – perhaps a vice-president of communications or of investor relations – tells them all the same thing. It would be unethical to do anything else. The analysts, in the next step, then call up major investors (institutional investors) who provide their brokerage firms with business, hence commissions, hence indirectly pay for their inflated salaries. A spin-off, independent research boutiques charging fees, also get into the act.

The institutional people, though, are analysts, too – "buy-side" analysts, they're called, as distinct from the "sell-side" analysts who work for the brokerage firms. Why be satisfied with one layer of analysts when two layers will do? Besides, sell-side analysts, trying to push their favourites of the day and generate trades, can't altogether be trusted.

Since the sell-side analysts all have the same information, their job is to devise an imaginative angle on it, or to be first on the line to investors with a bit of news, and generally to jockey for influence. It's a kind of bureaucratic product differentiation – economically useless again, but bureaucratically self-sustaining. "You're always on the lookout for a new angle," explains a Canadian analyst. "It's not enough to have the ideas; you have to market them. It has to be unique to get attention." Another spends about 90 per cent of her time "trying to think of things in a new light." They don't want to get too far away from the crowd, though; that would be bureaucratically risky.

Brokerage analysts' "buy" recommendations abound, regardless of reality. For a start, most of the analysts' information comes straight from the corporate officers. The latter aren't going to be too critical of their own companies and help to lower their share value by triggering "sell" recommendations. An industry may be decaying under the surface, like the U.S. automobile industry in the 1970s, and the telltale signs will go unobserved altogether by analysts.

Moreover, if analysts are too critical of a particular company and loudly issue "sell" recommendations, they risk offending their source of information in the company and being cut off or bumped to the end of the line for phone calls. An analyst, moreover, may work for a firm that serves as the company's investment banker – handling new share issues for the company or advising it on takeovers, at hefty fees. Some analysts even get involved personally in this investment-banking work with the companies they cover, or try to enlist these companies as investment-banking clients. Analysts in many brokerage firms are pressured to turn up investment-banking possibilities in the course of their work. There is no point in putting this lucrative business to risk with a categorical "sell" recommendation on the company's shares. Occasionally an analyst who transgresses gets the boot or otherwise has to leave. The others get the message.

A "buy" recommendation, by contrast, is more positive and optimistic than a "sell" recommendation – more likely to keep investors hopeful and in the market, and above all, generating commissions, which is the point of all this effort. Scuttlebutt puts the ratio of buy recommendations to sell recommendations at 50 to 1.

If a sell recommendation is required, the analyst may use doublespeak like "hold" or "fully valued" (meaning "don't buy," in other words, "you might think of selling"). "Swap" is the latest euphemism for "sell." "It's a better four-letter word," admits one brokerage executive. "May underperform the market" and "source of funds" are other such euphemisms for "sell." Of course, the analyst can let selected clients, such as large institutional investors, know what he or she really thinks, privately. Only the odd, maverick research boutique openly works on negative news.

Recommending stocks is the easiest part of the industry analyst's job, though. The next step is to go out and sell the idea so the price of the stock will increase and prove the analyst right. "Road shows" – whirlwind trips where analysts meet local brokers and push their chosen shares – are part of the exercise.

Base salaries for analysts, in the United States, range from US$100,000 to $200,000, plus large bonuses for hitting the right stocks. Top analysts can still command $500,000 to $600,000 or more a year, with the upper rung hitting seven figures – up to $2 or $3 million in cases, especially if they have been made a partner in their firm. So being an analyst in an investment bank has advantages over doing analysis in other bureaucracies, like the civil service, which don't have the bureaucratic leverage to siphon off such tribute. Canadian analysts, meanwhile, don't do badly either – somewhere "north of $100,000," as one put it modestly in 1989. (How much the take had fallen since 1987, when a quarter of a million was within reach and a few even made $500,000, wasn't mentioned.)

Not to be discounted in all this are the corporate investor-relations cadres who tell the analysts what they want the analysts to be told. Originally the method was to take analysts out to lunch and tout the stock. The more expensive the lunch, the better. It was crude, old-fashioned public relations, but still relatively simple. As the analysts' section expanded and became more elaborate and esoteric, however, investor relations was expanded in counterpoint: one bureaucracy feeds another. Then it was realized that press coverage influenced analysts and shareholders, in a loop. So resources were added to handle the press – public-relations resources this time. Another feedback loop was finding out what analysts, money managers, and brokers were thinking about a company, its management, its annual report, and so on. So opinion research was added: more bureaucracy. Now analysts and brokers grumble about all the surveys they're supposed to answer for investor-relations cadres.

Investor-relations cadres also work the media indirectly through analysts, who are interviewed as "experts," "mavens," or "gurus" by reporters. The analysts need to be prepared to say something authoritative when a reporter calls. Investor-relations cadres call this the "mantra," which they and company executives supply. The mantra is then "chanted" independently by the analysts to reporters, bringing with it the extra credibility of a third-party endorsement.

Advertising is another stratagem for influencing investors. Business magazines in particular abound with corporate image advertising and with balance-sheet presentations explaining how well companies are doing. This coincidentally helps feed the advertising branch and its cadres. Corporate image advertising, much of which, although not all, has an investor-relations function, eats up about US$3 billion annually in the United States.

Best of all the stratagems are the junkets, otherwise known as "show-and-tell tours," where a corporation takes analysts, fund managers, business writers, and others to chosen operations, occasionally in far-away places like the Northwest Territories or South America. One notable junket was a lavish trip aboard the *Queen Elizabeth II* to the opening of the Come by Chance refinery in Newfoundland in 1973, thrown by refinery owner John Shaheen. One thousand guests were invited. The ship itself cost a reported $97,000 a day ($244,000 in today's dollar value). Unfortunately, the refinery rapidly went bankrupt.

A junket by Allied-Lyons PLC in 1987, for eighty or so analysts, fund managers, and business writers, was more successful. The tour visited the recently acquired distillery operations of Hiram Walker – London to Scotland, then to Toronto, Windsor, New York, and southern France aboard a chartered Concorde aircraft. The meals were lavish, as suited the study trip. The "liquor" analysts became liquor analysts in more ways than one. The cost was a mere $1.2 million, or more than $13,000 per head. Columnist Diane Francis in *Maclean's*, who was on the junket, gushed over the "booze cruise . . . a great success and everyone had a jolly good time" and exclaimed enthusiastically that it was "the kind of posh flamboyance that most Canadian multinationals would be well advised to emulate."

Next to the brokerage and institutional analysts and investor-relations functionaries are analysts who look at the larger picture. Among them are the prima donnas and gurus of stock-market analysis, many of whom, in the United States, publish their own newsletters and also manage portfolios and investment funds for clients. There are also economics gurus, who muse prophetically about interest rates, inflation, expansion, recession, and other omens. And there is everything in between.

What they do in common, directly or indirectly, is predict – try to predict – the future of the market. In North America, there are twenty thousand analysts (about fifteen hundred in Canada) who are members of analysts' societies alone. Since there are so many of them, some of them are going to be right in their predictions at any given time. Particularly if they publish their own newsletters – have their own devout congregations – they will attract attention and notoriety and may become, if only for a brief moment, media celebrities. This powerfully enhances the illusion that stock-market analysts are not, in their essence, bureaucrats playing self-cancelling, circular games with traditional bureaucratic elements – words and numbers on paper – but are, instead, romantic individualists fulfilling some important and dramatic historical function. As one star analyst passes back into bureaucratic obscurity, another comes into the light.

Remember Joe Granville? "Guru Joe," he was called. In 1981 Granville was celebrated for having correctly predicted a decline in the Dow-Jones index and recommending "sell everything." His public reputation, and his influence with his eleven thousand market-letter subscribers, who began selling, helped make the prediction come true. Barbara Frum on "The Journal" was tickled pink to have him on the show. In 1982, despite his system, he was making the wrong calls – spectacularly wrong calls – and was all but forgotten. Al Frank, the highest-ranked analyst in the U.S., sometimes asked by strangers for his autograph, missed the October 1987 crash altogether and lost a lot of money for his clients and himself. "I'm embarrassed and ashamed," he said. He apologized abjectly in his newsletter, *The Prudent Speculator*.

One who did predict the October 1987 decline long before it happened – some said too long – was a Canadian "market adviser," Ian McAvity. His subsequent sales-spiel meetings overflowed with distraught investors. Everybody seemed to have forgotten that in the early 1980s he had predicted that gold would go to $3,000 an ounce by 1986. It stagnated instead in the $430 to $590 range. McAvity once did a study, based on his charts, claiming that there was a direct correlation between the Dow Jones and the phases of the moon. For that matter, a top Wall Street analyst predicted in 1981 that oil would hit US$100 per barrel by 1990. The highest it got after 1981 was $33, briefly in 1990, in the days prior to the Gulf War.

Robert Prechter, the oft-interviewed and most closely watched analyst of the mid-1980s, whose specialty was time cycles, missed the timing of the 1987 fall and then predicted that the Dow would plunge below 400 in the early 1990s, a decline of 85 per cent from its 1987 peak (as of this writing, in mid-1991, it's at the 2900 mark).

The same goes for individual stocks. Institutional analysts don't help at all. During the 1980s, investment funds that bought a package of stock reflecting a major stock market index (say the Standard & Poor 500 in the United States) – representing, in effect, the stock market as a whole – outperformed most funds that relied on analysts to select individual stocks.

Earlier, in the 1960s, some American theorists argued it was a mug's game to make predictions about the market, either based on past market behaviour or on a current study of companies. Analysts were outraged. Did this mean that throwing darts at the financial pages was as good a way of picking stocks as any other? The theorists' answer was an unequivocal yes. A couple of public figures tried it, and did outperform mutual funds. It became a fad. But the theory was irrelevant to the bureaucratic function of analysts: to help keep the machine turning over.

The analysts' paper wanderings have become more involved and elaborate than ever, thanks to the data-generating capacity of computers. Take the "chartists." The premise of a chartist is that one doesn't need to know anything about the companies one buys into. One just needs to chart past market action, using graphs, by which one can also predict the future. This is called "technical analysis," although it is worlds away from technical analysis in the ordinary sense, like analysis of welds in a pipeline or of pesticide residues in soil. It is really bureaucratic model-building. The practitioners call themselves "technical analysts" or just "technicians," or "trend and cycle analysts," or "wave theorists."

The movements on a chart are interpreted in the symbolism of tides, waves, and ripples. The technician's job is to recognize a change in trend by watching the "trend line." Bureaucratic jargon about the trend line increases to fill the interpretive space available. There are primary trends, uptrend lines, downtrend lines, up-curving trend lines, down-curving trend lines, necklines, head and shoulders (above the neckline), reverse head and shoulders (below the neckline), aborted head and shoulders, deformed heads, multiple heads and shoulders, two heads with one shoulder, double tops, double bottoms (both upward- and downward-sloping), triple tops, triple bottoms, diamond wedges, simple pennants, exhaustion gaps, fan movements, flags, flags flying at half mast, rectangles, saucer bottoms, coil bottoms, climactic bottoms, spike tops, breakouts, breakaway gaps, exhaustion gaps, golden crosses, and other verbal siblings concocted by the chartist subsection. New chart methodologies are forever being concocted, in the best make-work fashion – generating more jargon.

There is the wave side of technical analysis. That, too, goes back a long way. It began with a British economist in the nineteenth century who related sunspots and magnetic storms to the fluctuations of commodity prices. The Russian Nikolai Kondratieff devised the Kondratieff wave (the "long wave") about business cycles, based on commodity prices, and predicted the business decline beginning in 1929. This, perhaps more than anything else, enhanced the standing of wave theory. An obscure American accountant, R. N. Elliott, applied cycle theory to the stock market, based on a numbered development series found in nature (the increases of branches on a tree, for example). This numbered series was first spotted by an early-thirteenth-century Italian, Leonardo Fibonacci, in trying to figure out the architecture of the Great Pyramid at Giza. This, in turn, connects directly to the present. Robert Prechter, the pre-eminent stock-market guru of the 1980s, is a convert of Elliott's, having stumbled across his work. Prechter co-wrote a book on Elliott wave theory. The basic premise is that predictable waves of investor psychology (pessimism and optimism) steer the markets, with natural ebbs and flows. Prechter, when he graduated from university, spent four years playing for a rock band – productive entertainment work – before joining the bureaucracy (Merrill Lynch, in his case) as a junior technical analyst.

Wave theory, like chartism, lends itself to open-ended elaboration and complexity. It is, in other words, bureaucratically expansionist. Wave and cycle identification abounds unto exotica, like the skirt-height theory of stock price movements, otherwise known as the "skirt-length effect" or, more correctly, the "hemline indicator." Short hemlines indicate stock-market peaks; 1929 and 1968 hemlines are cited, along with 1987 when high hemlines combined with white dresses. People buy stocks when the social mood is upbeat, goes the theory. The trick is to predict when the good mood will peak – when the "major mood top" will be reached – after which a bear market begins. Lots of leg showing on the streets of New York is the sign. Another sign is new Crayola crayons, like the "wild strawberry," "vivid tangerine," "fuchsia," and others added in 1990, according to wave-theorist Prechter. After all, the last time new colours were added to the Crayola box was in 1972, and the following year the Dow Jones declined 24 per cent. Similarly, factoring in the movement of heavenly bodies, hence tide fluctuations, variant behaviour under full moons, lunar eclipses, and sunspots or ionizing radiation – the electromagnetic school – is quite common in chartism.

Chartists are continually discredited. Aside from the fact that they regularly fall on their faces, computer analysis has shown no correlation between the signals of the charts and subsequent market movements. Analysts of other schools call them names – unproductive mooches on society, astrologers, practitioners of hokum and foolish nostrums. These detractors suggest reading tea leaves would be better. Not too long ago, reading the charts was dismissed as "witchcraft." But the chartists became more prosperous and numerous anyway, especially in bull markets when guessing activity increases. In the 1980s, investment dealers hired them in increasing numbers. Chartists have one great bureaucratic virtue. Almost every system they concoct involves in-and-out trading, which produces commissions. In the early 1970s, an acerbic Princeton University professor, Burton Malkiel, observed, "The technicians do not help produce yachts for the customers, but they do help generate the trading that provides yachts for the brokers." This allusion as to who got the yachts became a common reference. It made no difference.

During the inquiry into the failure of the Principal Group of trust companies headquartered in Edmonton, it was revealed that a daughter of the group's chief and founder, Donald Cormie, was paid C$288,000 to do archeological research exploring the historical links between world weather patterns and economic cycles. The depth of Lake Wabamun, just west of Edmonton, was also of importance. Cormie's contention was that from the depths of the lake and from precipitation records he could better gauge the credit-worthiness of farmers and foresee the movement of commodity markets. Lawyers at the hearing could hardly keep back their laughter. Cormie, alleging that such studies had a business purpose, became a figure of ridicule. The poor man, though, was just trying to elaborate on the Kondra-tieff wave, one of the inspirations of technical analysis.

The other main subsection of analysts is the "fundamentalists." They are the larger school of the two. Fundamentalists focus on the fundamentals of companies themselves – their earnings and dividends, their price-earnings ratio (stock price to earnings), their book value, the quality of their manage-ment, the prospects for particular industries, and detailed information about the economy. The fundamentalists keep getting things wrong, too. In a bear market, stocks of companies can plummet while their earnings (a key "fun-damental") rise impressively. Average price-earnings ratios (of all companies listed on an exchange) can vary wildly with market swings, defying the "fundamentals." The fundamentalists also mistime the peaks and bottoms. Thinking in packs, they are also liable to miss developments that fall outside the group way of looking at things.

The chartists and other technicians, dismissed by the fundamentalists for practising witchcraft, themselves dismiss the fundamentalists as backward-looking charlatans. Nine times out of ten the fundamentalists' mistimed data has nothing to do with where stock prices are going, snort the technicians. Market prices reflect hopes and fears, guesses and moods, the rational and irrational ideas of hordes of buyers and sellers – factors that defy analysis and for which there are no statistics, the technicians charge. Nevertheless, like the fanciful technical analysts, the fundamentalists' sub-section inflates too, with its denizens in their warrens daily cogitating, collecting, and sifting reams of data and statistics, calling sources, some-times making field trips, applying their analytical principles, and writing their investment reports and newsletters in endless circles.

Analysts who try to combine both schools indulge in even more bureau-cratic complexity. These analysts rely heavily on computers. The ability of computers to screen and analyze data has generated a third school: quantita-tive analysis. Since one can sift and rearrange data in a computer to no end of complication, this school has open-ended possibilities for occupying minds.

Taking the measure of both the technicians and the fundamentalists, and later their quantitative offspring, a new and perverse stratagem sur-faced: "contrarianism." The idea was to do exactly the opposite of what everybody else was doing. That was all – a case of bureaucratic *reductio ad absurdum*. The premise was that nobody could predict the market, and that it was dishonest to pretend otherwise and to get people to invest their money as a result. More than that, stock analysts and money managers frequented each other's company and followed each other's tracks. This produced "groupthink." Groupthink prevailed for individual investors, too. Many institutional investors, moreover, were driven by the fear of failure and acted together, finding safety in numbers – another classic bureaucratic character-istic. Even specialists – say, analysts of the automobile industry – didn't have any private knowledge that would give their clients an advantage, and weren't immune to parroting the conventional wisdom. The effect of this advising and investing in packs was to overly inflate the value of stocks – puff them up with air, in the jargon – or overly deflate their value instead.

Contrarians, by simply doing the opposite, set out to make the most of it, inspired by such wise counsel of the financial press as *Barron's* in 1921: "General Motors common," *Barron's* intoned at the time, "cannot be con-sidered an investment." Another brilliant analyst's counsel, by distinguished Yale economist Irving Fischer a few days before Black Tuesday, 1929: "Stocks are now at what looks like a permanently high plateau."

Some contrarians became renowned. They produced books and news-letters of their own. Worst luck, though: Too many people became contrar-ians, even in Canada, and even among respectable investment managers. American writer John Rothchild, in his picaresque account of trying to play the market, *A Fool and His Money*, complained that contrarianism was so rampant, the truly contrarian approach wouldn't be contrarian. "My own research had left me logically paralyzed," he protested. Only in the most spun-out, self-centred, and unproductive bureaucracies could backwards become forwards and forwards backwards, and the participants nevertheless be so intensely serious about themselves.

In the larger investment-dealer firms there are economists, sometimes even an economics department, although, as one survey found, economists' ability to predict such variables as inflation or interest rates is no better than opinions collected at random. Theoretical, otherworldly, dogmatic, and narrow-minded, economists are not much good on the practical side of economic activity, either, but they are accomplished bureaucrats. U.S. con-trarian economist Ravi Batra observed that his colleagues kept changing their forecasts every few months, and still turned out to be wrong – and still, it should be added, lost no status in the bureaucracy and pocketed handsome paycheques. With their bureaucratic ranking, they are also often interviewed for thoughts on the market and the impact of the economy on the market – thoughts passed on reverently by the respectful media.

Writer John Rothchild tells of his tracking of Henry Kaufman, "the dean of the economic forecasters, the famous spokesman from [investment banker] Salomon Brothers, the man whose speeches make the front page of the *New York Times* and whose opinions move the world markets." "When Henry talks, people listen," *Executive* magazine in Canada once said rever-ently of Kaufman. Kaufman had made a famous announcement in 1982 correctly predicting a break in interest rates. Less well-known was that in 1981 he had got the direction of interest rates wrong and that in the mid-1980s he had also been embarrassingly wrong about interest rates and inflation (mention of the losing streak, Rothchild naughtily points out, is omitted from a book by Kaufman). Kaufman continued, nevertheless, to head up the Salomon Brothers' research department and to be in great demand for predictions, commanding big audiences and a big salary. He also had a spreading bureaucratic infrastructure at his beck and call. About three hundred and fifty people had some professional input into his work. They were supported, in turn, by the office resources of Salomon Brothers. Rothchild decided that, based on respective records, a stock-market astrologist he had interviewed, who often made specific correct forecasts, was more reliable.

As well as the chartists', astrologers', and economists' macroprognostication subsections, the analyst section also occupies itself with trying to figure out, day in and day out, why the market moved up that day, or down, or why it did nothing at all. This is more fodder for the stock-market branch, and is generated regardless of whether it's right or wrong or of any earthly importance. A columnist for *Newsday*, during the 1980s bull market, colourfully described this fodder as the analysts' "baloney-sandwich explanations." "They didn't have the foggiest idea why the bull market was going on so long. But they couldn't actually say that out loud. . . . The gamblers might stop coming to the casino."

Conflicting forecasts? More and more of them, *Canadian Business* once complained – forecasts blatant in their opposition to each other, on every damn thing from interest rates to the Dow Jones. "Take your pick," said a Wall Street column in the *Toronto Star*, documenting the same disarray of conflicting opinions. "Market forecasts conflict," read the headline in the business pages of the *Vancouver Sun*. The complaints are irrelevant because the analysts' section keeps producing the pointless, conflicting forecasts anyway.

The analysts subdivide and grow further. Contrarianism, a subdivision in itself, had a Zen dimension, then spun off a psycho-contrarian subsubsection. "We ask our people to think differently," the guru at one firm explained to *Forbes*. They are encouraged to relax, the better to sense the flow. Long vacations are also encouraged (maybe the greatest of all inventions of any bureaucracy). Staff members come and go as they please. Reading material includes the *Journal of Psychology*, *Memory & Cognition*, and the *Humanist*. It's a bureaucratic paradise. The members of this firm aren't undergraduates in a corner in a student hang-out, "finding themselves"; they manage about US$1.5 billion. Zen has its counterpart in Taoism, as in *The Tao Jones Average* ("Tao" is pronounced "Dow"), a book on understanding eastern thought and its application to the stock market. This generated a school of analysis.

There is a "whole-brain" analytic fashion, which advocates "using the unstructured complex right side of the brain along with the more rigid analytical left side." In other words, go with your intuition. It could be described as the "touchy-feely" or "New Age" school of analysis (or of non-analysis, if you like), or maybe the "coiffure" school, because hair is an important factor. CEOs with a winter tan and overstyled hair, for example, are regarded with suspicion – too impeccable and sybaritic – by many whole-brainers. Discount the company's stock, they say. Excessive gold jewelry on a CEO, known to veteran whole-brainers as the "Indian bride syndrome," casts a cloudy aura on a stock. There is also a whole-brain culinary principle of analysis, whose rule of thumb is "the better the meal [at an annual meeting or reception], the worse the deal." And a sub-principle: There is an inverse relationship between the presence of tiger shrimps at a company function and corporate prospects.

Stock-market analysis now includes traditional seers, mystics, and psychics. One New York practitioner, who uses tarot cards, astrology, and a crystal ball, got into it after correctly predicting the outcome of the 1987 Super Bowl. She charges US$100 an hour. She invites her clients to bring along their stock portfolios, from which she often gets vibrations. Some of her clients, she claims, are executives from high-powered brokerage houses, looking for a competitive edge. "They figure this is just as accurate as anything else," she says. The New York Stock Exchange, incidentally, is a Taurus, and the American Stock Exchange is a Cancer.

Another in this analysts' subsection, a professional astrologer, examines "numena" (the heart of things) rather than the superficial phenomena that preoccupy other stock-market analysts. Birthdays, mothers' birthdays, and the exact hour of birth are important for individual investors. Dates of incorporation and of stock splits throw light on the prospects of companies, as do birthdays of the company's principal officers. This data can be used for drawing up birth charts and checking their alignments against each other. Strict astrological aspects, like interplanetary relationships, solstices, and signs are, needless to say, also important.

This analytic offshoot isn't new. J. P. Morgan consulted an astrologer and so did a president of the New York Stock Exchange. Cornelius Vanderbilt held seances to raise the spirits of dead financiers to get stock tips from them. These cases may seem to be exotic, but where is the line between psychic or astrological counselling and, say, psycho-contrarianism or Fibonacci numbers of the analysts section proper? Which throws light on real economic activity (the production of goods and services) and which is only make-work? Is there any difference in absurdity between an Elliott wave chart and a birth chart, or between the abstractions of economists and the movement of the stars? An astrologer contacted by writer John Rothchild had studied economics in graduate school and found it to be a sloppy pseudoscience, full of irrationality, next to which astrology was much more rigorous, sensible, and practical. An electromagnetic (atmospheric) specialist interviewed by Rothchild, similarly, had studied math and come up through Merrill Lynch as a technical analyst. The move to atmospheric analysis was a natural progression.

There is a New York analytic boutique called Harmonic Research, whose president is a graduate of Harvard Business School and is occasionally interviewed by the media. A typical newsletter entry signals a "crucial day" when "we have the planet Mars going stationary direct in a major T-square (negative configuration) with Venus and the Saturn/Uranus conjunction." Also used are number-oriented philosophers such as Ptolemy and Pythagoras, the work of a "time and cycle" analyst strong on the "vibration of each stock," and a variety of number calculators called the "Octagon Chart" and the "Square of Nine," first developed in ancient Mesopotamia to determine the seasonal value of commodities. And so on.

One imagines a member of the old bureaucracy – say, an assistant deputy minister – preparing a white paper for Parliament, factoring in lunar eclipses, vibrations, and the Saturn-Uranus conjunction. The denunciations of "bureaucracy-gone-mad" can be heard just thinking about it.

Harmonic Research charges US$360 per year for its newsletter (eighteen issues) and $600 for its hotline service. The hotline service includes recorded messages three times a week, plus special updates on days of extreme volatility. Consultations with the president cost $30 per minute. These are the going rates for guru newsletters and newsletter gurus, incidentally. Hotline services are typical, too.

Every once in a while, in the past, some sardonic critic of stock-market analysis would suggest that the analysts should include the signs of the zodiac among their indicators or consult horoscopes. The critics were being satirical. In real life, the New Bureaucracy imitates satire.

In fact, it makes no difference to the productive economy whether an investment guru makes the right prediction or not, or whether contrarians are clever geniuses or prating fools, or whether the astro-physical analysts are right in their cosmic predictions more often than the stratospheric economists (with their stratospheric speaking fees) are right in theirs. What one investor gains, in this game, another loses. Analysts – their whole bureaucratic panoply, all the printer's ink and printouts, the citations, the endless telephone calls and reams of paper, the puffed-up incomes, the expensive office space, the road shows, the earnest television and radio talk, the seriousness and pretension, and the dignified luncheon addresses – cancel each other out in a vast exercise of making work for each other.

They do, however, play a bureaucratic role. By indulging in the game, and getting others to indulge alongside them, they help to inflate the stock-market branch. The more involved and elaborate the play, the better. Bizarreness, far from being a drawback, helps the process because it adds to the elaboration.

The analysts section is fed on the side by an academic subsection. One school of economists, for example, devotes itself to what it calls the "efficient markets hypothesis" – EMH in the jargon. According to EMH, stock prices always reflect everything known about a company's prospects and the direction of the economy. So the stock market is relentlessly logical, and functions like clockwork. A key tenet is that people trading in stocks act in totally rational fashion. The theory makes tarot cards look good. "It's as if believers in the Ptolemaic system were still trying to show that the planets revolve around the earth," jibed noted U.S. stock-market veteran David Dreman. The EMH, nevertheless, with its ideological gloss, has had great influence, helping to prop up the stock-market branch. Its proponents keep working on it assiduously.

The possibilities in this academic subdivision are limitless. Two Carleton University professors discovered that if you buy large-capitalization stocks at the opening on the last trading day of a calendar month and sell them at the close of the eighth day of trading of the following month, you'll do better than if you buy ten days ahead of month end and sell on the penultimate trading day of the month, although your advantage may be wiped out by commissions. (Did you follow that?) This was considered noteworthy. The findings, indeed, appeared in the *Financial Analysts Journal* and were discussed in detail in the *Financial Post*. Such articles and journals abound, with their many contributors and their own bureaucratic infrastructures – the editors, secretaries, printers, mailers, and suppliers who keep the stream of paper flowing.

Meanwhile, some universities are setting up laboratories where they run experimental stock markets. If that weren't enough, physicists and mathematicians are getting into the act, applying the "science of chaos" to the stock market in order to be able to forecast market changes. The science of chaos is part of a field of physics called "nonlinear dynamical systems." It identifies non-linear patterns, following deep underlying mathematical laws, in what appear to be random happenings. Research to find the hidden structure of non-linearity in stock and commodity markets is now being done in Canada as well as in the United States. One of the locations is the Los Alamos National Laboratory, of atomic bomb fame.

The money-manager branch and its advertising, including the retail marketing efforts of brokerage firms, also have a broad cultural effect which bolsters the stock-market branch. They propagandize the game of moving one's money around. "Go for these stocks," the advertising says, in effect.

"Try this industrial fund." "Gold's coming back." "Gold's going out." "Get into the market now." "Get out of the market now." "Go to cash." "You'll just get poorer in cash." "Here's how the mutual funds rate." Whether the advice is taken or not, the pressure to participate, with an appeal to acquisitiveness, is maintained.

Game-like cultural devices, which prop up the mythology of stock markets, are used. One is stock-picking games with simulated transactions. The Toronto Stock Exchange and Toronto-Dominion Bank's Green Line Investor Service sponsor annual stock-market competitions for university and college students – including business schools – and in the TSE's case, also high-school students. For the general public, there are annual entry-fee, cash-prize contests, both in Canada and the United States; the United States has at least five, including a futures contest. These games carry the implicit message that such playing in real life has something to do with business, not just with self-cancelling speculation and bureaucratic waste. In the United States, where the ideology protecting the New Bureaucracy is most entrenched, there is even a summer camp where young kids are sent to play stock-market games and learn other ways of playing with paper.

Technical exotica multiply. Their portrayal in the media adds glitz and fashionability to the imagery even if the devices are not widely used. A feature in the *Financial Post's Moneywise* magazine, for example, showed a sweatered professional late at night in his study, a full moon shining through the window, family pictures on the desk, looking into a computer monitor and, with his keyboard, "touching [a] database." He could also play endlessly into the night with his portfolio-management computer program. Then, the next day, he could plug directly into stock exchanges and into wire services with stock-market information. If we were properly sophisticated and upwardly mobile, the picture said, we would all be doing it.

Young moderns can go one step further and get a printout of selected stock prices by subscribing to a phoneprinter, where pushing a few buttons on the phone will do the trick. A *Forbes* magazine report showed a smiling Monterey, California, resident holding such a printout. He's sitting in his pajamas, on the edge of his bed. "Even before he brushes his teeth in the morning," the magazine recounted, he "crawls out of bed and gropes for his Schwabline Phoneprinter to check his investment portfolios." The phoneprinter apparently comes before his bladder, too.

One of the latest in accessories is portable stock-quote systems, which also beep or vibrate when a stock price or when turnover in a particular stock hits a certain level. Discount brokers like to market these items since they boost share-trading by their owners, by as much as 60 per cent or more. Don't leave home without it, is the idea.

Also feeding the stock-market branch are the mass media on their own.

Reading the entrails of the previous day's stock market activities, as if they actually meant something, is just part of the cultural feed. General-circulation newspapers devote entire pages every day – extremely valuable mass-media space – to stock-market listings. On the odd occasion, routine stories about the day's trading activity will even turn up as the lead story on the front page. Television prattles on about the stock market on programs like "Venture" (the CBC) and "Wall Street Week" (PBS), and flashes stock-market indexes (and gold and sometimes silver prices!) on its news broadcasts. Television, like the newspapers, also reports what the analysts have to say – the analysts' serious pretensions give the coverage pretension and the coverage's serious pretensions give the analysts pretension. In the United States, an entire cable-programming network is largely devoted to the stock market and related activities. Canadian cable systems devote a channel to stock-market listings. Radio runs stock-market reports. All this culturally supports the stock-market bureaucracy – represents a kind of cultural capture of the public – and through it, indulges the bureaucracy's waste and excesses.

In the back corners of the stock-market branch, away from the main body of cadres, less fashionable kinds of bureaucratic make-work endure. They batten on to, and work, the edges. They seem to be shady, and sometimes are, because they often ignore bureaucratic niceties, although they are no less bureaucratic themselves for all that. They hearken back to the past. Their endurance would be astonishing, except that all bureaucracies have their edges, and edges on their edges, and economically wasteful bureaucratic cells can be ingenious and tenacious in keeping themselves going.

Short-sellers dwell in the branch's back offices. Short-selling is a bet that the price of a stock will decline. Short-sellers borrow shares from a broker (shares bought by clients on margin, for example, and held in the broker's account). They then sell the shares into the market at the current price. The idea is to replace the borrowed shares when the price goes down, buying them in the market and pocketing the difference.

The practice dates back to the days when stock markets were unregulated. A pool of speculators would buy up a stock to hoist the price and then make a killing on it. Another gang, seeing the price rise beyond reason, would decide to sell the stock short, break its inflated price, and make the killing themselves. The two sides would go at it hammer and tongs, furiously expending time, money, and energy to no economically productive purpose at all, although generating lots of notoriety.

The current generation of short-sellers purport to sell stock that is actually overvalued, and thereby benevolently "correct the market." To encourage the share price to go down regardless, however, they use bureaucratic devices of their own. They say nasty things about the stock. There is even a short-sellers' newsletter in the United States, the *Overpriced Stock Service*, and a short-sellers' hotline. After a negative report is out for a while, publicists may be hired to spread the negative analysis. One of the great hallmarks of short-selling is ganging up on a stock to drive it into the basement whether or not it deserves to be there.

These manoeuvres work best with relatively small companies or companies whose shares have limited trading, where the muscle of a short-selling syndicate can have an effect, even if the stock isn't overvalued. If the short-sellers have a reputation as successful vampires, the reputation itself will help push the price down, in which case their gambit becomes a self-fulfilling prophecy.

However, those who stand to lose by the decline (money managers, investment advisers, and their clients, for example), or just those who see a speculative opportunity, may strike back, supporting the stock by buying up shares and thereby raising the share price. This is called "squeezing the shorts." In that case, the short-sellers have to cover their commitment at a higher price. They get caught in a wringer. Their purchases of stock to cover their position helps push the price up even faster, putting any remaining exposed short-sellers in an invidious position. The anti-shorts may tighten the squeeze by taking out large advertisements and running a publicity campaign of their own.

In one case, in the United States, the share price of a company went from $10 to $40, down to $16, back to $40, back to $16, up to $60, and down to $18, as shorts and anti-shorts played their corresponding games. In another case, a short squeeze ran a stock up from $19 to $190 in six months, after which the squeeze fell apart and the stock tumbled back to where it was before.

Taken by individual cases, short-selling may appear to be risky. Given the necessary capital and research, though, short-selling is just another layer of bureaucracy. Some brokerage firms run short-selling subsections for clients. One American short-selling syndicate has managed as much as US$900 million in short positions, for partnerships of investors and for pension funds. The syndicate hires private detectives to get useful dirt on potential victims. Detectives have also been hired by the other side – to get useful dirt on a short-seller. More money is spent.

Short-sellers are sometimes denounced with colourful epithets – "vultures," "bottom feeders," and *"tontons macoutes."* A more accurate description would be "bureaucratic feeders," who make extra work all around. An overvalued stock would eventually decline in value without short-sellers, as stockholders sold it off in the conventional way. Short-sellers nevertheless would be hard put if there wasn't an inventory of excessively overvalued stocks that they could go short on. Here, the main section of the stock-market branch helps out, with its "buy" recommendations, its group-think, its pushing of fashions and its puffery. Again, one bureaucratic section feeds another.

There are still other feeders. Stock-lending to the short-sellers subsection by brokerage firms – which is how short-sellers get the necessary stock to sell – is an inflated and remunerative subsubsection. The brokers collect a slice of interest on these loans. Takeover activity helps inflate this subsubsection. Takeover artists turn to stock-borrowing to strengthen their hand in forays. Risk arbitrageurs, meanwhile, in competitive takeover situations, often short the stock of the contender they think will lose, as well as buying the stock of the contender they think will win. They need to borrow stock for the short-selling. From 1980 to mid-1989, as M&A activity spiralled, stock loans outstanding in the United States rose from US$6.6 billion to $32.6 billion. In record takeover year 1988, U.S. investment banker Shearson Lehman alone had fifty people in its stock-loan department and was taking in more than $100 million from stock-lending. The head of the department, for this clerical function, earned more than $1 million that year. The stock-loan subsubsection, in turn, has spun off a subsubsubsection – "stock-loan finders," who help brokers find extra passles of shares when they don't have enough of their own to lend and can't locate any.

Another venerable make-work device, enduring in the bureaucratic backwaters, is stock promotion. It shelters under the ideological umbrella protecting the stock-market branch overall. Stock promotions involve initial public offerings and secondary trading of shares in "junior" companies, whose prospects rest more on promise than on past performance. These are the "penny stocks," often not listed on an exchange. In a so-called "speculative" market like the Vancouver Stock Exchange (VSE), brokers depend on promoters to churn up interest and buying in such stocks and hence generate brokerage commissions for them. Brokers also collect as "underwriters" of the original stock offering. If they guarantee the offering, they are given stock warrants as a consideration, which they can cash in as the stock price rises. This is is in addition to the underwriting commission. The brokers and promoters work in tandem.

The process is routine, bureaucratic – and the routine is simply repeated. The function of stock promotions is to pump up the price of these intrinsically worthless or marginal shares, by generating an initial rise in the price and interest in the stock. Then, when the "story" behind the stock wears thin, the promoter, the brokers, and the insiders sell out at or near the top price. The promoter allows the share price to collapse.

The process can be recycled. After a while, the promoter may be able to pick up or collect a block of those collapsed shares at their new low price and then start flogging them again. A broker can do the same. Since the stocks are priced so low to begin with in this recycling – sometimes as low as a few cents a share – even a small gap between the buyback price and the resale price can represent a huge percentage take. The idea is to "ride" a stock up and down, and up and down again.

There is another variation. If a company is listed on an exchange, but its share price has collapsed, it qualifies as a "shell company." A promoter can buy the shares for the nominal price to which they have fallen, give the company a new lease on life with a changed name and a news release, perhaps some new assets (different mining claims, a "breakthrough" technical process, a new joint agreement) picked up directly or through a merger, and go through the promotional routine again. The company benefits by the stock-market listing while avoiding the nuisance of having to meet listing requirements again. At one point, less than 2 per cent of the companies listed on the VSE had been untouched by a name change, a merger, or a delisting in the prior decade.

Or a syndicate can use the same company name but keep floating different news about it, riding the stock each time. Possible or purported joint agreements with other companies known or unknown are a useful huckstering device. One minor bureaucratic prodigy VSE-style, CTI Technologies Corp., went through an eclectic variety of ostensible products – pilotless airplanes, swimming pool alarms, securities systems for parents with toddlers, pizza chains, cellular telephones, and condoms (the "Love Gasket") – in just a few years.

The excuse for this make-work is that it raises money for new ventures that couldn't get the money elsewhere. But the bureaucratic overheads eat up most of what is separated from the "mooches" or "fish" (the suckers), with top promoter cadres themselves each raking off two to three million dollars a year on average, from the process. A study in the 1960s, focussing on the Toronto market, which was a haven for such promotions, found that only 18 per cent of the money raised for such promotions (in mining, at the time) actually got into the company treasury, and the 18 per cent wouldn't be too well-spent either. A study in 1979 done for the B.C. government, covering the prior fourteen years of the VSE, found that despite claims of procedural reform, only half the money invested in new shares in listed companies was received by those companies (the promoters, property vendors, and particularly brokerage firms took the first half). Of that, according to David Cruise and Alison Griffiths, in their exposé *Fleecing The Lamb*, as little as 21 per cent on average, or 10.5 per cent of the investment overall, might go to the purported working purpose of the company, based on Ontario findings. In some cases none of the investor's money ends up directly applied to its intended purpose. The B.C. study was so incriminating that the provincial government refused to release it. The study did not cover what is eaten up in brokerage commissions and in manipulated prices in the "aftermarket" trading; money thrown at stock after it has been originally issued, as promoters generate interest in it, doesn't get into company treasuries at all. Factor that in and the economic product as a percentage of money spent would be even more minimal – a barely perceptible trace.

Because of stock-market mythology, nevertheless, the promoters are seen as free-enterprise individualists. They are credited with such heroic qualities as having nerves of steel. Skirting the rules or the law doesn't necessarily distract from this imagery; it may enhance it. Occasionally a promoter will have delusions of grandeur – will actually try sustaining a dud stock – and lose money as a result. This adds "risk" to the image. All this is supposed to constitute a wild stock-market frontier. In reality, it's low-grade bureaucracy, with set routines played out over and over, securities lawyers and accountants doing the prospectus and other paper work, predictable ploys within rational rules set down by the regulatory agency, repetitive sales techniques, evasive action to avoid regulatory and legal checks – a warren generating waste in one corner of the stock-market bureaucracy.

People familiar with the scene have long known that stock promotions and their aftermarket trading exist only to keep feeding this extraordinarily wasteful and silly bureaucracy, at the expense of the naive or of habitual gamblers drawn into their transactions. Exacting cash for trash is the broker's ancient art. Here it is transparent and freely talked about, in private, by the practitioners. Every once in a while, a scathing book about it is written, or there is a burst of indignant magazine articles. "Half the companies are out and out scams . . . and most of the rest are rig jobs of some sort," commented Vancouver writer Adrian du Plessis, formerly a VSE floor trader and since become a leading expert on the exchange. John Woods, editor of *Vancouver Stockwatch*, has mused that just 1 per cent, or perhaps at best 2 per cent, of junior companies that go public with a new listing on the VSE actually evolve into "real" companies that may be around for a few years. The record for Vancouver is the CHoPP Computer Corp., which hit a total market value of $275 million on the basis of a supercomputer it never built. CHoPP eventually delisted itself and migrated south of the border. Tillex is another notable case, from among many. Listed on the VSE in 1985 at thirty cents a share and traded mostly in the United States, it was pumped up to $78 in eighteen months before trading was halted and the stock delisted, which rendered the shares virtually worthless.

On occasion, a company being promoted will, almost inadvertently, actually make a mining discovery or otherwise become a viable operation. Stock promoters, with all possible swagger, will point to such cases to justify their own existence and their waste and also, not least, to help hype whatever promotions they have in the hopper. Mining discoveries, like the Hemlo gold find, are particularly useful since their value is established suddenly, which creates a sensation. Stock promoters can trade on such happenings indefinitely. The greater the sensation and the hype about windfalls from these odd cases, the more low-grade bureaucracy can be created behind them.

Whatever is incidentally produced by stock promotions in the real economy would, of course, be far better financed in another way without the almost total waste of the mechanism. Stock promotions "are an inefficient way of raising money," a mining promoter (as distinct from a stock promoter) explained to the *Financial Post* in 1989. "If it costs more than 5% or 10% [the capital] should not be raised because it's probably a bad prospect." The scam side of it – taking people for a ride – is undesirable in itself. In the mythology, however, stock exchanges are automatically, magically, taken as a linchpin of free enterprise – a sacred expression of it. So this wasteful, diversionary low-grade bureaucracy endures.

In Canada, even the most outwardly respectable of national brokerage firms (investment dealers) indulge in this bureaucratic variant. Their Vancouver offices have taken full advantage in fattening themselves on the waste. As members of the exchange, they could change the rules to eliminate the waste, but that would also eliminate the exchange itself – a good idea economically but not, of course, to these cadres. The promotional routine itself has become impersonal and bureaucratized – so much so that promoters will often hire technicians specializing in a single area of promotion, like taking control of and renovating shell companies.

Just how mechanical and bureaucratic is this variant is illustrated by a U.S. brokerage firm dealing in penny stocks called Blinder, Robinson, which flourished in the 1980s. Some of the firm's own salespeople called it "Blind 'em and rob 'em." The time period, with its general bull market and grandiose free-enterprise mythology, was particularly conducive to inflating such bureaucratic workings.

Blinder, Robinson's headquarters were in Denver, Colorado. At its peak, in 1987, it had 1,700 brokers in sixty-one offices, ranking tenth in the U.S. in the number of "account executives." New recruits went to a three-week "state of the art" training school ("boot camp"), where, as *Forbes* reported, they were rigidly schooled in cold calling and other procedures. The 1,700 brokers averaged 100 calls a day each – 170,000 per day in total, 850,000 a week, over 40 million a year, based on a straight-line calculation. They were managed by a cadre of some 130 branch managers and assistants with a discipline that *Forbes* commented would do the old German general staff proud.

The firm handled "housebrand merchandise," whose share prices it could push up and down. Typically, it recycled stock it had previously promoted and then allowed to sink into oblivion. It used all the available mechanisms, like crossing the profits of early investors into other stock in the stable, or crossing buy-backs at a low price with sales of the same shares to others at a higher price. Through various agreements and mergers, it got its hands on seemingly limitless amounts of low-priced shares which it then proceeded to push through the machine (one small company promoted by the firm authorized 900 million shares).

Raided by the Internal Revenue Service, battling the Securities and Exchange Commission, and hit by a lawsuit from a fellow penny-stock broker, Blinder, Robinson filed for bankruptcy. The Blinder, Robinson style of bureaucratic organization was typical of the major U.S. penny-stock brokerage houses which fleeced investors in the 1980s. Most of them ultimately ran into trouble with regulators and the law, touching off a regulatory crackdown in the process.

These and similar curiosities in the bureaucratic backwaters are interesting cases, although they don't begin to rate, for bureaucratic waste, with the main sections of the stock-market branch.

Illegality and fraud, or the threat of illegality and fraud, eat up time and resources in surveillance and prosecution. The regulatory and prosecution cadres who do the work, including those on the public payroll, constitute a subsidiary bureaucracy of the stock-market branch.

The New York Stock Exchange alone, in just the enforcement of its own rules, spends about US$80 million a year in surveillance. The U.S. National Association of Securities Dealers allocates $90 million annually, most of its budget, to regulation. The U.S. Securities and Exchange Commission (SEC) has an annual budget of $169 million, a substantial part of which goes to enforcement. At that, the SEC can't cover the territory properly. It has to pick and choose its cases to try to make strategic points. Provincial securities commissions are the corresponding agencies in Canada. A New York securities lawyer, writing in the *Wall Street Journal*, estimated total U.S. regulatory costs, including compliance expenses, at $1 billion annually, or more than $10,000 for each of the eighty thousand active stockbrokers in the country.

A third level of surveillance and investigation handles criminal prosecutions: the Department of Justice and U.S. government attorneys' offices. In Canada, RCMP commercial crime squads get into the action. Trapping an Ivan Boesky or anybody else requires a great deal of time and money. "This is probably the most complicated form of law enforcement in terms of preparing and proving a case," admits an RCMP inspector. "It's quite common for us to examine 20,000 documents, and then have to sort and match them." In the E. F. Hutton cheque-kiting case in the United States in the early 1980s, the firm, in response to subpoenas, submitted seven million documents. An SEC investigation into a suspected insider-trading conspiracy headquartered in Zurich, which began in 1981, was still underway in 1990 and still at the speculative and circumstantial stage. Investigation is just the first step. Then comes the decision whether or not to prosecute in light of the difficulties and, if prosecution goes ahead, the lengthy and complicated court case.

The surveillance bureaucracy on one side expands the legal bureaucracy on the other. With the attempted crackdown on insider trading in the United States, the already lucrative field of securities law became even more lucrative for securities lawyers, particularly if they had surveillance and criminal-law experience. Rates of US$300 an hour are commonplace, with top cadres charging $400 an hour. These lawyers may be retained just to hold the investment banker's hand. "Sometimes they hire you out of anticipation, sometimes for comfort," one lawyer explains.

The costs easily mount up because the large investment banks' bureaucratic power to allocate resources to lawyers is even greater than the bureaucratic power of the government prosecutors to add to their resources. This makes the legal process exceedingly costly. Before investment bank Drexel Burnham Lambert capitulated to charges on six felony counts, in late 1988, its legal and related costs in preparing a defence had reached an estimated US$175 million.

Meanwhile, investment banks (covering both brokerage and investment-banking functions) have beefed up their legal staff to try keeping their employees in line and to help themselves legally finesse what they want to do. The lawyers' job, as one of them put it disingenuously, is to assess risks for the firm's business managers. Merrill Lynch's legal staff in the United States in the late 1980s comprised 128 attorneys and Shearson Lehman was up to 90 lawyers – enough from which to draw plenty of watchdog opinion.

The watchdog lawyers hired by the investment banks almost invariably come through the revolving door from the surveillance side – lawyers who "graduate" to high-paying Wall Street law firms or to the investment bankers after they have learned the ropes working for the prosecution (the old bureaucracy). The investment banks, through their cash flow – and that's the source of their bureaucratic power – can retain or hire the best surveillance lawyers available. In a matter of months, during the heated action in 1987, U.S. investment banks hired two former members of the SEC, the top securities regulator for New York State, the former regulatory chief of the New York Stock Exchange and a former associate director of market regulation for the SEC. Outside lawyers working on the defence side in criminal cases in the late 1980s included a former SEC general counsel, a former director of the SEC's general office, and several veterans of the U.S.

Attorney's office for the Southern District of New York. To remove the taint of its cheque-kiting conviction, investment bank E. F. Hutton (since disappeared in a takeover) hired a former U.S. attorney general. "Unheard-of" salaries were being offered, one astonished securities lawyer commented in 1987, when a hiring rush occurred. In-house lawyers also often share in executive bonuses.

The bureaucratic power of the SEC is no match for the investment banks when it comes to salaries and hiring. A senior SEC official recalled meeting with a group of Wall Street lawyers. He stood there with the cream of his staff, who made US$50,000. His own salary was $75,000 at the time. "They had kids making twice as much as me who didn't say a word," he recounted. Even entry-level salaries at the SEC were less than half those paid by top New York law firms. Its pay levels are so low it has trouble hiring beginning secretaries.

The same holds in other warrens of the stock-market branch, down to shady stock promoters in Vancouver. "Manipulators, con artists and thieves" working the VSE, David Cruise and Alison Griffiths reported in *Fleecing The Lamb*, have "got a battery of lawyers, accountants and brokers to help them slide around the rules and cover their tracks. After all, if they come across a little wrinkle that flummoxes the cops, they stand to make millions with impunity." The *modus operandi* of rules evasion in these cases is that stock-in-trade of bureaucratic machination – creating an endlessly complex paper trail, helped along by the common practice of using nominees. In one recent case described by the RCMP, the manipulators had more than a hundred trading accounts at thirteen brokerage firms.

Against this armament on the stock-market side, the surveillance side has to put more time and people into preparing a case if they want it to hold. At that, it is extremely difficult to make illegal insider-trading and stock-manipulation charges stick or, for that matter, to make judges and juries understand what is involved. This raises the level of bureaucratic cost and complexity all around.

The stock-market branch generates these costs prolifically, organically. It's a bureaucracy, but with an acquisitive rather than a public-service ethic. The regulatory rules devised to keep it under check run against the grain of its cadres' natural impulses. Violations and illegalities thereby spill-out naturally. They are reported in terms of rule-breaking, fraud, and swindle. Occasionally they draw outrage. This moralistic and legal condemnation misses the illegalities' essential nature: bureaucratic spillage.

Shouts of dismay and indignation, for example, accompanied the Boesky scandal and associated insider-trading cases involving seventy Wall Street members. Righteousness grew when Drexel and Michael Milken were charged. The Ontario Securities Commission laid 281 charges against the principals of Osler Inc. and others for breaching the securities act (this was in addition to the 114 charges laid by the Toronto Stock Exchange, for which Osler Inc. was found guilty on 91 counts). Other cases in the last few years, in the United States, have involved charges of misappropriating securities, money laundering, cheque kiting (mail and wire fraud), insider trading, stock manipulation, withholding commission rebates, lack of disclosure, keeping false records and violating margin rules, conspiracy, miscellaneous other securities frauds and rule-breaking, as well as inquiries into suspected illegal kickbacks (including sexual favours and drugs) and cases dealt with in civil proceedings like "bucketing" (skimming off some of the money from profitable trades made for customers). Large and seemingly respectable investment banks as well as petty swindlers were involved.

But none of this was novel. Illegalities and rules violations are a working offshoot of the stock-market branch and always have been, going back to the 1930s, the 1920s (before the Securities and Exchange Commission was established), and further into the nineteenth century (although most of the manipulative games in those days weren't transgressions because there was little in the way of securities regulation to transgress against). The stock-market branch worldwide now generates at least US$5 billion annually in losses to investors from fraud, of which $2 billion is siphoned off in the United States alone. Fines, suspensions, and criminal prosecutions are a routine part of the functioning of the Vancouver Stock Exchange and associated stock promotions – as regular, it seems, as the opening and closing of trading every day.

The mushrooming of top securities-law firms in the United States followed naturally from a step-up by the SEC of enforcement. Among the first to realize that securities defence work was going to expand and become more lucrative was a former crusading SEC chairman who, returning to private practice, began beefing up the securities side of his law firm. This reciprocal bureaucratic expansion works at lower levels, too. The history of Blinder, Robinson, the now-defunct penny-stock brokerage firm, for example, was an absurdist accumulation of complaints, fines, adjudication processes, suspensions, court cases, and, ultimately, a criminal proceeding. When holding company Blinder International Enterprises went public (that is, when some of its shares were put on the market), eight of forty-five pages in its public prospectus were devoted to litigation against the firm. When the SEC banned the Blinder, Robinson boss from the securities industry, he hired one of Washington's top securities lawyers, who succeeded in court in having the ban sent back to the SEC for a rehearing. The lawyer used to be with SEC enforcement. Another partner on the lawyer's team was a former SEC associate enforcement director. The team included four partners and a staff of twenty other lawyers. By the time the SEC managed finally to issue the suspension again, in the face of legal skirmishing, the case was ten years old, and even then the penalties were stayed pending an appeal.

According to one convicted penny-stock swindler turned state's witness in the United States, large segments of the trade in over-the-counter stocks are "controlled by organized crime." This adds more evasion complexity and, necessarily, more surveillance complexity.

Turn the heat on to check the stock-market bureaucracy and it adds other layers of bureaucratic activity in response. Rules evasion and rules surveillance are a bureaucratic subsection in their own right – part of the myriad bureaucratic spill-out from the stock-market branch.

The mythology of the stock market holds that its doings are a reflection of the real world. "A mirror of the economy," is the metaphor trotted out by commentators. The "verdict of Wall Street" is another. The "verdict" is supposed to be omniscient and all-wise. Even when it goes bonkers, it is supposed to have some superior meaning.

Behind the mythology – and propped up by the imagery – is bureaucracy. Wasteful bureaucracies build on their own patterns and possibilities. They have a life of their own, departing from outside reality, often at odds with it. The more intensely the bureaucratic games are played, the more elaborate they become. The more elaborate they become, the greater is the unreality.

Sometimes the unreality is too much even for the bureaucracy's followers. "Meltdown Monday" in the stock markets, October 1987, was such a case. Canada's finance minister, Michael Wilson, himself an investment dealer by trade (ex-Dominion Securities), was driven to disassociate the goings-on of the stock market from the real world of the economy. Stock-market commentators, who religiously reported on the slightest twists and turns of share prices, admitted that whereas the "real world" concerned itself with how productively we can turn out goods and services, it had "only a little to do with the bouncing around of prices for stocks, bonds and pieces of paper." Peter Newman in *Maclean's* wrote unkindly of the "hard-eyed moneymen who populate Bay and Wall streets" who had "taken leave of their senses." They treated equity stocks "like lottery tickets instead of pieces of paper representing the ownership of corporate entities whose employees are real people producing real goods and services."

The public was newly instructed by various commentators not to allow "the strange happenings in the unreal world of paper to scare us to death" and "to keep the fire storm from spreading beyond the stock exchanges to the economy at large." These commentators were probably more surprised than anybody that the 1987 stock-market "crash" had so little effect on the real economy – hardly was noticed by it – may, indeed, have indirectly helped the real economy by taking the gloss off the stock-market bureaucracy as different from productive economic work.

A spate of analyses appeared in the "business" press and elsewhere to explain how it had all happened. The silly efficient markets hypothesis (EMH), which saw the market as logical and rational, had been given a merciless drubbing by events. "Where was the [all-wise] invisible hand during the crash?" a feature commentary in *Business Week* exclaimed, perhaps feeling a bit betrayed. The commentary pointed out that there had been no significant news the day of the crash or the preceding week about the real economy of corporate earnings and interest rates that would have caused such a cataclysm.

The prophets of EMH fought back with *chutzpah*. They defended the crash as a rational stampede in which nervous investors, after finally digesting the information around them, simply pushed prices down to a new and more "efficient" level – in record time! The crash was to be applauded, they said. It confirmed the theory. The market was wiser than mere mortals. How proponents of EMH then explained the subsequent recovery of stock indexes, and why that was suddenly more "efficient" again, wasn't gone into. It reminded one of Orwell's Ministry of Truth – in this case not describing war as peace, but describing the economically irrational as rational.

The theoreticians of market irrationality were suddenly in demand for their comments. An economics professor at Yale disclosed that 40 per cent of 1,000 investors he had surveyed had, on Black Monday, suffered symptoms of emotional stress – sweaty palms, tightness in the chest, irritability, or rapid pulse – rather than acting with cool rationality. Human emotion, then, was the culprit. This news about the anxiety of investors as the value of their holdings plummeted was considered a profound finding.

This same worthy, as if a professor of medicine, was also exploring how epidemics and plagues spread. The object was to help construct a workable stock-market model. He and his fellow explorers suggested that individuals "infect" one another with enthusiasm for a stock, and that when the contagion becomes more widespread (that is, buying of the stock increases and the price rises), some investors are "cured" (that is, they sell out or stop buying) and the progress of the "disease" abates. The professors had failed so far, however, to reduce their plague theory to a mathematical formula which, for economists like themselves, means failure. And the price movements they studied didn't resemble the hump-shaped pattern of a typical epidemic.

A quartet of other professors, like anthropologists in the jungle, had identified a class of irrational investors known as "noise traders." "Noise," in the parlance, is news that bears little relation to real economic facts like a company's earnings. If the efficient markets hypothesis held, these "noise traders," because of their "irrationality," hence "inefficiency," should have been driven out of the market. Instead they often moved the market and made money . . . although they were wrong! (The notion that they might be making money by cleverly playing a paper game, and hence were "rational" rather than "irrational," and that it was the game itself that was economically irrational, wasn't talked about.)

Others focussed on the role of tips, hunches, gossip, rumour, fads, fashions, guessing, mob psychology, social pressures, and cultural influences. Whatever the shortcomings of plague theory, it was clear that speculative bubbles are often produced, and panics do follow as prices plunge. Here the metaphor was the market as a "crapshoot." The head of the Center for the Study of Investor Behaviour in Chicago, an economist, was solicited for his opinion. Several psychologists doing similar work were interviewed. "Investor behaviour" had become a growing field of study. At the same time, the old work on speculative bubbles, Charles Mackay's *Extraordinary Popular Delusions and the Madness of Crowds*, first published in 1841, was reread for any illumination it might provide.

The Economics Research Lab at the University of Arizona was also doing profound work, that is, work that was cited as profound. It undertook closed experiments using shares of stock in a fictitious company. The company's economic status was fixed. Price fluctuations were based solely on trading activity. Sure enough, the investors in the experiments continually generated boom-and-bust cycles, bidding up prices far beyond the company's actual value. When, as a control against the students' youthful inexperience, the experiments were conducted with businesspeople instead, the bubbles were even bigger. These experiments were mentioned in the Black Monday aftermath.

Researchers in "chaos theory" who had been doing work on stock markets were also asked for their thoughts. One of the key concepts of the "science of chaos" is the "origin of turbulence." The concept envisions how even a tiny shift in a single variable can result in a dramatic transition from stability to chaos. It's called the "butterfly effect" – as in the theoretical possibility that the beating of a butterfly's wings over Mount Fuji could ultimately produce a hurricane in the Caribbean. Perhaps that was the answer for Black Monday, it was surmised. "As yet," admitted a chaos guru, "chaos theory doesn't do anything for you formally. But it gives you inspiration . . ."

All this suggested that the stock market's disconnection from economic reality, with its mania, speculative fever, breakdowns, faddism, tail-chasing, second-guessing, attempting to anticipate other speculators, and the desire to make money out of nothing, was something new. Of course, it wasn't, as inhabitants of the stock-market branch always knew. The very phrases "bull market" and "bear market" embody the notion of the pack running one way or the other, at odds with or departing from economic reality. Since investing in the stock market – really "speculating" – is essentially guesswork, following the herd is a natural tendency.

Explanatory "baloney-sandwich" reporting, reflecting the gameplaying, adds to the unreality. It reports facts that purportedly explain price changes – good news for price rises and bad news for price declines – while not bothering with other facts that bear in the opposite direction. This exaggerates expectations that the changes will persist. In one experiment with students under simulated market conditions, the investors without news to explain price changes did better than those who had the benefit of financial commentary.

The stock-market branch, being an incestuous and convoluted bureaucracy, can make strange things happen simply by turning over. On one day, in early 1987, the Dow Jones leapt upwards, plunged downwards, and then moved back towards where it was when the bell rang in the morning. "Madness! A flight from reality," spluttered one regular stock-market commentator, apparently embarrassed by it all. "Values, and sensible perceptions of values, don't change that way. It's a temporary eclipse of rationality by unbridled emotion and knee-jerk reactions." Or was it? "The New York asylum was variously called berserk, total confusion, silly, impossible, frightening and lemming-like," he went on. At first, program trading (trading triggered by computers) was blamed. Then it appeared instead that the market "had made fools of the computer programs." Or had it? Crazy Friday, the day was called. Several individual stocks went up and down like yoyos (Pepsi, at one point, was "worth" 20 per cent more than it had been just an hour earlier). "You have to be able to distinguish between what's rational and what's happening," offered one economist pompously. The NYSE trading-volume record was broken that day – more than double the volume that had broken the record just five years earlier in a similar, inexplicable episode.

Sometimes the economic news goes one way and the stock market, because of its internal gameplaying, goes another. "News of economy's strength slows stocks," read one headline, describing such a case, or, conversely, "Stock markets surge as the economy slows down." Low unemployment – a good economic sign – may affect the stock market negatively. It touches off a whiff of speculation about higher interest rates and money flowing from stocks into bonds. "The [stock market] rally was subverted by the [declining] unemployment figure," is how an analyst explained one such conjuncture.

Another kind of disconnection from reality occurs with individual stocks. One such case is recounted by a Canadian analyst trained as a "fundamentalist" (evaluating stocks according to estimates of earnings, dividends, and other real economic measures). In the bear market of the early 1960s, IBM and Xerox earnings were going up by 20 per cent, but their stocks were falling by 50 per cent. "'Excuse me,'" he recalls thinking to himself. "I thought when earnings went up stocks went up. I learned in 1962 that that didn't happen at all." Like a disillusioned choirmaster who becomes a warlock, he converted to technical analysis (chartism and wave theory).

Tail-chasing in a circle – cadres trying to guess how other cadres might react – is a major part of stock-market make-work. And it can be triggered by anything – from a government announcement to some remote but sensational event – regardless of its bearing, if any, on economic reality. When some tail-chasers guess wrong about other tail-chasers, they have to recover ground by reversing direction – so there may be heavy buying in the morning and heavy selling in the afternoon, or vice-versa, by the same people. More churning.

The bureaucratic workings also produce "magical" or "supernatural" effects, at odds not just with economic reality but with astrology, numerology, Kondratieff waves, microwaves, and sunspots. One is the "January effect." Stock-exchange markets tend to rally in January. Another is the "holiday effect," really a "pre-holiday" effect. A U.S. study showed that 35 per cent of the market's entire appreciation between 1963 and 1982 occurred on just eight pre-holiday-weekend trading days each year. (The rise before Thanksgiving Day is called the "turkey rally.") There is the "turn-of-the-month effect." A survey of the Dow Jones Industrial Average for trading days from 1897 to 1986 showed returns are appreciably higher from the last day of one month through to the third day of the following month than they are for other days. There's also the "day-of-the-week effect." Mondays as a rule are a down day except before a Tuesday holiday, when the holiday effect takes over. The "Blue Monday effect" was so strong during the Great Depression that, according to one study, the entire market crash took place over weekends, from Saturday's close to Monday's close. The stock market actually rose on average every other day of the week.

Naturally, if there is a turn-of-the-month effect and a day-of-the-week effect, there is bound to be a "time-of-day effect." And so there is. Prices on the NYSE rise for about the first forty-five minutes of the day; most of the rest of the day is flat; and there's a little rally at the close. These effects are called "calendar anomalies," in the scholastic jargon of analysts' journals. They can be graphed, and one can see that whatever the progress of General Motors in selling cars and IBM in devising new computers, 3:30 p.m. on Monday (a double whammy of day-of-the-week effect and time-of-day effect) is not the time to sell shares.

These mysterious effects continue to puzzle all and sundry in the stock-market bureaucracy. They ask themselves why, if these anomalies are so well-known, traders don't take advantage of them and arbitrage them away. One erudite study, plumbing the depths of other studies, ends up fuzzily referring to "human nature," "behavioural predisposition," and "psychology." These factors make people behave in peculiar ways when they hit "cusps of time" – weekends, holidays, first-thing-in-the-morning, and the end-of-the-day. One ingenious explanation for the "weekend effect" is that individual investors buy stocks uniformly over weekdays at their brokers' urging (hence prices rise Tuesdays to Fridays) but often make sell decisions over weekends when they can mull things over on their own (hence the Monday declines).

None of this makes any difference to the world of productive work but, in the stock-market bureaucracy, it exercises minds. One nine-page article on the subject in the *Financial Analysts Journal* had eighty-one footnotes, many of them including multiple references in turn. And if one can bother with such effects for share trading on the NYSE, one can do the same for T-Bills and orange juice futures. More esoteric analysis is produced.

Maybe the best-known supernatural phenomenon is the "Super Bowl effect." According to the mythology, when a team that originated in the old National Football League wins the Super Bowl, the New York stock market, as measured by the Dow Jones Industrial Average, will finish ahead that year. When a team from the old American Football League wins, it will be a down year. The stock market followed that pattern for twenty-three straight years to 1989, before running afoul in 1990, but the myth was good while it lasted. There are lesser-known effects. One has to do with "Pittsburgh Phil" – an aging Pittsburgh resident whose name is actually Alexander. Legend has it that when Pittsburgh Phil visits the floor of the New York Stock Exchange, which he does occasionally, stock prices rally. Or, on any Friday the thirteenth, according to the myth, the Standard & Poor 500 index goes up (whether it does or not). In degenerate bureaucracies that are more and more occupied with second-guessing and fanciful surmising, superstition has a fair field: If a pigeon flies into the trading room of the New York Stock Exchange, there will be a stock market crash.

Endless games devolve into endless smaller games. The bureaucratic patterns and syndromes, though, can have serious consequences on the productive economy. The rise of the stock-market bureaucracy in the United States, starting in the 1950s, has had a destructive effect on the American economy.

American author David Halberstam, in *The Reckoning*, his sweeping chronicle of the Japanese and U.S. post-war automobile industries, described the process at work at a critical juncture, the bull market of the 1960s. These were the "go-go" years, exemplified by a particularly successful money manager called Jerry Tsai. The "old stock market" of the "fuddy-duddies" was turning over at 10 or 12 per cent. The "new one" of the go-go stock-market hotshots was turning over at 40 and 50 per cent. (This was a reference to the trading by the "dazzling young men" themselves.) The leading players would skim quick profits off the top of the churning, like separating cream from milk.

This rising new bureaucracy aided and abetted, and was aided and abetted by, the conglomeration movement – the application of financial strategems, creative bookkeeping, tax avoidance, and stock-market leverage instead of productive economic work. The conglomerators found, for example, that by merging two companies with different financial characteristics (one with a high price-earnings ratio and one with a low price-earnings ratio), the result looked better and flew higher on the go-go market than either of the originals. "Paper, rather than reality, was emerging from an economy like this," wrote Halberstam, "and illusion rather than production preoccupied the successful new manager." The conglomeration movement was a disaster.

A greater negative consequence for the economy was that the excitement and action of Wall Street covered over the real economic world of production, education, technology, and co-operation, where the Japanese were innovating and progressing while the American industrial heartland was beginning to decay (Nissan and Ford were the respective companies Halberstam chronicled in detail).

Still more serious was the impact of the stock-market branch on the decision-making process of corporations. The expression "short-termism" became part of the English language, to describe it. Playing the game of the stock-market branch is, by its nature, short-term in perspective. Institutional investors and individual players move in and out of stocks, sometimes frantically, looking for advantage and trying to maximize their gains. They have no compunction in dumping one stock and buying another based on the latest financial results, turn of events, announcement, or stock-price shift. Price-earnings ratios and dividend pay-outs of companies receive particular attention; they are objective measures in a sea of information and speculation. This information comes out quarterly, a drastically shrunken time-frame. Perspectives can be even shorter, down to weeks and days. "It's more a casino operation," admitted a Prudential-Bache vice-president in the mid-1980s. "In most companies there are no long-term stockholders anymore," Gulf & Western's CEO exclaimed, in the same period.

The stock-market short-termism put pressure in turn on corporate managements to adopt income-maximizing short-term profit strategies – to produce the steady quarter-to-quarter increases in profits that so please the stock-market players. They feared that otherwise the "market" would punish them by undervaluing their stock and might also leave their firm vulnerable to a takeover. Even when a dividend was reduced or omitted for specifically stated investment purposes, or because earnings were down for cyclical reasons, the share price would usually take a hit, although the company's long-term prospects were as good as ever and it had a strong technological capability.

Also, the pay-offs to executives themselves were becoming stacked with stock options, which were tied to the stock-market price. Increased status and all that goes with it, like higher basic salaries, also came with a higher stock price. So there was a personal incentive, as well, for executives to respond to the stock-market's short-term orientation. However, entrepreneurship and economic development, with their high up-front costs in technological development, worker training, design, and market development, are long-term – an altogether different kettle of fish.

The retrograde effect on enterprise could happen insidiously. In many of the large U.S. industrial companies, efforts were made to drive up the price of stock, sometimes by buying back stock, which used up capital that could have otherwise been allocated to investment. Preoccupation with the share price tilted the balance of power within companies towards finance people and short-term priorities and away from production and marketing people and economic creativity; the effects could be lethal. American engineering professor Seymour Melman, in his seminal 1983 book, *Profits Without Production*, discussed how many older industrial corporations, under such influences, simply gave up in some areas under competitive pressure from Japan and Europe rather than undertaking the difficult, expensive, and long-term job of increased productivity, product innovation, and development of new technology. Financially oriented corporate chieftains didn't have the know-how or inclination for it, in any case. It was much easier, too, for sustaining short-term profitability and the share-price, to pull back in troublesome areas (divesting subsidiaries along the way) and make acquisitions in other areas instead.

In some cases, research and development was cut back or the introduction of new products was delayed or abandoned, to boost current earnings and the stock price. Or immediate higher profits were chosen over a strategy of reducing prices to increase market share or to enter new markets. The way management related to the workforce was also affected. If a company resisted lay-offs in downturns or spent more time training its workforce, rather than just maximizing shareholders' return, the cost might cut into the quarterly numbers and the stock end up discounted, although the company's approach, promoting loyalty and knowledge in its workforce, was good entrepreneurship. This conditioned company behaviour.

Corporations could try ignoring the stock market, but particularly in the United States, the stock-market culture was part of the corporate culture, even if some executives complained about it.

One result of this short-termism in the 1960s and 1970s was that, in the 1980s, the United States began running up a huge merchandise trade deficit and became the world's largest debtor nation. In automobiles alone the trade deficit rose to almost US$60 billion in 1987. Consumer electronics, machine tools, semiconductors, and copiers were other product areas in which it had been outpaced. In computers, its export surplus vanished. Not all companies or sectors were affected in this way, and the stock-market bureaucracy was only one of the factors that contributed to the short-termism. But it was a potent one. A capping irony was that the bull market in the 1980s, in American stock markets, coincided with this rising trade deficit and external debt. A broad-reaching commission on industrial productivity, organized by a concerned Massachusetts Institute of Technology – whose findings were published under the title *Made in America* – targeted short-termism as one of the economy's basic problems.

The rise of the stock-market bureaucracy and also the mergers-and-acquisitions bureaucracy hurt the U.S. and Canadian economies in another way. It attracted overly large numbers of business-school graduates and other young talent to its bureaucratic paper games and away from productive work. Its lucrative, often fantastic, salaries and its fast track were a ready lure. The M&A activity at investment banks – "I-banks" in business-school jargon – was a big drawing card, but brokerage was also hot. On the corporate side, the fast track was the financial end of management. That the productive economy loses out, in terms of talent, from the growth of the paper-entrepreneurialism branch and the stock-market branch shouldn't be surprising. It is inevitably what happens when an unproductive bureaucracy gains presence and influence, and expands.

The "only money counts" mentality of the investment-bank cadres – the Ivan Boesky "greed is good" mentality – helped cover for this bureaucratic growth. It was put forward as the governing principle of capitalism and entrepreneurship and as a hallmark of free-enterprise individualism. In the real world, however, it is nothing of the kind. Unvarnished greed runs counter to the spirit of creativity and long-term commitment that economically productive entrepreneurship requires. This was the case for the Industrial Revolution and for early American entrepreneurship as much as it is today. Unvarnished greed, whether in paper games or inflated executive compensation, also destroys co-operation, needed in complex modern enterprise. It mocks the commitment of people at large to productivity, steady application, invention, and practical education, which does produce advanced economies. As doctrine for the New Bureaucracy, though, it was perfect, in the best Elmer Gantry fashion. It rationalized the most outlandish bureaucratic self-indulgence behind a belligerent free-enterprise, anti-bureaucratic mystique.

Bureaucratic power and, most of all, the ideology propping it up has managed to hide how crudely wasteful of time, people, and money the stock-market branch is. It is taken for granted that all the myriad, endless exercises of its cadres – all the fuss and fawning – have some economic function. Otherwise why the fuss and fawning in the first place?

Perhaps the fact that the trading is in shares of companies that are producing goods and services has something to do with it. The economic purpose of the productive companies rubs off on the stock-market branch, by an association of corporate images. Well-known company names – IBM, or GM, Exxon, Ford, BCE, or Canadian Pacific – conjure up powerful, images of computers, cars, oil wells, telephone lines, railways, and what else. There they are, in the stock-exchange listings. In any case, the fawning continues.

But all the trading of stocks to and fro – the turning over of the elaborate bureaucratic machinery – does not produce anything, at least not directly, other than make-work. No investment goes into company treasuries in the action of people buying and selling shares through an exchange. Shares simply change hands for cash, in endless repetition.

The main rationale for stock exchanges is that they allow companies to raise new capital by issuing shares to the public. This happens indirectly. Most new shares are not issued through an exchange. However, because there is subsequent trading in the shares through an exchange (the "secondary market" or "aftermarket"), investors, particularly small investors, will be more inclined to buy a piece of a new share issue. They know that, with the exception of very large blocks of shares, they will be able to dispose of their holdings easily at any time, through the stock market, although they might not always like the price.

Moreover, because investment-dealer firms, in their brokerage function, handle trading in stock, they have a ready-made relationship with institutions and speculators for selling them shares in new issues. They know who has money to play with and who wants to play. Without this relationship, the distribution of new shares would be more difficult. The trading action, by bringing more people "into the market," expands the possibilities of raising capital through share issues.

Finally, original investors in an enterprise can cash in by listing their company on an exchange and offering shares to the public. True, they can always sell a piece or all of their company privately. Sometimes, however, the calculation is made that a stock-market listing will result in a larger pay-off, particularly if only a minority percentage of the shares are being sold. And, if the new share ownership is distributed widely, the original investors can keep control of their company with a smaller ownership share while still cashing in most of their stake. This listing of a company on an exchange and the sale of shares held by the private owners doesn't add new capital to the enterprise. It does, though, add to the number and variety of companies listed on the exchange and hence the scope of the secondary market and its contact with investors. Theoretically this makes it easier to issue new equity if necessary, not just in the newly listed company but also, incrementally, in listed companies in general.

What the rationale boils down to is that the securities markets, thanks to the secondary trading through stock exchanges, raise the capital that fuels capitalism. They are the lifeblood of capitalism. Stock exchanges have a totemic significance.

Reality, however, is quite a bit different. The raising of capital through new issues of common stock is just a small fraction of the stock-market bureaucracy's overall activity (new issues and share trading together). In the ten years 1981-1990, for example, a banner decade for equity issues in Canada compared to other years, new issues of common stock through Canadian securities markets averaged C$4.5 billion annually, according to Investment Dealer Association figures. This came to only 6 per cent of trading turnover and new issues in Canada combined, excluding the role of convertible preferred shares (which may later be converted into common stock) and private placements (share issues without an investment-dealer intermediary). Even adjusting for these, the fraction of overall activity represented by common-stock issues would be small. A figure for *net* new common-stock issues, taking into account retirements (equity removed from the market), would be even less.

In the United States, *net* equity issues represent an infinitesimal part of combined activity (new issues and share trading) as measured in dollar value – just 0.5 per cent for the period 1980-1988. For non-financial corporations taken alone, the figures are even lower. In only three of those years was the net equity issue positive, and then it was marginal. In the other years in that period, and also in 1989 and 1990, there was a *loss* of listed equity of non-financial corporations, through removals from the stock market. That is, in each of those other years, for non-financial companies taken together, there wasn't even an infinitesimal raising of net new capital through the stock-market branch and its vast apparatus, but a drainage instead.

That is only part of the story, however. The costs of subsidies and overheads have to be deducted. An appreciable slice of the new equity issued in Canada in the 1980s, for example, was accounted for by the Quebec Stock Savings Program with its extraordinary tax-giveaway provisions – a dispensation of public money of about $870 million over the decade. The special federal capital-gains tax exemption, introduced in 1985, helped considerably for issues in general. So did the federal tax gift in the form of so-called "flow-through" shares, for mining issues – via a deduction from taxable income of as much 133 per cent of the outlay, for most of the 1980s. This isn't to mention the cost of accountants and lawyers on all sides figuring out how to best take advantage of the flow-through provisions. Aside from the artificial propping up of the financing in these cases, there was a loss of tax revenue in favour of already privileged high-income individuals, increasing financial inequity and the public debt along the way. This was a retrograde way of raising capital for enterprise.

Next come the bureaucracy's costs. These are impossible to track completely. Columbia University law professor Louis Lowenstein, however, in his 1988 book, *What's Wrong With Wall Street*, calculated total trading costs in the United States, based on commission rates and related factors, at US$25-30 billion annually. Economically, this cancelled out virtually the same sums generated by common stocks sold for cash, on average. But remember that, in those years, retirements of equity were greater than equity issues, for non-financial corporations, leaving a net equity deficit. The bureaucratic machinery was burning up $25-30 billion a year and not even keeping even – indeed, as we'll see, was helping to create the deficit.

Also to be added are the applicable costs of all the non-investment-dealer cadres, from gurus to newspaper reporters, plus their infrastructures, plus the cost of institutional investors' and speculators' time in playing the game. These costs as well are too myriad to track, but in total they would be considerable. All such overhead costs make the raising of equity capital through maintaining a large stock-exchange bureaucracy not such a brilliant idea.

That isn't all of the story, either. When a company issues new shares to the public while at the same time paying dividends of a like or greater amount, it raises no new capital; the payout of the dividend, for cosmetic purposes, cancels the share-issue capitalization. The company could as easily have kept the money used for the dividend (it would be entered in the books as retained earnings) and not bothered with a share issue. The same applies when a dividend is paid out in the form of new shares (a "stock dividend"): No new money is raised. Similarly, when one corporation buys part of another corporation's stock issue (maybe the issue of a majority-owned subsidiary), no new capital is added to the corporate sector. When a takeover company issues new shares to help finance the takeover of another company, no additional capital is added to enterprise (what is put in by the new share issue exits in the pay-out for the takeover). Restructuring in the other direction, in which a company divests itself of a stockholding in another company by a "secondary" share offering, doesn't add to common stock, either. Privatization share issues, which have inflated the figures in Canada, also just shift equity around.

Stock buy-backs funded by debt, LBOs (often "taking companies private"), and other mergers and takeovers funded by debt or retained earnings end up reducing the amount of corporate equity (common-stock) in the economy. These are new share issues in reverse – shareholders are paid money to surrender their shares. Call it "de-equitization." The stock-market bureaucracy plays as active a role in this process as it does in the share-issue process. These buy-backs, LBOs, and other financial engineering were the major reason for the "deficit" in new issues in the United States in the 1980s. Factor that in, and the raising of capital for enterprise, by the stock-market bureaucracy, becomes even less significant. All the rest, meanwhile, simply shifts share ownership back and forth.

At that, raising capital through the securities market is unreliable. In bear markets, in particular during recessions, share issues lose popularity. Stock markets are too sluggish. Yet that may be the very time when injections of fresh capital into enterprise are needed.

This brings us, finally, to the heart of the question: The financing of enterprise in any case, contrary to the popular idea of the stock-market, is mostly done by retained earnings, depreciation (the other part of "cash flow"), bank loans, bond issues, and private investment instead. For that matter, companies listed on stock exchanges represent only a part of modern economies with their diverse private sectors and large public sectors. More than that, and again contrary to the imagery, the most creative periods of economic development for different countries have been when their stock markets either were marginal and did not count or when their pressures could be ignored. As a rule, historically, stock markets have bureaucratically battened on to surges in industrial and technological development – the real work of enterprise – after they have taken place.

Take the case of Japan, whose post-war enterprise, investment, innovation, and development were so successful. Almost all the capital – about 70 to 80 per cent – for its postwar industrial expansion was in the form of loans from commercial banks. A crucial part of the financing came in the form of "overloans" to the commercial banks from the Bank of Japan, which the banks passed on to industry. In effect, the central bank, as well as supplying substantial capital of its own, acted as guarantor and manager for the whole "two-tier" system, which underwrote from scratch a phenomenal period of "high-speed growth." In the crucial early part of this period – the early 1950s, what might be described as the "entrepreneurial" phase – the commercial banks were "merely a channel through which the central bank fed industry with investment funds," as one Japanese banker himself declared.

Another tier of financing was provided by eight specialized publicly owned banks, the most important of which was the Japan Development Bank (JDB). At one point, in the early 1950s, they supplied as much as 38 per cent of industry's capital, over and above the overloans from the Bank of Japan. The JDB played a particularly important role in strategic industries like electric power, ships, coal and steel, and, later, industrial robots. The source of the JDB's capital was the postal savings system, which was to become the largest deposit organization, by assets, in the world.

These were the key financial players in Japan's remarkable economic recovery and surge forward, a period, moreover, when capital formation as a percentage of gross national product – the raising of money for investment – reached what was described by economic historians as "an almost unbelievable" level (42.8 per cent in 1961). The Tokyo Stock Exchange, meanwhile, as a capital market for industrial financing, remained stillborn until the 1970s. Public share offerings hardly left a trace, hitting a low point in 1965 of only one billion yen (C$3 million) for the whole country. That year, incidentally, the Tokyo stock market came close to collapse when the market slumped.

The largest part of share ownership, moreover, is closely held by banks, insurance companies and other corporations, most of which have a group connection to the issuing company; about 60 per cent of the stock of listed companies is virtually never traded. In Chalmers Johnson's classic work on the Japanese postwar economy, *MITI and the Japanese Miracle*, published in 1982, the index doesn't even have a "stock exchange" or "stock market" entry.

Another major and growing source of industrial funding, in addition to the banking system, was, of course, internal: retained earnings (profit not distributed as dividends) and depreciation. Retained earnings form part of a company's equity; they build up the equity side and provide leverage for further loans. The more successful Japanese companies eventually built up such large reserves that they constituted pools of capital; automobile manufacturer Toyota became known as the "Bank of Toyota."

It wasn't just that stock exchanges were marginal, financially, in Japan's entrepreneurial development. Because they didn't count – and more importantly, because they didn't have much presence – their bureaucratic culture didn't intrude on enterprise. Shareholder influence was weak. Japanese industry was free of the pernicious short-termism and paper games of the stock-market branch. Japanese firms could concentrate on export-market penetration, quality control, long-term product development, technological and engineering experience, and the development of their workforce's capability.

Sweden, like Japan, turned from being a backward, remote, largely agricultural country to a highly successful, technologically advanced industrial leader. It did it by private, crown, and co-operative investment, a banking system, and retained earnings. This continued right through to the post-World-War-II period. In the late 1960s, for example, share issues amounted to only 3 per cent of company financing – "extremely insignificant," commented Swedish economist Rudolf Meidner, in a note on the period.

As for the Stockholm Stock Exchange, it was mostly a sleepy place, especially in the post-war years. Turnover (volume of trading) was low – in the 1970s, a mere 3 to 5 per cent of capitalization. Through to the end of the 1970s, fewer shares were traded on average than in the interwar period, and there were only a dozen-and-a-half stock-exchange members. For most of the postwar period, not many more than a hundred companies were listed. Even by 1987, when the exchange could take advantage of the rising profile of stock-exchange bureaucracies elsewhere and of a bull market, there were only 157 listed companies. This was for a full-bodied, technologically dynamic economy. Compare it to the Vancouver Stock Exchange, almost entirely a bureaucratic fabrication – providing, over and above its make-work, mostly newspaper copy about hand-wringing, regulations, fines, suspensions, and court cases – where there were about twenty-four hundred listed companies; the actual economy of British Columbia, meanwhile, suffered from severely limited manufacturing, technology, and design.

The Industrial Revolution in Great Britain was financed privately without publicly traded stocks and stock exchanges, except for canals and, later, railways. The rise of industrial manufacturing historically preceded, rather than followed, stock-market activity. The entrepreneurial capitalists, in this case, were merchants, bankers, and inventors, who provided seed capital on their own, often through partnerships. The increase in output generated by their factories paid for additional capital costs. Most of the trading on the London Stock Exchange, by contrast, was in government securities.

Even when regulatory impediments to forming limited liability companies (corporations as we know them) were eliminated in the 1850s, by far the bulk of British investment came from retained earnings. Meanwhile, the spread of stock exchanges after the incorporation laws did nothing to stop Britain from going into relative decline, starting around 1880. Indeed the stock-exchange mentality may have contributed to the decline. Britain in the late nineteenth century had thirteen provincial stock exchanges, and in the early twentieth century, twenty such exchanges, plus the leading exchange in the City of London. It had the most developed stock-exchange bureaucracy anywhere. However, the culture of stock exchanges, again, is to buy paper, to speculate, to get a financial return on somebody else's enterprise. Actual innovation and entrepreneurial commitment – in leading areas of manufacturing, like chemicals, the electrical and engineering industries, and new steel-making processes – fell behind.

In the remarkable postwar economic reconstruction of West Germany, stock exchanges again played virtually no role. A study of West German capital formation from 1950 (for which share-issue data is first shown) through to 1960 found that new share issues accounted for only 2.3 per cent of business capital. Funds came almost entirely from internal sources (depreciation and retained earnings), bank credits and direct government credits. Figures for the 1960s and 1970s paint a similar picture.

The underwriting and distribution of share issues and the handling of share-trading were dominated by the large "universal" banks, in their investment-bank and brokerage capacities. More important was their "culture." Like the Japanese commercial banks and, earlier, the Swedish trading houses, they functioned as instruments of industry and were heavily involved in business decision-making. Because of their industrial commitment, primarily as lenders and directors, they had little interest in the short-term, disconnected, paper-shuffling games of the American stock-market branch.

So the small stock-exchange bureaucracy didn't inflate much beyond its actual, minor economic function. The largest of the exchanges, in Frankfurt, operated only two hours a day. Only in 1990, with all the foofaraw of stock-exchange expansion elsewhere, were the Frankfurt and other German exchanges pushed into formally extending their hours – to three hours a day. Similarly, as of the mid-1980s, there were only an estimated 150 financial analysts in the whole country, compared to about 18,500 in the United States. Only a quarter (or about 450) of the country's joint-stock companies were listed on any exchange, and only about half that number on the largest, Frankfurt exchange. Numerically they were less than a fifth of 1 per cent of the 300,000 limited liability companies in the country. There were actually more domestic companies listed on German exchanges in the 1950s and 1960s.

Even that overstates the role of stock-exchange listings because many of the listed companies were tightly controlled, often family-run, and put few shares on the market. Often, too, the issues were of non-voting preferred stock, which is a form of debt. More than half the West German stocks were held in large blocks that were rarely if ever traded.

But stock exchanges were always marginal to Germany's economic history. The industrial banks (later to become the "universal" banks) were the major financial underwriters. The ploughing back of profits was another important factor (most particularly in the chemical industry, which, in its entrepreneurial phase, financed itself internally). Another, much ignored but potent, driving force in Germany's economic development was public enterprise – in everything from railroads, mines, iron and other industry, utilities, forestry, even large-scale farms, through to banking. By the time of World War I, the extent of public ownership was not far behind private ownership. This source of capital and enterprise was also a major force in the post-World-War-II period, in such companies as Volkswagen, VIAG (a holding company controlling more than 120 companies in turn), VEBA (energy, chemicals, and trading) and others – upwards of four thousand companies in all, in West Germany, before considerable privatization.

Similar stories of stock-exchange marginality hold for other western European countries. The Paris bourse, in the postwar years, became what one financial journalist described as "a house of slow death," at times barely turning over. Yet, in the very same period, the French achieved an economic "miracle" equal to the West German one. As elsewhere, internal financing and then loans were the major sources of financing. Net capital raised by equity issues was slight.

Italy also had its *miracolo economico*. In the mid-1960s, its economy was the fastest-growing in Europe. Internal financing, as always, provided a big part of business capital, especially for the many small firms that make up a large part of the Italian economy. Banks and Italy's special long-term credit institutions (for industry and agriculture) provided the bulk of external financing. Share issues were a minor source of capital, and only a third of share issues in turn, as measured by market value, were listed on the stock exchange in Milan. Companies were the major buyers of stocks (in the 1970s, accounting for 60 per cent of stock-issue purchases); large companies control other companies which control other companies, in Russian-doll fashion. These corporate stock purchases added no new business capital to the economy. As for the bourse in Milan itself, it was, as The *Economist* described it, a "financial backwater," a small club of banks and insiders, with a limited number of listed companies, and active trading probably in no more than a dozen of them. Even after the exchange was expanded in 1985-87, it didn't amount to much.

In Switzerland, industrial financing has been self-financed for centuries. Foreign trade produced capital reserves. Widespread savings meant there was plenty of bank credit. The Swiss stock exchanges have reflected this, through to current times.

Two other of the great postwar economic success stories in Europe, although lesser known, are Finland and Austria. Their stock exchanges were inconsequential, indeed barely existed in that period. The small Helsinki stock exchange had fewer than fifty listed companies – a smaller number than in the 1920s – and went through extended *longueurs*. "Pessimism and inactivity," reads its self-description for the 1960s. "*Via Dolorosa*" was how it saw itself in the mid-1970s. Total value of shares traded on the exchange was a hardly perceptible $8 million in 1960 and $15 million in 1970, compared to $1,749 million and $5,331 million for Canadian exchanges. As a ratio of each country's respective gross domestic product, the Finnish stock-exchange turnover came to just one twenty-eighth and one forty-second of the Canadian one for the two sample years. Finland now has a higher per capita gross domestic product than Canada.

The Vienna Stock Exchange, meanwhile, was a relic of an old and discredited world. Its most memorable "achievement" was its own crash in 1873, in the days of the Austro-Hungarian Empire, after a period of crazy speculation over railways. "Ramshackle financial constructions took the place of investments in real railways and real factories," one historian described those events. In the post-World-War-II period, the exchange was virtually non-functioning prior to 1970 and remained so marginal in the subsequent fifteen years that, as The Economist put it, "it was easy to forget it existed at all." A "mausoleum," the magazine described it.

In both Finland and Austria, in the postwar period, the leading entrepreneurial force was public enterprise, far removed ideologically and practically from the bureaucratic stock-exchange culture. Public enterprise also played a leading role in France and Italy, as well as in West Germany and Japanese banking, as already noted. It was also, along with co-operative enterprise, a significant, although lesser, factor in Sweden.

When the marginal stock-exchange bureaucracies began to inflate in these and other countries in the 1980s, sometimes with dramatic increases in share turnover, the real economic work of enterprise, financing, technology, and innovation had already been done. There were now surplus savings and expanding corporate profits – the fruits of the real economic work – that the stock-market branch could feed on.

Economic development in North America was no different: Stock-exchange bureaucracies battened on to real economic and technical surges after they had taken place. In Canada, in the early nineteenth century, the Welland Canal and other canals were underwritten largely with public funds, before stock exchanges existed. When the first railways were being built, stock exchanges still didn't exist, and most of what stock trading there was involved shares of banks. The exchanges that followed – the Board of Brokers in Montreal and the Toronto Stock Exchange – were actually just small, rudimentary groups of brokers meeting in each other's offices for about half an hour a day, trying to supplement their other income. Only a small number of companies were listed. Sometimes as few as two or three transactions were handled. At one point, the Toronto Stock Exchange had to scale down to a weekly gathering, and, in 1867, closed altogether for two years, for lack of business. But the real economy carried on as usual.

Manufacturing in Canada flourished without stock exchanges. Most companies were family-owned or raised equity capital through the sale of shares to friends and employees or in communities where they were located. Massey-Harris, the largest multinational company in the British Empire, was an example. It wasn't until well after 1900, when this industrial structure was in place and shares became more widely owned, that the listings of the Toronto and Montreal stock exchanges began to reflect the progress in manufacturing. And not until the speculative excitement of the 1920s was manufacturing stock widely traded. Indeed, up to that time most investors regarded stocks of any kind as novelties. The mainstay of many an investment-dealer firm was municipal bonds!

A book on capital formation in those years (*Capital Formation in Canada 1896-1930*, by Kenneth Buckley) doesn't even mention stock markets or stock exchanges other than to note, in passing, that "an adequate market for new equity issues" did not appear. R. T. Naylor's two-volume *The History of Canadian Business 1867-1914* has a nine-page section on "the stock exchanges, the bucket shops, and the money market," mostly illustrating how marginal and manipulative their activities were.

During World War II, an era of tremendous economic expansion and of technological and manufacturing progress for Canada, the raising of investment capital by equity issues played no role at all. Common-stock issues of 626 large companies plus subsidiaries, for which consistent reports were available in the period, averaged a nominal $6 million per year for the five years 1940-1944, and that meant very little, for dividends paid out at the same time averaged $202 million annually. Meanwhile, share trading declined to minimal levels.

As in western Europe, public enterprise (crown corporations) – again bypassing stock exchanges – has been a major entrepreneurial force in Canada.

The United States was no exception to the rule. Stock-market activity in the formative era prior to the civil war was isolated, primitive, and slight. Part-time brokers arrived at periodic call times (there was no continuous market), did their business quickly and departed. Most of their business was in government securities, with trading in banks and insurance companies on the side – not, in themselves, the doings of entrepreneurship.

The market staples for the rest of the nineteenth century were canals and railroads. The canals and early railroads, however, had been largely underwritten by governments – federal, state, and local – either with direct financing or with indirect financial underpinning in the form of massive land grants and other subsidies, grants, and privileges upon which bond and stock issues could be levered. Meanwhile, in the latter half of the century, the United States was undergoing a period of revolutionary industrial innovation and expansion, which was soon to make it the most economically powerful nation in the world. Its stock exchanges, while this was going on, were back in the railroad age. In 1885, only one industrial stock was listed on the New York exchange, the Pullman Palace Car Company, and its listing wasn't properly a "manufacturing" one, since most of its assets were railroad sleeping car companies. Not until 1910 did industrial stocks become favourites of investors and speculators, replacing the rails for the first time. By then, industrial America had already been created and was self-sustaining.

U.S. economic development, from the fur trade through to Henry Ford and the Ford Motor Company, and the whole kaleidoscope of industry and invention in between, was financed not by public share issues supported by stock-exchange trading, but by grubstakes, savings, loans, partnerships, accumulated profits from other endeavours, the participation of friends, private syndicates, well-heeled backers, occasionally an inheritance, and most importantly perhaps, retained earnings. The family-owned or closely held company was predominant.

Stock-exchange trading in corporate shares, meanwhile, hardly came into the picture. It did have notoriety, but only because of its gameplaying with money. Throughout the nineteenth century, as U.S. business historian Elisha P. Douglass summarized it, the stock exchange in New York "was a speculator's rather than an investor's market. . . . Bonds and preferred stocks had varying degrees of investment quality, but most common stocks had very little intrinsic value and became mere instruments of speculation." The speculators were of two kinds: "wealthy and powerful financiers capable of directly manipulating the market," on the one hand, and "a shifting, transient horde of petty gamblers who merely responded to market fluctuations" on the other. Since the volume of a company's shares available for purchase was relatively small, it was always possible to rig the market. Endless but intense and deadly games were played between bulls trying to corner a stock and bears, selling short, trying to break the corners.

Nobody mistook these paper games for capitalization and the real work of entrepreneurship. "There are such creatures as investors," wrote the *New York Times* sarcastically in 1887, of the stock-exchange scene, "though a broker may pass a busy life without falling in with one." Speculative promotions, meanwhile, were mostly swindles, marginal speculations, or, at best, inflated hopes of unrealistic stock "jobbers."

When the rush of industrial stock-exchange listings finally did occur, around the turn of the century, the entrepreneurial work of building those industries and the necessary raising of capital for them had, again, already been done. A major impetus for these listings was the conglomeration movement – the first of its kind – exploiting what industrial entrepreneurship had accomplished. Investment banks and bankers, such as J. P. Morgan, realized that if you combined several companies, made up a corporate giant, and put a battalion of promoters and public relations artists to work, you could flog a lot of watered stock in the new company and make a fortune for insiders, as well as rake off huge fees for putting the deal together (shades of the M&A bureaucracy of the 1960s and 1980s). Since the promoters and underwriters in this way could offer the original company owners more than their companies were worth, somewhat like the premiums paid in later conglomeration manoeuvres, the latter were only too willing to cash in handsomely and let the devil investment banker take his due.

The formation of U.S. Steel, from a merger of several companies, is an example. The financing of actual enterprise wasn't a factor in the exercise. Except for a nominal administrative transaction, none of the proceeds from the selling of shares to the public represented a capital contribution to the corporation itself. The automobile industry is another instructive case. It was financed largely by reinvested profits, supplier credits, shares to suppliers and privately organized investment, roughly in that order of importance. The Ford Motor Company didn't "go public" until 1955.

Stock exchanges, in broad cultural terms, do not create economic activity but follow it, as a bureaucratic or manipulative and predatory overlay, and at a respectful distance.

Even in terms of raising capital for established sectors or established companies – as a bureaucratic financial intermediary – and even in the United States, the stock-market branch has been a minor factor. From 1901 to 1952, net stock issues (issues less retirements) of U.S. nonfinancial corporations represented only 10 per cent of capital raised. In the immensely productive wartime and immediate postwar years, 1940-1952, net share issues represented only 5 per cent of sources of capital.

For the period 1953-1983, a time of unprecedented economic progress, similarly, net equity issues provided a yearly average of only 5.5 per cent of the capital of U.S. nonfinancial corporations (and just 3.2 per cent on an aggregate dollar basis). Retained earnings, on the other hand, supplied a yearly average of 17.6 per cent and depreciation 45.7 per cent. One American study isolated capitalization figures for the key manufacturing sector, in two periods 1952-1959 and 1960-1968. It found that net equity issues provided only a nominal 1.8 per cent of capital for the first period and accounted for a negative -0.3 per cent for the second period.

In the late 1980s, during the biggest bull market in history, mergers, takeovers, and share buy-back programs (sometimes as a defence against takeovers) – often leveraged with a great deal of debt – took large amounts of equity *out of* the stock market and out of non-financial corporations. The net equity drain for the period 1984-90 inclusive was an estimated US$655 billion. Adjusting for inflation, this equity deficit for non-financial corporations would be triple all net equity issues in the 1953-1983 span. Remember, again, the inflated rate of share trading in this period. To add to the irony, the equity taken out of the market had been produced largely by the real economy in the form of retained earnings, and not by stock issues, in the first place. "An equity market is supposed to be a place where industry raises capital," grumbled Anthony Harris, the *Financial Times of London* correspondent in New York, "but Wall Street has become a market where industry gives capital back, and on a huge scale." As the statistics show, however, corporate America has always raised most of its capital internally, and most of the rest through debt, as have corporations everywhere else.

The myth persists, however, that stock exchanges have to do with enterprise rather than with bureaucracy. Commentators talk approvingly of how one stock market's turnover has been "stirred" by some incident or activity, like a takeover, or they frowningly puzzle over how hard it is to "rouse" a particular stock market. Stock exchanges themselves boast of increases in turnover. One can imagine the reaction to a government department boasting of going through double the motions that it used to and incurring almost double the overheads to provide the same service of a year or two earlier. Conversely, declines of stock-market activity and the lay-offs of brokers and analysts are treated as economic tragedy rather than as a long-overdue, and inadequate, reduction of deep-rooted bureaucratic waste. A stock exchange that opened a couple of hours a day, like the West German exchanges until recently, or a couple of hours a week, with minimal turnover and only occasional mention in the mass-media (and listings left to financial sheets) – a bureaucracy appropriate to an exchange's minor economic function – would do as well.

All the rest is structural bureaucratic waste, make-work, short-termism, and – unto chaos theory and horoscopes – silliness and absurdity in the extreme.

5

The Derivative-Paper Branch

Cheek by jowl with the stock-market branch is the derivative-paper branch of commodity exchanges, foreign-exchange speculation, and similar bureaucratic expansion – more abstract and contrived yet, in its invention and make-work, than the stock-market branch itself.

At the centre of the derivative-paper bureaucracy are the commodity (futures and options) exchanges. Their *modus operandi* is the creation of "new products" – not "products" ordinarily understood like milk or automobiles or perfume, but derivative, symbolic products that are invented, passed back and forth, and sometimes discarded (if not enough people are drawn into the shuffling) in a bureaucratic world of their own. The branch, in this fashion, has managed to establish colony after colony of paper-churning make-work. The "ultimate crap game," a veteran U.S. investment manager complained in 1984, when the expansion was in full throttle. "It's not *doing* anything." But, bureaucratically, it was; it was making work for cadres.

With their often crowded trading pits and their "open outcry" (shouting) and hand signal methods, futures exchanges project an image of frenzy and disorder. Floor traders and brokers on a hectic day jostle amongst themselves. There are occasional fights and cases of broken bones. A few traders wear helmets. The din is loud; the most common occupational injury in futures trading is a sore throat. Buying on margin (putting up as little as 12 per cent to 1 per cent of the value of the contract), which is how futures trading is done, adds to the intensity. By committing oneself to a large contract while covering only a small fraction of the cost, one can win big or lose one's stake very quickly when the value of the contract changes. Futures exchanges are often described as the last outposts of free enterprise because of this combativeness and because speculating in the futures market is risky, which automatically elicits the free-enterprise mythology of risk and reward.

In reality, however, futures exchanges are just another make-work section, except more so. Their progress suggests a strange bureaucratic law at work – that the more excited the image, exotic the paper processes, speculative the aura, and free-enterprise the mythology, the more wasteful, make-work, and mundane is the actual activity.

The person who sells a commodities future agrees to deliver a given amount of the commodity by a certain date in the future. A producer of soybeans, for example, in selling soybean futures, is thus assured a certain price for his soybeans regardless of what happens to the market in the intervening period. The buyer of the futures, meanwhile, is speculating that the price will go up in the interim, in which case he'll sell the soybeans at the higher price (in actuality, a paper transaction through the exchange) and make a gain. If the price goes down instead, he'll take a loss. Trades are made in standard quantities, depending on the commodity. Each such quantity traded is called a "contract," after the nature of the arrangement between seller and buyer.

Options are another paper variant. An option gives the buyer the right to buy (in case of a "call" option) or sell (in case of a "put" option) a commodity or stock at a preset price by a certain date. If the price goes up, for example, the holder of a "call" option can buy the commodity or stock at the lower, option price, and cash in the difference, or can pocket the gain by selling the option contract itself. If the price doesn't go up or declines, the holder of the option simply lets it expire. Meanwhile, the original seller, or, in the jargon, "writer," of the option makes his money by charging a premium for the option (the cost of the option). If the option is exercised (and it will only be exercised to the buyer's advantage), the seller has to make up the difference and absorbs the loss. If the option ends up "out of the money" and isn't exercised, the premium is all profit.

Selling options is really an exercise in collecting premiums and using the premium revenue to come out ahead in the end. A spread between the existing price and the option's "exercise" or "strike" price, when it is initially set, adds a margin of safety for the seller. Because the price of an option (the premium) is just a sliver of the value of the stock or the commodity it controls, the option represents a high degree of leverage. Futures and options contracts can be traded back and forth any number of times, their values fluctuating with events, until they expire.

Those are the mechanics.

Until the 1960s, futures trading in Chicago, the leading futures locale, was limited to contracts in a few agricultural products such as grains, corn and soybeans. But those weren't doing well. At the Chicago Board of Trade

(CBOT), the wheat and soybean trading pits were sluggish because of a grain surplus. Its members were desperate. The rival Chicago Mercantile Exchange (CME) was heading for oblivion. It attempted to diversify into livestock and meat futures ("pork belly" futures date back only to then), but that didn't help much. Egg futures were drying up because there wasn't enough price fluctuation to keep speculators interested. Without price fluctuation, futures trading has too little to play with. The Mercantile Exchange then tried an onion futures contract, but that didn't help either. Price manipulation was so bad, in fact, that farmers petitioned Congress to ban the onion contract, which it did. The affair was known as the "Onion Scandal." The only other contract left was potatoes. If, at one point, the Mercantile Exchange's board of governors hadn't bought extra memberships, to put money into the exchange, it might have gone under.

So the exchange members began dreaming up new futures contracts to keep their bureaucracies alive. At the CBOT it was plywood, then gold and silver, then options on equity stock (shares in corporations), then futures on interest rates (on mortgage-backed certificates). The options operation branched out on its own, becoming the Chicago Board Options Exchange (CBOE). At the Mercantile Exchange, it was futures on foreign currencies, then on a stock index (the S&P 500, reflecting a composite of stocks on the New York Stock Exchange). The latter contract dates back only to 1982. Then the CBOE began trading options on a stock index (the S&P 100). Interest rates, foreign exchange rates (after fixed exchange rates were abandoned), and stock indexes all fluctuated, which maintained sufficient speculative interest to keep the action going. The volume of trading exploded. The two exchanges, like alchemists, seemed to have discovered the magic formula for inflating their bureaucracies out of nothing.

Once the formula was discovered, there was no stopping it. Other exchanges rushed in so as not to lose out on the bonanza, even if getting started – getting enough speculative action going – was difficult because futures trading is a zero-sum game. For every dollar that one speculator makes, another speculator loses a dollar. The New York Stock Exchange established a futures exchange. So did the Toronto Stock Exchange, scrambling to be first in Canada. Languishing provincial stock-exchange bureaucracies in Montreal, Philadelphia, Boston, and the Pacific Stock Exchange in San Francisco and Los Angeles (a seat on the exchange traded in 1978 for 25 cents) went about propping themselves up with options of various kinds, stock-index futures, and whatever other concoctions they could think of. The larger exchanges also got into options where there were options left to get into. Bad bureaucracy chases worse bureaucracy.

There are now, in the United States and Canada, futures on U.S. Treasury bonds, ten-year Treasury notes, five-year Treasury notes and three-month Treasury bills, Canadian government bonds, foreign exchange, Eurodollars, bankers acceptances, all manner of stock indexes (including a Japanese index), a municipal bond index, the thirty-day interest rate, the one-month London inter-bank rate, mortgages (mortgage-backed bonds), a commodity futures index (inevitably, a future based on other futures!), a currency index (the U.S. dollar not relative to another currency but to a whole pot of them!), cross-rate foreign-currency futures (the Deutschmark relative to the Yen, for example), interest-rate swaps (derivatives in themselves), the grain standbys (including soybeans, flaxseed, and canola), the livestock and meat standbys (cattle, hogs, and pork bellies), cocoa, coffee, orange juice, and sugar, precious metals (including platinum and palladium), industrial metals, crude oil, heating oil, unleaded gasoline, propane, natural gas, lumber, and cotton.

Because the S&P 500 stock-index future, used in conjunction with playing the stock market, generated such a high volume of paper shuffling and the commissions and arbitrage profits that go with it, considerable energy went into concocting other index futures that might be floated. Everybody had to have one. Four U.S. futures exchanges have a composite-index contract, each of them different. One futures exchange tried using two indexes (a 2,000-stock one and a 3,000-stock one) originally devised by a pension-fund consultant.

At different times contracts have been proposed or actually launched for an international stock index, over-the-counter stock indexes, stock-index subsets (such as high-tech, consumer staples, energy), retail new-car sales, an earnings index, housing starts, computer chips (Drams), the Consumer Price Index, pollution credits (regulatory allowances, dubbed "smog futures"), high-fructose corn syrup, grain sorghum, residual fuel oil, palm and coconut oils, and ocean-freight. The Toronto Futures Exchange once tried launching a contract on a package of *American* industrial stocks (the same basket of stocks, in fact, used to calculate the Dow Jones Industrial Average) in a desperate attempt to reverse sluggish trading.

"They're kind of writing these things [new futures contracts] as fast as they can be written," admitted a director of research at one futures brokerage. Writer John Rothchild wondered sardonically if there were going to be futures on rainfall, the Democratic primaries, the Nielsen ratings, and hospital occupancy. The elaboration of stock-index "products" by different exchanges was becoming embarrassing. "They've become like 'pet-rocks' – everyone thinks they have to own one," rasped the futures executive who, as a younger man, had invented the first interest-rate future (based on mortgage-backed bonds) and helped start the proliferation in the first place.

The idea is to get enough people to speculate in a new "product" in order to generate sufficient volume in order to get still more people to speculate in it. To get over the hump, exchanges spend more and more on promotion, sometimes running into the millions of dollars. Most new futures "products" fail, which does nothing, however, to stop futures exchanges from attempting to expand their territory with such concoctions. Or, in the words of a futures exchange cadre, it's a matter of throwing spaghetti against the wall to see what will stick.

Then there are options, not just on stocks but also on foreign currency, commodities, stock indexes, Canadian and U.S. government bonds, and anything else they can be grafted onto, including one based on the stock portfolios of major institutional investors. If one can concoct futures of all kinds and options of all kinds, why not futures options? And so there are – options on the futures of all the things there are futures of. These are derivatives of derivatives – sometimes derivatives thrice removed – but they serve a make-work purpose just as well. Indeed, when it became clear in the late 1980s that most new futures contracts were going under – that the spaghetti thrown against the wall wasn't sticking – one futures *éminence grise* in New York recommended the introduction of options on futures that didn't already have them, as an alternative make-work solution.

All this proliferating bureaucracy, except for a few agricultural and other commodities, has been generated in the last twenty years, mostly centred in Chicago. Many foreign exchanges, seeing how it was done and what a good thing it could be for them, began to copy the example.

Bureaucracies need excuses for their make-work. In this case, it is "hedging." Farmers, for example, are said to sell futures contracts in the spring, assuring themselves of a fixed price for their commodity, rather than be caught by an unexpectedly low and disastrous price in the fall when they deliver their product. The futures market absorbs the risk for them. It is a kind of insurance. And in order to have a futures market for that purpose, you need speculators and speculation, so that there will always be buyers for sellers and vice-versa.

This was the excuse for the original commodities exchange bureaucracies in Chicago in the nineteenth century. American farmers, however, don't normally hedge. A study done for the U.S. Commodity Futures Trading Commission in the mid-1970s found that only 5.6 per cent of farmers used the futures market, and less than 1 per cent overall were actually hedging rather than speculating (how much less was a matter of surmise). Most of those who indulged, in fact, traded in commodities they neither used nor produced. As the chairman of the Mercantile Exchange himself once explained, by the 1960s "the cycle of production was such – year-round – that the futures market wasn't really needed anymore." Besides, why pay money to a Chicago bureaucracy? Futures aren't much in the way of insurance, either, since futures prices parallel actual cash prices for commodities. A trend one way or the other is eventually going to hit, or benefit, the producer regardless. In Canada, farmers organized wheat pools and then fought for the establishment of the Canadian Wheat Board, which averages out price fluctuations, in order to bypass the Winnipeg Grain Exchange. The idea itself of an exchange bureaucracy and its speculators making money on the back of productive work offended Canadian farmers.

But, early on, futures markets quickly became bureaucracies, moving paper back and forth with only incidental reference to the commodities themselves. Most commodity futures contracts are now settled before expiry by other transactions, without actual delivery of the commodity to the buyer taking place. This is the case not least because the seller is usually a speculator just like the buyer, and not a producer of the commodity at all.

Financial "products," led by interest-rate (bond) futures and including foreign-currency and stock-index futures, have now come to dominate the futures section, replacing the old agricultural commodities. Banks and some large investment institutions, as well as the large securities firms, have become major participants. Futures exchanges, blessing their good luck, have begun to push the line that institutional investors need to hedge their investments in bonds and stocks by buying futures, just like the fictitious farmer who needed to hedge the value of his growing wheat. Strained pitches are made to institutional money managers about their need to cover their behinds by hedging – another case of one branch of the bureaucracy playing off the anxieties of another branch in an attempt to inflate itself. Great use in these pitches is made of the word "prudent," as in a CBOT pitch about "key benefits of using futures for the prudent financial manager."

The general estimate of the number of genuine hedgers in these and other futures markets, however, is not much higher than for farmers, just 10 per cent, and that figure may be exaggerated on the high side, too.

The actual function of futures and options exchanges is (a) to keep turning over and to expand, (b) to make money for its traders who are members of the exchange, and (c) incidentally to make work for a growing infrastructure (from janitors to managers of futures funds). It does this by gathering money from the public in the form of individual and institutional investors. About 90 per cent of individual investors (really "speculators") lose money in futures, money which goes to large traders and to exchange overheads. A study by Michael L. Hartzmark, then at the University of Chicago, showed how it happens. The analysis covered trading in nine futures markets (seven in agricultural commodities, two in treasury paper) in 1977-1981. Large "commercial" traders (commercial companies, large investment banks) made in total US$728 million. Large non-commercial traders (speculative firms without a commercial facade, futures funds) made

$125 million. Small traders (floor traders who close positions overnight, Joe and Jane Citizen, and small hedgers) lost $853 million. Five large traders, or 0.1 per cent (one-thousandth) of the sample, made 58 per cent of the profits. This doesn't mean that large traders cannot lose, too. One Kansas savings and loan bank, a decade later, took a $119 million hit in futures-contract trading. It went into receivership.

Brokerage houses freely admit that the average lifetime of a personal futures account is less than a year, as people give up with their pockets lighter. A former chairman of the Commodity Futures Trading Commission, interviewed by author Rothchild, put it a different way. "These markets are like a dinner," he explained. "The diners are the traders, the arbitrageurs, the brokers. They feed off the public customer, who is the dinner." The exchange bureaucracy's task is to keep enough dinner on the table. The more "new products" it can dream up, the wider the sweep in collecting money from the public.

Investment dealers (investment banks) have enthusiastically joined the feeding. Some of the biggest pay-off is on the brokerage side – collecting commissions on sales – particularly where aggressive tactics (including cold-calling) and the other usual tricks in the repertoire are used. When interest in stocks wilted after the 1987 stock-market fall, brokers began looking desperately for ways to make new work for themselves. Suggesting to customers the idea of buying futures was one of them. They pushed the potential for spectacular gains while glossing over the down side (spectacular losses) – and did make some extra work for themselves. Large U.S. investment banks now have their own institutional futures departments, brokering trades for institutional investors and underwriting futures funds.

There are also specialized commodity brokerage firms in the field, some with short life spans. Their telephone sales procedures may seem shady and hence anarchistic to lay people, but they are just as routinized and rehearsed as the cold calls from "financial consultants" at prestigious brokerage firms. The *Wall Street Journal* once went to the trouble of listing the routines: the hard-sell, the hot tip, the good-old-boy routine, the high-tech pitch, the old as new, notes from the front (trading sound effects drummed up in the office to carry over the phone and add verisimilitude and excitement), the chance-of-a-lifetime line, the "don't-worry-any-idiot-can-do-it-with-my-help" line, and the guilt trip. They're all familiar, as if from a manual. The usual one-two calling method is frequently used as well. The first call, by a "qualifier," makes contact and lines up the customer. The second call comes from a salesperson who, by being the follow-up caller, can assume authoritative airs.

In a sample case of a futures account described by *Forbes* in 1989, commissions and fees in one year amounted to more than a third of the client's deposit with his broker. In three years, at that rate, the client's capital would have disappeared. The account would have had to make a 35 per cent profit (and, this, in a zero-sum game) just to break even, and a 42 per cent profit to cover lost interest on the capital as well. The brokerage firm explained that a commodities account, by its nature, requires a lot of trading. The case, as the article pointed out, involved a well-informed investor served by a competent broker. What if the broker had been incompetent or dishonest? "Heads you lose, tails you lose even more," *Forbes* concluded. As if to answer *Forbes* question, a news item appeared of a cartoonist in Britain who lost C$53,000 in commodity futures in a short three months; her brokers charged $21,000 in commissions on the various transactions. In juxtaposition, a commodity brokerage executive, also in Britain, at the age of twenty-eight, pulled in over $6 million in earnings and dividends one year, far ahead of the most lucratively rewarded corporate executives in the country.

A few lawyers in the United States have created a subsubsection – suing brokers who have churned futures contracts on behalf of clients, in which the client ends up losing money while the broker does well. "My personal opinion," said one such lawyer who advertised the service, "is that unless you're a floor broker on one of the commodity exchanges, you'd have to have loose marbles to trade in commodities." The lawyers, presumably, do well in turn providing the antidote.

There are now, also, managed futures funds (pooled funds) offered to the public. In the United States there are over two hundred such publicly managed funds, each with its general partner, its underwriters (often large investment banks), and its trading advisers. A study published in the *Financial Analysts Journal* covering the years 1980-1988 – good years and bad – showed that the average annual return for such funds was a meagre 2.3 per cent, much less than the cost of capital and little over a quarter the return on Treasury bonds. Collectively, by this measure, the publicly managed futures funds were a futile circular exercise, making work for their bureaucracies and wasting the time and energy of their investors – exactly what one would expect. If they did make money, moreover, it would simply be at somebody else's expense. These fund losses in total are just a common-sense reminder that bureaucracies cost money and that a make-work bureaucracy wastes money.

Inevitably, however, by the law of averages, the machinery produces some big winners – the playing is highly leveraged. These big winners are a few managers of private pools. Private pools are organized for large investors and manage about US$9 billion in assets. Because they have lower sales costs than public funds, their odds are somewhat better. Best of all, the managers pocket not just their management fee of 2 to 6 per cent (average, about 5 per cent), and not just the returns on their own investment in the pool, but also a hefty chunk – from 15 to 20 per cent – of the rest of the take, if there are any gains. This latter slice is euphemistically called an "incentive fee." Such leverage attached to a winning streak adds sensation to the winning managers' incomes and reputations, gives lustre to the bureaucracy, and helps the feeding continue.

One of the better known, in the United States, was a Richard Dennis, who managed a huge personal portfolio (estimated at US$100 million) plus two private syndicates and a co-managed fund. In 1986, there were glowing features about his strategic muscle and tactical agility. He personally made $80 million that year. "The ranking titan of futures traders," *Financial World* described him. *Business Week* ran a story on his magic. In 1988, there were equally animated features about where he had gone wrong. Losses for his funds and his personal account in 1987 and early 1988 were estimated variously from $70 million to more than $100 million. He lost $8 million trading soybean contracts in just one week. The "legend in his own time" had become a loser. His funds, having reached their loss limit, were closed out.

For every star in the descendant, however, there is another one in the ascendant. One of them was George Soros, author of a book called *The Alchemy of Finance*. From 1985 to 1990 he took home an estimated US$380 to $440 million, some of which came from futures markets. Another who did well was Paul Tudor Jones II. In 1987, he raked in somewhere from $80 to $100 million, in good part by unloading stock-index futures just before the October crash and then buying back in the aftermath. He was thirty-three at the time. In 1988, he slipped badly to a miserable $30 million, although recovering to $65 million in 1989 and $70 million in 1990. Yet another, Bruce Kovner, pocketed more than $200 million in the two years 1989 and 1990.

These returns look like alchemy, indeed. But they are just the aggregate losses of many others, using the leverage of buying on margin and special fee arrangements (for funds under management) as mechanisms. The greatest leverage of all is the inevitability that where there are losers there will also be winners, and some big winners among them, as long as there is enough fluctuation in the commodity markets to keep the machinery turning over.

Add to the brokers, fund managers, and trading advisers the equally inescapable advisory newsletters, analysis boutiques, hot lines (nightly telephone advice), and also, in this case, "trading systems." Trading systems are mathematical, computerized programs that indicate when traders should buy or sell contracts. Over sixty of them have been developed in the United States and offered to the public for futures trading. They're pricey, some costing US$3,000. They come with catchy codes names like TradeFinder,

Volatility Breakout, Dual Diagonal Day Trader, ProfitTaker, Triple Trailing Trigger, or acronyms like QUANTUM, SPECTRUM, QUAD, SCOOPS, and PEPS. Some are slickly marketed. One trading-system creator, getting the hang of it, had produced nineteen of them as of mid-1989 – a mini-bureaucracy in his own right.

The trading systems, alas, aren't much good for anything, except taking people's money and keeping them involved. An author of a text on technical trading explained, "If I had developed a truly successful trading system, why would I sell it? Instead, I would sell my house and trade [with the system] for myself." The newsletters, whose performance record is woeful, have the same bureaucratic function.

These subsections in turn make work for other subsections. The existence of trading systems inevitably led to a newsletter that rates the trading systems, at US$225 per year for six issues ($50 for a single copy of its Master Performance Table). Naturally, somebody also came up with a system tester that purports to test trading systems. There is even a newsletter called *Club 3000 News*, for people who spent at least $3,000 for a trading system only to discover that it didn't work. There are, in the United States, at least two newsletters that track the performance of commodity funds and commodity-trading advisers. There are trading consultants (advisers) and technical experts. Chartism, with its strange technical vocabulary, its bar graphs, and its trend lines, is big in futures; a satire of itself. Financial publications add space and resources. *Futures*, a U.S. monthly magazine, has established a Commodities Educational Institute, which runs a travelling "Futures & Options School" – pricey, and marketed with a hard sell.

In 1986, the U.S. National Futures Association proudly declared that the number of cadres providing futures trading services had more than quadrupled in the previous decade, and the ranks since then have only continued to inflate. Similarly, U.S. futures trading volume (number of contracts) in the years 1978-1990 increased 373 per cent, as compared to the gross domestic product which, in real terms, went up 24 per cent. A more useful comparison would date back a decade earlier, when the cadres had just begun to expand their territory with newly contrived contracts. From 1968 to 1990, futures trading volume increased thirty times or 2,873 per cent, while the real economy, measured by GDP, increased 65 per cent in constant dollars, a ratio of 44 to 1.

Volume of trading in options contracts shows the same pattern. Stock-index options provide an illustration. They did not exist until 1983, when the S&P 100 options contract was introduced by the CBOE with wine and cheese parties. An S&P 500 contract was also established. In their first year, 10.6 million contracts were traded, mostly in the S&P 100. Three years later, in 1986, 114.8 million contracts were traded, or more than a tenfold increase in three years, before falling off dramatically to 62.3 million contracts in 1988, after Black Monday. In 1990, trading was up to 80.9 million contracts. Overall trading in options contracts in the United States, which began in 1973 from a combination of happenstance and make-work envy, managed 1.1 million contracts in its first year, and hit a high of 305.2 million contracts in 1987 after fifteen years of progressive inflation.

The futures-exchange bureaucracy is protected by ideology and protects itself bureaucratically. First, it needs to sustain the image of a freewheeling and hence somewhat glamorous and exotic mart. Charges by critics that behind the excuse about hedgers and insurance there is really just a big gambling casino don't necessarily hurt. Playing the markets is understood to be a kind of gambling, so the accusations are essentially free advertising. Complications like margins and options don't hurt either. They add intrigue and suggest there is something intelligent about the exercise.

The media help. Article after article appears about the excitement of the futures pits and the brand of young trader in them. There are breathless features on investing in commodities and other futures (from soybeans to platinum). These articles may raise warning signs – telling readers, for example, that most small investors in futures lose money – but this doesn't detract from the aura of the game. The media, in sum, describe futures transactions as risky, that favourite free-enterprise word suggesting reward and fortune as the prize of risk, rather than describing the dealing for what it is essentially – a low-grade bureaucratic "tax" on suckers.

For political purposes, the exchanges have also had to overcome or at least blur a reputation for manipulation and legalized theft. Every once in a while, a notorious case of dubious goings-on surfaces and an exchange is denounced by a Congressman or a judge as a "cesspool" or "ripe for corruption and abuse." The exchanges attract their share of shady characters. Employees of wayward commodity brokerage firms have been indicted or faced administrative charges for fraud, racketeering, abusive sales practices, just plain cheating, and other counts of not so nicely separating suckers from their money. Over and above that, rule-breaking is endemic. The "Chicago sting" in 1988, where FBI agents penetrated the CBOT and the Mercantile Exchange and uncovered market manipulation and fraud was, given past history, more amusing than shocking. The futures section, in other words, contributes its share to the annual US$10 billion in investment fraud, as estimated by the National Futures Association.

Most of all, though, the futures exchanges have had to overcome the notion (reflecting the fact of the matter) that futures trading is largely unproductive shuffling of paper, designed to put money into the cadres' pockets.

To protect their waste and to gloss over any malpractices, futures exchanges use a variety of bureaucratic devices. They pay substantial fees to academics who conclude that futures serve a useful economic purpose ("greedy academics," a former regulatory agency chairman described them). Packages of glorified promotional literature are produced; hedging, the excuse for futures, is given considerable place. The CBOT itself has a book-publishing wing turning out, among other things, a trading manual that can be used as a university text and an open-ended series called "Readings in Futures Markets" in which esoteric articles by academics and others are brought together. The CBOT also publishes an academic journal called *The Review of Futures Markets*. This adds gloss.

The CBOT's education department also produces videotapes, slide/ cassette packages, a long list of booklets and leaflets, and a high-school instructional program complete with "student book," teacher's guide, and end-of-chapter tests. The Mercantile Exchange established a US$1 million chair in finance at the University of Chicago. Advertising is also used, freely plugged with doublespeak. Shortly after the FBI sting operation was made public, an inventive full-page CBOT advertisement appeared in business publications, pushing interest-rate futures. "Unparalleled integrity" was touted in the ad.

Where the derivative-paper branch really excels bureaucratically, though, is in lobbying ("congressional relations programs"). The Chicago futures exchanges and their registered traders and brokers have well-heeled political action committees (PACs) which together gave more than US$2 million to Senate and House of Representatives members in the short period 1987-1990 alone. Counting their other disbursements (to presidential candidates, political party committees, and so on) and funds held in reserve, the total allocation would come to about $5 million in that period, according to Federal Election Commission records and disclosure statements. This is exclusive of prosperous traders pouring personal donations into the political coffers of the Washington powers that be. Exchanges educate their floor members on the importance of making campaign contributions, indirectly through their PACs and directly as individuals, knowing what side their bureaucratic bread is buttered on.

The exchanges also paid "personal appearance" fees to Senators and Congressmen who dropped by, before the Senate and House belatedly changed their rules to prohibit acceptance of such fees. The going rate, as of 1987, was US$2,000 for a Senator and $1,000 for a House member. "Every year," the *Wall Street Journal* reported in 1987, "dozens of lawmakers flock to Chicago to collect." According to an official of futures broker

Lind-Waldock, cited by John Rothchild, some got the fee just for driving their cars past the exchanges.

An indication of the lobbying intensity the futures section is capable of occurred in 1988, when futures were under attack for their role, real and alleged, in the 1987 stock market collapse. The chairman and president of the CBOT alone made twenty-seven trips to Washington to meet with Representatives and Senators. This pace was maintained in following years. An earlier meeting, in late 1987, had taken place with then vice-president George Bush. A total of 164 members of Congress availed themselves of these visits in 1988. Exchange directors and staff travelled to Washington to explain the workings of the market to congressional staff. More than a hundred members of Congress visited the exchanges in Chicago itself that year, presumably picking up those lucrative appearance fees (if so, it would be a record pay-out). In one political skirmish, Senate offices had each received three visits from the Chicago futures bureaucracy before the other side even got started. "One of the wealthiest and most effective lobby groups in Washington," *Common Cause* magazine summed it up, ". . . a textbook example of what's wrong with the legislative system."

Having liberally sprinkled Washington with its largesse, the futures bureaucracy finds "no shortage of defenders," the *Wall Street Journal* noted, even when moderate reforms are proposed. Within the exchanges themselves, brokers' groups have extra power because they are among the biggest contributors to the exchanges' own PACs. Exchange officials meet privately with Illinois legislators in Washington – "war councils," in effect – to try to ensure that nothing is done to deflate their ballooning bureaucracy, described for the occasion as one of the state's biggest "industries" and compared to United Airlines and Caterpillar.

One of the fastest growing new bureaucratic activities has been foreign-exchange trading. The banks, with their foreign-exchange departments, are in the lead. The trading also feeds the activity in currency futures and futures options handled by exchanges. Average *daily* volume of currency trading as of late 1989 was an estimated US$500 billion a day. This compares to the record high of only $21 billion in securities traded on the New York Stock Exchange on October 19, 1987 (Black Monday), and a daily average in 1989 of only $6.1 billion. The $500 billion average daily volume was 18 per cent greater than in 1987 ($425 billion), 67 per per cent greater than in 1986 ($300 billion), 233 per cent greater, or more than triple, the figure for 1985 ($150 billion), and close to 600 per cent or almost seven times what it was in the late 1970s ($75 billion).

As of mid-1988, only an estimated 10 per cent of that trading was directly related to foreign trade or investment, of which, in turn, an indeterminate smaller fraction was for hedging. Less than 2 per cent of the heavy foreign-exchange trading of Bankers Trust, a major player, reflected customer service, according to a source close to the firm. The total transactions, up to US$100 trillion a year, completely eclipsed the world's trading in real goods and services of a mere $4 trillion. "A sometimes frightening gambling casino," *Forbes* magazine called it. A multicurrency betting parlor," said *Institutional Investor*. *Forbes* allowed the trading had a life of its own. It also had a bureaucratic growth pattern of its own.

By the early 1980s, major U.S. banks and others were making fat profits in currency trading, not least as a result of growing speculation in currency, the transactions for which were cleared by the banks. These currency profits were badly needed because of Third World loan difficulties and a gradual decline in the corporate-loan business. Other banks and agents, seeing the margin taken out by this easy clerical work (buying at the bid and selling at the ask, with a spread in between), rushed to join the fold until there were thousands of dealers. This both reduced the spreads and cut the paper bounty into smaller pieces.

To make up for this loss of profit, many banks began speculating in foreign exchange on their own accounts as well, since they were already at the centre of the action. This added to the speculation already being done by corporations (in managing their cash reserves), individuals, and players of the currency futures market. Bankers Trust earned US$593 million from currency trading in 1987, a particularly good year. The big players that same year collectively took out an estimated $5 billion net in foreign-exchange operations. The top eight U.S. money-centre banks alone earned $2 billion in foreign exchange, as agents and principals.

The currency option player responsible for most of the take by Bankers Trust, Andrew Krieger, quit in disgust after receiving a bonus of only US$3 million! (He was also having second thoughts about what he was doing, and the mere $3 million didn't help. When he tried to explain his job to his six-year-old son, the son interrupted, "Well when are you going to do something that helps people?" Krieger, who had once almost finished a PhD in Indian philosophy, considered teaching Sanskrit. He told a *Wall Street Journal* reporter that he was troubled by the fact that there was "an absence of people on Wall Street who think about why they're doing what they're doing." Despite these reflections, he couldn't actually bring himself to leave the bureaucracy, and continued foreign-exchange trading elsewhere.)

The investment banks, seeing how the money-centre banks were doing, had earlier plunged into foreign-exchange dealing. This was stepped up. The investment banks (in Britain, merchant banks), unlike the commercial banks, didn't have Third World loan losses to make up for, but they had problems of their own: the fall-off in brokerage business and profits after Black Monday. Foreign-exchange trading was looked to, to help fill the gap.

Large corporations had become major speculators. At one point, most Japanese financial institutions, from trust banking to insurance and trading houses, were making more money from foreign-exchange dealings than from their main businesses. Several major corporations, among them British Petroleum, Kodak, IBM, Imperial Chemical Industries, and Union Carbide, set up foreign exchange operations of their own. They had already been managing considerable foreign funds. Establishing speculative foreign-exchange profit centres was a natural next step. British Petroleum Finance International (as BP's new section was called) had reached US$5 billion a week of currency transactions by mid-1988, almost all of it trading for profit rather than to service its oil business. Reuters, the primary foreign exchange data network, had installed 145,000 terminals by early 1988, with demand more than tripling over the preceding five-year period.

As more and more dealers joined the multiplying foreign-exchange warrens, larger positions were taken to keep the take up to the level to which the banks had become accustomed. For this and similar purposes, a new banking discipline sprang up called "risk management." Its objective was to show the way to taking the largest possible positions within maximum risk limits. A bank would buy currency options, for example, to hedge its position, allowing that position to grow larger. This newfangled discipline required a subbureaucracy of its own. It drew in turn on a subdiscipline called "quantitative analysis" – the application of formal mathematics to market positioning – developed by several Wall Street investment banks.

The somewhat complicated and abstract foreign-exchange game was, in the process, made infinitely more intricate by risk managers and their stratagems. "Fiendishly complex," said a bank regulator. "There are some extremely sophisticated strategies that look riskless but can make their risk quotient explode," said a former foreign-exchange trader, describing bank management's ignorance of what may be involved in certain stratagems. "There aren't a lot of people who understand [these complex money instruments and techniques]," admitted a federal government banking official. The complexity, it seemed, was getting beyond even the regulators and bank management. Not that these elaborate technical systems necessarily did the job, either, or were fail-safe. "The currency options hedges many banks use today don't work," commented a finance professor at the University of California, Berkeley. There was only "a lot of folkore . . . that says they do."

But all this continuing elaboration, complication, and high-paid help, increasingly abstract, generating a private language with esoteric terminology, trillions of dollars changing hands, thousands and thousands of cadres vying with each other (increasing their own numbers and compensation in the process) – was unproductive make-work to begin with, generated by its own processes. Whether it is done with the aid of folklore or science makes no difference.

Once in a while a photograph of foreign-exchange traders appears in the papers, the traders gesticulating usually wildly, their faces rapt and sometimes twisted with intensity. Or there will be a feature story of foreign-exchange traders in different cities around the world, making split-second decisions (buying and selling electronically, sometimes) as the scene changes across time zones and as, in the words of the *Institutional Investor*, this protean mass of money "ricochets through a global network of telephones and computer terminals." A trader may buy a few million dollars and then sell them a couple of minutes later (Andrew Krieger of Bankers Trust fame, typically made two hundred trades a day). A currency will fall in value because of some news and will keep falling the next day because of opposite news. The newspaper reader is meant to believe there is some higher economic logic, rather than just bureaucratic logic, to it.

Volatility is the name of the make-work. Without it, the game slows to a mere regular churn instead of a high-speed one. "We want volatility, we thrive on it, that's how we make money," a Barclay foreign-exchange trader exclaimed. There can never be enough volatility, traders confess. "Intraday" trading – the fast and furious buying and selling of positions in the same day – in particular requires volatility as well as huge volumes, so that slight or even minute percentage gains can constitute a respectable profit. When, for example, in the first quarter of 1989, the market ungenerously became less volatile, the foreign-exchange income of Citicorp, a major player, slumped one-third.

There are two varieties of volatility. One is short-term. Explosions, hijackings, or political speeches – even merest rumours of events – can send currencies in any which direction, as traders try second-guessing each other. Their reaction to a relatively minor but speculatively important announcement, and then reaction to their own reaction, can send a currency reeling. The other variety is the trend. "The trend is your friend," is a catch-phrase. The idea is to ride it – ride it, ride it – playing your winnings and leveraging the ride with options. This works as long as you call the big turn when the trend starts going the other way. If you miss the turn, the other guy wins and you lose.

The bureaucratic charm of the derivative-paper branch, and particularly of its foreign-exchange section, is that the attempt to skin the market adds volatility to it, which increases the possibilities of the game, which draws more parties into the game, which intensifies the activity, which generates more volatility, and so on, in a make-work circle. Trends work the same way. The players, riding the trend, feed the trend by so doing, which they can then ride harder, and so on until, of course, the turn, when they start riding in the other direction.

Currency values are supposed to reflect the relative economic health of countries. Changes in economic health are usually gradual and long-term. Currency values should slowly change in step. Foreign-exchange traders, on the other hand, playing with often huge credit limits and making profits on marginal fluctuations, are quick to move with any piece of news they think might get other traders to move, in their vast exercise of chasing each other's tails and of over-heated guesswork. The mass psychology of thousands of traders is what rules, particularly in intra-day trading and its minute-by-minute judgements. The old guidelines for establishing currency values – trade flows and purchasing power – and other, short-term, factors like interest rates and capital flows take a back seat next to this rank speculation. As a McKinsey & Co. director and foreign-exchange expert put it, "What determines FX prices is what traders think is important, period. Trading psychology rules in the short term; trade flows take years to have effect."

The Montreal-based *International Bank Credit Analyst* reported in 1989 that as much as 75 per cent of the turnover in foreign-exchange markets follows daily trading models, where money is invested according to charts and the babble of technical analysis, that is, according to the readings of the market's own entrails. Similarly, a 1987 *Euromoney* survey of foreign-exchange forecasting services found that, of twenty-one services, none at all offered pure "fundamental" forecasts (forecasts based on real economic factors), five used fundamentals for the longer horizon and technical analysis for the short term, three combined the two techniques, and thirteen offered only technical analysis. "Economic fundamentals [the real world] do not enter into most traders' behavior," observed Jeffrey Frankel, professor of economics at the University of California in Berkeley and an expert on foreign exchange. Even if some non-conformist traders think the real world should count, if they act accordingly in a market dictated by technical-analysis tail-chasing, they'll get clobbered.

The banks, investment banks, and commodity exchanges flog their foreign-exchange devices to corporations and institutional investors who have been made to believe that "you pay the man [to hedge your foreign-exchange exposure] or risk disaster," as *Forbes* magazine put it. Some of the slickest magazine ads run by the derivative-paper branch are by banks and investment banks pushing foreign-exchange products. Catchy phrases with a sophisticated ring, like "currency exposure management" and "hedging packages" are in vogue. In Canada, the Royal Bank of Canada and the Bank of Montreal have pushed their foreign-exchange risk-management services. Many institutional investors are sceptical. Logic tells them that, in the end, the gains and losses from their foreign-exchange exposure (say, in holdings of foreign stocks) will average out. Hedging with options merely adds the cost of the options to their overhead. But the derivative-paper branch, like any expansive bureaucracy, continues to talk up the techniques and to formulate esoterically complex strategies which always conclude how good these manipulations are. Above all, the derivative-paper cadres play to investment advisers' bureaucratic insecurities. The hedging subsection grows.

Part of the make-work is concocting new "products." Cadres in "product development" or "derivative products research" at the large U.S. banks and investment banks work overtime to concoct a variety of stratagems which can be piggy-backed onto a sales pitch. Options are a basic ingredient, similar to a soup stock in a kitchen. Premiums for foreign-exchange options aren't cheap, rising to as high as 6 per cent of principal for an "at-the-money" option lasting a year, and the option, of course, may never be exercised. Then the combinations begin. A customer, for example, may buy an option from an investment bank and sell back a slightly different one, so as to hedge for the most part and gamble slightly at the same time. Many clients want to gain a windfall from favourable currency movements and not just protect themselves against unfavourable movements, or they can be enticed into so wanting. This adds to the product variety.

These multiplying devices, combinations, and techniques have generated a language of their own: option cocktails; delta hedging, gamma, theta, vega, eta (mathematical derivatives) synthetic or structured products; caps; floors; collars; swaps; range forwards; participating forwards; and brand-name investment-bank acronyms such as "minimax," "fox," "scout," and "cylinder." Acronyms are in, in the investment-banking world. "Solutions looking for a problem," is what some jaundiced observers called these last creations and, as it turned out, they haven't proved too popular with customers, maybe because the customers can't quite figure out what earthly use they are.

By mixing option cocktails to specific tastes – by encouraging something more than a basic-option slug – the banks collect higher fees. The concocters, though, aren't called bartenders. They're called "financial engineering groups." What they engineer, in the end, is getting corporations involved and paying the fees. Banks found they could make more money by generating transactions ("peddling products") whether they were really needed or not. Corporations and institutional investors, meanwhile, need financial engineers of their own to work through the intricacies, play the margins, and, not least, figure out whether their banks are giving them good advice and good rates. The investment banks "are selling black boxes [mathematical trading strategies] based on calculus to people who can barely speak algebra," one knowledgeable observer remarked. Inevitably, a separate subsection – foreign exchange consultants ("risk management" consultants) – has sprung up selling their ability to speak this algebra. It's another cottage or "boutique" bureaucracy. These boutiques, according to reports, expect to take the lead in constructing both "plain vanilla" and exotic synthetic hedges – in other words, yet more elaboration. Investment banks, never ones to leave any bureaucratic territory to others, have also begun moving into the consulting subsection, among them First Boston Corp., a once celebrated M&A operator. Fallen on hard times with its M&A make-work, it was looking to foreign exchange to help prop itself up. "Strategic foreign exchange consulting" is its consulting *schtick*.

Naturally there are also, now, foreign-exchange software producers (a large branch of the futures-trading-systems subsection) who, since they had acquired the expertise, expanded into the foreign-exchange consulting boutique subsection. Moreover, bureaucracies, by their nature, suffer from pangs of uncertainty. New cadres spring up to produce words and numbers to assuage such trepidation. There are technical forecasters to whom professional market-makers pay subscriptions of US$25,000 a year, although the subscribers don't understand the forecasters' techniques, let alone trust them.

Generous marketing expenditures by money-centre banks, over and above advertising, help keep interest up. Under the guise of teaching its more valuable customers, as well as its own staff, how to deal in foreign exchange, Citicorp established what it calls the "Bourse Game" – a mock foreign-exchange market with competing teams set up in the wing of a hotel at US$3,500 per guest – for promotional purposes. Chemical Bank had a similar game. Entertainment is a big marketing item. Money-centre banks in the City of London spend so much money on restaurants, indulging their foreign-exchange clients, that restaurant prices have become a topic of discussion. The virtues and costs of sports events versus nights at the opera are debated in terms of their bureaucratic effectiveness. American banks invite clients to the races *and* provide pocket money to bet with (maybe to get them in the mood for foreign-exchange dealing as well as to entertain them); British and Swiss banks consider this uncouth. Barclays Bank, one of the foreign-exchange powerhouses, is enthusiastic about free tickets to soccer games for economy and effectiveness; rubbing shoulders with one of the teams, if it can be arranged, is considered superior, for making an impression on a client, to any American bank's three-day trip on the Orient Express.

Exchanges dealing in currency futures and options add to the playing back and forth. The currency futures market which, in the form of the International Money Market (IMM), had rescued the Mercantile Exchange in Chicago from atrophy, expanded by leaps and bounds (about eighteen-fold) in the dozen years 1978-1990. Add to futures the currency options activity at the Philadelphia Stock Exchange and in London. It also inflated spectacularly.

Different "suckers" feed this bureaucratic section. The small speculators lose. Probably most corporations lose, if indirectly, in the spreads and premiums they pay. Only some of the largest corporations are active foreign-exchange participants trying to milk the market, and so have the necessary cadres. Beyond them, "the corporations don't know what they're doing," one trader confessed. Plenty of "suckers" are found willing to buy or sell at less than competitive rates. Second-tier corporations that suddenly have to trade currencies "[get] terribly ripped off by [their] banks," a former trader, holding back his laughter, disclosed. Multimillion dollar blunders by corporations playing the foreign-exchange game occur from time to time.

The biggest payers for the foreign-exchange bureaucracy, though, may be the central banks, intervening to cushion the swings caused by speculative trading. They buy into panics and sell into booms. It's called "leaning into the wind." It doesn't make casino sense, but the central banks feel they have no choice if they are to offset the economic damage of fluctuations and of speculative runs at weak currencies. Sometimes the major central banks, particularly if they get together, can ambush and clobber the traders. Usually, though, the best they can manage is to bring a swing to a halt or catch it at a turn. The traders themselves, anticipating central bank intervention, are not then likely caught unawares.

The traders use the central banks in this way, the *Institutional Investor* remarked, like pool sharks using the side cushions of a pool table. Most central banks by themselves are no match for the weight of currency hurtling through trading space. "Sheer wall of money," "avalanche," and "gargantuan tidal forces" are other metaphors for it. The total amount of U.S. dollar reserves held by all the central banks is less than a day's trading volume. One single trader – the man who made a fortune for Bankers Trust before quitting – was able to frustrate the Bank of England on one occasion.

Foreign exchange "would be a zero-sum game if the central banks weren't there," one specialist commented. "Little wonder," the *Institutional Investor* added, "that bank traders privately view central banks the way Las Vegas dealers treat half-drunk wildcatters from Texas." "You do have a general loser," said one bank's foreign-exchange chief. "It's the central banks. They're looked on as the suckers." Or, as yet another specialist put it, "The banks are making [foreign-exchange profits] from the general public."

Not everybody thinks the central banks are losers. Studies are contradictory. A central bank may lose in the short run but simply wait for the wind it leaned against to change direction, maybe several years – wait, in effect, for currency values to get back into something approaching equilibrium – and then recoup its losses. Inasmuch as the central banks are manhandled by the inflated foreign-exchange bureaucracy, however, the public ends up paying through its taxes – paying just as surely as it would for ranks of civil servants passing the time playing chess or pinochle. But the public pays for wasteful and unproductive bureaucracy, wherever it is, one way or the other.

The foreign-exchange practitioners themselves, of course, do not want this waste to stop. "What I'd really be afraid of," says one senior trader, "is that the market stops moving." He would be aggrieved, it turns out, even if the market stopped moving by itself, without government intervention. Worse, managed exchange rates or a return to fixed exchange rates would shrivel the foreign-exchange bureaucracy to almost nothing. "That would certainly screw up banks that are depending on FX profits," said a foreign-exchange sales chief, "and screw up our traders who've got Porsches to buy." He keeps "a cottage up in Scotland," just in case his bureaucracy is shut down in that way. "Traders react to proposals to fix exchange rates or even to craft very narrow trading bands like vampires confronted with a crucifix," *Institutional Investor* remarked humorously.

The commodity exchanges that trade in currency futures and options would also be terribly deflated. To help ensure that doesn't happen, the American Coalition for Flexible Exchange Rates (ACFX) was formed. One of its leading founders was the chairman of the Mercantile Exchange, which, through the International Money Market, brought currency futures to the world.

Another mushrooming bureaucratic section has been created by trading in government and corporate bonds, bond futures, and options on bond futures (really, interest-rate futures and options), taking advantage of interest-rate volatility. There used to be a day when people bought fixed-income government and corporate bonds as a long-term investment, locked them away in a strong-box, and didn't bother with them except to clip and cash in the interest coupons. Now a whole, arcane bureaucratic section has been built on the back of bonds.

The value of bonds varies inversely with interest rates. When interest rates go up, existing bonds decline in trading value because, by putting equivalent money into new bonds, one can get more interest. There is no advantage in selling the old bonds, however, since they will already have been discounted. Down the road at maturity, moreover, one receives the face value of the bonds regardless (unless there is a default). The unproductive shuffling of bonds back and forth is caused by an altogether different factor. Interest-rate volatility offers the prospect that by analyzing the direction of future interest rates correctly, before anybody else does – by guessing right, in other words – one can make a killing in bonds. The bond-trading section expands to fill this empty speculative space.

The bond-trading section also plays off the stock-trading section. If, for example, independent of interest rates, the stock market drops through the floor, then of course it is better to have been in bonds or in cash. Moreover, a stock-market drop is supposed to bring recession and hence a lowering of interest rates in order to get the economy moving again. Fixed-interest bonds, pegged before the interest rates drop, then look even better. On the other hand, if the stock market takes off, bonds lose their lustre. Ingrate bond-holders will abandon them for stocks. The stock-market branch and the bond-trading cadres churn in counterpoint. The churning, however, involves not just bonds against stocks and cash. Long-term bonds (whose value swings more with changes in current interest rates) and short-term bonds are played against each other, with the players "lengthening" and "shortening" their portfolios, in and out, like playing a trombone.

Alas, trading bonds back and forth, like trading futures, is an unproductive zero-sum game, or rather a minus-sum game, because every time the bonds are traded a spread or brokerage commission is taken out. Where investment funds are involved – a bond fund with pension money, for example – management fees are also taken out. What one side gains in guessing right about future interest rates, the other side loses. But the bond traders and fund managers – the bureaucratic cadres – do well again.

Take the case of one particular American bond management firm at the time of the stock-market plunge in October 1987. The very morning of Black Monday, the principal's gloomy forebodings about the bond market appeared in the *Wall Street Journal*. He was all "in cash." By 1:00 p.m. the unexpected (for that day) stock-market fall had been so precipitate that he totally reversed his gloomy prognosis about bonds (they would be going up as stocks went down). By 2:00 p.m. he was all in bonds, even if the newspaper ink explaining his previous, contrary outlook was hardly dry. But the recession that the stock-market crash was supposed to cause didn't happen. It wasn't such a brilliant idea to get back into bonds, after all. By the end of the first quarter of the following year, just a few months after the stock-market collapse, the bond-fund manager had sold out his entire bond position and was completely back in cash again. Bond traders took their slice in and out. The bond management firm and its principal, meanwhile, continued to manage and pronounce in their well-fed bureaucratic way.

Other managers of "fixed income" also adjusted their positions back and forth, although in not quite such an extreme way. They and their economist colleagues produced the usual volume of baloney-analysis reflections on the bond market, purporting to explain what was going to happen and changing their opinions conveniently as they went along. Although uncertain about their predictions, they nevertheless kept trading (they're supposed to do *something*, after all, for their keep). They swapped issues and switched sectors when they thought they saw an opportunity to pick up some yield advantage. Others with whom they were swapping and switching presumably "saw" an advantage in doing the opposite. Their trading, like all bond trading, mutually cancelled itself out. So did the advice of the sophisticated and highly paid bond analysts and economic seers. In fact, bond-fund managers collectively have underperformed bond indexes. The money under their management would have been better served if they had spent their time playing bridge in the back room instead.

Bond trading is now described as "hot and heavy," "volatile," and "risky" – "no longer a placid backwater but a place of turbulence" – just like stock trading. "In a single day, the market might be down, up and down, or up, down and then up," a managing director at Morgan Stanley told *Fortune* in 1987. "That's as much movement as traders used to see in an entire year." Investment banks trade in bonds for their own accounts (proprietary trading) – indeed, they make most of their trading profits in bonds. This helped fill a bureaucratic gap when M&A activity declined at the end of the decade.

Bond brokers can egg on clients and churn accounts just as stockbrokers do. In one U.S. case that went to court, the plaintiff, a municipal government that lost more than US$6 million, cited churning as the cause and alleged that a thousand transactions had been made by the brokers in twenty months. This augments the rake-off from trading which, together with the primary rake-off from the sale of new issues, feathers the bond traders' nest. Incomes of over $1 million are commonplace, and incomes of several millions a year, especially for department heads, are not at all unusual. One Salomon Brothers' department head, who had received $4.75 million in 1990 (and $10 million over three years), still was dissatisfied because traders in other divisions made more!

Michael Lewis, an art history graduate who went to work for Salomon Brothers in the halcyon late 1980s, described the scene in his trenchant account, *Liar's Poker*. His job purportedly was to advise investors on which bonds to buy, but the real trick was to persuade them to buy bonds Salomon couldn't sell otherwise and didn't want to be stuck with. Those who succeeded in peddling the unsellable received the "Big Swinging Dick" award. The Salomon maxim was that investors had short memories. The bond markets – particularly, for Salomon, mortgage-backed bonds – "puked money." The main trading game at Salomon wasn't stocks or commodities but interest rates, played on the bond-market desks. ("Liar's poker" was a bluff-and-call poker game played with the serial numbers of dollar bills, which the top traders indulged in most afternoons for a few hundred dollars. Gambling with their own money, rather than just the firm's money, made the day complete.)

The trading in interest-rate futures, options, and futures options has mushroomed spectacularly. It's like trading bonds themselves, but with the leverage of buying on margin added. The interest-rate, or "financial," futures, you'll recall, were invented in the mid-1970s to prop up the Chicago Board of Trade. The instruments used were Government National Mortgage Association mortgage-backed securities (Ginnie Maes). The Ginnie Mae futures have since faded away, replaced by futures on U.S. Treasury bonds, Eurodollar bonds, and U.S. Treasury notes and Treasury bills, in descending order. Speculators now play the spreads between different interest-rate futures – buying Treasury-bill futures and selling Eurodollar futures, for example – sometimes juggling different expiry dates for the two sides of the transaction. This complication adds to the game.

Fifteen years ago, interest-rate futures did not even exist. Now they account for 45 per cent of all futures trading in the United States as of 1990, or 123 million contracts. Options on interest-rate futures did not exist either, until 1982 (how did the world get along without them?). By 1990, 35 million such contracts were traded. The interest-rate options market (options as distinct from options on futures), run by U.S. banks, has reportedly grown even faster.

Interest-rate futures, options, and futures options, like their foreign-currency conterparts, expand exponentially the paper-shuffling possibilities. As with other futures and options, their ostensible *raison d'être* was to provide for hedging, in this case against interest-rate fluctuations. Again, they quickly became burgeoning speculative markets in themselves, with banks and investment banks keeping book and running options operations.

Here the same kind of esoteric mathematical models are used to manage the banks' risk, with the same high-paid "quant" practitioners (quantitative-analysis cadres) drawing them up. "Rocket scientists," they're also called, in the parlance. Like the programs for managing risk in foreign-exchange speculation, the computer programs don't do what they are meant to do. "There is no theory that encompasses the real world of interest rate options," declares a New York specialist. But that's not important. Its impressive, "scientific" complexity is all that matters.

Shelves of "new products" are devised here, too, in order to generate fees and pay margins. One such new product was stripped bonds and stripped mortgage-backed securities – abstruse concoctions that could end up baffling the bureaucracy itself. They provide as good an illustration of the process as any.

In coupon (bond) stripping, the coupons (interest) were "stripped" off the principal of a Treasury bond, bizarre as the idea sounds. The two were then sold separately in derivative form (as "deposit receipts," which, like baggage checks, reflected the fact that there was a bond stored away somewhere, on which all this was based). The investment bank took a satisfying margin along the way and a trust company got a fee for holding the original bond. The receipts or certificates were given fancy marketing acronyms, like TIGRs (Treasury Investment Growth Receipts), CATs (Certificates of Accrual on Treasury Securities), and COUGARs – together known as "felines" – or, in Britain, ZEBRAs (Zero Coupon Eurosterling Bearer or Registered Accruing Securities). They could be traded like conventional bonds and – of attraction to speculators – they were highly volatile in value. The value of the interest-coupon receipt (fixed interest) would vary inversely to changes in the interest rate, like a bond, except, without the constant face-value of the principal attached, it would swing even more than a bond. The stripped principal, meanwhile, in effect a bond without interest, would also be more volatile. With a regular bond, one could re-invest the annual interest at new interest rates, somewhat offsetting any swing to that point. Stripped principal, however, did not allow that. The cadres had invented a couple of new games.

Once the investment banks discovered they could create a new product in this way, it was only a matter of time before it occurred to them that other "new products" might be possible. Theoretically one could strip coupons from one kind of security and "paste" them on to another, or mix and match other components of securities. The investment banks duly came up with stripping mortgage securities (bonds based on pooled mortgage loans). The two strips were called IOs (interest-only) and POs (principal-only). An investment bank could sell the two paper strips for more than the underlying mortgage security, earning a fat premium in the process.

These strips, also interest-rate "synthetics," were even more exotic and unpredictable than TIGRs and CATs. They had an extra wrinkle: the behaviour of mortgage holders. When interest rates went up, pre-payment of mortgage principal slowed down, so bondholders had to wait longer for their money (mortgage holders, if they had extra cash, would invest it instead, to take advantage of the high interest rates). The value of POs, reflecting this longer-than-expected wait for principal repayment, and also taking a beating from the rising interest rates themselves, plummetted doublefold. The IO (interest-only) strip, on the other hand, went up in a value or declined less than otherwise. A slowdown of prepayment meant that interest (the IO pay-off) would be paid for a longer period.

This was so complicated that even experts found the stripped mortgage securities hard to figure out. One of the greatest users of this "instrument" was a young Merrill Lynch hotshot with a Harvard MBA, Howard Rubin. More to his credit, he had once been a professional gambler, counting the blackjack cards with such skill that he wore out his welcome at the Las Vegas casinos. As a trader at Merrill Lynch, he made a lot of people very rich, including himself (US$1 million a year plus a slice of profits; probably several million in total). "He was a god," one colleague said. Then he got caught with an estimated US$900 million in PO strips unsold, with interest rates going the wrong way. Merrill Lynch took a $377 million trading loss. It shamefacedly hunkered down with "incremental analytical work and systems work" – public-relations jargon for more bureaucratic calculation – to try to prevent such a mess from happening again.

Merrill Lynch wasn't the only case of the bureaucracy concocting something so complicated that the cadres weren't quite sure how it worked, while going through the motions anyway. Prudential-Bache, as solid as the Rock of Gibraltar (the Prudential logo), dreamt up synthetics they called Residual Income Stream Equity – acronym "Risers." Synthetics are "products" pasted together from other things. The Risers, alas, didn't rise as they were supposed to, to the chagrin of out-of-pocket client innocents. The sales force that flogged them hadn't figured them out either. The bureaucratic cells where these paper confections are pasted together are known derisively as "rocket shops."

Bond-fund managers, artful bureaucrats in their own right, have been forced to add or retain rocket scientists of their own to cope with the concoctions of the new-product cadres. It's yet another instance of bureaucratic inflation feeding bureaucratic inflation to the point of Kafkaesque absurdity. Not that the bond managers do keep up. The slicing and dicing of bonds into weirdly complex confections "has gotten carried so far that no one knows what anything is worth anymore," the managing director of a U.S. fixed-income investment specialist complained to the *Institutional Investor*. "It's a case of technology gone mad."

Almost any device can be taken a long way, the derivative-paper cadres have realized. Take "swaps," for example, which surfaced in the early 1980s. The original idea for interest-rate swaps was fairly simple. Companies, for reasons of mutual convenience, would swap a fixed-rate payment obligation for a floating-rate obligation. A bank or investment bank acted as intermediary, managing a "swaps book." It brought the parties together and took a nice margin for its trouble. Of course, if interest rates went up, it was better to have fixed-rate obligations, and if they went down, it was better to have a floating rate. One could even bet on the prospects. This was a futures market in the making. Before long, with the cadres making book, the swaps market was full-blown. By 1988, interest-rate swaps were being arranged at a US$550-billion-a-year rate globally and currency swaps at $120 billion. By 1990, combined swaps in place had a face value worldwide of nearly US$2.5 trillion. Naturally, the swaps cadres chattered about "risk management," hedging, and insurance, and traded on the institutional-investor cadres' preoccupation with covering their behinds. This fed buckets of money into their bureaucratic mill. Inevitably, too, new "products," combinations, and arcane strategies issued forth. A synthetic swap, for example, could be created out of a "strip" of futures, the *Financial Post* reported enthusiastically. "The permutations are boundless," the report exulted. "A speculator's playground," *The Economist* described the swaps market, but it's really a bureaucratic playground. One insurance-company swaps chief took home more than US$8 million in 1989.

Equity "synthetics" – derivative paper whose value rises and falls depending on what's happening in the stock market, but which isn't itself a stock or basket of stocks – are being touted as the next wave of new "products," and a way to help fill in the make-work gap after the stock-market collapse of October 1987. Here, as with swaps, providing the derivatives to clients, and trading in them for a profit, overlap. Top traders in these and other derivatives now make an estimated US$700,000 to $900,000 a year, with the exceptional manager of one derivate shop hitting a reported $25 million.

These are all premium-gathering or margin-gathering exercises. Like the rest of the branch's make-work, they resemble making book on the point spread of football games, except they are done by established bureaucracies, are reported on positively (and promoted by) a press bureaucracy, and most importantly have the simulacrum of something to do with business. The trick, also like book-making, is to pump up traffic, in order to pump up the rake-off. This is where the creative scope of synthetic, or "New Age," paper bureaucracy comes in handy. Its confections can be made to appear new. They are complicated enough to be intriguing and to hold out promise. By the time people begin to realize that the derivative paper is a proxy for a bureaucratic collection scheme, and become disillusioned – or, alternatively, when the cadres' rake-off margin declines – new "products" will have issued forth from the bureaucracy's cells. "Brokerages have created another cycle – the product cycle," *Business Week* cheered.

With the creation of stock-index futures, "index arbitrage" appeared, another elaborate waste of time, money, and energy. Index arbitrage plays on the difference between the price of stock-index futures, traded in Chicago, and the underlying real shares, traded in New York. The two prices parallel each other. When the two markets become misaligned, the fund managers and investment bankers go to work, buying in one market and selling in the other, and locking in a guaranteed profit. There is an added bureaucratic quality: The arbitrage is computer-triggered and computer-aided in its execution. Hence its other name: "program trading."

Some of the billion-dollar state and corporate pension funds engage in this program trading through their investment banks, which collect an appropriate fee. Corporate treasurers, managing cash balances, also may take a ride on it. Program trading accounts for approximately 10 per cent of all trading on the New York Stock Exchange, and at times in the trading day can hit as high as 30 per cent. It doesn't actually produce anything, other than motion. "Scalping the market," it's called. Huge profits have reportedly been made.

On some days, the Dow Jones goes up and down violently without economic reason. This nevertheless produces the usual headlines suggesting some powerful and mystical force at work (an "Invisible Hand" or an inscrutable but omniscient "Verdict of Wall Street"). It turns out that the supposedly dramatic, traumatic, and profoundly meaningful agitation of the market is just the result of program traders going through their motions. The individual investor, meanwhile, with small-scale trading, gets run over if he or she is in the way. One long-time Wall Street commentator called it "dancing in the dark with elephants."

A similar, more discrete kind of arbitrage can be done among government bonds, mortgages, and the interest-rate futures market, playing the computers endlessly with quant programs. The bureaucratic rake-off, though, is not so discrete. In 1990, for example, the bond-arbitrage group at Salomon Brothers split a US$60 million year-end bonus. The leading cadre took home $23 million of the pot. Salomon's bond-arbitrage group uses, on average, not one, but five different strategies at the same time.

"Portfolio insurance," which many people blamed for the 1987 stock-market crash, is a program-trading spin-off. On paper, it's a work of bureaucratic genius – the "key [to risk-free profits] that investors [have] sought for centuries," as *Forbes* sarcastically put it. When the Dow Jones, or a basket of shares, dips more than a certain percentage, the stockholder – say, an institutional investor – sells S&P 500 futures to hedge against a further fall. What may then be lost with a further decline in the actual stocks is gained by being able to meet one's S&P 500 futures-contract obligation at a lower price. That, at least, was the idea. In October 1987, however, when a stock-market decline triggered the "portfolio insurance" mechanism, the resulting sale of S&P 500 futures was so great that it drove the price of futures down below the price of the underlying stocks, putting the stocks out of line. This triggered in turn, by "automatic pilot," the sale of stock by arbitrageurs. These sales caused stock-price declines, which triggered yet more futures selling by the "insurers" – so much so that not enough buyers could be found, and the market "crashed."

The critics, for their part, were caustic, sputtering away at the "super quant computer kiddies" – the wet-behind-the-ears bureaucratic engineers who didn't seem to realize, or care about, the damage they could do to the stock market and who hadn't the faintest idea of, or interest in, the productive economy. Instead, they played ever-more abstract games, creating a "make-believe ghost market" in the process – the "symbolic economy." What the critics wouldn't, and couldn't, admit to themselves was that the conventional stock-market bureaucracy, of which they were reverent defenders, doesn't intrinsically care about productive economic work, either, and that, given technology, the quants were inevitable: were a direct progeny.

This index-arbitrage paper shuffling was all made possible by the creation, by the Mercantile Exchange, of the S&P 500 stock-index futures contract – a champion of make-work. It hadn't yet been dreamt up in the 1970s. In 1982, it managed 2.9 million contracts. By 1986, just four years later, it hit the 19.5 million mark, for an almost sevenfold increase. Even in 1990, with the bull market subdued and with index arbitrage under an odour for its role in Black Monday, the S&P 500 still managed 12.1 million contracts, or four times its 1982 level.

Program trading and similar computer-assisted games don't end with playing off stocks against stock-index futures, or bonds against interest-rate futures, however. They can also be played between stocks and stock options (and stock-index options) and between options and futures of all kinds. ("Portfolio insurance," incidentally, has added the use of options.) Highly developed bureaucratic cells have evolved where cadres spend their days combining these variables over and over again. While speculators in futures and options, who believe in free enterprise and "risk and reward," are losing their stakes, these bureaucratic "money machines" gather in what's to be had, almost risk-free – something like collecting a private tax or picking up money off the floor. The leader in refining the machinery was a company called Chicago Research and Trading Group (CRT). *Circa* 1988, it was executing more than US$2.5 billion in trades each day.

It was all done with the aid of a highly refined computer model that evaluated futures and options according to volatility, time remaining until contracts expire, and similar factors. The computer programs deciphered subtle changes in price relationships, enabling the firm's traders to lock in minute profits (but multiplied by huge volumes) trading in different markets simultaneously from Singapore to Chicago. The trading company might, for example, buy options and sell futures in the same commodity (say, Treasury bonds) at the same time. CRT avoided having to risk guessing the direction of the market and could even cope with, and profit from, volatility. As a bonus, it occasionally made a lot of money quickly. By using margin money and option leverage, it was able to control as much as US$750 million in end value with only $3 million, according to the *Wall Street Journal*.

This one firm often accounted for more than 5 per cent of the multi-billion-dollar trading in the S&P 500 stock index and U.S. treasury-bond futures, and an amazing 30 to 40 per cent of the volume in most exchange-traded options markets including those outside the United States.

None of this was remotely like productive economic enterprise. The leading principal of CRT was a philosophy graduate, a former bible-school student (where he spent three years), and a mathematical genius. The company occupied three floors of the Chicago Board Options Exchange Building. It provided its staff of nearly six hundred employees with free meals, served by five on-staff chefs. Top employees could quickly earn six-figure salaries. The founder's hero, for the twentieth century, was Walt Disney.

CRT executed 100,000 trades daily, according to the *Wall Street Journal* report, which is a lot of churning of paper. So protective a screen is the ideology around it, however, that no one dreams of a governing authority acting to eliminate the waste of it. That would be revolutionary and unAmerican. Only unusual natural forces need to be feared. A newly hired CRT president and chief executive was particularly concerned about the effect of a possible steep recession. "The thing we need as a machine is activity," he said. "Our biggest worry is a slow bleeding to death if the markets dry up." CRT, not unexpectedly, became the envy of the rest of the derivative-paper bureaucracy.

Another U.S. company, Mint Management, a futures fund acting for investors, took the method one step further. All trading decisions were made by two mainframe computers programmed to run seven automated trading systems, trading in about fifty-five markets to diversify risk. The senior partners in charge never second-guessed their computers' decisions. In fact, they had a binding contract among themselves not to override their system.

But computerized trading strategies – in effect, program trading strategies of all kinds – are now, as we have seen, the bureaucratic fashion. Not just companies like CRT but also the major investment banks have plunged heavily into the genre, labelled "high-tech," pumping up the rake-off for their own account ("proprietary trading"). These programmed machines are increasingly dominating world "markets." The continuous devising of new products by the quant cadres plays in counterpoint. It both generates sales income and creates new trading volume – volume on which their firms' proprietary trading can batten in turn. There are glimpses of a bureaucratic El Dorado in which the machinery turns over regardless: "the promise," as *Business Week* put it, "of solving the Street's oldest problem – the boom-and-bust syndrome in trading volume."

The combinations of stocks, futures, and options can be played every which way. The bureaucratic mentality being what it is, they are, indeed, played every which way. Brokerages, for example, have encouraged retail clients to try "spreads" – buying one future and selling another, or buying and selling the same commodity through futures contracts expiring on different dates – hoping that one "leg" of the spread would make more money than the other leg loses. In effect, people buy and sell the same thing at the same time. An increasingly arcane bureaucracy doesn't notice the absurdity, and collects its commissions. Similar complicated strategies, with gimmicky names, are encouraged, where the "investor" takes a risk and then uses a combination of other measures to offset the risk, leaving not much in the way of anything in the end except a finely calibrated "perhaps" (and, then, "perhaps not") and much wasted time sorting it out; but the cadres collect their commissions.

As for options in themselves, "Get the hell out of those right away," Peter Lynch, the well-known American investment expert, once said. "Options are really expensive. It's a tragedy all the money that is wasted on them." But brokerages peddle them anyway, for exactly that reason.

The face value of trading in the S&P 500 futures contract just by itself matches the dollar value of all stock trading in the United States, and far outstrips trading on the NYSE. Because futures speculation is so highly margined, it is more volatile, too – more sensitive to what is euphemistically called "market forces," that is, rumours, tail-chasing, guru pronouncements (depending on who is in fashion), and the slightest movement of the investment herds. This has a feedback effect on stock markets. The febrile bureaucracy of futures trading is consequently now touted as the leading edge of the stock market – where the cosmic decisions of "the market" are now made – although the stock market itself is still doing what it used to do. "The floors of Wall Street and Bay Street are becoming mere senate chambers for decisions made on [futures] markets," maintained one enthusiast.

The highly-levered option markets are the same – a more attenuated variation of what investors in stocks, bonds, and money instruments (Treasury bills, and so on) have always done. Some clever cadres, indeed, have concocted a way of using stocks and cash to produce the same results as options – a synthetic synthetic. Most fruitful, bureaucratically, options lend themselves to no end of paper manoeuvres. They cover, in complications and mathematical gloss, unproductive games, played day after day by highly paid cadres, that would raise storms of indignation if the time, energy, and money were wasted more plainly with cards games in the staff lunchroom.

However, in their own bureaucratic terms, the exchanges and brokerage firms which have devised options and the new futures, and pumped up their trading, do have a lot to be proud of. They can rightly be boastful. They have managed a bureaucrats' *tour de force* – creating an entire second bureaucracy when one (conventional stock markets) was more than enough.

6

The Money-Manager Branch

Banks, insurance companies, and trust companies were the money managers of old. Banks collected deposits at one rate, lent at another, and followed their own rules. Their top executives became rich and powerful. Their shareholders also prospered. Banks and insurance companies managed money very well – on behalf of their own bureaucracies. Insurance companies were particularly wasteful of the economy's resources. One American book on insurance companies, catching their structural waste, had chapters appropriately entitled "Too much insurance," "Too many lawyers," "Too many underwriters, too many agents," and "Too many salesmen." The "whole life" insurance sector was especially notorious for the high up-front commissions it paid out to salespeople, in order to sell policies. Their bloated ranks and all the time they spent was paid for by the poor policy-holder in surrendered policies (lost premiums) and abysmally low average returns.

The New Bureaucracy has its own money-manager branch – institutional investors and financial counsellors – of which the old money managers are also a part. This money-manager branch is a sister to the stock-market branch. As it inflates, it feeds the stock-market branch in turn.

Atop the money-manager branch are the institutional investors. They include pension funds, mutual funds, stockbrokers (doing their own proprietary trading as well as acting for others), and the banks, trust companies, and insurance companies, which manage pension-fund, mutual-fund, and other moneys. The largest institutional investor in the United States, as of the *Institutional Investor* ranking for 1990, is Prudential Insurance. The second largest is the American Express group, operating through eleven subsidiaries. Of the top twenty, eight are banking (including trust-company) groups; four are insurance groups; three are investment banks (brokerage firms) or, like American Express, have investment-bank subsidiaries in their mix; two are public pension funds; two are mutual funds (Fidelity, Dreyfus); and one is an independent money-management firm.

Together, the institutional investors dominate stock markets. In the United States, they control close to half of all public-company stocks and upwards of 55 per cent of the stock of S&P 500 companies. They account for about 75 per cent of the trading on the New York Stock Exchange, measured by value. In Canada, institutional ownership of widely held companies is in the 50 to 70 per cent range, and institutional investors, including investment-dealer trading departments, also account for about three-quarters of all stock-market trading in the country, by value. Of the institutions, the pension funds carry the most weight.

Investment advisers (the people who manage pension-fund money) and mutual-fund managers aren't just clerks processing forms or accountants looking up actuarial tables. They move huge blocks of money from one stock to another, or in and out of the market altogether, "huffing and puffing," as *Business Week* once described them, as they try to beat the averages. This is where most of the churning on stock markets comes from – unproductive moving back and forth of paper in the classic sense. What one institutional investor gains, in this churning, another loses, except what is taken from the pockets of individual speculators and hapless ordinary investors. As it happens, institutional investors – taking the Americans as an example – do slightly worse than the average as measured by stock indexes. In the process they have generated their own bureaucracy, with its gurus, analysts, quants, and computer trading models, brokerage outriders, academic journals, and meditators reflecting on the stock market miasma and sometimes on their own navels.

The churning in the 1980s bull market was immense. Investment advisers (managing private corporate pension money) and mutual funds in the United States were replacing an estimated 60 to 65 per cent of their portfolios every year, as of 1986. Even after the bull market frenzy had fallen off, equity turnover by investment advisers still averaged in the 45 per cent range, with the very top churners hitting 300 to 400 per cent.

It wasn't always like this. In the past, stockbrokers, who were the main custodians of a family's shareholdings, would turn over a portfolio perhaps 5 per cent and at most 10 per cent a year. All this changed with the mad market of the late 1960s and the enormous success of the "go-go" fund managers. Jerry Tsai, the most noteworthy of the group, turned over his portfolio more than 100 per cent annually, and in 1965 reached 125 per cent. This new breed of fund managers weren't just addicted individual speculators. They had large funds under their management. They bought and sold in huge blocks as they caught stocks on the rise, dumped them when they levelled off, and moved to other shares. This gradually became the model: the "performance game." Aggressively churning one's portfolio, as one sought to outwit the other players, was how it was done.

Never mind that, when the stock market tumbled at the end of the decade, the high-performance go-go funds unceremoniously took a steep fall and the star fund managers retreated to the shadows (one of the bravura performers, later traced by *Business Week*, had ended up running a singles bar). Tsai's own, famous Manhattan Fund crashed ingloriously, loaded with dud stocks; more than half of them had either lost 90 per cent of their value or gone bankrupt within a year (no problem for Tsai who had already sold his management company, which owned the fund, at the top of the market). Never mind, also, that the exercise is a self-cancelling game; all the players together are the "market" and, as the market's own adage has it, "the market cannot beat itself." Never mind, too, that half of all institutional investors being rated against each other are going to be in the bottom half.

Even in terms of the game itself, the increase in churning has no practical basis. The possibilities for using one's cleverness to make gains by shifting funds from one stock to another have increased only marginally over the years. These possibilities lie in the number of listed companies. The more companies there are, the more the opportunities for the fund manager to discover "over-valued" or "under-valued" shares and to get the march on his or her competitors. From 1985 to record year 1987, the number of listed companies on the New York Stock Exchange increased 7 per cent. The number of reported transactions, however, increased 55 per cent, a whopping eight times as fast. From 1975 to 1985, the number of listed companies actually declined slightly, by 1 per cent, but the number of transactions, instead of declining in correspondence, still rose 55 per cent.

A study by American pension-fund analysts Stephen Berkowitz and Dennis Logue took the analysis further. It looked at the variation in price increases and decreases among different stocks. The greater the variation, the greater the possibilities for making gains by buying stocks on the rise and selling stocks about to languish or fall, at the expense of other fund managers and speculators. Hence the greater reason to trade. For the years 1964 to 1984 (the years of the study), however, there was no upward trend in such variation. The shuffling of paper back and forth by the money-manager branch increased dramatically anyway.

The study then charted the possible gains to be made from shifting in and out of the market – moving back and forth from common stock to Treasury bills – with "perfect foresight." This moving in and out of the market is called "market timing." A large variation in possible gains this way would provide a rationale for the increased turnover in stock trading. But there was no explanation there, either. The opportunities from market timing went up and down, showing no trend, in a pattern quite unlike the ballooning inflation in stock-market transactions.

It also turned out that throughout the 1980s up to the 1987 crash – a period when the bureaucratic churning of common stock rose by leaps and bounds – the low-turnover portfolios outperformed the churners. All that clever and complex calculation of the churners, plus the extra transaction costs incurred, went for nought except to expand their bureaucratic section.

For every bureaucratic syndrome of the stock-market branch there is a money-manager connection. Take short-termism which leads to the churning – the buying and selling of stock according to the quarter-to-quarter numbers, with little or no regard for a company's long-term objectives or for defending a domestic industry against foreign competition. *Myopia quarta-lia hysteria*, is the joking clinical description. The institutional investors are behind most of it.

Most professional investors are still paid to beat the market every quarter, or at least every year. Now that computers are available to tote up trades and track fund returns, even their weekly and daily results can be tallied and compared with that of their colleagues. They have little patience to wait out the effects of long-term investments or changes in management policies for companies going through a bad patch. "Even if you're certain a company will have a payoff on its investment in three years," explained the executive editor of two Value Line publications, "you have to consider the present value of your investment. . . . Either you pay less for the company now or you put your money elsewhere for three years and switch it to the company then." Of course, three years – the long-term framework which is too long for most money managers – is itself a short term, entrepreneurially speaking.

The negative effect this short-termism may have on enterprise doesn't come into money-managers' stock-selection process. "[The short-term emphasis] which makes us quicker on the trigger to dump a stock ultimately hurts the whole economy," admitted a senior equity-investment manager in 1984 when the issue broke out of the closet in the United States. And, he added, "I don't know what you can do about it." Investment advisers are bureaucratically removed and indifferent, changing their portfolios according to the numbers – in many cases, using a computer model fed with the numbers. An added irony: Some of the worst offenders are corporate pension plans under the control of corporate officers who deplore short-termism when it comes to the shares of their own company.

Investment advisers and other fund managers, similarly, are only too happy to cash in on takeovers and the premiums they add to the share price of target companies in their portfolios. The boost to their results makes them look good. The effects of hostile takeovers on entrepreneurship and on the economy, or the waste of paper entrepreneurialism generally, are of no concern to them. Led by the large state-employee pension funds, U.S. institutional investors have also been involved in the takeover game at the other end – providing junk-bond capital for LBOs and, in many cases, participating in the LBO syndicates themselves with equity contributions, most notably in the Kohlberg Kravis fund used for the RJR Nabisco takeover.

Risk-free profits from "scalping the market" by index arbitrage (program trading between index futures and the stock market)? Pension-fund managers are the major financial partners, giving the investment banks' program-trading groups access to billions of dollars. With that muscle, they can move the market while they're at it – they have the "ability to push stocks up and pull them down at will," charged one Wall Street commentator – and skin that margin, too. "Notorious . . . a handful of big institutional investors today control the market," he described it. "Monster institutions," added another. Not that the speculators and smaller professional traders who get scalped, particularly in the futures market, and who complain bitterly about this "jerking around of the market," deserve any sympathy; they make their cut by scalping the market themselves in their smaller ways.

Institutions were also the big players in "portfolio insurance" – the strategy of selling stock-index futures when the stock market begins to decline, to offset any subsequent losses in the stock market itself – which strategy, in October 1987, helped plunge the market into its downward spiral.

Behind the churning and futility, and superficial drama of stock-market action, are the bureaucratic cadres themselves. Collectively they produce nothing other than the waste of their own bureaucratic overheads. Even as paper shufflers, they are not quite sure what they are doing and often simply go wrong, not least from following each other's tails. All players together cannot beat the market in any case.

Not only have the high churners (the most active, vain, and aggressive money-manager bureaucrats) done less well than the low churners. Between their overheads and miscalculations, the U.S. money-manager cadres as a whole regularly underperform the averages, as measured by the S&P 500 stock index. For market cycles 1966 to 1974 and 1975 to 1982, and thereafter year by year to 1990 with one exception, the median performance of U.S. pension equity funds (as tabulated by SEI – Capital Resource Corporation, a leading performance measure) fell behind the S&P 500. Only in 1988 did it beat the index and then by only 0.2 per cent. Other tabulations show the same kind of results. Over any extended market period, less than a third of all money managers will beat the market averages, according to a *Barron's* report, and those that do typically founder in subsequent periods.

U.S. contrarian David Dreman, in his 1979 book *Contrarian*

Investment Strategy, added another perspective. He reviewed fifty-one surveys of professional investors' choices of specific stocks, from 1929 to 1976. Seventeen of the studies measured the performance of five or more stocks that the experts had picked as their favourites. Despite the advantages of diversification (five or more stocks), fifteen of the seventeen portfolios so chosen underperformed the market – a "failure" rate of close to 90 per cent. The choices that came out on top in the other thirty-four surveys did not do appreciably better. Overall, the favourite stocks and industries of large groups of money managers and analysts underperformed the market on thirty-nine of fifty-one occasions, or a failure rate of 76 per cent. "Throwing darts at the stock pages blindfolded or flipping a coin to decide what to buy would give you a fifty-fifty chance," Dreman couldn't help remarking. "Using a financial professional would reduce your odds considerably."

Similarly, a survey of bank trust departments (then the largest institutional common-stock investors) over the years 1953-1976, based on choice of favourite industry rather than favourite stock, showed a failure rate (underperforming the market) of 67 per cent. Another survey asked investment managers for six favourite stocks and one favourite industry, and six least-favoured stocks and one least-favoured industry. The favourite stocks and industry subsequently underperformed the S&P 500 while the "worst" stocks and single industry did better than the S&P. A later analysis, by Arnold Wood, investment writer and president of Martingale Asset Management, covered the 1980s. It dealt with Wall Street analysts' earnings estimates for the thirty big-name corporations in the Dow Jones Industrial Average. Their ten *best* buys would have provided a return of 5.6 per cent compounded while their ten *worst* buys would have provided a 10.5 per cent return.

Despite this woeful record, the money-manager bureaucracy grows. The number of registered investment advisers in the United States in 1989 had ballooned to three times what it was at the beginning of the decade, while pension assets had grown much less rapidly. Hundreds of new money-manager "boutiques" sprang up in the late 1980s – many of them started up by refugees from the 1987 Wall Street crash trying to keep themselves in the luxurious style to which they had become accustomed.

Part of this growth was caused by a specialization mania. Corporate pension officers were disappointed by the performance of "balanced" managers – staid managers who bought baskets of stocks and bonds so as to balance risk and didn't play around too much. In the early 1970s, they began replacing them with crews of specialty firms. They were soon to be frustrated with them, too. (Eventually they turned to various kinds of "basket investing," a strategy not a little reminiscent of the balanced managers they had cast off in a prior generation!)

The money managers, meanwhile, harvest a rich fee structure. Salaries for managers of public pension plans in the United States can easily exceed US$100,000. In-house corporate pension-fund managers undoubtedly do much better. And neither is a match for what outside investment advisers pull down – in the mid-1980s, as much as five to ten times what laggard public pension funds were paying. Fees for "active" equity-fund managers – outside investment advisers – run from 0.4 per cent to occasionally as high as 1 per cent of assets under management. The fees for managing a $2 billion active fund at 0.5 per cent, for example, would come to $10 million. Stephen Jarislowsky of Jarislowsky Fraser in Montreal, Canada's top investment counseling firm, reportedly took home $15 million in 1988.

Money managers can manipulate their compensation bureaucratically, too, just like the corporate cadres. One new wrinkle, borrowed from the corporate branch, is "performance" or "incentive" bonuses. The ostensible idea is to improve performance and to control fees. But, like stock bonuses for corporate executives, the performance bonuses are more a convenient way the cadres have of increasing their take. A typical configuration is bonuses on top of salary for beating the benchmark, but only in a few cases, and then ever so slightly, a small cut in salary for negative performance.

The critics grind their teeth in vain. "Paying double doesn't mean that performance doubles," muttered one U.S. pension specialist. A fund will end up paying extra for performance it is supposed to be getting anyway, another grumbled. "If these managers aren't going to outperform the market, why are they in business in the first place?" But, it should be added, by the nature of the exercise, most managers don't beat the market even when they are trying for all that they are worth.

Every once in a while bureaucratic angst slips out: a confession, sometimes inadvertent, of the ludicrous illusion of it all, and a revealing portrait of the bureaucratic character of the branch. In one baring of soul in the *Financial Analysts Journal*, the president of a U.S. asset-management company, trying to explain the investment advisers' collective failure to beat the benchmark, talked about their "fatal attractions." Here are "ostensibly reasonable" people, "by and large, highly educated (many of us hold certificates nearly as demanding to come by as MDs)," and yet, by the results, they are "consistently poor at our profession." This is a dilemma, particularly if one doesn't want to admit that the exercise of money management is circular. The unhappy writer, plumbing the depths, told how money managers' "feelings overcome . . . reason," how they "take shortcuts that violate logic" and, worst of all, how they "don't learn, or want to learn, from experience."

He made a list of "causes of irrational, and occasionally bizarre, behavior." "Mindless routine" came first. "We are steeped in ritual," he explained. When things go well, it is taken by money managers as a reward for their persistence. Evidence that contradicts this notion is dismissed. Psychologists call it "cognitive dissonance." Locked in this syndrome, members of the money-manager tribe can overlook the obvious.

One by-product of ritual and routine is "comfort" – "feelin' good" by latching on to familiar or jazzy catchwords and concepts and tossing them back and forth with colleagues. The infatuation with "factors" – the endless theoretical ways of measuring stock value – particularly exercised the author. At one professional updating program, the word "factors" was used 222 times (he counted them). This lemming-like seeking of comfort in factors was too much for the writer.

Money managers, trying to better their competitors, also collectively suffer from "information overload." In their search for avoidance of risk and something solid to stand on, and in their vanity about their analytic abilities, they make money management increasingly complex and tortured – producing, through analysis, an endless number of variables – so much so that it blocks their ability to grasp the essentials and make logical decisions. Snap judgements might do just as well, if not better. But the analytic production gives the investment advisers greater confidence in themselves, albeit false confidence.

"Follow the leader" is another syndrome, rooted in ordinary psychology, which plagues investment advisers. "Why do we all read the *Wall Street Journal*?" the writer complained. These and other foibles were dolefully recounted, in navel-gazing fashion. Hope is expressed that help will be found in research in "behavioral finance," a new-fangled discipline. One confession, though, is avoided: that money managers constitute an inflated and wasteful bureaucracy in themselves. That would produce just too much angst among the cadres.

The illusions and "irrationality" of money managers have, in fact, long been known and documented, with analogies to psychological and crowd-behaviour studies showing the folly of human nature. Institutional investors, for example, have habitually followed the pack in their market timing. Surveys of the 1960s and 1970s by the U.S. Securities and Exchange Commission and others show that typical institutions bought at market peaks (in 1967-1968 and 1972) and sold at market bottoms (1966, 1970, and 1974) – exactly the opposite of buying low and selling high that experts are supposed to be capable of. "The great majority of funds," a Merrill Lynch survey concluded, "lose money as a result of their timing efforts, and when the effects of commission costs are included, virtually everyone loses money." "They're all sheep," snorts one corporate CEO. "Herd instinct" and "group-think" are other epithets. "Money managers, who eat at the same clubs, work in the same buildings, read the same journals and watch each other like hawks, wind up thinking and acting alike," writer Andrew Allentuck described it, in the *Financial Post Magazine*.

But fear as well comes into it. Fund managers fear being a "bad dog," as one asset manager described it. The fund manager who underperforms the benchmark is called onto the carpet by his or her "client" – a corporate pension fund, for example. "Bad dog," scolds the corporate pension officer. After all, one of the reasons for hiring outside investment advisers is to be able to blame them for not performing, à la George Steinbrenner. To make matters worse, the outside investment adviser more often than not gets paid more than the corporate officer. To make matters worse still, while the performance of an investment adviser is easy enough to measure, by the numbers, the skill of the adviser isn't. The investment environment is so capricious – where the "experts" continuously get things wrong – that underperformance can mean almost anything. In the old bureaucracy (the civil service), one can at least assess skill based on working together. With investment advisers, though, so much of the craft is abstract and, in the end, comes down to guesswork, that the pension officer may not know what to make of the investment adviser.

This is a relationship prone to emotional outbursts by the client and apprehension by the money manager. Daily performance data (measurement of money-manager performance) is now available on-line, so that pension plan officers can look over a manager's shoulder. This creates more bureaucratic torments. The Big Brother atmosphere can cloud the poor manager's judgement, some of them complain. At the same time, the corporate pension officer may be harried by the corporation's chief financial officer. The "bad dog" money manager is filled with anxiety and worries about his or her ability. It is a classic bureaucratic syndrome.

"At least half the institutions are driven by sheer fear of failure," says a Toronto securities analyst handling institutional accounts. "They act together because there's safety in numbers." Or, as an investment adviser put it, "Get the money and then just don't do badly enough to lose the account."

Inevitably, one thoughtful financial analyst found inspiration in the Taoist "Wu Wei" principle – the "principle of not doing." The principle states that going with the flow and not managing too hard wins the day. Or, "Action through inaction is sometimes the best course." Translation for money managers: "Constant activity – the work you're supposed to be doing – only racks up commission costs so why bother; take it easy and collect your fees anyway."

But how, amidst this futility, does the bureaucracy maintain itself in such style? By its own momentum. In any sample of pension-fund managers there are going to be some, at any given time, who guess right or pick the right strategy, and beat the average, sometimes quite impressively. If they're clever, they market this "success" and increase the funds under their management. "Differences in income [of portfolio managers] seem to reflect mainly marketing skills," confessed one manager. When their reputations crumble, others will be around to replace them. The very devising of an average means there will always be somebody in the sample above average.

One American portfolio manager, in a moment of frankness, used the metaphor of a roomful of monkeys, a thousand of them. Each is trying to predict the direction of the market. At the end of ten predictions, one monkey has a perfect record of ten straight calls. She starts her own investment firm. Ten other monkeys get nine out of ten predictions right. They're hired by large investment counsellors (blockbuster outside managers). The forty-four who went eight for ten go to the bank trust departments, which can't afford to hire "top talent." (Unmentioned, but in the scheme of things, many of the remaining 945 catch on anyway or become "financial planners.") The hapless ones stay home and make another ten predictions.

Some institutional investors scorn market timers. One American holding-company president, Robert H. Jeffrey, who sets policy for several outside money-managers retained by his company, went so far as to write a learned article mathematically proving the "folly of stock market timing." Analyzing the years 1926-1982, he found that "the maximum downside risk from timing was more than twice as great as the maximum upside reward." According to his figures, tables, and graphs, the market-timing strategist "has tremendous natural odds to overcome." It was akin to "driving on what seems to be the wrong side of the road just when the opposing traffic is the heaviest," in order to get to one's destination more quickly.

But market timing is a great marketing device if one is among the lucky monkeys. "Successful" market timing has the aura of superior and masterful knowledge. Large and numerous pension funds claim to make some use of market timing. One of the most "successful" and daring of market timers in Canada was Milton Wong of M. K. Wong Associates in Vancouver. He was known as a "superstar," a "cult figure," "The Maestro of Money." Clients flocked to him. Assets under his management increased exponentially, hitting $3.5 billion. Then, with the October 1987 crash, he missed the turn. But it was most lucrative while it lasted.

The fund managers help feed an entourage of economists, analysts, and traders, as well as sundry other researchers and suppliers. They keep the analysts and economists of the large brokerage firms well remunerated, through brokerage fees and research commissions, and also keep the many research boutiques in business. The money managers in Canada (buy-side analysts) select the "All-Star Analysts" line-up (sell-side analysts) published in the *Financial Post* every year, in ritual recognition of their relationship. In the United States, the "All-America Research Team" is saluted each year in the *Institutional Investor*.

But the bureaucracy doesn't end there. Given there is a bureaucracy, it was inevitable there would be consultants for the bureaucracy – pension-fund consultants. The largest, in the United States, has over nine hundred employees and associates worldwide and upwards of US$100 million in revenues, including the revenue of its own investment-management subsidiaries. Pension-fund consultants run searches on money managers – helping clients to choose them – and monitor their performance. Clients include pension officers of large blue-chip corporations – "sponsors," in the lingo. Consultants in the United States typically charge sponsors a hefty $20,000-$30,000 for a money-manager search. Actuarial and brokerage firms have also gotten into the act. In 1989, there were more than a hundred pension-consultant firms in the field in the United States – not bad considering that pension-fund consultants did not even exist a couple of decades earlier. One almost needed a consultant to choose a consultant. Profits in pension-fund consulting have soared.

This subsection has its own bureaucratic wrinkles. Legislation in the United States made pension officers liable for pension-fund mismanagement. The consultants played endlessly on this liability theme, equating the retaining of consultants to "due diligence," *Barron's* reported in a probing article on the cadres. "You need to hire us whether you need to or not," was the message, in effect. In fact, prosecutions involved only cases of gross mismanagement and fraud. But shaky corporate officers swallowed the consultants' bait anyway. Besides, the fees for the consultants did not come out of the pension officers' pockets. When the legislation went through, "signing up new clients was like shooting fish in a barrel," a former pension consultant recalled. Lawyers and actuaries are also retained.

Most important of all, perhaps, the consultant "offers the security of a cover-your-tail, third-party policy endorsement," commented *Barron's*. Faced with thousands of managers and a profusion of investment alternatives to choose from, the pension officer has the consultant as a cover, if things go awry: the "crutch" factor. The consultants, meanwhile, can't be hung either. The buzzword phrase in the bureaucracy, to describe their relationship to their clients, is "have influence over." It's a delightful example of "consultant boomfog," *Barron's* observed, "for 'influence' implies performance of a valuable function without responsibility for the investment results."

Like other consultants, pension consultants are highly creative when it comes to adding on make-work. There are now "full-service" pension-fund consultants, just as there are full-service investment banks, full-service management consultants, and full-service public-affairs groups. And, where there are full-service consultants, naturally there are consultant boutiques, too. Between them, they've dreamed up a whole catalogue of supplementary services, like "portfolio characteristic analysis" and "investment-program structure assistance," some of which are little more than voodoo, but all of which generate make-work and fees.

Other "products" are aimed at money managers themselves. One of these services is called "personal-style analysis" – purportedly trying to help the managers understand their strengths and weaknesses. The exercise used to be called "holding hands" or "a good talk," but as "personal-style analysis" it can be charged for at US$50,000-$60,000 annually (performance data and analysis document included). Another is "tactical asset allocation," the bureaucracy's doublespeak for market timing, typically developed in connection with some big-name quant from academia. High-quant bond-management consulting, using arcane mathematical analysis, is also in. One leading bond consultant, with a "product menu" of roughly twenty computer programs, charges clients up to several hundred thousand dollars a year *per service*. Whatever these models and analytic systems do or don't do, they "serve to 'stir the pot' and inspire fee-generating manager searches and portfolio revamps for consultants," *Barron's* commented.

Because money managers taken together cannot beat the market and end up uselessly shuffling paper back and forth, "passively" managed stock-index funds were born. These are collections of stocks based on stock indexes, usually the S&P 500. They don't try to beat the market, just reflect it. This dispenses with buying and selling different stocks, which dispenses, in turn, with analysts who look into the entrails of stocks. It also reduces administration and transaction (churning) costs. In this basic form, it really does cut down on bureaucracy. About 30 per cent of U.S. pension-fund assets invested in equities are in passive or semi-passive pools, according to consulting firm Greenwich Associates.

Bond-index funds were also created, for similar reasons. Active bond managers as a whole were getting regularly beaten by bond-index benchmarks. Bond-index funds were not so bad, however, for trading cadres. First, a pension plan's bondholdings had to be rejigged to match the index: trading profits. Then it had to be kept in sync because of maturing and called issues, downgrades, and so on: more trading profits. Annual turnover could hit as high as 40 per cent.

The inhabitants of the money-manager branch call the stock-index funds "no-brainers." A new subsection has arisen: the "closet indexers." These are so-called "active" managers, who allocate most of their portfolio outlay to index stocks (so they can't be embarrassed by the S&P 500) and who don't bother juggling the mix (just like proper indexers), but who collect the higher fees for "active" management.

Traditional money-manager gurus and analysts denounce indexers, if for no other reason than indexers have no use for the gurus and analysts. The latter call closet indexers "sheep-like" (this is a worse epithet, in the money-manager branch, than "crook" or "fraud"). One portfolio manager, describing his avocation as an "art form" – because it certainly wasn't science and what else is there? – dismissed index funds as "the artistic equivalent of painting by numbers." As indexation becomes more popular, the index becomes the market. This is derided as "investment socialism," as if calling it by that most wicked of all names, in the New Bureaucracy, was enough to damn it. Another epithet, "unAmerican," is almost as bad.

Indexers are also attacked as "parasitic" – with the indignation that only other parasites can muster. The active managers argue that with their analyses of companies and their stock bets, they price stocks properly and make the market "efficient." Those who play the game, but underperform the average, are as if martyrs to this higher purpose. The indexers, by contrast, simply batten onto the process. Stock-exchange officials, such as the president of the New York Stock Exchange, denounce indexers for putting brokers out of work and for casting a pall on Wall Street.

The anti-indexers, however, comfort themselves with thoughts of revenge. They reason that when the index becomes a factor in the market itself – with index funds, in effect, following their own tails without reference to underlying values – the anti-indexers will play against the indexers and reap the reward when the index ultimately corrects itself. The indexers, on the other hand, see the anti-indexers as financial luddites. They have also enhanced their own status by that most time-honoured of bureaucratic devices – giving themselves a high-sounding name. They call themselves "structured managers."

While this intrabureaucratic squabbling goes on, another phenomenon appears: the impulse of indexers themselves not to leave simplicity and common sense alone, to make things complicated – and to raise their fees accordingly. Index fund managers want to attract money (and hence fees) for their particular warren, so in search of an edge they "actively manage" the "passive" funds, in classic make-work fashion. One fund, for example, uses a bankruptcy screen; it decides whether to hold stocks of bankrupts or near-bankrupts in the fund, although they are part of the index and should be held regardless. Also, the index funds, while not playing stocks against each other, play futures and stocks against each other instead (remember "index arbitrage"?). Index-fund managers also use stock-index options to try to enhance returns.

Sitting in their offices, busy making work, institutional money managers have also concocted a new index "product" called a "tilted fund." A tilted fund is jargon for a custom-made index, with selected inclusions and exclusions packaged together to compete against a conventional index. Ordinary indexes allow for some proliferation of index funds, but the funds are colourless and the management fee is miserable. Tilted funds, on the other hand, are tutti-frutti next to the plain vanilla S&P 500. The swirls and nuts and colours allow for endless combinations. Index funds are now created to replicate a "management style." Instead of playing stock against stock, the tilted fund managers play index against index. This occupies their time and boosts the fee to around 0.25 per cent of a portfolio, or as much as ten times the lowest management fee for a plain vanilla S&P 500 index.

"Tactical asset allocation" (TAA) – high-quant computerized market-timing strategic models – is another money-manager fashion. Instead of playing stocks against stocks, TAA managers play stocks, or stock-index funds, against bonds and Treasury bills ("asset classes," they're called). Once started, endless elaboration follows. Progressively complicated models come out of the box. "You customize a program for each [client]," says a proud money manager. Futures, options, and endless hedging strategies are added. TAA, with its proliferating asset classes and its "styles" and "sectors" within them, ends up with much of the complication of choosing stocks.

By moving in and out of stocks, bonds and other instruments, TAA also generates more brokerage fees. TAA managers, in communion with their computers, may move funds as often as once a month – no slouches as churners. One Los Angeles tactical allocator changes the mix on average every two weeks. "Some tactical asset allocators," the *Institutional Investor* remarked, "appear to be applying an electric beater to turnover." Best of all, the management fees for TAA, estimated in the 0.6 per cent range, are higher than for passively managed index funds. They're not quite as high as the top range of traditional active-management fees (0.7 to 1.0 per cent) but they're getting there.

The bureaucratic elaboration wasn't quite finished yet. The derivative-paper branch also saw the possibilities of playing to the insecurites of institutional investors. Institutional money managers had used stock-index futures for index arbitrage and so-called portfolio insurance and had also used related options strategies. As the 1980s ended, the call went out to get the institutions involved in futures and options in all their complexity and endless variations. The talking up of the derivatives' wonders and virtues increased exponentially, not least on the part of the new layer of "risk management" consultants, whose own fees would multiply the more that institutional investors got tied up trying to figure out the derivatives. The new "new products," with their dazzling hues and catchy names – "dynamic hedging," "option replication," and so on – had a particularly useful quality for the purpose: They seemed to promise, without necessarily doing so, that they could capture all of the possible gains on the upside while risking none of the possible losses on the downside. Of course, just like perpetual motion, it couldn't be done, but that wasn't important.

Every little bit helps. *Fortune*, in 1988, estimated that American companies, not to mention public pension plans, were forking over US$30 billion each year in fees to a "growing gaggle of service providers" – pension-fund consultants, brokers, money managers, lawyers, actuaries, and other cadres who inhabit the pension-fund section of the money-manager branch.

Mutual funds are another bureaucratic overlay. They didn't exist anywhere until 1924, when the first one was put together in the United States, and a few followed to take advantage of the stock market frenzy. The speculative delusion was so wild at the time that talk about the stock market's wonders spread beyond the narrow confines of the usual stock investor and gave the early mutual-fund sellers a hook. In 1940 there was only US$448 million in mutual-fund assets spread over approximately sixty-eight funds. In 1950 there was $2.5 billion in assets in ninety-eight funds. By contrast, in 1990 there was $1.1 trillion in 3,122 funds (of which $245 billion were in equity funds). In the decade 1981-1990, the number of funds increased by almost five times.

In Canada, similarly, mutual funds, totalling just C$638 million in 1961, hit $4.5 billion in 1980, shot up to to $12 billion in 1985, and then skyrocketed to $34 billion by the end of 1990 ($40 billion, including insurance funds). The *Financial Post*, as of that date, listed 532 different funds (643, including insurance funds). Some mutual-fund cadres are grandiosely predicting $200 billion in assets in Canada by the end of the decade, including money-market funds. "Fund management," said a New York investment-bank analyst in pre-crash 1987, "is an international growth industry."

In all these cases, economic development and the savings for it came first. Mutual funds came later, at the tag-end in terms of economic history, like the flea on the wart on the frog on the bump on the log. Their bureaucratic machinery and endless trading don't add equity capital to enterprise, except when a fund buys a segment of a share issue and the share issue is actually for a productive rather than a paper-shuffling purpose. But then, as we've seen, stock markets in general have played a small or negligible role in raising money for enterprise.

The ostensible function of mutual funds is to help people with modest savings and little or no expertise make a killing, or at least to do better than if they invested elsewhere. The original mutual funds bought common stocks. Although now, in the United States, both money-market and bond fund categories are larger, measured by assets, the equity funds are still special and beckon the public with glimpses of the pot of gold at the end of the rainbow. They draw on the myth and ideology of stock markets. They allow small investors to get into the stock market and capture the same rewards as the wealthy player and the speculator. Professionally managed, they also eliminate the risk of individual investors being taken for suckers because of inadequate or belated information. The investors are saved having to deal with brokers or having to keep an eye on stocks or doing much of anything at all other than placing their money. The mutual fund pools the work and handles stock trades in bulk at lower per-share commissions.

Not that they do particularly well for investors. Like pension-fund investment advisers, mutual fund managers struggle to keep pace with the market. Lipper Analytical Services is the leading mutual-fund measurement service in the United States. Its performance tables and listings appear quarterly in *Barron's*. For the decade 1981 to 1990 inclusive, the average cumulative return of U.S. equity funds reinvested trailed the return on the S&P 500 by 26 per cent, and the broader Wilshire 5000 index by 12 per cent. For the last five years of the decade, it trailed the S&P 500 by 32 per cent. A calculation done by *Forbes* for the two market cycles June 1983 to June 1989, taking in the 1980s bull market, showed that only one in ten domestic American stock funds beat the S&P over that period.

Measured in terms of principal invested, mutual funds as a group typically underperform the market by an average of 2 per cent a year, *Business Week* summed it up. Sometimes the funds forge ahead for a period. When, for example, the stocks of the large companies in the S&P 500 languish and the stock prices of smaller companies rise faster, the mutual funds, with their broader holdings, reflect that difference. This doesn't mean that fund managers have suddenly become more clever, however. Next to a more representative benchmark, like the Wilshire 5000, they may still be trailing. These measures are exclusive of sales charges that set back the funds' net performance even more. Moreover, several of the worst of the stock funds had been merged out of existence and thus erased from the records. If they had been included in the analysis, the average performance of the stock funds would have been even less impressive.

Inevitably, by the law of averages, some mutual funds do extraordinarily well in a given period. For every one of those, however, there is another one that does extraordinarily badly. The former can be marketed heavily. The latter can be forgotten. This gives the impression that mutual funds are just a little short of miraculous and that their managers are benefactors of mankind.

The performance of Canadian equity funds is much the same. The *Financial Post* Mutual Fund Performance Survey for the decade ending

December 31, 1990, showed a ten-year average annual compound rate of return of 6.9 per cent. The market benchmark, the TSE Total Return Index, came in at 7.6 per cent. The five-year performance record, similarly, was 4.3 per cent (equity funds) as compared to 5.8 (TSE benchmark). This lagging mutual-fund performance again is calculated without sales or redemption charges being taken into account, which would tarnish performance results further.

In other words, if you had substantial savings to invest, you would have been better off, on average, investing in a basket of stocks yourself and letting the eggs in that basket grow instead of supporting some mutual fund's overheads. (In fact, the TSE has devised a basket product for just such a purpose, but stockbrokers have given it a fish eye; it earns them only half the commission of a mutual-fund sale.) Even if mutual funds together did outperform the averages, however, they would simply be capturing profits for the benefit of one fraction of the population at the expense of another fraction of the population – more paper shuffling.

The underlying function of mutual funds is to support a bureaucracy of managers and dealers who create, manage, and sell the funds. They feed on the overhead fees. There is a "load fee" for most stock-based (equity) mutual funds in Canada. The traditional load fee is a "front-end load" – a percentage of one's investment paid at the beginning. For equity funds in Canada in the 1980s, it ranged up to 9 per cent (9.9 per cent of the net amount left over).

The pitch to customers is that the fee is a one-time payment. This makes it a bit easier to swallow. But mutual fund investments are continually being redeemed (people pulling out) while new mutual fund purchases are being made. Each time people pull out, they leave their load fees behind. Each time somebody makes a new fund purchase, another load fee goes into the pot (unless it involves just a transfer from one fund to another in the same group, in which case the load fee is waived or a smaller transfer fee is paid). With this taken into account, the cost to the customer of front-end load fees averaged about 2 per cent of the investment per year in the 1980s, based on a sales charge of 8 per cent and an average hold of four years.

Most of the front-end load fee goes to paying commissions to the dealers, brokers, or in-house salespeople who peddle the mutual funds (split between the dealer organization and the salesperson). Mutual funds are sold, not bought. It's a little like the old life insurance business. Economically wasteful up-front commissions are allocated to keep agents busy and to keep sales going, thereby to keep assets piling up and the whole of the machinery turning over.

On top of the load fees are the expense fees – a "management fee" to the fund-management company (from which it takes a profit, in turn), plus a supplementary *pro-rata* charge covering custodial, legal, and audit fees and similar costs. This "expense ratio" cuts into the fund's return, hence is indirectly borne by the investor. For the largest equity funds in Canada (over $600 million in assets) it ranged from 1.88 per cent to 2.5 per cent as of 1991. A few equity funds have expense ratios of more than 3 per cent. The average for all front-load funds is about 1.75 per cent.

When the high 8 to 9 per cent front-end load fees began meeting too much resistance, after the 1980s' bull-market excitement abated, the charges were reduced. On a middle-sized investment, say $5,000, 5 per cent is now a typical front-end load. Some funds eliminated sales charges altogether or offered new funds or optional arrangements without acquisition fees. In most of these cases, however, there is a redemption fee, paid when the customer leaves the fund. This is known as a "rear-end load" or a "back-end load." The redemption fee declines slowly, eventually to zero, the longer the customer stays in the fund. These back-load funds proved popular and now account for the vast majority of sales of independent fund companies.

The mutual-fund organizations, however, made up for the reduced front-end loads with higher annual management fees. As for the shortfall or delay on back-end loads, this was compensated for by even higher management fees, on average. Fortunately for the back-load funds, too, redemptions occur on average while part of the rear-end load fee is still due. A rough calculation, reported in the *Financial Post*, showed (surprise!) that the average rake-off from rear-end loads was more or less exactly what it had been from front-end loads.

Mutual funds are supposed to be particularly suited for small investors but, as *Canadian Business* once described it, a small investor who starts with a high load fee, and carrying the annual expense charge, has some catching up to do. A healthy return in the first year is necessary just to get the investor's holdings back to the original outlay. The most successful equity fund, moreover, has bad years, which have to be swallowed. Depending on how well stocks do generally compared to interest rates, the small investor may have to hang in for a long, long time, paying the overheads, before getting ahead of conventional investments like term deposits, but still falling behind the stock-market benchmark. Rear-end load funds end up adding the same burden, but more indirectly.

The cost of the expense fee and the load fee (annualized), plus brokerage commissions for the fund's stock transactions, works out to something like 3.65 per cent on average, a hefty slice. Net of the charges, the average annual compound rate of return of Canadian equity funds, including dividends, was 4.9 per cent for the ten years ending December 31, 1990, based on data from the *Financial Post* Mutual Funds Performance Survey. Canada Savings Bonds, by comparison, reflecting high interest rates in the 1980s, averaged 17.9 per cent compounded in this period. Discounted for inflation, the compound return on equity funds, net of all fees, was just 2.8 per cent annually for those years. The overhead costs of the mutual-fund bureau-cracy were greater than the real net gain of their clientele. Even using the ten years to the end of 1989 as a measure, before the stock markets tumbled in 1990, the real return, discounted for inflation, was only 4.2 per cent annu-ally – not much better. At the same time, the value of the investors' principal was being undermined by inflation, leaving them with a net loss overall, in constant dollars. Somebody who invested C$1,000 in a Canadian equity fund at the end of 1980, and held on, ended up, on average, with just $870, in 1990.

If, for the purpose of selling to the customer, load fees and redemption fees can be passed off as a one-time payment, the annual expense fees can be finessed because they are small in percentage terms. A bureaucracy, however, needs only a small percentage annually of a large pool of assets to keep afloat and to grow fat. And as long as accumulated assets don't fade away through massive withdrawals, the fund-management companies collect their annual management fees indefinitely, like an annuity. "Mining the lucrative mutual fund market," a Canadian Press business reporter once innocently described it.

"Somewhere along the line the client must pay the commission," a mutual-fund executive put it baldly. In 1986, a particularly good year, the top Canadian mutual-fund salespeople pulled down $750,000 each in com-missions. "My income is outrageous," one admitted. Not surprisingly, enrol-ment in the mutual-fund dealers course shot up, adding to the ranks of stockbrokers, independent dealers, insurance-company salespeople, and the countless cadres in banks and trust companies who sell the funds.

Fund-management companies, other than those with an in-house sales force like the Investors Group, compete with each other to get brokers and dealers to sell their funds. To a large extent, they sell to these cadres rather than to investors. It helps to have a good performance record, but it helps even more to treat the cadres right. Freebies for better performers, such as trips to exotic locations, were used in the 1980s in Canada to generate enthusiasm for particular funds, before regulatory pressures put a damper on them. Another wrinkle is trailer fees – small percentages that go out to dealers and brokers annually on sales they have made which stay with a fund – an annuity for the dealers. This gives the dealers an incentive, in turn, to keep people tied to a fund or fund group. Yet another device is to pay above-average commission rates to stockbrokers. Fidelity Investments Canada did this in 1990 and, lo and behold, sales shot up dramatically; a survey soon showed Fidelity was rated first overall by brokers. Does this mean that the brokers or dealers, supposed to be independent advisers, might push or defend a particular "product" rather than another in order to fare better themselves? No matter. This conflict of interest, between advice for the client, on the one hand, and revenue for the broker advising the client, on the other, is an integral part of the stock-market branch, as it has been all the while for life insurance, so why not let it pass for this money-management sister branch as well?

In the bull market of the 1980s, everybody rushed to get into the act. U.S. investment banks established their own funds. *Business Week* reported how pressure was put on brokers to sell their firms' high-commission in-house products, in order to boost gross commissions as well as add to lucrative management-fee income. (To add to the injury, most of these house-brand funds have turned out to be dismal performers.) Commercial banks, trust companies, and insurance companies created their own funds. Insurance agents doubling as mutual-fund dealers began selling double-barrelled mutual-fund and insurance packages all at once, where the mutual-fund placement is financed with borrowed money and the insurance covers the borrower's life.

There is room at the bottom as well as the top. One Wall Street firm, First Investors, sells door to door, much like life-insurance sales of old. As described by *Forbes* reporters Matthew Schifrin and Laura Walbert, in a 1987 exposé, First Investors' army of low-paid and inexperienced salespeople waltzed into people's living rooms and spouted a carefully rehearsed sales pitch. "Front-end load" became "method of plan deductions," in the spiel. There were scripted responses to most questions. The sales force was rigged pyramid fashion. Sellers recruited other sellers and took a slice of the commissions their recruits earned. Top managers, getting slices of everybody else's slices at the end of the chain, did particularly well. (Predictably, one of the principals had a private plane, a farm in the Midwest, a condo in Florida, and a house in Nantucket.)

First Investors aimed at people who saved $100 a month, people whom other brokers weren't interested in and who were also, usually, more naive. For ordinary sales, they charged a top load fee of up to 8.5 per cent. Great emphasis, though, was put on contractual plans where, for example, the client agreed to put $100 a month into one of the funds for fifteen years. Over the full fifteen years, the sales commission could amount to 10 per cent, a healthy take. But, on top of that, a disproportionate part of the commission was paid in the early years. Half of the first year's "investment" went to paying commissions. The unfortunate clients were hard-pressed just to break even, forgetting about inflation, unless they kept contributing for five years or more. Worse still, the funds in the group had been largely poor performers, even given the general mediocrity of mutual funds.

But the best part for this mutual-fund subsection was the drop-out rate. The excuse for the contractual plan was that it aimed at people who needed discipline to save. The dropout rate, though, was around 50 per cent. The high up-front commissions, left behind, fed the pyramid.

First Investors, with slightly lower charges but with its contractual plan intact, continues to peddle mutual funds today.

The First Investors' manner of selling funds is extreme, but its general objective is much the same as the object of mutual funds as a whole – to gather commissions and fees by appealing to people's lack of investment ability and often to their greed. Also like First Investors, mutual funds use sophisticated advertising with selected details to capture customers. And, again like the First Investors' operation, albeit less so, there is a regular dropout rate, in the form of redemptions, leaving the up-front or redemption fees in the dealers' and the fund company's pockets.

Trading costs, which are charged against a fund, pile up, too. Equity mutual funds are great portfolio churners, if U.S. figures are any indication. According to Chicago-based Investment Information Services, the average U.S. equity fund turns over an extraordinary 92 per cent of its portfolio annually. This feeds the stock-market branch. Annual turnovers of 300 or 400 per cent are common. Some go even higher, into the 500 to 700 per cent range. A sample edition of the mutual-fund survey in *Barron's* turned up a growth (equity) fund with an annual turnover of 929 per cent and a fixed-income (bond) fund with a turnover of 999 per cent! Mind you, high-turnover funds, with their higher costs, do less well than low-turnover funds, just as churning pension-fund managers do less well than non-churners.

The dealers, brokers and in-house salespeople steadily, insistently, expand the mutual-fund section, through sales. The section also inflates, however, by creating new funds and then variants of new funds. In the late 1980s, when people were becoming sceptical of mutual-fund managers' stock-picking abilities, stock-index funds were created. Then some companies altered them to make them sound better. Half of these altered index funds, in one U.S. survey, had expense ratios as high as actively managed funds. "If camels are horses designed by a committee, then some fancy new index funds are the camels of the mutual fund business," snorted *Forbes*.

Or take publicly available futures funds (in limited partnership form). Unlike equity funds, whose value can grow with corporate expansion, they play in a zero-sum game. A fund's return consists of whatever it can wring out of other professional traders and suckers, less whatever those other professional traders wring out of the funds, less the bureaucratic overheads and management rewards for which the funds have been created in the first place. Somebody has to pay for the bureaucratic motion and for feeding the derivative-paper branch.

This is what happens. The average return of 2.3 per cent in the years

1980-1988 (as covered by the study of the period) did not even keep up with inflation, much less match a savings account. Fully a quarter of such funds were wound up over the period, after an annual average return of minus 20 per cent. Given past figures, the odds of a fund dissolving within a ten-year period, from poor performance, were in the 50 per cent range. If mutual funds are a circular exercise, economically speaking, and are created and promoted out of bureaucratic momentum, futures funds, taken together, are the most patently futile, silly, and circular exercise of them all.

They do, however, make bureaucratic sense, which is the point. Management fees can exceed 5 per cent and management fees and transaction costs together range from 15 to over 19 per cent a year. Given those overheads, there has been a bureaucratic rush into the subsection. The major U.S. investment banks, trying to maintain cadres after the 1987 crash, eagerly offered new commodity funds despite their horrible general record. Futures brokers and other underwriters also rushed to launch new funds. As these new public commodity funds surfaced, generating sales and marketing efforts in the process, assets in this category in the United States rose from only US$140 million in 1980 to $1 billion in 1987 and to a sudden $3 billion by the end of 1988.

Fixed-income funds (mostly bond and mortgage funds) and money-market funds aren't much better, despite their low expense charges. Average performance of fixed-income funds in Canada, for example, trailed the benchmark (the ScotiaMcLeod Universe Bond Index) for the three-year, five-year, and ten-year periods ending in 1990. It even trailed Canada Savings Bonds, making up some ground only in 1991 when interest rates declined (and hence bond portfolios rose in value). Bond funds, nevertheless, are bread-and-butter for the mutual-fund bureaucracy. They can be sold as being ever so much safer than equity funds, but still benefitting from the magic of the fund manager's expertise. Clients can also be switched to bond funds when the goings-on of the stock market make them fear for the value of any equity-fund units they hold. The fees, in this manner, keep coming in.

Money-market funds (which invest in Treasury bills, for example) serve mostly to park money – a traditional banking function. In the United States, they are the largest category of mutual funds as measured by assets. They have been growing quickly in Canada, too. For the mutual-fund groups, the money-market funds bring in at least some fees, low as they are, and help to defray overheads. Forget that they, too, in Canada, like equity and bonds funds, have generally trailed their benchmark (Treasury bills) by more or less their expenses, the cost of which comes out of the clients' pockets. One Canadian investment dealer allowed that if you have $10,000 or more, you're probably better off investing the money yourself. Plays on currency exchange rates – another circular exercise – are dressed up as international money-market funds.

The mutual-fund section enthusiastically fed LBOs, with junk-bond ("high-yield-bond") funds or fixed-income funds with a junk-bond element, taking advantage of the LBO excitement. As late as 1983, junk-bond funds did not even exist. By 1988, at their peak, there were 102 of them in the United States, accounting for an estimated 30 per cent of all junk-bond money. Junk-bond mutual funds that helped leverage the takeover of Federated Department Stores by Campeau Corp., and of Allied Stores before it, lost a good slice of their value as those particular bonds plummeted and then defaulted. Junk-bond funds as a whole reeled from the LBO fall-out.

"Hybrids" were concocted. Hybrids combine several elements, each of which has a marketing angle that can be played on. Dealers could, for example, sell risk and safety at the same time, with a hybrid – say a futures fund with a guarantee attached, bizarre as it sounds. There is always a catch to these artifices, but only for the client; bureaucratically, they're wonderful. One early hybrid was a high-income, triple-bond, closed-end confection put together by a U.S. mutual-fund group. It invested in a blend of U.S. Treasury bonds, international bonds, and junk-bonds – upgrading the plain vanilla of separate funds in those areas into one super-duper combination, "Howard Johnson" style, as *Forbes* put it: "Strawberry, chocolate, tutti-frutti." Other concocters followed. One created a seven-sector bond fund. The idea is that management will cleverly alter the mix to generate higher yields – a little more chocolate this time, less tutti-frutti. The management fee for that cleverness has to be a little higher than most. Also, to do the required tricks, portfolio turnover has to be high, chewing up a chunk of the return in transaction costs. Naturally, for devising such a wonderful combination, there is also a substantial underwriting fee to begin with.

In one brilliant piece of hybridization, a mutual fund was created offering the combined genius of five well-known stock pickers. It bombed in performance. One marginal but aspiring Canadian futures fund similarly hired five advisers, which suggested that the fund wasn't all that risky (five advisers can't all be wrong at the same time). Their number also added pretension to the fund's image. Cynics might say that a mutual fund's virtue is supposed to be the wisdom of its manager, and that five managers cancel each other out, but that's not the point. Some funds, marketing themselves as "advisers' funds," will have as many as nine advisers managing them.

"Multi-asset" funds are the new wave. They combine everything under the sun, from short-selling to junk bonds to the most esoteric derivative-paper hedging strategies. Since different managers are required for different allocations, a small army of cadres is needed. One such fund had twelve managers for just the futures and options half of its assets. This bureaucratic flowering is the product of "volatility analysis." Volatility analysis is money-manager bureaucratese for immensely complicated, computer-fed, miles-of-print-out calculations which show that if you spread your bets . . . there is less volatility. Bureaucratic abstraction generates bureaucratic subdivision and the bureaucratese to cover it.

Another species in the same genre is the "asset allocation" fund, promising to make your fortune with that old nostrum, market timing. Here as before, and inevitably, the exercise is futile and pointless overall. "Worse than useless," *Forbes* jibed in a survey of the funds. But mutual-fund cadres, like pension-fund advisers, can flog the concept anyway under the impressive-sounding "asset allocation" name.

Alongside the hybrids are the special varieties, capable of endless proliferation – the "specialization jungle," one adviser called it. Sector funds split off into leisure, health care, biotechnology, even oceanography funds. Speculative funds exploit, in mutual-fund form, the same mythology that props up penny-stock promoters. One noted Canadian group of three speculative funds lost money just like any sucker. A $100 investment in 1979 in the most dismal of the three would have yielded only $49 a decade later in 1989, disregarding the added punishment of inflation and lost interest in the interim. A similar investment in Canada Savings Bonds would have grown to $278.

In 1987, pumped up by the heat of the bull market, the mutual-fund section in the United States added 146 new equity funds (an increase of 21 per cent in that year alone). In 1988, when several billion dollars were taken out of equity funds by disillusioned investors, the number of such funds increased even more as a way of maintaining the size and turnover of the section.

Meanwhile the proliferation was undermining some of the rationale of mutual funds. Fund managers had long preached the principle of diversification. Otherwise investors might as well pick a few stocks of their own and bypass the funds' expense ratio. The specialty funds, however, first introduced in the early 1980s to add turnover, violate that principle, leaving investors open to the same kind of volatility and losses they would risk by going it alone.

There are so many funds, it is almost as difficult now to pick a fund as to pick a stock or basket of stocks, defeating their purpose altogether. U.S. investment advisers like to say there are more stock funds than there are major stocks. There are four-fifths again as many mutual funds in the United States (3,122 at the end of 1990) as there are common stocks listed on the New York Stock Exchange (1,741). Even excluding money market and short-term municipal bond funds from the total, which leaves stock, bond, and income funds, the number of U.S. mutual funds still outstrips the NYSE listings.

Attempting to choose skilfully among the 1,133 stock funds or, in Canada, the 260 stock funds, requires the same licking of pencils and poring over of figures by the conscientious investor as does choosing stocks. Even the president of the Investment Funds Institute of Canada, the mutual-fund trade association, felt obliged to point out that choosing a mutual fund "requires a great deal of homework and soul-searching." He meant to underline how important and portentous investing in a mutual fund was. But mutual funds are supposed to be an easy way out, where somebody else does the homework.

Long-term and short-term rates of return, variability, expense ratio, load or redemption fee, who the manager is, and how long the manager has been around all have to be factored in when making a choice. This exercise too, however, like picking stocks, is quixotic, because past performance is no guarantee of future performance. Some experts warn against taking actual percentage growth figures (the measure of past performance) too seriously. They point out that all the new funds don't have a long-term record in any case, and stress the need to size up the managers of funds instead. But that is a quixotic exercise, too. "The funds are just travelling from one group of baffled people [managers] to another," opines one Toronto investment authority. "I don't think there's much distinction between fund managers and people. You have as many idiot fund managers as good ones. You can't tell which are which, reliably. By the time the track record is reliable enough to say something, the guy's too old."

To comfort the perplexed, the mutual-fund bureaucracy has spawned an inevitable newsletter subsection. These advisory newsletters, mostly in the United States, bear such names as *Money Fund Report*, the *Mutual-fund Letter*, the *Mutual Fund Forecaster*, the *Telephone Switch Newsletter*, *Mutual Fund Investing*, *Growth Guide Fund*, *No Load Fund-X*, *Professional Tape Reader*, or, in some cases, the name of the individual publisher. The newsletters do no better than the funds themselves, which collectively underperform the market. Indeed, they may do worse. In 1989, Mark Hulbert, editor of the *Hulbert Financial Digest*, which tracks newsletters, did an analysis for *Forbes* of investment-letter portfolios that advise on fund timing and selection. Of the twelve that had records going back two market cycles to 1983, only one beat the S&P 500. Following the newsletters' advice, an investor would have ended up with one-third less money on average than if he or she had simply bought an S&P basket. A thirteenth newsletter portfolio, of international mutual funds, underperformed its benchmark by 45 per cent. On the other hand, Hulbert noted wryly, the funds themselves, with only one in ten beating the market in that period, weren't much to boast about, either.

Analytic boutiques, like Lipper Analytical Services and Morningstar in the United States, generate reams of data and paper. Newspapers and magazines like *Barron's*, *Forbes*, *Business Week* and, in Canada, the *Financial Post* run mutual-fund data surveys, plus periodic feature sections filled with the latest chatter. Commentators opine on mutual funds from time to time in newspapers, business papers, and magazines. If that's not enough ink and paper for angst-ridden mutual-fund investors, there are also handbooks to be bought.

If that's still not enough, one can always ask a "financial counsellor" for mutual-fund advice, and pay for that, too. Or one can turn to a "fund-picking service" – yet another bureaucratic layer, a fringe one, but interesting. There are eight or nine such services in the United States. A couple of them have sprouted from mutual-fund newsletter operations – sub-subsections of a subsection. They take money under management and invest it in different mutual funds. Their particular bureaucratic genius is that they add annual percentage charges – more management fees – to the fees of the mutual funds in which they place money. They're mutual-fund bureaucrats' petty bureaucrats, "double dipping" into the investor's pocket. "The dumbest idea in years," *Forbes* described it.

The mutual-fund section as a whole, meanwhile, is pushed along by the weight of its own bureaucracy – impressive performers being paraded and, when they fade away, other impressive performers, arising by the law of averages, taking their place and maintaining the image. A company with a "family" of mutual funds can do this internally – prop itself up by pushing the ones that happen to be successful at any given time (today's stars may be tomorrow's duds) while keeping mum about, merging out of existence, or phasing out family members that don't do so well. This technique, among many others, was pioneered by the nefarious Investors Overseas Service (IOS) in the 1960s, which came to a sorry, scandal-ridden end. Similarly, sponsors of single-country closed-end funds can cite fabulously successful funds for particular countries as past examples, although the majority of single-country funds have done very poorly.

High-cost funds exploit the same mechanism. If they have a good year, and some inevitably do, they are able to push sales up despite their high expense charges and the law of averages, which dictates that most of them will fall behind because of their expenses. One such extreme case was a U.S. fund operator catchily named "44 Wall Street." It had a 19.3 per cent return in 1988, so it could pass off its expense ratio of 10.9 per cent, about seven times the U.S. mutual fund average, as unimportant. Its cumulative ten-year record, though, was a negative 53 per cent, and that in a bull market where the S&P 500 reinvested rose 354 per cent. The fund's cumulative five-year record was even worse – minus 78 per cent. The technique of "sawing off" embarrassing parts of the record was also pioneered by the IOS group.

Some hopeless funds, if they're not wound up, get passed around like orphans to different managing firms. Dismal performance doesn't necessarily mean the managers will get the boot or even that they'll take a reduction in their fee ratio. They'll protest to shareholders that their fees fall well within the average.

Banks and trust companies, by using their sheer bureaucratic muscle, can protect their own groups of mutual funds. Through their mail-outs, advertising, and regular contact with customers, they can prop up funds even if performance isn't wonderful. The largest independent group in the United States, Fidelity, had US$69 billion in retail mutual funds under management as of the end of 1990, plus another $50 billion in institutional funds (pension and trust funds), most of which goes into mutual funds. This mutual-fund money is captured in just over two hundred different funds, so that a client need never be lost to Fidelity's embrace. There are, as well, new funds in the deep freeze waiting to be warmed up, although after the two-hundred mark, there is not much new in the way of funds to come up with. Following the 1987 crash, Fidelity's sales slumped and it cut back its workforce by 30 per cent, but the number of funds was increased, by about sixty or seventy through to the spring of 1989 – an additional two-thirds – in an attempt to use the proliferation of new funds to retain and increase turnover.

Fidelity's special bureaucratic genius is that it has created a mini-stock-market branch under its own roof, from which it draws the overhead. Many of its new funds are sector funds. Fidelity encourages investors in these funds to pick an industry they think will be a strong performer, and then to switch as conditions change. There are also funds that specialize in over-the-counter stocks, undervalued assets, turnaround companies, high-growth (but risky) possibilities and out-of-favour issues. Investors in all these funds in effect play the market – contrary to the diversification principle of mutual funds – while Fidelity year in and year out collects a fee on their assets.

Meanwhile, customers distraught or nervous about stock markets altogether are recaptured in the "short-term end of the market" – Fidelity's money-market funds. When these customers look kindly on stock funds again, Fidelity will still have them in the stable, and collect the stock funds' higher commissions. Fidelity's revenues – taken out of funds under management, for overheads and profits – were US$1.3 billion in 1990. It had 6.2 million retail accounts, including people handling farmed-out pension money in their own name.

The father of Fidelity's current CEO and dominant shareholder, who built up the company in the post-war years, frequently laced his dissertations on the market with references to Chinese and Zen Buddhist philosophers to try to explain the market's vagaries. The reality is bureaucratic machinery: multiplying funds, computer analysts, myriad industry and stock analysts, masses of research reports (most of which go into giant trash cans), thousands of service and marketing employees working phones and computers, traders working their phones and computers, a thousand new PCs to run specially developed software, and MBAs coming out of the woodwork.

The fund managers work this paper and verbal machinery and buy and sell shares in their endless, and economically unproductive, cycle. Fidelity itself declines to release compensation information, even average figures. Salary plus bonuses for experienced fund-manager cadres in the United States generally, however, are reported to be in the US$300,000 to $800,000 range. Those who happen at any time to have a good record can do better. A few are comfortably into seven figures. Several million a year is not unusual. Fidelity's leading fund manager in the late 1980s, Peter Lynch, made $3-$4 million annually plus three-year performance fees that, in some of those years, could have as much as doubled his take, according to *Financial World* and *Business Week* sources. The firm's principal was pulling in around $6 million at the time. Analysts with only a few years' experience can make $150,000 at firms like Fidelity.

Turning this machinery over, and helping to produce these rake-offs, is advertising. It is the most important mutual-fund subsection of all. "Massive advertising campaigns" and "awesome marketing machine," is how *Fortune* has described the feeding method, in Fidelity's case. Fidelity's annual spending on advertising has been estimated as high as US$60 million, most prominently for a sledgehammer campaign of weekly full-page ads in newspaper business sections and, increasingly, for television. Dreyfus reportedly spends about $40 million, and the U.S. mutual-fund section as a whole, about $120 million. Fidelity uses direct marketing as well as media, including a monthly newsletter distributed free to all Fidelity accounts. The cost of getting a customer into the house comes to an estimated $100, mostly in advertising. It's a bit like selling perfume, Fidelity's marketing head explained. "People are buying hope and the future," he said. Inculcating the corporate "brand" – branding the market – is a key advertising objective, whereby a few big players commanding substantial advertising budgets can gradually dominate the section and have an extra margin to play with.

Fidelity had one hugely successful fund, the Magellan Fund. Exclude it and the group's equity funds on average did no better than the S&P 500. But Fidelity was able to advertise the Magellan Fund and any other hot performer, and ignore the laggards. "Magellan has done extremely well," complained one competitor, "but the rest is just tonnage."

The advertising and the concoction of new funds go together. "Fidelity views new funds the way Kellogg views new cereals: as another opportunity to further segment a market and lure new customers," *Fortune* described it. "There's no limit to the number of funds we can offer," Fidelity's marketing head chimed. Others in the field follow suit as best they can. Somebody has to pay for the advertising, fund proliferation, and other overheads. Fidelity, after the 1987 crash, gradually increased its various fees and added sales charges, without any effect on sales; advertising props up sales charges and fees, which prop up advertising and help other overheads as well. *Fortune*, in 1986, commenting on this process, observed that the more-expensive load funds had outsold no-loads by a two to one margin for years, although they performed no better. Even at the end of the decade, with no-loads having made inroads, load funds still outsold them.

In Canada, the Mackenzie Financial Corp., manager of the Industrial Group of Funds and the Mackenzie Group of Funds, is the best-known marketer among mutual-fund companies. It is the second-largest mutual-fund group in the country, after the Investors Group. Like Fidelity, Mackenzie has cranked up its take despite its load charges, in no small part because of its massive advertising and marketing campaigns. The marketing includes sponsorship of a racing car that competes on the North American Indy circuit. It dispenses an annual freebie junket in Canada to brokers and dealers, under the guise of an educational conference. Until regulatory pressure finally forced a change, the "conference" visited places like Nashville, New Orleans, Monaco, and Hong Kong. ("Once again this year our primary goal will be education, but who said education has to be dull?" the brochure advertising the Nashville excursion put it.) Up to 1,500 brokers and dealers have been invited to the outing. The very top sellers (the top fifteen) received such extra bonuses as a Mediterranean luxury cruise (valued at $18,500) and an excursion from Paris to Venice on the Orient Express. This helped to keep the dealers serving up Mackenzie.

When Mackenzie Financial's much-flogged Industrial Growth Fund had a lacklustre year in 1989 (they made a "big call on metals," which didn't "work for them"), they shifted their advertising focus to its twenty-year performance track record, from its ten-year record, to soften the impact on the numbers.

According to one specialist, about half of all mutual-fund buyers make their decision through reading or watching media ads, without bothering to glance at a prospectus, much less to ponder over all the baloney-sandwich advice in the money pages of newspapers or do the existential awareness exercises ("know your objectives") and complicated factor analysis the baloney slicers recommend.

The statistics themselves can be misleading. A fund may hit a lucky stock when it's small and the stock is a substantial part of its holdings, giving it an extraordinary percentage return for that year. This will be averaged on an equal basis with future years, although then the fund is large. This skews the long-term results upwards. It's known as the "Dreyfus effect." Dreyfus had a huge chunk of Polaroid shares, which led to spectacular results in its first few years. Eye-catching average rates of return are only good if the investor got in at the beginning of the time-frame mentioned – neither earlier nor later.

Adding another bureaucratic layer are the financial planners and personal money managers, the third section of the New Bureaucracy's money-manager branch.

There are financial planners who give advice, others who also manage funds, and others who give advice while selling "financial products" (earning commissions on those sales by getting people to take their advice). There is the seminar subsection, the newsletter subsection, and the media subsection, all helping to feed the activity.

Other sections overlap. Mutual-fund dealers act as financial planners. Insurance agents are transmuting into financial planners (and their companies' advertising works hard to show that the companies are not just insurance firms but plan all aspects of their clients' financial futures). Stockbrokers have always acted as financial planners of sorts, but in a limited way, mostly advising on what stock to buy. Now they too have seized the possibilities. Major firms (the "full-service" brokers) have busily repositioned themselves as financial planners and asset managers. In the revised bureaucratic nomenclature, brokers are no longer called "account representatives" but "financial consultants."

Part of the *modus operandi* is to keep people worried about what their money is doing. Without financial counselling, how are they to know that their savings are gaining as much as they might? It's a short step from there to separating people from a financial counselling fee or a sales commission, or getting their assets under deposit or management.

This ever-more-layered bureaucratic activity doesn't create new wealth. It has no working relationship to the growth of productive economic activity. It doesn't even provide entertainment unlike, say, a bar-room piano player. The underlying message – sometimes paraded as bait – is that people can make gains, indeed can become rich, by following the right advice about their money. At the least, they should make the most of their savings by seeking advice or by arranging for somebody in the field to manage their capital. But if this making of extra gains by paper activity is in fact the case, it can only happen by taking a margin out of the economy at the expense of others. Like the paper shuffling of the rest of the money-manager branch, financial planning economically is a self-cancelling exercise.

In *A Fool And His Money*, the account of his journey through the money-manager and stock-market branches, American author John Rothchild mused about how the shops in his neighbourhood in Miami Beach were all being replaced by banks, trust companies, and brokerage retail outlets. "If [the] trend continues," he commented, "soon there will be nothing to shop for except interest rates." He imagined a country of brokers and tellers, where people cash cheques and make deposits up and down both sides of their local shopping street twenty-four hours a day. "It had become easier to get advice on a stock at any hour of the day or night than it was to get a pizza," he realized. As it happens, he wasn't exaggerating. Larger money managers, like the Fidelity mutual-fund group, have phone lines open twenty-four hours a day, in their efforts to increase their territory.

Nobody knows quite how many financial planners there are. In the United States, in 1986, there were 50,000 to 150,000 of them, according to the *New York Times*. By early 1987, *Business Week* estimated there were 250,000 people claiming to be financial consultants. *Fortune*, in the fall of 1989, cited estimates of from 150,000 to 500,000. It depended, no doubt, on who was considered to fall into the category. Between 1983 and 1988, the number of investment-advisory firms registered with the Securities and Exchange Commission increased a whopping 160 per cent. By comparison, the productive economy in those years, as measured by gross domestic product, increased only 21 per cent in constant dollars.

The average financial planning practitioner was earning US$80,000 in this period, an extraordinary bureaucratic take when compared to the U.S. public service, where the *maximum* pay for all but a few dozen top jobs was $82,500, the average pay of accountants (dealing with finances and figures, and professionally qualified) was only $45,000, and the average pay of attorneys and engineers was in the $65,000 range. Financial planners' fees in the United States range from $100 for spot advice to as much as $12,000 for a complete financial plan, not to mention annual charges thereafter where a continuing planner-client relationship is established.

Organizations, such as the International Association for Financial Planning (IAFP) in Atlanta, have sprung up to represent and service these planners, knock off their rough edges and help their entrenchment as a full-fledged bureaucratic layer. Financial planners, as a separate bureaucratic species, have cropped up and proliferated seemingly out of nothing. There wasn't even such an animal fifteen years ago. A former chairman of the Canadian Association of Financial Planners has recounted how, in the 1960s, the category didn't exist, just a scattering of people calling themselves estate planners, usually from the insurance industry. There was simply "no perceived demand." Until the late 1970s, he could name everybody in the business where he was located (Vancouver). Then it "mushroomed." Financial planning became a "buzzword."

Membership by financial planners in an organization doesn't, by itself, guarantee anything. A dog named Boris Bo Regaard, for whom false information and a membership fee were filed, was once accepted as a member of the IAFP. An Albany, New York con artist, whose shop was shut down by the authorities, turned out to be an IAFP member. The association has no exams and isn't a licensing office. This layer of bureaucracy will ultimately be regularized – calls have gone out for licensing – in which case the bureaucracy and economic waste won't be any the less, just better organized.

There is not much more comfort where a planner has gone through some accreditation process. The trouble is, as a *Vancouver Sun* article pointed out, you really can't trust any of them, especially planners who earn all or part of their income from commissions, selling mutual funds, or insurance. Choosing among them is confusing. "The best approach," the article intones, "is self-defence: increase your own education on financial matters and don't rely on any one source for advice." In other words, do the work yourself and pay for outsiders' advice anyway.

It's not that people all of a sudden had savings that required the advice of financial planners. Canadians and Americans have always had savings. The relationship of financial planners to the savings rate in the United States, although not in Canada, was actually perverse. Personal savings in the United States as a percentage of disposable personal income was highest during World War II. Of the post-war decades, savings were highest in the 1970s. In the 1980s, on the other hand, they declined to their lowest post-war rate, and were extremely low in the years 1985-1988. The mushrooming of the financial-planning section occurred in this latter decade, when household savings, relatively, were falling off – bureaucratic self-inflation against the grain of the practical economy.

The financial-planning bureaucracy really came into its own during the 1980s bull market, when reportage about stock-market plays increased, when mutual funds expanded exponentially on the back of the bull market, when the idea of making money with money was popularized once again, and when the corporate takeover stars showed how it could be done on a mammoth scale, and were heralded and revered by the media.

These were also the Reagan years, when individual acquisitiveness was celebrated. In most other eras, even in the United States, there was a check on the idea that making money from the playing of money games was wonderful. People, using their common sense, correctly saw it as unproductive and parasitic on the mass of people. They withheld complete approval of celebrated financial wheeler-dealers, although they might envy them their wealth and power. Now that check was gone. More and more people began trying to make money from money. Not to do so, it seemed, was to miss out. The financial-planning section bureaucratically fed on this ideological development and, by the same token, suffered a fallout in numbers when the bull market and the ideology of the Reagan era subsided.

The cadres set out to generate make-work by insisting on various planning exercises and check-up visits to follow. "You can't just come to us with money," the president of a New York financial-planning firm explained to *Forbes*. "You have to commit yourself to the process." In this case the process was US$8,000 for the initial plan and $4,000 per year thereafter, until the sun stopped coming up in the morning. This was the *average* fee.

In late 1985, *Consumer Reports* sent a reporter and her husband to major financial-services companies to see what kind of financial advice they would get. "Almost all the plans contained a serious flaw," the magazine reported. "They usually suggested that the couple increase its spending on financial products and services," although where the money was going to come from, most didn't say, and the one that did overlooked or underestimated major expenses. And what kind of financial products were the couple advised to buy? "The recommendations almost always reflected the primary business of the company designing the plan." About 85 per cent of U.S. planners also sell products to clients, according to a recent SEC study.

Some planners charge a relatively low flat fee, but add commissions on transactions. These are, in effect, commissions on commissions. The more transactions, the more this variation of double-dipping brings a return to the planner. It's a temptation for churning. A full-service broker – acting as financial planner, salesperson, and trader at the same time – always has that temptation and, in the United States, has in-house, high-commission mutual funds to push as well. The client can end up paying 4 per cent or more off the top, plus 2 per cent and up each year, depending on how much trading the broker does. Some advisers offer "free" financial plans, whose commission costs for implementing them, however, can climb to as high as 8 per cent of assets. For advisers who draw up financial plans but don't actually handle downstream transactions, adding an annual monitoring fee brings in a regular stipend for subsequent years. Each bureaucratic post has its own layering methods.

Like the stock-market branch, the money-manager branch (financial-planning section) also generates sheer scam on its bureaucratic edges. Case histories abound, at least in the United States where reporters dig out the stories. Some involve crude and simple theft – a financial planner selling a fake bond to a client and spending the money, or "investing" the client's funds in his own account and disappearing. The amounts involved can be considerable. A San Diego planner was charged with cheating investors of US$69 million by selling them non-existent currency futures. Remember that financial planning is in good part lay-psychologist and clergy work, albeit in bureaucratized form – hand-holding, reassuring, looking after, understanding personal circumstances – just the kind of relationship that lends itself to misplaced confidence.

Other cases showed more finesse, and the rake-off was just as great. In Chicago, four thousand investors lost US$35 million over fifteen years to a group of planners who allegedly used their funds to buy twenty-two automobiles, eight motorcycles, four airplanes, and an aircraft hangar. "Financial Concepts," the firm was called, and no fooling. To tell customers of losses in their portfolios, the principals sent out letters with SORRY YOU LOST YOUR MONEY stamped on the envelopes. Some scams involve recommendations of transactions on which the financial planner or associates collect hefty commissions and inflated sales margins. In one such alleged scheme, good for a reported US$55 million, condos and old coins were the recommendations. "Pet the goldfish [the suckers]," the cadres were encouraged. The company promoted itself as "a family of professionals that will guide you on a direct course across our volatile economic waters." A 1987 estimate put losses from financial-planning fraud in the United States at a minimum $500 million, exclusive of the costs of policing, prosecution, defence, and trial.

In the United States – the ideological heartland of the New Bureaucracy – the money-manager branch naturally produces make-work for lawyers, too. Litigation against financial planners has been on the increase. "Many of those who think of financial planning as a free lunch may find themselves providing dinner for plaintiffs' attorneys," *Forbes* reported. When somebody loses rather than wins, the financial planner is the obvious target for discontent. Negligence appears the most promising line of argument. Naturally, too, where there are lawyers litigating, there are insurers insuring against lawyers litigating, hence another bureaucratic subsection: brokers and underwriters of financial planners' insurance. "Errors and omissions" insurance, it's called, in the branch.

Personal money managers do their own bureaucratic layering – sometimes very thick layering. Personal money managers are firms – from large full-service investment banks to private limited partnerships – that invest people's money on a discretionary basis. Minimum investments range from $100,000 to $5 million depending on the scheme. By one formula or another, the money managers extract 2 to 3 per cent of assets each year (their fee plus expenses or an all-inclusive "wrap" fee) for funds under their management. The process is machine-like. "Fees from managed assets accrue like clockwork," a Shearson Lehman executive explained proudly.

Some get the take up to as high as 5 per cent. The wrap-fee idea for large portfolios is the one being introduced by brokerages in Canada to make up for the decline in trading commissions.

Cadres take even a bigger slice out of many limited partnerships, particularly "hedge funds." A hedge fund uses options and other devices to protect its backside (hence "hedge") while it tries to crank up returns with leverage. Some of the private futures syndicates fall in this category. The fee structures are the same, too – the usual management fee plus a chunk of profits (that wonderfully named "incentive fee"), typically 20 per cent. Sometimes the incentive fee doesn't kick in until after a certain rate of return is achieved – 10 per cent, for example. Managers who have a good run for a few years, not necessarily through their own sagacity – and the run attracts more investors as it goes along – can make enormous amounts of money. When, on the other hand, fortune turns the other way, and the limited partnership takes a beating and perhaps falls into receivership, despite the hedges, well, it's one of those things. "Hedge hogs," a cartoon in *Forbes* joked. Other varieties of limited partnerships often have the same fee arrangement.

Inevitably, one U.S. outfit began a hedge fund to invest in other hedge funds – in effect acting as general manager of a multi-manager partnership. Naturally it takes a fee, and naturally it takes an incentive fee, too, on top of the fees and the incentive fees of the actual funds. This idea is being picked up by others. Finally, along the bureaucratic chain, for wealthier clients, come the money-manager consultants. Money-manager consultants don't pick stocks and bonds. They help people pick the personal money managers who then pick the stocks and bonds, just the way that pension-fund consultants counsel pension-fund officers on which investment advisers to choose. It's a bureaucratic law, after all, that where you have cadres, you also have consultant cadres. These particular consultants take their own slice – a finder's fee and then an annual monitoring fee. What the actual managers charge comes after that. Some pension-fund consultants have gotten into the act.

U.S. investment banks have combined this idea with the multi-manager partnership idea. They oversee a stable of money managers available to clients, do the administrative work, and proffer advice on which managers to choose or to switch to. The bureaucratic beauty of it is that both the money managers in the stable and the stable manager all take their cut from a regular wrap fee. The fee for a typical "select-style" equity fund of this sort starts at 3 per cent (declining for larger investments) – not bad for the cadres, given that managers on average don't beat the average. "Wrap bonanza," the *Institutional Investor* chimed.

The money-manager branch has one other major division – the do-it-yourself section. There is a publishing side and a seminar side. One of the best-known money-management publishers in Canada is Hume Publishing (or, as it has labelled itself, Hume Successful Investment & Money Management), because of its massive direct mailings. "Are you willing to get rich?" scream its leaflets and form letters. "No-Risk Registration Form," "no-risk invitation," "free offers," "yours free with your risk-free trial subscription," "receive reports FREE," "free book & free preview offer" and other such lures are packed into the glossy, multi-piece mail-outs. In the early 1980s, Hume Publishing also used costly full-page newspaper advertisements with blaring headlines: "Are you sincere about making $1,000,000?"; "The kind of money these men are making is almost unthinkable"; "How an 'average working man' went from a $30,000 a-year-income to a half-million net worth in just a few short years"; "You? A millionaire? Why not?"

The Hume Publishing bumf is full of testimonials of people with modest earned incomes who have accumulated huge assets by following the Hume programs. Until recently it had an advisory stable in Canada, whose stellar qualities it grandiosely extolled. Morton Shulman and Andrew Sarlos, since departed, were touted as a "Canadian investment legend" and a "Bay Street genius" respectively. One of the recurring leaflets is laid out in magazine style and called *New Millionaire*, refurbished from just *Millionaire*. Issues of the leaflet typically illustrate prosperous couples and families, along with testimonials. A motor launch, a sailboat, and a private swimming pool are favourite graphic props. The mail-outs appeal to dreams and greed. The object is to sell Hume's money management courses and its newsletter, *The MoneyLetter*. A typical course, "Successful Investing & Money Management," a $408 for a complete set of thirty-one lessons. *The MoneyLetter* costs $97 a year.

It makes no difference that only a few selected winners are cited and no losers. It makes even less difference that these kinds of exercises by people are unproductive wasted motion, economically. In the 1982 recession, adviser Andrew Sarlos and the money he managed took a bad tumble, Sarlos personally losing $20 million and nearly drowning under a mammoth debt burden. That need not be mentioned, nor need questions about Shulman's wisdom, like the 1987 article "Has Morty Lost His Touch?" in the *Report on Business Magazine*. One *MoneyLetter* subscriber, talking to *Canadian Business* magazine about these seers' predictions in an earlier period, humorously described their contradictions, their hedging ("the art of foolproofing your predictions"), and various canards. At the time, investments that had cost the subscriber $18,647 had a market value of $7,375.

Among the misadventures mentioned in the *Report on Business Magazine*'s article were two Hume Publishing mutual funds started in 1985 with classic Hume marketing. The funds were managed by Shulman, Sarlos, and two other "heavyweight" managers – "four of the best and brightest minds in Canada's investment business," an advertisement trumpeted. Management decisions were made at a breakfast meeting on Shulman's patio, to croissants and coffee. The lacklustre funds were sold in 1988 because of poor performance (minus 20.5 per cent and minus 12.1 per cent respectively for their last year). But they were generating management fees of about $3 million per year.

At its peak in 1987, with its mutual funds still in tow, Hume budgeted $30 million for its marketing programs, for both Canada and the United States, double the budget of the year before. It's now back to just a fraction of that. Still, subject to the mood of the times, a certain volume of paper sent out produces a given number of subscribers and keeps the machinery turning over. If one investment course fades, another can be packaged (Hume added a real-estate investing course, with the necessary thirty-two lessons, now at $13.90 a lesson, or $450 per taker). If advisers make too many wrong guesses, or their reputations fade, or their interests change – remember all those analysts who were stars today and forgotten tomorrow – they can be replaced. Shulman and Sarlos left the Hume stable and were replaced. By paying high enough advisory fees – buying a proper assortment of celebrity reputations – the organizer can always mount a good-looking panel or list of newsletter contributors. Hume advisory-board members in the United States, where the better part of the firm's revenue is generated, have included former secretary of the U.S. treasury William Simon and Louis Rukeyser, host of the U.S. television program "Wall Street Week".

Hume Publishing isn't alone among purveyors of investment courses. In the United States, mail-order investment courses of the most florid kind are even pitched on late-night television. Similarly, *The MoneyLetter*, grossing about $3.5 million per year on a circulation of 35,000, is just one of many of its kind offering stock-picking and other speculative advice. There were from eight hundred to fifteen hundred such newsletters in the bull-market days of the 1980s, according to different estimates. Depending on the ups and downs of the stock market, anywhere from five hundred thousand to more than a million Americans subscribe to the newsletters. The epistles of fashionable guru analysts are part of this section.

Newsletters are a minor layer of the money-management bureaucracy, but the rake-off can be a most lucrative one, once the publisher establishes circulation. A year's subscription typically costs between $100 and $300. A mere 1,000 subscribers, then, means $100,000 to $300,000 gross; 10,000 subscribers takes the gross into the millions. Usually from one-half to three-quarters of gross can be pocketed as profit, once circulation is established. The more specialized and technical of the newsletters can garner higher subscription fees. A top-priced specimen, published weekly, goes for US$1,095. Two medium-priced U.S. newsletters reached the 150,000 and

200,000 circulation marks respectively in the bull market. Less-established investment letters fade away when small investors lose interest in the stock market (about a fifth disappeared after the 1987 crash). Others spring up when the investors return.

This bureaucratic layer is not only expandable horizontally, it is also inflatable vertically. Speaking fees, hot-lines at high per-minute rates, and other additional rake-offs puff up the take. Newsletter publisher-writers can marry a money-management component to their newsletter function, taking in lucrative money-management fees. Or a money manager can start publishing a newsletter. One or more mutual funds or closed funds can be spun off from newsletter activity.

There are so many stock-picking newsletters that there are three newsletters in the United States that do nothing but track the other newsletters. There is a newsletter digest that publishes excerpts of other newsletters. Why not write a book about how to use newsletters? Somebody did. Again, it makes little difference that some newsletters are, for a while, uncannily right in their predictions, and their circulations go up, and others are uncannily wrong, and their circulations tumble. The newsletters economically are self-cancelling bureaucratic filler. When stock-market activity inflates, the newsletter bureaucratic layer inflates with it.

There is also the book-writing subsection. Morton Shulman made his reputation with *Anyone Can Make A Million*, which spent twelve weeks on the *New York Times* best-seller list. Another one entitled *Wealth Without Risk*, by an American personal-finance counsellor, was a number one best-seller among advice books, in 1989. Guru analysts and newsletter publishers write books, which they can sell along with their reputations. Mutual-fund stars can write books (Peter Lynch, the former manager of Fidelity's Magellan Fund, produced *One Up on Wall Street*). Broadcast personalities can spin off books (even Gordon Pape, a Canadian freelance broadcaster, and now a Hume Publishing contributor, has produced three books).

The book buyer may be under the impression that such inviting books have particular wisdom. The books and their wonderfully promising titles, though, are produced much like fodder. By reminding people to think about their money, they help to keep selling new books that come down the pike.

John Rothchild, in *A Fool And His Money*, ever-conscientious, described how he went to a library to find the best of all the investment books that had been written. These how-to books on making money took up three aisles. One of the books he found was written by somebody who had earlier produced *The Only Investment Guide You'll Ever Need*; the author had given in to the temptation to work that vein again. Rothchild's most pertinent finding, however, was that the books collectively, all written by authoritative and knowledgeable people, offered contradictory advice, cancelling themselves out. One guru, for example, recommended putting all one's eggs in one basket and then watching the basket. Another insisted that diversification was the only way. Rothchild arranged the contradictory advice in matching pairs. There were twenty-two listings: "Be flexible, change course quickly," for example, versus "be steadfast, keep a steady course"; or "study as much as you can, [for] the ignorant investor is a sure loser," versus "study nothing, since a little knowledge is a dangerous thing."

One thing the writers did agree on, however, was that the average investor was always wrong, which stopped none of them from writing hundreds of pages and flogging books to the average investor. Rothchild quoted a newsletter writer who suggested a sure way to make money from best-selling investment books was to note the advice and do the opposite. The newsletter writer claimed to have tested his theory through the entire twentieth century with convincing results (case after case is cited). Again, that's of no consequence. The real function in each instance – selling books – was successful. "Books without brains?" *Forbes* quipped about *Wealth Without Risk*. The magazine described the book as a "useless, misleading, error-filled heap of bunkum." The book's publisher, at the same time, was handing the author a reported US$3 million in advances to write another three books. Wealth without risk.

Seminars are another subsection in the same vein. Free seminars abound. Investment dealers offer them regularly, to draw in customers ("mine for clients," the *Financial Post* once put it) and to get them involved, generating commissions. Notice of these seminars appears in the "business" calendar of daily newspapers as if they were noteworthy business activities rather than the bureaucratic make-work they are.

Evening gatherings using a high-profile speaker and taking on a revivalist-meeting atmosphere – often in association with a mutual-fund company – are a variation of the genre. They can work a raging bull market (euphoria, intimations of magic wealth) or a market collapse (the answers to your perplexities and distress) equally well. "Money shows," in large venues like convention centres, with exhibits, prizes, and drawing cards – and sometimes mini-stock exchanges – are another routine. The man who started money shows in Ottawa and Toronto (the latter held in the Metro Convention Centre) had been a retailer whose business went under. He happened to attend a money show in Montreal. Instead of following all the advice proffered, he understood where the real opportunity was. "I am making more money now than I ever did with the clothing stores," he told the *Toronto Star* as his 1990 show was about to open.

The annual RRSP blitz, known as the "RRSP season," has a parallel acculturating effect and helps to prop up the money-manager branch. In sample year 1988, an estimated $30 million was spent on RRSP advertising in newspapers and magazines alone. Another $30 million was spent on seminars, trade shows, brochures, and direct-mail and telephone sales campaigns. Many RRSP advertisements feature tax breaks – "Invest $25,000 [in a Whistler Mountain hotel development] and within 12 months earn approx. $21,000 in tax savings alone!"; "Invest your RRSP funds in Ontario tourism and receive a 30% TAX-FREE CASH GRANT from the Government of Ontario . . . It's true!" RRSPs themselves are a tax break to be played on.

One of the functions of the money-manager branch is the exploitation of just such tax-avoidance possibilities, with the burden shifted onto the backs of all other taxpayers. Investment-dealer seminars play on the available manoeuvres. Financial-advice media personalities in the 1980s waxed ecstatic about the tax breaks from flow-through shares. Celebrated financial adviser Brian Costello ($2,000 for ninety minutes of tips and patter), at an Oakville mutual-fund seminar, proudly cited a woman he knew with a $2.5-million mutual-fund portfolio who paid no income tax. Tax-avoidance gems like limited-partnership vacations (sailboat and powerboat charters, houseboats, recreational vehicles) and shipping containers are touted at money shows.

The media's rush into investment advice – money pages, radio and television programs, money magazines (for example, the Financial Post's *Moneywise* and its annual Investor's Guide) – also reinforces the culture that helps feed the branch. Once past a certain threshold, it becomes a conditioning force, like lottery propaganda. This cultural underpinning of the bureaucracy, a derivative of the bureaucracy itself, has little to check it. Since many people have savings, basic information on what to do with those savings may be useful. Soon, however, this information begins expanding exponentially, turns in circles, keeps readers thinking about their money and possible permutations and combinations and hence keeps them as targets for more such elaboration (and the advertising that goes with it). Ex-journalists and transmuted journalists show up in the money-manager bureaucracy proper – go altogether bureaucratic – like Mike Grenby (ex-*Vancouver Sun*) and Gordon Pape.

Like the seminar pitches, much financial-advice copy is loaded with tax-avoidance chatter. Some of the "personal account" articles in *Moneywise* read like a guide on how to take advantage of the Treasury – really a guide on how well-off individuals or couples can take advantage of the less well-off who have fewer tax-avoidance possibilities. "The rich get richer and the poor get soaked," a star mutual-fund salesman once declared to his audience, encouraging them to get richer by soaking the poor. Money pages and money magazines help give this soaking of the poor legitimacy.

The image-laden television commercials of investment dealers help out, too. They are meant to drum up business but inevitably they have a cultural content as well. "This is what money is about," they say, "and the right way to pocket it, and who deserves it." As for people doing better with a fairer old-age pension or fairer tax system, or by being more economically productive by not wasting time with a broker, we never see those images, because there is no equivalent self-interested bureaucracy with an advertising budget and freedom of action to push them.

Aside from the wasteful bureaucracy itself, nobody counts how much time, energy, and productivity is wasted by this capture of the public's mind – by how much economically unproductive time people spend responding to the bureaucracy. In late 1979 and 1980, there was a brief period when attention to gold and silver speculation, rather than to RRSPs, mutual funds, stocks, and bonds, was being drummed up. Books were written on it, gurus commented, newsletters gushed forth. In short, the usual bureaucratic excrescence was produced. (Even today, reflecting the media's own cultural captivity, the price of gold is flashed on the local and national television news.) When the market suddenly rose, on one occasion, there was a six-hour line-up at a Toronto bank to purchase gold. It was reminiscent of the line-ups that happened in the Soviet Union for meat, which were so deplored – all those people wasting time waiting in line – except worse, in this case, it was part of an unproductive exercise. Going to investment-dealer seminars to learn about futures trading or poring over investment (really "speculation") newsletters and stock-market news is, in its time spent, unproductive economic waste, too. Yet given the ideology behind this waste and bureaucratic overlay, we are nevertheless supposed to venerate such activities, applaud them automatically, just as surely as if a state-controlled *Pravda* had given us the instructions.

The bureaucratic utopia – a post-industrial Brave New World – would presumably have everybody from spies to waitresses quitting their current jobs and devoting themselves to managing their money or becoming financial counsellors or mutual-fund dealers. Absurd as the notion is, it is nevertheless the cultural ideal. In keeping, a testimonial in Hume Publishing's glossy sales literature has a man boasting that he no longer works, but manages his investments full-time.

The money-manager branch of the New Bureaucracy, and the stock-market and derivative-paper branches, float on this cultural capture like a hovercraft floating on buffeted air.

7

The Advertising and Marketing Branch

Every once in a while somebody mentions the cost of the CBC as if it were a great problem. Federal cabinet ministers make sombre noises about it, and in the last few years have been cutting the CBC's appropriation in constant dollars. Michael Wilson, when he was finance minister, even told reporters that reducing the CBC's allocation was necessary to boost the economy and create jobs. Nobody, on the other hand, talks about the cost of broadcasting in general in Canada or the cost of advertiser-financed broadcasting. The latter cost is ignored, as if mentioning it were taboo. In the hazy ideological fog surrounding and protecting the advertising and marketing branch, advertiser-financed broadcasting is somehow considered to be "free" – it just seems to come out of the sky – although it's obvious, when one thinks about it, that such broadcasting does cost money and that we all end up paying for it. It's a charge on the economy like anything else that takes up time and resources.

In fact, we pay for advertiser-financed broadcasting without having a say in the matter. Its financing is collected much as if it were a private, arbitrary tax. At least in the case of the CBC's public financing, democratically elected representatives decide on tax levels and on how much of the revenue generated should go to the network. With advertiser-financed broadcasting, by contrast, the financing decision, using money that comes out of our pockets in consumer decisions, is private and autocratic. One would have to become a hermit, not buying or patronizing anything advertised on television and radio, to avoid altogether this private bureaucracy's "taxation" method.

More than that: While the funding of broadcasting publicly is highly efficient, as we'll see, the financing of advertiser-allocated broadcasting (including the commercial revenue of the CBC) has extraordinarily wasteful overheads. First is the cost of making commercials. Then there are advertising-agency commissions and fees, and media sales commissions (for their sales forces). Also at the expense of the economy are the in-house costs of the companies which advertise (including pricey executive time), associated hefty salary costs of executive cadres in broadcasting companies, the auxiliary expenses in the way of office space, secretaries, and other overhead costs, plus assorted research expenses. Public- or subscriber-financed broadcasting simply dispenses with these wasteful bureaucratic sections.

In Canada, for television alone, this waste of the commercial financing mechanism comes to $690 million annually, as of 1989. This money goes to the overheads of collecting the funds for television, and not to television (programming, distribution, associated administration) itself. It works out to 55 cents down the drain for every dollar left for providing television programming proper. This is an astonishing overhead cost which no other business – short of shady stock promotions, perhaps – would even countenance. By contrast, the cost of raising money publicly for the CBC, through the tax collection system, is 1.6 cents for every remaining dollar. Indeed, the incremental cost is nominal, since the tax system has to be operated for other reasons.

Along with the extraordinary overhead waste comes the intangible but heavy cost of being beaten over the head with repetitive propaganda for up to twelve minutes for every programming hour. If the old, government bureaucracy bombarded television viewers with twelve minutes of exclusive, expensive, and manipulative propaganda every hour, to help inflate their own activities, there would be hell to pay. The advertising and marketing branch, though, protected by ideology and its own bureaucratic weight, does it with impunity. People may grumble and point to better ways of financing television, but against a bureaucracy both entrenched and ideologically sheltered, there is not too much they can do. Restraining the expansion of advertising or cutting it back isn't even discussed, much less implemented.

What applies to television applies to the advertising and marketing branch as a whole. It is extraordinarily wasteful and extraordinarily intrusive. Unlike the old bureaucracy, it is virtually unchecked. And it benefits from a rare, and powerful, bureaucratic immunity: ideological cover.

The branch expands leap-frog fashion. The more advertising and marketing there is, the more advertising and marketing are required to make an impression, and so on in an intrusive and wasteful spiral. Over a certain minimum threshold, moreover, advertising propaganda has little or nothing to do with the operation of a free market for goods and services. The protection of brand names, about which so much of advertising is concerned, subverts an open market which is based on competition over price and quality, free from the interference of brainwashing.

Because this propaganda is for things that are made and sold, and because making and selling things are part of the economy, there is an association of ideas between the propaganda and economic activity. From there it's a short step to the claim that if you restrict advertising, you hinder economic progress. It's a phoney claim. Most propaganda is for things people would buy and use anyway: detergents, cars, gasoline, shampoos, beer, cigarettes, toilet paper, sanitary protection, motor oil, packaged food, furniture, clothing, headache remedies, coffee, tea, banking services, and so on. Or the advertising is in product categories that cannot be pumped up anymore, and the expenditure is a circular struggle for market share. Or it's in categories where, if people bought less and used their money for something else, they and the world would be no worse off and might be better off: beer and other alcoholic drinks, cigarettes, lottery tickets, soft drinks, sugared cereals, gimmicky toys, candies and chocolate bars, and so on. Ironically, for some categories, like beer and cigarettes, where the advertising and marketing branch is on the defensive, the cadres themselves argue that their advertising doesn't increase overall consumption, only moves it around.

In economically advanced countries, there is no relationship between the volume of advertising propaganda and differences in wealth, except perhaps a negative one. Advertising as a percentage of gross domestic product in the United States was an enormous 2.4 in 1989, based on figures from market-research firm Starch INRA Hooper in their *World Advertising Expenditures* survey. By comparison, it was only 1.3 per cent in Japan and Canada, 1.6 in the U.K. and Switzerland, 1.0 in West Germany, 1.1 in Sweden, 0.9 in France, and 0.5 in Italy.

Six countries that year had higher GDPs per capita than the United States and two others were at about the same level. They all had much lower rates of advertising expenditures. The countries with less advertising benefited in another way: The percentage of GDP saved in lower advertising and marketing overheads was available for more productive purposes. The inflated American advertising expenditure, now at US$129 billion a year, is all the more striking when one takes into account the economies of scale of the American market, which should reduce the percentage spent on advertising in the United States. Also to be kept in mind, in the comparison, is that advertising in the lower-spending countries is itself inflated.

Another measure: In several of these countries in the 1980s – the U.K., Japan, West Germany, and Switzerland in particular, as well as the United States – the advertising bureaucracy, in terms of advertising expenditures, grew appreciably faster than GDP. For the period 1981 to 1990, U.S.

advertising expenditures increased almost twice as much as GDP, on a percentage basis, in constant dollars.

Using the advertising ratios of the higher GDP-per-capita countries as a guide, the United States could have eliminated more than half (or US$63 billion) of its advertising in 1989, and with it more than half of the advertising and marketing bureaucracy, and been none the worse economically – indeed, been better off because of the resources made available for other uses. So great is the waste in this bureaucratic branch in the United States that in 1989 the country spent more in advertising than the other sixty-one nations in the survey combined!

Not all of the inflated advertising expenditure is wasted, inasmuch as it helps finance media, which would still cost money if financed otherwise. The waste, however, is nevertheless enormous. It includes the applicable costs of the advertising and marketing branch, associated advertiser and media in-house costs, excessive media costs (for performers' salaries, for example) tied to their function as advertising vehicles, media outlets without enough merit to be financed differently, and non-mass-media advertising vehicles (outdoor and location advertising, direct mail, and so on). Advertising expenditures American-style, in short, have little to do with economic practicality and everything to do with bureaucratic self-inflation and the waste that comes with it.

This bureaucratization brings with it other problems. Inasmuch as the advertising and marketing branch pushes things people would buy anyway, it is wasteful and unnecessary. But where, on the other hand, it creates wants and forces spending, it twists economies out of shape. The United States has an extremely low savings rates and many people – particularly people culturally most vulnerable to advertising propaganda – are asset-poor. With less spending and more saving, the United States might be better off economically and socially. Worse, the materialist, self-indulgent imagery of advertising propaganda discounts what is really important in political economies: investment, enterprise, education, self-discipline, patience, co-operation, individualism, creativity, public services, public works, and above all, now, environmental priorities and the ecological survival of the planet.

In his history of American advertising, *Advertising, The Uneasy Persuasion*, sociologist Michael Schudson described the cultural role of national advertising in the United States as "capitalist realism" – the American equivalent of the old Soviet Union's "socialist realism." It is not official, state art (read "propaganda"), but given American governments' tacit support and approval of it, it could just as well be.

If one stands back and looks at advertising propaganda from the outside, Schudson's description of it as "capitalist realism" is provocatively apt. The comparison with the Soviet Union is apt in another way. The advertising and marketing branch is as wasteful, intrusive, unalterably narrow-minded, and self-serving as any Soviet-style bureaucracy, drumming us with privileged one-way propaganda day in and day out, out of touch with real needs, arrogant in its pretensions, absurdist in many of its practices, rife with excesses, and protected by ideology and power. "Capitalist realism," then, doesn't quite do. Capitalism, after all, invests capital, invents technology and produces things, and did so long before there was propaganda of this sort. The advertising propaganda, on the other hand, portrays only the consumption of things. "Bureaucratic realism" might be used as a description, after the branch of the New Bureaucracy that creates the propaganda, or "huckster realism," named after the purpose of it, or "buying-things realism," or "brand-name realism," after what it actually portrays.

The waste and excesses are rampant. There are the category wars – the "car wars," "hamburger wars," "beer wars," "cola wars," even the "sneaker wars." Take the "car wars" case history. In 1988, General Motors spent an enormous US$1.3 billion on advertising in the United States alone, a 34 per cent increase over the previous year, according to *Advertising Age*, although it was already the third largest advertiser in the country. That resulted in a declining "share of voice" for Ford, as the Ford ad manager explained to the magazine. So Ford upped its ad budget for the 1990 model year. Dealers also got into the leapfrogging. On one sample night in New York in 1989 there were two hundred different car ads on television, primarily paid for by dealers. In the five years 1984-89, automotive ad spending increased 107 per cent, that is, more than doubled.

"The money being spent is ludicrous," complained the director of marketing for Porsche Cars North America. "Car advertising is becoming a continuing blur." "Category clutter," it's called, in the jargon. The greater the category clutter, the more that has to be spent to break out of the clutter, and the greater becomes the clutter. "Ad gridlock," *Advertising Age* reported. One way to break out of the clutter is to generate a new brand name. This requires more ad expenditures in turn. Then competitors produce more brand names. As of mid-1989 there were 315 "nameplates" in the automobile and light-truck category in the United States. More gridlock.

Niche producers (smaller, specialty producers), like Range Rover, whose participation in the market provides real choice, are overwhelmed. "It's like guerilla warfare [for us]," said the agency for Range Rover of North America. The guerillas rarely, if ever, win. "Clever cents will never beat dumb dollars" is the rule. More executive time is also taken up. "We spend a lot more time in media planning than we ever did," volunteered the director of field and consumer marketing for GM's Oldsmobile division, discussing the fight against ad gridlock.

This is all for a product that people would buy anyway, of which there are too many in the country, that produces its own transportation gridlock and the economic waste in time loss that goes with it, and that encourages urban and industrial sprawl and hence the using up of agricultural land. It is also the largest contributor in North America to urban air pollution, is a significant contributor to the greenhouse effect, and, in vulnerable areas, increases low-level ozone destructive of vegetation and contributing to respiratory illness.

The "fast-food war" generates similar waste. Like cars, fast-foods are a "mature" sector – that is, a sector where sales have levelled off or begun to decline. Its advertising increases anyway. In a mature industry, the logical first strategy is to increase advertising or to encroach on somebody else's territory, which also involves increased advertising. McDonald's forked over US$764 million for advertising at home in 1990 (the eighth-largest spender) and about $1 billion worldwide.

Canadian beer advertising went into a compulsive upward spiral in the 1980s, although sales were flat and per capita consumption was declining. In the mid-1970s Canadian brewery advertising, substantial as it was in its own terms, was in the C$20 million range. By 1982 it was up to $52.4 million, and in the two short years to 1984 shot up to $87.8 million. By 1985 it was a reported $100 million, including commercial production costs. With non-media promotional spending added, it was an estimated $200 million. Meanwhile beer consumption per capita (fifteen years and over) had gone in the other direction, declining to 104 litres from 117 litres a decade earlier. Total consumption 1980-1985 had risen only marginally despite the increase in population.

The excessive levels of advertising and promotional spending continued from there. Breweries in Canada spent more on advertising and promotion than any other sector of the economy except the auto industry, a remarkable feat of wastefulness for an industry that size. By 1990, advertising and promotion spending by the two major breweries was an estimated $350-$400 million, while consumption per capita was still stagnant. This is for a beverage that people drink enough of as it is, whose taste from one mainstream brand to another is virtually identical, and which is a major contributor to serious family problems, physical and sexual abuse, homicide, traffic accidents, illness, workplace inefficiency, worktime lost, and other misery and tragedy.

Absurd as the waste is, it is an ordinary outcome of the bureaucratic process. The advertising and marketing branch functions in a mature sector like beer by trying to slice a little bit of market share off somebody else's share. From there the process becomes more and more Kafkaesque. All the furious time and energy of the brewery marketing cadres, plus their expenditures, end up moving market share back and forth by only minuscule amounts. Anything more than a 1 per cent gain is considered a major breakthrough. The cost of the waste comes out of each company's revenues. Either the shareholders lose in lower dividends or beer consumers lose in slightly higher prices (this small private "tax" on each bottle of beer adds up). "You are chasing the cost curve, and everyone's no better off," complained the president of Molson's, who then had to chase the cost curve anyway.

Try something new to get an edge and it only ends up costing money all around. The manoeuvres on one side are cancelled out by reciprocal manoeuvres on the other. One such idea was to introduce a new beer in a non-standard, long-necked bottle, as a marketing ploy. By the time the stratagem had been worked through, the major brewers had written off a $59 million inventory of stubby bottles, spent approximately $120 million buying new glass, paid higher distribution costs because of the different bottle sizes, and spent untold millions in advertising and promotion to push the change. "I think it's quite clear that they've all lost – I don't think there's much doubt about that," a brewery industry analyst in Toronto commented.

The pattern for massive beer advertising and marketing in Canada came from the United States, the bureaucratic leader. In 1970, Philip Morris acquired Miller Brewing and applied the marketing techniques that it had developed for cigarettes. The number-one brewer, Anheuser-Busch, responded. In one five-year period, 1975-1980, its ad spending more than quadrupled. By 1989, a peak year, it was spending US$592 million on advertising, according to *Advertising Age* figures.

The self-expanding factor at work in the car, fast-foods, and beer advertising sections is at work across the landscape. The "cola war" between Pepsico and Coca-Cola has become more tiresome than even the most tiresome of fast-food advertising campaigns. Kellogg's, of course, dominates the cereal wars, but others aren't shy: General Mills and Quaker Oats allocated nearly US$100 million in marketing in one year for an "oatmeal war" against each other – that is, for just for one kind of cereal and derivatives. The athletic-shoe war (Nike versus Reebok versus L.A. Gear) is, for its market size, an even more notorious case of leapfrogging, with expenditures in one three-year period jumping by huge increments and more than doubling.

It happens in smaller sectors, too. Duracell hikes its ad budget 34 per cent; Eveready adds another 41 per cent. Ragu levers up another 26 per cent for ad spending; Prego, trailing, doubles its ad budget. And pizzas? "Pizza ad battle mushrooms," *Advertising Age* announced over an article on spiralling ad spending.

Other sectors are also known for their high ad spending: toys and games, snacks, crackers and cookies, beverages, detergents, soaps, other toiletries, cleaning preparations, cosmetics, disposable diapers, perfumes, non-prescription drugs, airlines, cigarettes, and liquor among them. When a new brand or variation is introduced, the costs go even higher. In the United States in 1990, US$2.3 billion was spent on toiletries and cosmetics advertising (excluding local ad spending), as calculated by *Advertising Age*. Almost all of that was for image, which is a lot of waste, leaving aside the extra costs of overblown packaging and excessive retail space. "When people are living in a world where bombs are exploding, they want to surround themselves with the perceived best," said the executive director of the Fragrance Foundation, the U.S. perfume industry group, not in the least aware of how fatuous her statement was.

Note that the reference was not to "the best" but to "the perceived best." More than eight hundred fragrances compete for attention, producing gridlock. Relentless promotion offers a chance to temporarily break out of the gridlock, and to charge more in order to pay for the relentless promotion.

This particular bureaucracy has created its own Catch-22. If, for the sake of economy and the free working of the market you don't throw money around, you get punished. Kraft General Foods once tried pulling back its advertising and promotional support for Maxwell House coffee, on the theory that coffee had become a commodity and people would buy on price. Folgers, a Procter & Gamble company, stepped in with unrelenting, heavy advertising and promotional efforts and supplanted Maxwell House as number one. Maxwell House began sinking back into the dreaded "commodity swampland," otherwise known as the free market or the rational market. Kraft General Foods responded by itself "heavying-up" on media advertising and promotion for Maxwell House. The weight of this media barrage "moved the needle" back several market-share points.

Advertising Age, with a bit of a guilt complex for this waste, felt obliged to try to explain it away. "There are those, of course," an editorial declaimed, "who will complain that GF's return to brand advertising for Maxwell House is simply another example of a big company buying, or renting, market share. As if it's somehow improper to spend money on advertising and promotion in order to increase sales. To them, we would ask: Is there an alternative somewhere? . . . One wonders how else market share can be gained these days. . . . Why apologize for it?" Why, indeed? In the bureaucracy's own terms, there is no alternative to the waste.

Most of these products being flogged so heavily are old products, variations of old products, or resuscitated products brought back from the grave. The advertising bureaucracy, when it feels the need to justify itself, likes to claim that advertising speeds the introduction of new products. Otherwise we might be waiting forever. Advertising, the argument continues, creates enough sales volume for new products to cover expensive development costs and to bring prices down. If this were really the rationale for advertising and marketing, however, most of it would be eliminated tomorrow.

Look down the list of leading advertising categories. Only the odd one, like "computers and office equipment" and "electronic entertainment," suggests anything markedly new. Most of the workings of the advertising and marketing bureaucracy have nothing to do with real innovation. Innovation of significant value sells itself if there is no propaganda wall blocking it. "If I discovered a cure for cancer I could say it in a ten-second commercial," one New York advertising agency president put it bluntly. In fact, he could do all the advertising he needed in just a few minutes on the national news, and without paying for it. Other innovation is deterred by the bureaucratic barrier. If, for example, the automobile market had been subject to independent consumer information and to a low advertising ceiling, how much more quickly would seat belts have been introduced in North American cars – a rare major innovation that really counted? How much more advanced would public transport be today? As for consumer packaged goods, "most would-be entrants simply cannot afford the huge advertising outlays required to penetrate the existing noise level and break down loyalties to entrenched brands," concluded journalist Kent MacDougall, in a probing series in the *Los Angeles Times* – in 1979, when the noise level wasn't nearly what it is today!

It is exactly for products that aren't particularly needed, on the other hand, or that aren't much different than others, that advertising is laid on in continuing and endless waves. This outParkinsons Parkinson's Law. One might call it the Law of Advertising Make-Work: The less information that has to be transmitted, the more advertising that has to be done.

One expression of this waste is popularly known as "product differentiation" – creating a new package or a superficially different product that can be plugged for market share. In the old days, this meant establishing a superficial difference between two makes, say a Chevrolet and a Ford that were both technologically stale gas-guzzlers. The more alike two competing brands were, the greater the advertising effort required. This made the waste and pretension of it even sillier. Product differentiation was ridiculed.

Moreover, it could only be taken so far before stalemate set in. Inevitably another kind of product differentation became fashionable: variations of existing products. These are called "line extensions" or sometimes "flankers," in bureaucratese. Like package redesigns, they are a way of keeping old brand names alive. Most "new" products are line extensions. They have added a whole new section of make-work to the advertising and marketing branch.

Several of seven "new" cookies and crackers introduced by Nabisco with a US$100 million propaganda launch in 1989 were line extenders, like Triscuit Bits (one-inch versions of Triscuits) and Honey Maid Honeycomb Graham Snacks (mini-graham snacks in three flavours). A couple of years earlier it had introduced eighteen "new" cookies and crackers. In one blitz, General Mills added twenty-two "new" items in a single brand (Betty Crocker). Shampoos have great line-extension possibilities. In 1985, a particularly good year for shampoos bureaucratically speaking, $202 million was spent in the United States on rolling out new lines. There are now 1,300 shampoos in the American market. The lines can also be extended vertically into conditioners, hair sprays, gels, mousses, and dandruff formulas. Cereals and cold, cough, and sinus-congestion remedies are good line-extenders.

Line extensions themselves can be line-extended, as in Hamburger Helper being extended to Tuna Helper, being extended to new Buttery Rice flavour (and a US$11 million campaign, to extrude the last extension).

Line extending itself, however, like everything else in the advertising bureaucracy, is subject to the leapfrogging effect. Introduce a line extension here to capture a little more of market share, and a competitor will introduce a countervailing line extension of its own – in effect, it has no option. Everybody is back to square one, except the advertising bureaucracy, which has been puffed up another layer. The tactical response may devolve into the minutest details. When Procter & Gamble concocted Sparkle Crest for Kids and then the animated rocking 'n' rolling "Sparkles" character to push it, Colgate-Palmolive came up with Colgate Junior toothpaste and the animated "spokes-star" "Colgate Junior Superstar" to promote it.

The most powerful advertiser or brand-name company in any category can use line extensions pre-emptively, filling up shelves with its own products and ensuring that in any segmentation of the market it will still come away with the largest share. Unilever, for example, has around ten different brands of margarines in most American and European supermarkets.

Open-ended line-extending, by adding so many variations, has helped to increase the size of supermarkets to football-field dimensions, and larger. This also cuts into store productivity. In 1960, the average supermarket in the United States and Canada reporting to the Food Marketing Institute (largely major chains) carried 6,000 items. By 1980, it was 14,000 items, a seemingly incredible figure at the time. By 1990, it was 30,000 items and, in U.S. member stores alone, 33,500 items. New items were being introduced into the market at a rate of almost 1,200 a month or 14,000 per year, about five times the rate just five years earlier. Each line-extension requires its advertising and marketing cadres and their expenditures to support it, and to support it indefinitely if it hangs on, producing a permanently enlarged bureaucracy.

Quite apart from the bureaucratic enlargement caused by the leapfrog effect, most of the time and money spent to launch new products and new line extensions is wasted in terms of its own objectives, because most such "new" products fail. The failure rate is generally estimated at 90 per cent. One 1989 U.S. analysis found that less than two hundred packaged-good products introduced in the past ten years had more than US$15 million in sales, and only a handful produced more than $100 million in sales. This worked out to a failure rate of a bit more than 99 per cent.

"Bizarre," says Alvin Achenbaum, a U.S. marketing strategy consultant. The astonishingly wasteful creation of endless new products that fail, though, isn't the result of trying to satisfy a consumer need. It's a function of corporate and marketing cadres following their own bureaucratic imperatives. "Brand managers feel compelled to move new products forward – come hell or high water," Achenbaum explains. "Promotions and raises come from making things happen; there's little room for objectivity." More absurd, the strategy chosen to make a new product sell is more often than not to push it with a full-bore propaganda campaign, which means that unless the product gets a large share of market – which is highly unlikely – it is doomed to financial failure. Or, as one securities analyst put it, countless brands and line extensions are on "life support, kept alive by brand managers who want to keep their jobs."

Another leapfrogging mechanism is advertising in new media. New media, created to facilitate or to incite the advertising bureaucracy's expansion, range from a transnational satellite television network down to a new city magazine and newly rigged panels on shopping carts. Once one category member – say, a soft-drink manufacturer – uses a new outlet, others in the same category are impelled to follow. This is known as "vertical media inflation": using more media to reach the same audience numbers.

Although, because of new media, existing media such as network television may reach fewer people, their revenues keep rising anyway. The reason? Parallel leapfrog inflation continues: category wars, for example, or the attempt to break through clutter by spending more. This applies to print media as well as to television. Clutter, in the trade, is also known as "noise level." How can one rise above the noise and actually get people to see and remember an ad? Use full-page or multi-page ads and use colour (four-colour ads increase readership by 53 per cent over black and white), the president of a New York marketing-research organization recommends. This works until everybody catches on or has to follow out of self-defence, leaving the reader in a morass of full-page and multiple-page four-colour ad layouts.

This progression follows what might be called the Law of Advertising Propaganda Noise: The noise level of advertising propaganda in general continually rises to blur any individual increases in propaganda. Meanwhile agency commissions and ad-production costs go up another fraction.

Occasionally somebody in the advertising branch, or on its edge, will complain about clutter. "It is indiscriminate as a destructive force; everything gets tainted," wrote a senior advertising-industry reporter. But, of course, the clutter only gets worse.

Only in one way is most such advertising not circular. By protecting brand-names, it helps protect the bureaucratic power of the corporate branch (the companies doing the advertising) against the workings of a free market. The whole idea of using advertising propaganda is to be able to charge more for a product (in effect, to collect a "tax" over the market) and to collect or retain a larger market share. This happened in the 1980s with a vengeance. Cereal manufacturers, for example, were able gradually to double their prices in the decade. Operating margins of brand-name packaged-food companies were fattened. Profits went up even faster, and with them, stock prices, and with them, in turn, the huge compensation from stock options for the likes of the chairman of Heinz. A recent survey of consumer businesses by the Cambridge (Massachusetts)-based Strategic Planning Institute statistically confirms that businesses or brands with a dominant or major market share do spend more on advertising, can command a higher price (no surprise there), and have by far the highest profits. Correspondingly, the firms that dominate kitchens and homes – Procter & Gamble, Unilever, and Philip Morris – are interested only in owning one of the two top brands or groupings and are massive advertisers. The chairman of NutraSweet, talking of the power of their brand name and logo, once said the company's goal was to be able to keep customers "even if a competitor offered sweetener for free." The cost to consumers of being overcharged, meanwhile, is huge.

This bureaucratic "taxing" of the consumer (collecting a "premium price" is the euphemism) is all the more ironic because the advertising branch, which makes it possible, uses free-enterprise ideology as a cover. The advertising branch does the job by building a cultural wall around brand names. Its method, of course, is untrammelled brainwashing which manipulates perceptions of a thing's worth.

The English writer Eric Clark, in his book *The Want Makers*, describing this function, writes that advertising no longer creates the image that helps sell the product. It *is* the product. He cites the managing director of a London advertising agency on how this works for beer. "The many competitive brands," the man explained, "are virtually identical in terms of taste, colour and alcohol delivery, and after two or three pints even an expert couldn't tell them apart. *So the consumer is literally drinking the advertising, and the advertising is the brand.*" (Clark's italics.) Even if differences between products exist, it is often better to sell the image anyway. The reason, Clark goes on, is simple: "The product can easily lose its real edge if a competitor comes up with something better; it cannot lose its image because it is not dependent on any actuality."

In the old days, keeping a brand image healthy involved constantly modifying the product behind it, even just cosmetically, so the advertising would have something to work on. Now, when the brand *is* its advertising, as Clark points out, modifications are made not so much to the product, or to the content of the advertising describing the product, as to the image itself.

Consumers think they have real choice, as the carefully tailored images bombard them in their colourful variety. What they are given, though, is a choice of perceptions often dominated by a tight oligopoly of major advertisers. Advertising cadres themselves use the term "perception" to describe what they do. The chairman of a New York agency, for example, implored his colleagues, at an awards ceremony, not to slide into defeatism amid the clutter. "If [they] can increase the *perceived* value of a brand," he intoned, they will be accomplishing their mission. This successful inculcation of perceptions translates, in turn, to a higher ownership value attached to the brand itself. Increasing the clients' equity in their brand names, through advertising propaganda, is the advertising cadre's job, he explained.

He cited, in order to dismiss, a widespread alibi used by ad agency cadres to excuse their failures: that they had "too little news to work with, too many parity brands." (A "parity brand" is a brand that isn't any better than the others on the shelf.) "This is nonsense," he declaimed. ". . . There is no such thing as a parity product. There is only parity advertising. . . . A brand can have *technical* parity – parity taste, parity texture, parity smell, parity price – and still rise above *perceptual* parity. It is our job, it is our mission, it is our only hope – with our ideas, our insights, our strategies, our positionings and our advertising – to keep parity from happening." That is, it was their job to keep "perceptual parity," the Darth Vader of the advertising bureaucracy, from appearing on the scene.

It takes just one party trying to get an advantage by making its brand name important, through advertising propaganda, to touch off a round of bureaucratic inflation and to make the market for a product subject to that inflation and its "tax" forever. In 1989, for example, WestPoint Pepperell in the United States announced it would spend up to US$20 million over the next year to advertise its bed and bath products (sheets, towels, and so on). This was an unheard-of figure. To that point, WestPoint's annual ad budget was only $2.5 million and the total ad spending for the whole category (all participants) was estimated at no more than $12 million. Even *Advertising Age* used the verb "inflates" to describe what WestPoint was doing to its advertising. Others would have to follow.

Unlike colas and cars, the market for bed and bath products was still relatively free of the advertising and marketing bureaucracy prior to the

WestPoint announcement. Advertising was modest. What there was focused on print ads of beautiful towels and linens. There was plenty of choice. People bought according to their tastes in patterns, texture, and quality. Brand awareness – as measured by "unaided awareness levels" – was low, WestPoint's advertising agency found. So was brand loyalty.

Now came the bureaucratization. The aim of the eight-times increase in ad spending was to build consumer brand-name recognition. "We want to change the way consumers shop [for sheets and towels]," said the agency's CEO. ". . . We're trying to change consumers from going to look for a specific pattern, so instead the first thing they look at is a name." The idea, added the vice-chairman and chief creative officer, in connection with one of the lines, was to go beyond pattern and colour and "decommoditize" it.

There goes another category.

Fresh meat and poultry, accounting for 16 per cent of supermarket sales, is the next targeted category, in the United States. "A marketing person's dream," a food industry analyst exulted. "Imagine the opportunity to add value to a commodity product through branding such a huge industry." Also on the cadres' agenda for branding and for higher prices: produce.

If the accumulated cultural encrustation from years and decades of propagandizing a brand name allows its owner to charge more for products ("tax" the market) and still hold a major, perhaps dominant, market share, then that ownership is going to be worth a lot of money. This was brought home in the late 1980s. Astronomic prices were paid for brand names. Nestlé bid US$4.5 billion to acquire Rowntree (five times the company's book value). Philip Morris paid $12.9 billion for Kraft, four times Kraft's tangible assets. Kohlberg Kravis Roberts laid out $25 billion for RJR Nabisco.

The high failure rate in launching "new" products and the high cost of building a national brand from scratch give existing major brands a double value. Indeed, in consumer-goods markets, full of expensively-backed brand names already, it is almost impossible to create a new "megabrand." Only major supermarket chains, putting their clout behind house brands, have some countervailing leverage of their own. As for using innovations in products to invade established territory, they can be quickly matched by dominant brand-name owners, with the exception of technological breakthroughs protected by patent. Given the daunting cost and low success rate of creating an equivalent brand from the bottom up, corporate bureaucrats choose to pay huge premiums for existing brands instead.

The corporate cadres, in turn, more and more become not producers of goods or sellers of goods but "brand-name managers" – bureaucrats managing perceptions behind which they can nudge up prices. The brewery Heineken, in describing itself as "a marketing company with a production facility," was only recognizing bureaucratic reality.

The holder of this kind of bureaucratic power can even dispense with the production facility altogether – can actually fail in the marketplace as a producer and seller of goods – yet carry on managing the brand name. Eric Clark points out, for example, that when Ronson, a producer of cigarette lighters, shavers, and electrical products, collapsed, its name was acquired by others who then licensed it to manufacturers of various products, including cigarettes (which the real Ronson had never produced). Fruit of the Loom and Stetson are two other companies that don't make anything. They rent out their names, which add an *apparent* difference to products, in return for royalty payments.

Meanwhile, as ever, the cadres in the corporate branch, who commission the manipulation, are ahead of the game. The extra margin they can charge the market makes it easier to keep profits up and to collect those extraordinary salaries, bonuses, stock options, and perks.

That's the structural economic waste of the advertising branch. Within that structure, the machinery of the branch generates more waste, not to mention extravagance, self-indulgence, and silliness so extraordinary that if it occurred in the old bureaucracy – say in the department of health and welfare or in the motor vehicle branch – it would spark outrage and the most heated, bitter ideological denunciation.

No excess, it appears, is spared. Television or movie-theatre commercials costing $1 million or more to produce are now commonplace. One, for Timex, called "Under The Red Sea," was filmed, of course, under the Red Sea. Another, for Peugeot, shot mostly in the Canadian Rockies, involved a French ad agency, a Canadian production house, locational and travel costs to Kananaskis County, Alberta, and Innsbruck, Austria, a crew of fifty (French and Canadian) for the Canadian segment alone, three 35mm cameras, a Hercules aircraft, a sixty-five-foot parachute, a helicopter, a shell of the Peugeot with flotation devices (to be lowered by the helicopter as if it were zooming out of the Hercules), actors, and miscellaneous paraphernalia. One forty-five-second and one sixty-second commercial were put together out of seven hours of filming, or a shooting ratio of 240 to 1.

Another commercial, for Jovan Musk, used 27,000 feet of film, or about three hundred minutes, for thirty seconds of commercial, or a shooting ratio of 600 to 1. The average thirty-second spot is culled from 3,000 to 4,000 feet (thirty-three to forty-four minutes), itself an extraordinarily high shooting ratio of 66 or 88 times to 1.

A four-part Pepsi commercial featuring Michael Jackson, and an added "teaser," produced in 1987 – five-and-a-half minutes of finished footage in all – reportedly came in at more than US$2 million for production costs, excluding agency costs and Jackson's own stupendous fee. Costly special effects are freely used. For one Pepsi commercial featuring Michael J. Fox, a look-alike actor wore a US$100,000 plastic mask of Fox's face, among other special effects used.

Commercials costing more than US$500,000 to make are even more commonplace. A limited survey covering 2,498 spots shot in 1989, conducted by the American Association of Advertising Agencies, found that the *average* thirty-second spot, including regional cheapies as low as $1,800 in the mix, came to $178,000 ($190,000 for national spots). One well-known producer referred simply to anything from $250,000 to $1 million as the average cost of a high-quality commercial.

The average remuneration for commercial directors that year, for national ads, was US$13,000 for each shooting day. One top director commanded $34,000 a day. A much sought-after still photographer, pulling down $100,000 a year, turned himself into a commercial director and after a few years was earning $750,000 annually. The average production-company charge for location shooting was $117,000 a day, exclusive of performers' fees, agency charges, music, and editing. Even lowly food stylists – the people who spray pancakes with Scotchgard to keep the syrup from soaking in and disappearing, who "tighten" sour cream, and do other such tricks – manage up to $600 per day. Sometimes an extra is added to the extra: Back in the late 1960s, a well-known producer of commercials hired a staff astrologer to help them with difficult decisions. "American business must, more than ever before, utilize every tool at its disposal to turn out superior services and products," said the production firm's president. The astrologer's remuneration wasn't disclosed.

With that kind of money available both for paying the director and crews and for production technique, some big-name movie directors have deigned to come to the trough. Among them, George Lucas, Woody Allen, Leonard Nimoy, Joseph Losey, and Federico Fellini (whose first commercial had a cast of fifty-two and a budget of US$450,000, almost enough, said quipsters, for a Fellini movie; Fellini's own fee, on top of that, was kept a secret). "They paid me honours and attention such as popes and princes must have reserved for important artists during the Renaissance," Fellini told reporters. Woody Allen's fee for writing and directing five spots for an Italian grocery chain was estimated by the Italian press at from US$1.5 million to $5 million.

Even in second-tier Canada there is impressive bureaucratic indulgence. David Cronenberg was hired by The Partners' Film Co. Ltd. of Toronto to direct a series of commercials at a fee of C$80,000 for ten days of shooting. Imperial Oil (Esso Petroleum) put out $500,000 for a special-effects spaceship commercial (produced by a Los Angeles company) and a similar amount for its "Trouble in River City" spot (filmed in England). Nor is

Imperial Oil alone in Canada for underwriting commercials at that level of cost.

Add to these expenditures the cost of celebrity performers, where they are used. In the United States, even minor stars on a network TV series can command US$250,000 for each commercial, according to a Los Angeles-based broker who matches celebrities with advertisers. Tip O'Neill, the former Speaker of the House of Representatives, took in $100,000 a day for flogging American Express and Miller Lite and for rising from an open suitcase on the bed of a Quality Inns motel. That is as much per day as his annual salary was as Speaker. The late John Wayne reportedly received $2 million for spots for a mere savings and loan company. Sometimes these six-figure fees are paid for a cameo appearance, sometimes even without lines.

Michael Jackson picked up US$5 million for Pepsi sponsorship back in 1984. Then he took home US$15 million ($10 million in cash and an estimated $5 million in tour support) for the multi-part commercial produced in 1987. Gossipers chortled that Jackson, described by *Rolling Stone* as a health-food devotee, was loathe to be shown holding a Pepsi, much less drinking one. The outlay for television time, by Pepsi in this case, was estimated at another US$50 million worldwide. Later Jackson signed a US$20 million deal with L.A. Gear, the footwear maker.

Michael J. Fox got a reported US$6 million for three commercials, one per year, also for Pepsi. Madonna managed $5 million for a single two-minute spot for Pepsi, which promptly axed it because of religious protests. Jackson, Fox, and Madonna, for these few commercials, each grossed many times more than the CEO and second-in-command of Pepsico each received in *annual* compensation. In that sense, at least, the advertising and marketing branch appears to have more bureaucratic power than even the corporate branch.

Rank and file actors do well, too. Actors working in television and film in the United States make more than 35 per cent of their income from commercials. Voice-over announcers are also paid indulgently. Top voice-over announcers in Canada make more than C$400,000 a year. The second-rate, a group of fifty to one hundred, make a measly $70,000 to $100,000, and still have all the time they need for their other, proper work. Most voice-over announcers try to keep their rake-off quiet for fear of antagonizing peers. Their U.S. counterparts reportedly pocket ten times as much, which would take a few of them up to the $4 million range. "The fact that I'm paid as much as I am is insane," a Canadian voice-over announcer working in New York volunteered to a reporter.

If television spent as much money per minute of finished product on programs as advertisers spend on commercials, the quality and extravagance of television programming would be mind-shattering (US$22 million *average* hourly costs and $185 million for a one-hour Michael Jackson special). "By screen time per pound, commercials productions make *Heaven's Gate* [a notorious case of film-making waste and extravagance] look positively cheapskate," an American director of commercials once declared.

Cases of indulgence within indulgence are common in the trade, though little known outside it. In one instance, an art director rejected a dining-room table, although it would be covered with a cloth. "I would know what's under the cloth," he explained, "and it wouldn't be right." A modeller of hands in Britain was retained at her special fee – for a commercial for rubber gloves, a pair of which she wore the whole two days of the shoot. "They might as well have used a gorilla," she said. A director shooting in a bar in New York hired sixty extras to make sure there would be a teeming crowd wherever the camera looked, but only twenty extras could fit into that particular bar and only fourteen or fewer could be seen at any given time by the camera.

But such cases give only a slight taste of the awesome extravagance – and economic waste – in the production of commercials. Crews, casts, and assorted attached persons take off to Hawaii, Venice, the Greek Islands, or the Bahamas – staying in first class hotels and eating in the most expensive restaurants – to get just the "right light" or the right ambiance. Scenes are shot four ways – the ad agency art director's way, the director's way, the producer's way, and the client's way – so that the ad agency art director can postpone making up his mind and cover his behind.

For an American commercial produced in Spain, showing Century 21 salespeople lifting a house (it was done from behind by two forklifts), a "typical American suburban house location" was created, including a three-walled exterior set (the house itself). Special American-width sidewalks and curbstones were built. Special trees and fire hydrants were brought in. Astroturf set on a concrete slab represented the lawn (tiny bits of Astroturf were even used between the squares on the sidewalk). Cast, crew and other personnel numbered a hundred, not counting agency and advertiser personnel left behind in the United States. Five weeks of preparation and three days of shooting were required, plus the usual post-production time. The house was lifted about thirty times. All this for one thirty-second commercial. Even with Spain's relatively inexpensive crews and construction costs, the commercial came in at well over half a million U.S. dollars.

The cost of producing commercials in the United States in the early 1980s rose more than twice as fast as the Consumer Price Index – as much as 25 to 30 per cent in a single year, according to one estimate – and kept on rising, five times the rate of inflation, in 1988. Those were average increases. In some product categories the increases were much higher. The same happened in Canada. When, in 1989, the average commercial production cost for national advertisers in the United States increased only twice as fast as inflation, albeit from levels that were already airborne, it seemed almost like restraint.

The leapfrog effect at work in the branch at large is also at work here, with advertisers trying to best each other, hang on to viewers, and break through clutter. "In an age of commercial zapping and clutter an advertiser has to 'drop his drawers,'" a former ad-agency director put it.

Similar bizarre excesses occur in print advertising, over and above the overuse of full-page and multiple-page four-colour spreads, and over and above "peel and sniff" strips (for perfume, liqueurs) and actual eye-shade samples. Some liquor companies, in Christmas advertising, have run musical magazine ads, which play well-known carols when the ad is opened up, thanks to microchips and money. One Absolut Vodka musical ad campaign cost in the neighbourhood of US$1 million, including the magazine space. For another ad, in France for IBM, plain music coming off the page apparently was not good enough; it used both music and blinking lights.

The apogee of these "technology-driven" ads, as they are called in the jargon, was a Hennessy cognac bottle-in-a-box popping out of a Christmas stocking, in *Time* magazine. Production costs alone amounted to US$1 million, over and above $389,000 for the advertising space. Holograms are also in (Finlandia Vodka). All this in an attempt to arrest a decline in consumption of liquor as people looked to their health. The ultimate in sniff-strip indulgence was an insertion in *Architectural Digest* by which readers got a whiff of a Rolls-Royce leather interior.

The production costs of print ads in general should not be forgotten, either. A sizeable part of the money put out for print advertising goes into physically reproducing the ads, starting, of course, with cutting down trees, going through the paper-making, design, and printing phases, and ending with the costs of disposal and reforestation. Busy readers flip through most magazines without paying much attention to the ads to begin with.

One rationalization for this waste is that the advertising propaganda heavily "subsidizes" magazines and newspapers, making all the editorial content possible. This doesn't make the waste any the less. It merely moves the charge for it to consumers of products and away from subscribers and readers. The rationalization in fact offends the very free-enterprise doctrine behind which the advertising and marketing branch hides. The price and the amount of editorial content should not be determined by the volume of propaganda it carries but rather by what the reader is willing to pay for the editorial content.

Especially with controlled-circulation magazines and newspapers, which are financed entirely by advertising, the effort and cost of selling advertising space, designing the ads, reproducing them, distributing them, and administering that side of the operation is quite out of economic proportion with the editorial content the publications are only nominally about. In some cases, the editorial content is nothing more than subservient filler, appended to the advertising. For paid-circulation magazines and newspapers heavily dependent on advertising, the imbalance is different only in degree.

Ben Bagdikian, a University of California communications professor, now retired, went to the trouble of actually measuring allocations of daily newspapers. He found that the cross-subsidy to the subscriber-as-reader from the subscriber-as-consumer (through advertisers) wasn't what it was imagined to be. American newspaper readers in 1980 were paying more than twice what they were paying in 1940 for pro-rated editorial content, factoring for inflation, despite the great increase in advertising volume in the interim. "The difference," Bagdikian noted in his book *The Media Monopoly*, "is mainly the money charged to readers for the added advertising pages delivered to their homes. Readers in 1980 were not getting the paper for less than cost; they were paying for the advertising." Lawrence Soley and R. Krishnan, advertising professors at the University of Minnesota and the City University of New York respectively, in a study published in 1987, arrived at a comparable conclusion for U.S. magazines. "The results," they wrote, "provide no support for the hypothesis that advertising lowers the selling prices of magazines . . . [or] the price per page of editorial materials to the consumer."

Either way, though, the bureaucratic waste remains.

The advertising agencies themselves are another major section of the advertising and marketing bureaucracy. Traditionally they took 15 per cent of whatever was billed to advertisers (by tacking on about 18 per cent to whatever advertisers paid for media time and space). The agencies also took a commission on production costs. The higher the cost of producing a commercial, the more an agency gathered in, with its added slice. They waxed prosperous.

Recently the 15 per cent billing has been under attack. Many large advertisers now reportedly pay 12 per cent or less, with bonuses for best performance, or they negotiate fees on a cost-plus basis, or they use a combination of the commission and fee system, or a sliding scale tied to results. Agency functionaries, despite some grumbling, still wax bureaucratically fat. As of January 1, 1989, CEOs of U.S. agencies with billings of over US$100 million were earning an average of $384,200 (subsidiary) to $438,500 (independent) in salary and bonuses annually. The top earner that year took in $1 million. Presidents were in the $271,000 range (top earner, $677,000); branch-office managers, executive vice-presidents, chief financial officers and creative directors were in the $185,000 range (top earners $546,000, $350,800, $459,500, and $820,500 for the four categories respectively).

Add to that, particularly for CEOs and other top personnel, all the usual, variable perks. Later in 1989, a major U.S. agency offered a senior creative executive a five-year package, which, with all the perks but leaving out the unpredictable value of stock options, came to US$2 million per year.

Side by side with advertising agencies are other bureaucratic sections: first, the media salespeople who flog airtime and advertising space and, second, media company executives whose work is totally occupied or is inflated by advertising sales. It is impossible to separate this waste statistically from general media operations – there is no bureau collecting statistics on private-sector structural waste – but some available statistics do offer clues.

For commercially financed television in Canada (excluding the mixed CBC), the cost of selling commercials (largely in commissions and salaries) and related administrative and overhead expenses came to approximately 12 per cent of all operating expenses, or about C$149 million, in 1989. This is a major contributor to the overall $690 million in waste incurred by financing television commercially in the country. Similar costs for commercially financed radio, at $270 million, were even greater and represented an astonishing 35 per cent of overall operating expenses.

Transfer that order of expenditure to the United States, where broadcasting and cable together had advertising revenues of US$36 billion in 1989. One is looking at enormous bureaucratic cost within broadcasting organizations just for this slice alone – something in the order of $8 billion annually – plus the even greater bureaucratic costs of the advertising-agency and commercial-production sections.

Next come the related cadres in the advertiser companies themselves (the CEO and executive committee, the vice-president of marketing and/or marketing director, and diverse associated personnel and overheads). In a world where a manufacturer can consider itself a marketing company with a production facility rather than vice versa, such costs represent a thick and growing bureaucratic layer.

Professional athletes and television performers, although not bureaucrats themselves, constitute another section of the advertising and marketing branch. They, too, feed on the branch's use of the mass media and on its bureaucratic power over markets.

Athletes draw on two bureaucratic layers simultaneously. First are the endorsement and promotion contracts allocated to them directly by the branch. Second is the branch's purchase of television rights to games and other events, at higher and higher prices as advertising expenditures leapfrog; this inflated margin is passed on indirectly to athletes in their contract-bargaining with team owners and in prize money at events.

The take from these layers of bureaucratic fat is considerable. Basketball player Michael Jordan's endorsement fees were estimated in 1991 at from US$15 million to $20 million yearly, and Magic Johnson's (before his retirement announcement) at as high as $12 million. Golfers Jack Nicklaus, Greg Norman, and Arnold Palmer have been picking up $7 to $9 million a year each from endorsements and promotions. Wayne Gretzky is well down the list at C$5 million.

Add to this the extra margins in salaries, bonuses, and prize money, flowing from the advertising branch. Salaries in the 1980s rose dramatically parallel to the spiral in advertising expenditures. Top U.S. baseball players now receive as much as US$3 to $5.8 million annually, sometimes in long-term contracts, with performance-bonus and endorsement income on top of that. Basketball players are not far behind. "I'm letting my family and my friends around me get all excited," Boston Red Sox pitcher Roger Clemens said when his record-breaking four-year $21.5 million contract was announced. The same holds for the athletes' aggregate feeding on the advertising branch. About 70 National Basketball Association (NBA) players earn US$1 million per year, and predictions are that $1 million annually will soon become the *average* salary in the league (as of 1990-1991, it was $900,000). More than 150 baseball players earn $1 million or more, and almost 40 of them, $3 million or more, with the figures rising. Franchise owners have also profited immensely from the feeding by the advertising and marketing branch, with aggregate league revenues skyrocketing. The NBA's revenues, for example, have multiplied about six times in less than a decade (1981-1982 to 1990-1991).

U.S. television performers of all kinds are also "subsidized" by this "tax" taken from consumers by advertisers. Network news readers routinely get more than US$1 million. In fact, some individual station news readers get that much. Dan Rather (CBS), Tom Brokaw (NBC), and Peter Jennings (ABC) are allocated US$2.5 million, $2 million, and $1.8 million respectively. Diane Sawyer, for anchoring an ABC news show, is reportedly receiving $2.5 million annually. For the economy as a whole (television as a whole imparting information), any group of reasonably proficient newsreaders, paid modestly, could do as well. To the bureaucracy, on the other hand, the ability of one news reader or another to earn extra rating points is extremely valuable. Interview-show host Oprah Winfrey, meanwhile, has reached the $42 million mark, almost all of which comes from television. Bill Cosby is in the $55-60 million range, mostly from his television show and from commercials and endorsements.

The bureaucratic dispensation also allows program budgets overall to inflate. "Cheers" is up to about US$2.3 million per episode. Historical dramas are propped up even more. "War and Remembrance," nicknamed by *The Economist* "Waste and Remembrance," came in at US$3.4 million per hour of television time.

Market research, another major bureaucratic section, adds a further layer of waste. Consumer-product companies and others, over and above the market research they do themselves, spend an estimated US$6 billion a year worldwide, mostly in the United States and Western Europe, hiring outsiders to try to plumb the depth of consumers' psyches and habits – all the better to manipulate them with line-extensions, advertising and other marketing techniques. This bureaucratic layer in the United States puffed itself up, and up, and up in real terms, year after year without a break, through the 1970s and 1980s, far outpacing GDP growth. Market research contributes its own brand of excess and silliness to the advertising and marketing branch. For using techniques of measuring and probing, it ranks with police states for bureaucratic enthusiasm.

Market-research doctrines go in and out of fashion as its cadres head in one direction and then another while their ranks, meanwhile, expand regardless. The great fashion in the 1950s was "motivational research." Psychologists were first recruited by ad agencies following World War II. The idea was to help advertisers latch on to people's dreams and desires, even unto the dark lusts and envies lurking in their subsconscious. Psychoanalytic theory seemed to provide answers and, as one veteran recalled, every ad agency would have its resident "motivation" expert. "You'd got all these psychologists and psychiatrists doing depth interviews and making recommendations. They'd come up with brilliant ideas in Viennese accents. They'd tell you the Freudian significance of your product. These guys could charge many thousands of dollars for a single appearance."

Symbols were a big part of the fashion. Eric Clark, in *The Want Makers*, from which much of the following detail is drawn, discussed how psychoanalytic theory applied to cars. "A car failed to sell," according to motivational research, "not because of the way it performed, nor because of its price, but because it had a blunt [hood]. And because a car is a phallic symbol, this car lacked potency and penetrating power!" The leading guru was psychologist Ernest Dichter, whose work was made public by Vance Packard in his best-selling exposé, *The Hidden Persuaders*.

Then came demographics – finding out about people's disposable incomes, their educational levels, their occupations, whether they were homeowners, where they lived, and other indicators of their socio-economic level. A magazine, or television program, or television network, could boast about having "good demographics" – having, among the people it reached, a higher percentage of high-income, free-spending people, or the kind of people more likely to buy particular products.

Then demographics went out of fashion. It was declared not good enough. "Psychographics" appeared. The idea was to take demographics one step further and group people according to their tastes, habits, styles, and preferences – their level of sophistication, how informed they were, whether they were style-conscious, their buying preferences, what they read and drank (and whether their alcohol was imported or not), the games they played,and anything else of "psychographic" interest.

Meanwhile, motivational research, which long ago had been declared out of style, turned out to have another life. The old guru Ernest Dichter was still in the saddle. One of Dichter's recent projects, Eric Clark discovered in an interview, was trying to find out why some people save shopping coupons and some don't. "What's behind it?" Dichter mused. "Are coupon users more of an anal character or are non-users afraid of being identified with cheap money grabbing? Coupon saver – greed or a sign of love?" Another project involved research on Heublein ads for Black Velvet whiskey with, in one case, an overtly sexy woman and the slogan, "Felt any velvet lately?" "I told them they may have built in some porn," Dichter said. "Maybe the one's saying, 'Felt any pussy lately?'" These profound reflections cost money and occupy minds.

The bureaucratic beauty of these changing doctrines of market research – of trying to get behind people's defences in general – is that there is no limit to how far, and how complex and elaborate, the market research can go, other than the patience of ad agencies and advertisers who commission, or themselves undertake, the exploration and measuring.

Literally tens of millions of people every year are asked countless questions by polling and market-research companies and boutiques in interviews over the telephone, in person and in group sessions, perpetually inflating the mass of information available to advertisers and marketers. In 1990, in the United States, 72 million people were surveyed. The interviews may deal not only with their subjects' demography, habits, and preferences but also query whether they had noticed and remembered particular advertisements. As well, because people may lie or not really know what they want, other bureaucratic warrens are established to go beyond polling and surveys.

One New Jersey market-research company aptly called Perception Research Services gives eye-tracking tests. It does this to about forty thousand people a year in several test centres throughout the United States. Each volunteer, in a small darkened booth, chin on a rest as if locked in a pillory, looks at pages of a magazine on a small screen. An invisible beam of infrared light, focused on the volunteer's eyes, records direct onto computer tape the position of the eyes' pupils every sixtieth of a second. The computer record shows the research outfit what part of each advertisement, if any, the volunteer looked at, and for how long. Ads not yet used can be tested in the same way, mixed up with a clutter of others. Brain-wave measurements are also used. The technique is to clip sensors to people's scalps and monitor their brain waves while they watch commercials.

It's all in aid of, say, helping one liquor company to make subtle changes to its ads so that it might, just might, thereby steal a bit of market share from another liquor company, which, however, has retained another eye-tracking firm or is using other perception and attitude-measuring techniques, and is trying to do the same thing. And so on, in a circle.

Also used for getting at what people are really feeling and thinking, rather than what they say they are feeling and thinking, are psychogalvanometers (similar to lie detectors), measuring the involuntary actions of the sweat glands. Measuring heart rate is another technique. There are tests for measuring the production of saliva (for food advertisements). There are voice-stress analysers (another form of lie detector, measuring sub-audible tremors) supposedly pioneered by the CIA. One British firm, called Hypnoscan, uses hypnosis (light trance) for the benefit of clients. There are a variety of button and dial handset systems by which people watching commercials can indicate their approval and interest or disapproval and lack of interest, linked, of course, to computers for a scene-by-scene record.

Psychologists are retained to ask probing questions of sample volunteers willing to reveal their innermost desires, drives, weaknesses, ambitions, and fantasies. Dichter, to back up his theoretical musings about the Black Velvet ads, planned to do one-on-one interviews. He also wanted to stage psychodramas involving men and women playing the roles of the kinds of women (sexy and not-so-sexy) depicted in the ads. Clark referred to "an air of unreality building in the room," as these possibilities were discussed. "Sometimes I get frightened myself," Dichter said of the variety of ongoing studies he had contracted to do.

"Focus groups" have become a much-used way of conducting interviews. U.S. toy marketer (more accurate a description than "toy maker") Mattel interviewed 70,000 children and adults in one year alone. The group-research office of a major U.S. advertising agency was up to four hundred group sessions per year, as of 1987. Focus groups may be asked not only to talk, but to act, to play, even to paint or to model. A woman in a focus-group drama, described by Clark, acted the part of a kitchen sink, by which to reveal her innermost feelings about cleansers. Two other women portrayed competing brands of cleanser. The proceedings were secretly observed and videotaped through a one-way window. To these "psychodramas" and "psychodrawings" add what might be called "psychosculpture" – people free-modelling in clay their feelings about brand-name products.

Focus groups have subsidiary bureaucratic functions. They add spice to cadres' routines. They're the touchy-feely part of marketing, as one practitioner put it. They also help advertising agencies and corporate marketing directors to cover their behinds. As one expert, a psychologist and former advertising-agency researcher, described it, focus groups really provide "a comfort mechanism for decision makers. Its sociological function is to provide hypotheses or confirmations which spread the responsibility of action."

With psychologists and psychiatrists in the bureaucracy, it was inevitable anthropologists would also show up and establish territory. One American cultural anthropologist started a company called Planmetrics, in New York. Among his techniques: television cameras in houses to record what people do. He also had them playing construction games with toy building blocks and household items. Another practitioner uncovers cultural archetypes (the "imprint" people pick up as children), using small focus groups and relaxation techniques. He charges US$100,000 per archetype study and nets a reported $1 million per year. Some of these cadres call themselves "ethnographers," an anthropologist subset, and reflect earnestly on how, for example, consumers "bond" with cornflakes.

Once it's established what kind of people might buy a particular line-extension or "new" product or, conversely, what kind of commercial, print ad, image, symbol, or package to use for particular kinds of people, one has to find out how many of them there are and where they are. Here's where demographic and psychographic research comes in. Since there is no end to how finely drawn the identification and grouping of people can be, there is no end to the schemes, systems, jargon, ingenuity, theoretical musings, intellectual games, and, above all, make-work of the subsection doing the groupings.

One system, for example, divides people into thirty-eight groups, or forty-four, or forty-seven (according to neighbourhood types), using a technique called "cluster analysis"; another divides them into forty groups (according to different parts of the country); another into six groups (by social grade); others into groups according to one criterion and then again according to another criterion; and so on, in endless variation.

Having divided the population into groups, market-research cadres can also, then, subdivide the groups. One "qualitative" research subsidiary divided "yuppies" (young urban professionals) into seven subgroupings. Ingenious cadres can also divide subgroupings into subsubgroupings. A marketing professional duly divided yuppy "dinks" (double-income, no-kids couples) into U-dinks and L-dinks, for upper- and lower-class ones. There is no need, bureaucratically, to stop there, either. Each subsubgrouping can be divided into finer and still finer subsubsubgroupings. In the bureaucratese, it's called "micromarketing," now a fashionable buzzword in the marketing branch.

The catchy names for the groupings help attract potential subscribers – namely advertisers, media companies and advertising agencies – to the classification systems. The best-known psychographic system in the United States is VALS (for Values and Lifestyles), concocted by the Stanford Research Institute, now called SRI International. The original VALS categories and groups were the need-drivens (survivors and sustainers), the outer-directeds (belongers, emulators, and achievers), the inner-directeds (I-Am-Mes, experientials, and societally conscious), and the integrated. VALS, explained its literature, was put together with "heavy reliance . . . on the works of personality theorists working in the area of developmental psychology. . . . A wide range of psychological and sociological theorists were consulted."

It's also possible to regroup the groups according to their attitudes and behaviour regarding a certain kind of product – food and beverages, for example. This is called "segmenting" – in effect dividing the other guys' segments crosswise. Segmenters produce their own categories, catchy labels, and jargon.

Nor does that end the proliferation. Category names and concepts, after a while, as people get used to them, can lose their novelty and sheen, and hence hurt a psychographic system's marketability. Also, although the theory as well as the category language has fashionable bureaucratic appeal to begin with, in practice the system doesn't quite work out the way it was meant to. "I agree with the theory 100 per cent," said one consumer-products research manager, "but it was impossible to act on as a marketer." The damned consumers rarely fell within the psychographers' neat groupings. VALS went out of fashion, and the bureaucratic machinery turned over again. SRI, for example, created VALS 2, not much different than VALS 1 but in a new and improved package of categories – a kind of market-research line extension. The clients go to work learning a new language. Research staff are retrained. Data bases are replaced.

Not that anything helps if the bureaucratic complexity defeats the market-research cadres themselves. A recent study of British socio-economic research showed that around a third of all consumers in each sample were put in the wrong social class and another third changed into a different class within a year. To make matters worse, the NPD Group, a "nutritional segmenter" in Port Washington, New York, found that about a quarter of the population exhibited an "inconsistent attitude" and couldn't be neatly typed. It called them "moderates" – the only name it could think of it, it appears, for such unseemly anarchists.

Critics within the advertising and marketing branch itself snigger at the pretension and artificiality of these new-age systems. "Hoax," "mumbo-jumbo," and "pseudo-science" are some of the terms used. Useful or useless as classification systems may be, however, they have caught on with advertising agencies for intrabureaucratic reasons. "They made headway in the agencies because [the agencies] need gimmicks to show they understand the consumers," explained Dr. Herbert Krugman, a leading market-research pioneer. The psychographic paper constructions provide the gimmicks.

To put these apparatuses to work – to fit populations into the categories and subcategories – requires apparatchiks, a bureaucratic machinery of its own, and mountains of information. The mailing list of Donnelley Marketing, in Stamford, Connecticut, for example, contains 85 million households, covering more than 90 per cent of the U.S. population. Donnelley claims to able to measure difference *within neighbourhoods*, right down to the individual household making the purchase decisions. The data base includes, as well as names and addresses, the sex of household members, dates of birth, phone number, car make, model and year, household wealth indicator (estimates to the nearest $500), head of household, length of residence, and derivative categories (oldest member's date of birth, for example). A similar British-based system provides psychographic details for small sections of neighbourhoods down to what people eat and drink ("heavy on vegetables and ice cream, ground coffee and pasta . . . higher on the gin," Eric Clark reported, of the data on one wealthy London area).

Interviewing people in order to create a psychographic system in the first place requires a small battalion of apparatchiks. One such modest exercise involved in-depth interviews with 4,000 people. The original VALS survey asked 1,635 people eighty-five pages of questions!

"Almost frightening, isn't it?" one direct-marketing consultant told Clark, of the purported "rifle-shot" ability to pinpoint people's lifestyles (including, in the VALS survey, sexual habits), all the better to manipulate them with marketing. "The more one learns," Clark himself reflected, "the more it has the feel of Big Brother about it. . . . It is interesting to contemplate the outcry if any government intelligence agency was known to have such computer data on all its individual citizens." A Quaker Oats promotions director talks easily about how new targeting and cross-referencing techniques, applied to promotions and direct marketing, will "allow us to manage consumer behavior on a household-by-household basis." The ever-expanding data banks, by their pinpointing ability, virtually destroy anonymity. This is the bureaucratic mentality at work with mindless devotion – mindless except for its own rules.

Nor is that all. Once an advertising or other marketing campaign is devised, aimed, and launched, other cadres try to measure what effect it has. They also try to measure the impact of individual television commercials.

Did people who saw them recall at least one or two things about them and did they buy the product as a result? Did a particular actor or slogan or image, chosen on the basis of brainwave measurements, or eye-tracking, or focus-group psychodrawing, actually get more of the "achievers" or the "heavy grazers" to buy the product the way he, she or it was supposed to get them to do?

Some marketing experts claim that as many as fifty different factors can affect sales and that, as a result, one can't isolate the effect of a commercial anyway. Another leading expert says there is no point in measuring recall of a commercial because commercials work subconsciously. Others say that recall measurement doesn't go far enough; the only thing that counts is whether attitudes were changed. Post-commercial recall surveys abound regardless. Complicated mathematical evaluation models have come and gone in an attempt to sort out what factors do what and to make predictions.

New technology, like scanning and microprocessor telemeters, only adds to the bureaucracy's machinery, as it struggles to find out the details of what everybody is doing. In one application, sample groups of housewives are recruited and given identification cards. Each time they pass through their supermarket check-out counters, information about their purchases is fed into an electronic works. A detailed record, cardholder by cardholder, is thereby passed on, through the scanner, to the market research firm. Other panels of consumers use electronic wands at home to record purchases, so that those made outside of supermarkets are recorded as well.

The results purportedly tell client companies how well advertising efforts are doing immediately after the advertising appears; nothing so crude as looking at store reorders of the product. Computer models ("marketing effectiveness models") are used to analyze the data or customize it for individual clients.

Because there are now "people meters" that record when the television set is on, who is watching it, and what channel it is set at, the electronically recorded purchases can also be matched to the programs and commercials watched in the cardholder's household. This allows psychographic cadres to determine whether people in the same demographic or psychographic category, but who watch different programs, shop differently for whatever hidden cultural and psychic reasons. One such survey allegedly determined that "Dynasty" watchers were better targets for grocery commercials than "Dallas" watchers, although they were demographically similar. Another, as *Fortune* reported breathlessly, found that "Search for Tomorrow" fans buy 27 per cent more spaghetti sauce than average, but 22 per cent less V8 vegetable juice, whereas devotees of "All My Children" feel so-so about spaghetti sauce but purchase 46 per cent more V8 than the norm. An "extraordinary appetite gap," *Fortune* called it. In terms of a bureaucracy's fascination with its own games, these are momentous discoveries, even if the cadres don't know what to make of them. "We've been looking for an explanation [of the divergences in taste]," said the director of media services for Campbell's, "but it's still a big mystery."

The newest technology on the horizon is an electronic passive meter digitally programmed to monitor people's faces. It will constantly scan the room with a small camera and check who is actually watching the television screen rather than smooching, falling asleep, or heading for the refrigerator. Bright minds and unstated sums of money will be tied up on that one for at least five years before it comes on-stream. The ideal, as one market research company's marketing vice-president explained with bureaucratic zest, is a sensor system that not only identifies each watcher but also records their physiological reactions.

It also takes cadres to interpret data. The more the data – and the mountain keeps growing – the more time and energy of cadres is required to go through it. "So much scanner data, so little time," sighed a report in *Advertising Age*. This has spawned, as if biologically, another bureaucratic addition, to break down, sort, analyze, and synthesize the data and to retrieve certain particulars and combinations of particulars. It begins with a subsubsubsection of market-research cadres who produce the necessary software. This software is used, in turn, by cells of advertiser cadres, with important names like "decision support services."

Other, boutique cadres offer something called "database enhancement services." Database enhancers overlay externally compiled information on client databases, and apply sophisticated analysis techniques, to make the client databases more useful. One such database enhancement shop advertises a US$30 million computer facility. It has enhancement data on over 85 million U.S. households – 200 million U.S. consumers.

The more that data can be played with, alas, the more that cadres are impelled to produce more data for the playing. A 1990 survey by the U.S. Advertising Research Foundation of sixty-eight companies, mostly research operations and marketers, found that "data overload" was the "most characteristic" attribute of market research. Nobody appeared to be happy about it – or knew what to do about it. "Nightmare," "hard to control," and "just too many numbers" are descriptions that surface when cadres talk about the data inundation.

The original rationalization for this marketing bureaucracy, and one still resorted to, was that marketing represents a higher order of things in the commercial world. It doesn't just create new products and flog them by bombarding households with advertising. That was mere, backward "selling." Marketing finds out what people want and then makes the right product. "Authentic marketing," pronounces a standard American textbook on the subject, "is not the art of selling what you make so much as knowing what to make." Starting in Britain, the doctrine was built into a new high-fashion called "account planning," where an account planner leads the way by "digging deep into the mind of the consumer" and adopting the consumer's voice and way of thinking for each advertising account. One exponent even proclaimed that "the power of advertising has shifted from the hands of the advertiser into the hands of the consumer."

But from the beginning, as the marketing bureaucracy developed its techniques of gathering information and of persuasion, it inexorably got more and more involved in trying to create wants and needs, defend and expand the power of brand names, build images and devise the most effective propaganda. For the most part, its findings on what the customer wanted and how the customer thought and what the customer did, down to sexual habits, was used to help figure out what cosmetically "new" product might get a little more market share or what images in an ad would work best. Marketing was "selling" under another, bureaucratically elevated, name. In fact, it always had been "selling." That was the whole point of it. Nor did it change the wasteful advertising bureaucracy. It added elaboration. The "account planning" vogue, in turn, was just a more intensive and manipulative way of setting people up for propaganda – "[finding] a critical insight on which to build a powerful strategy," as an account-planning proponent put it – another convenient way for the bureaucracy to lie to itself and do what it wanted to do anyway.

Ironically, even in terms of the wasteful advertising bureaucracy, market research is wasteful. If market research is so good, advertisers ask themselves, why do 90 per cent of "new" products fail? If marketing skills are the key for creating image, why are companies paying megalithic sums to take over other companies for their brand names instead of relying on marketing skills applied to brands of their own? Not much more than a decade ago, market research determined that the personal computer would never sell. Research almost killed off the original Coca-Cola, told Sony there was no future for portable stereos, and informed Xerox that secretaries were quite content using carbon paper. Research, said one jaundiced advertising pioneer, is "something that tells you a jackass has two ears." Of course, it's had its "successes," too, like letting Perrier know that the shape of the bottle was more important than what was inside it – for the bureaucracy, a memorable finding.

As with advertising in general, the allocation of resources to market research (including public opinion polling) has no relationship to economic performance, only to how far the bureaucracy has inflated in any particular country. The worldwide revenues of major U.S. research organizations increased almost 200 per cent in constant dollars from 1975 to 1990. The increase for domestic U.S. research spending was much the same, about 185 per cent. U.S. GDP, by comparison, increased only 43 per cent.

Advertising agencies, commercial production companies, media companies, and market researchers aren't the only parts of the advertising and marketing branch. Sales promotions actually make up a far larger portion of marketing expenditures than advertising. Packaged goods companies in the United States, according to Donnelley Marketing, Stamford, Connecticut, spend only 31 per cent of their marketing dollars on media advertising, but 25 per cent on "consumer promotion" and 44 per cent on "trade promotion," or 69 per cent on sales promotion over all, as of 1990.

Those packages of cents-off coupons you get in the mail or in newspaper inserts (called Free Standing Inserts, or FSIs) are part of sales promotion (although they are also included in advertising figures). So are sweepstakes, games, and contests. The woman in the supermarket who offers you a bite-sized sample of a "new" product, one almost certain not to make the grade and to disappear into oblivion, is paid out of a promotions budget. Money-back offers, mail-in premium offers, in-package or attached premiums, cents-off promotions, bonus packs, and couponing in retailers' ads are part of this section. Event marketing – advertiser "sponsorship" of sports, music, and other events – is a growing subsection. Incentives to sales agents and to dealers (bonuses and prizes in merchandise and travel) raise the ante.

At the centre of this section are the sales promotion agencies, many of them belonging to large advertising agencies, including the mega-groups. The largest single part of their work is also the most bureaucratic: consulting, planning, and strategy. There are other bureaucratic warrens. Agencies or boutiques may specialize in sweepstakes, for example, or in event marketing. Graphics need to be produced, for promotions and mock-ups. The number of audio and visual productions inflates. Those redeemed cents-off coupons, rebates, and premiums have to be handled by stores and then honoured, involving countless bureaucratic ranks. It's called "fulfillment" and, yes, there are "fulfillment consultants." All those mailed-in entries for sweepstakes have to be opened and their numbers checked. There are even boutiques in the United States that specialize in placing products on TV game shows. There are media linkages: Major brand-name promotions and their gimmicks are advertised on television and elsewhere.

Of all the advertising and market bureaucracy, the sales promotion section in particular inflated in the 1980s. In some years it grew at a rate two-and-a-half times faster than general advertising. Leading U.S. sales promotions agencies in 1988 ran up an amazing 23 per cent increase in revenues. (GDP, that year, increased only 8 per cent), and almost as striking increases of 17.4 per cent in 1989 and 14.1 per cent in 1990, as charted by *Advertising*

Age. Individual promotional-company increases ran as high as 328 per cent in a single year. Revenues from event promotion in 1988 jumped 82 per cent, the highest individual-category inflation. The US$108 to $140 billion spent on sales promotion in 1990 – the figure includes conventions and trade shows – now rivals or exceeds advertising spending, depending on where the line between the two is drawn.

The connection between sales-promotion expenditures and the productive use of money is altogether coincidental. Sometimes the spending is so indulgent, it catches one's attention. On Halloween night 1989, Chrysler Canada treated 2,100 potential Imperial buyers to *The Phantom of the Opera*, at a cost of $150,000. Extravagant as the promotion might have been, it was treated in the bureaucracy much like any other promotional stunt. Bureaucratic indulgence in Canada, as elsewhere, had come into vogue. A couple of years earlier BMW had rented Roy Thomson Hall in Toronto, hired the Toronto Symphony Orchestra, and laid on wine and smoked salmon for 1,200 potential customers of its 12-cylinder luxury sedan. During the Ross Johnson days, RJR Nabisco paid golfer Jack Nicklaus US$1 annually for half-a-dozen appearances and spent up to $60 million a year for sports sponsorships overall; Philip Morris in the same period, 1988, spent $85 million and Anheuser-Busch $50 million for sports sponsorships. The marketing bureaucracy and its sales-promotion section considered these expenditures quite normal, indeed admirable.

The bureaucratic inflation in sales promotion happened when media advertising was inflating as well. It worked by leapfrogging, too. A "brand manager" – the corporate person in charge of a brand – resorts to added promotions to provide a quick fix for a brand that's suffering from weak blood or to seize an advantage over a competitor. There is another motive. Brand management is a fast track into general management. The quick spurt in sales that comes from promotions redounds to the brand manager's credit, helping him or her rise in the corporate branch.

The trouble is that competitors, if their brands are threatened with losing market share, quickly make matching offers and concoct matching gimmicks. The various promotions cancel each other out. Moreover, consumers often use cents-off promotions to buy brands they would probably have bought anyway at the full price. The few extra customers that might be garnered in the short term by any one side rarely pay for even the promotional costs. The only quick fix for these eventualities is – more promotions. Sales promotion becomes a kind of brand-manager bureaucratic addiction. Indeed, one packaged-goods company has compared using cents-off promotions to heroin addiction, with nobody able to kick the habit. The waste of it, meanwhile, escalates.

In 1980, in the United States, more than 96 *billion* packaged-goods coupons were distributed. That ate up a fair amount of paper, ink and energy, plus the time of production crews, printers, and distributors (not to mention the added cost of garbage collection, waste-disposal management, and their environmental overheads). By 1990, according to Carolina Manufacturers Service, that already elephantine distribution figure had mushroomed to 280 billion coupons, an increase of 190 per cent. The population in the same period increased only 10 per cent. Redemption rates, meanwhile, kept falling, from a miserable 4.0 per cent in 1980 to an even more miserable 2.6 per cent in 1990. More and more coupons were being distributed just to get the same number of redemptions. In Canada, according to Nielsen Promotion Services, packaged-goods couponing rose from 6.5 billion coupons in 1985 to 23.4 billion in 1990, or an increase of 260 per cent in five years, with a 45 per cent increase in 1990 alone. Dominant brands, in couponing, have merely extended their category wars into sales promotion as well.

Add to these numbers all the other coupons – from oil companies, local merchants, and others – those coupon books, packages, and sheets that help fill up the mail box. Marketing cadres won't even hazard a guess as to how big the whole couponing bureaucracy is.

Flyers and other free-standing inserts (FSIs) proliferate. As many as a dozen may drop out of midweek and weekend papers. The same flyer may appear in the daily paper and local free-circulation paper, or be separately delivered in addition to daily newspaper insertion. This duplication accounts for much of the coupon-distribution increase in Canada, where supermarket inserts carry most coupons. One Canadian FSI specialist estimates that perhaps only two or three out of ten flyers are read, much less acted on.

Another section of the advertising and marketing branch, overlapping advertising and sales promotion, is direct marketing. This includes addressed advertising mail (solicitations from credit-card companies, automobile dealers, department stores, magazines, book clubs, mutual-fund companies, stockbrokers, investment newsletters, charities, political parties, and so on); coupon packages and mailed samples "to householder"; telemarketing (flogging by telephone) and "tele-media" (use of 1-800 and 1-900 numbers); direct-response advertising (TV, radio, and newspaper); videocassettes (distributed direct-mail fashion); catalogues; and interactive cable television and videotext (still in their early stages). Advertising-agency branches and separate direct-response agencies specializing in the field have proliferated, most coming on to the scene in the last ten years.

These bureaucracies have their offshoots in turn, like name-list providers (redubbed with the more elevated name of "list brokerages"). Cadres who write letters ("direct-mail copywriters") form another subsection. The *average* fee in the United States for writing a direct-mail piece, as of early 1990, was US$5,900. For those complex sweepstakes mailings, the cost is in the $40,000-$48,000 range. This is just for the writing, before the elaborate multi-part production, packaging and distribution takes place. Several of these cadres take away annual incomes in the seven figures.

In Canada, expenditures on direct mail and catalogue advertising, the two largest parts of direct marketing, hit the C$1.8 billion mark in 1988, exceeding both television and radio advertising and just a shade behind newspaper advertising. By 1986, there were already 200,000 cadres in this section alone, as compared to only 60,000 in 1981. In the mid-1970s, only one Canadian ad agency had a direct-marketing arm. A decade later, as many as twenty-five direct-marketing agencies (either branches of ad agencies or independent) were in the field. Direct marketing has also mushroomed in the United States. Direct mail itself jumped from US$7.6 billion in 1980 to $23.4 billion in 1990, an increase of 200 per cent.

Direct mail suffers the same fate as coupons. According to a U.S. Postal Service Household Diary Study for 1988, less than half of it is read, and almost all of it is discarded. As the number of pieces received has gone up over the years, the percentage read has gone down, and more is thrown out without being looked at. A response rate of 1.5 or 2 per cent is considered good. Computerization, which has made selective direct marketing possible, has ended up with companies flooding their markets in the hope of getting some response. American households received an average of 540 pieces of addressed advertising mail in 1989, about 50 billion pieces in all. In less-bureaucratized Canada, the average household had to contend with only 106 pieces. Whatever usefulness direct mail has is offset by repetition, volume, and waste.

This section of bureaucratic inflation will only increase further as major brand-name advertisers, building up data bases, add addressed or more finely targeted direct mail (including videocassettes) to their repertoire, as they have begun to do. Packaged-goods companies, the mainstay feeders of media advertising and sales promotion, are seen as the next big growth clientele of direct mail. As this volume continues to increase, and the percentages read and acted on decline, each mailer, including charities, is going to have to increase frequency, gimmicks, items, or glossiness to get attention, and so on, in a circle.

One of the costs that isn't included in statistics on the working of these sections is the time households spend going through and handling coupons and direct mail (including sweepstakes, many of which are deliberately complicated and rigged to go on from one stage to another). In the United States, households in aggregate deal with perhaps 350-400 billion pieces a year, counting coupons individually. None of this household time makes the economy more productive or saves consumers money in the end. The allocation of this time is not considered a cost because it is culturally induced (hence "voluntary") and incurred by households, but it represents waste nevertheless. One group of recipients that does sometimes look at these costs, corporate business locations, are beginning to cut off pass-through delivery of junk mail, including free (non-subscription) magazines. They can no longer stomach the wasted time that looking at the stuff means, even to throw it away quickly after a glance, although their own companies may use junk mail themselves.

There is a delicious Kafkaesque irony in this leapfrogging. Advertisers had pumped up their promotional and direct-response spending in the first place because they had already generated so much commercial clutter on television and, to a lesser extent, in print. The innumerable coupons, profusion of promotional gimmicks, and streams of inserts only replicated the same self-defeating clutter – a "vicious circle of promotion and pricing escalation," as a leading Procter & Gamble marketing executive admitted. All the marketing participants, however, were now locked into this cycle, too. The escalation jumps from one part of advertising and marketing to another and within the parts, at the same time.

There is no relationship between increased sales-promotion expenditures and productive economic activity except the negative relationship of added bureaucratic waste. In 1989, International Marketing and Promotions, London, a unit of advertising agency D'Arcy, Masius Benton & Bowles, did a survey of European sales promotion regulations. Denmark, Finland, Sweden, and West Germany had the most stringent regulations. West Germany, for example, did not allow in-pack premiums, mail-in offers, purchase-with-purchase, cross-promotions, sweepstakes, money-off coupons, and next-purchase coupons, and had restrictions on cash rebates, contests, multiple-purchase offers, and extra product offers. The very countries that restrained their sales-promotion bureaucracies – that, in effect, maintained more disciplined markets – happened to be the ones with the highest GDP per person.

Other bureaucratic cells are generated around the edges of the advertising and marketing branch, and begin growing on their own. There are futurist think-tanks, whose inhabitants talk about megatrends for the benefit of the cadres. There is the *de rigueur* seminar subsection and its subsubsections (the Burke Institute in Cincinnati does nothing but market-research seminars), at the usual astronomical fee levels – US$900 for two days is typical. Marketing also is now a fashionable subject in university business schools and in colleges, as befits bureaucratic entrenchment. A marketing professor on one's corporate board is a sign of keeping up with the times.

Inevitably, there are advertising-agency consultants, who conduct agency searches for advertisers. And there are public-relations cadres – sometimes brought in from the outside, in which case they are "media consultants" – who have created a new section of their own: getting publicity for products indirectly through news coverage about commercials about products. Ads rejected by different media, for example, far from being an embarrassment, are a godsend. Controversy can be cranked up, getting news coverage. Exposure in the news can be worth many times more, in advertising terms, than the expenditure on the advertising campaign itself. The public-relations cadres who flog these news "events" constitute the "free-media" section of the advertising and marketing branch. Alas, their efforts can cancel each other out, too. The cadres worked so hard generating publicity for their respective commercials on the 1990 Super Bowl broadcast – the "Super Bowl of commercials," one cadre called it – with one advertiser starting advance pitches almost three months before the game, that it all became too much. A new term entered the branch's lexicon: "hype clutter."

The advertising and marketing branch exhibits the usual negative characteristics of an entrenched and ambitious self-serving bureaucracy, except more so: intrusiveness, arrogance, and impunity.

The branch interrupts television programs and televised sports events mercilessly and repeats its propaganda on end – tortures viewers with "repetitive gaucheries," as television critic Roy Shields put it. Its crudely barking commercials may also, in the process, cut into moving, finely drawn, or thoughtful programs or be interspersed in the reporting of horror and tragedy – destroying mood, mocking and trivializing the content of programs and events – the content of people's lives.

The bureaucracy also arrogates to itself people's leisure time. Average adult viewing time ranges from 24.5 hours a week in Canada to 30.6 hours in the United States. If viewers watched all the commercials while their sets were on, they would lose five to six hours per week of their time, or two-and-a-half to three years of adulthood (based on sixteen hours per day waking time), on the commercials alone. Most viewers in fact avoid or ignore a good percentage of commercials. Let's assume they sit through half of them. If this lost time in the United States alone were assessed at the rate of the average hourly wage (approximately US$10.25 per hour at the end of 1990), the cost would come to $303 billion annually, for the adult population eighteen and over. Children lose several hours per week of fun, sports, and homework time watching commercials.

The cadres attack viewers through technical adjustments. The loudness of commercials doesn't exceed regulatory limits as measured by a sound-level meter, but the loudness is deliberately concentrated. Advertisers in this way can keep the noise level up to the allowable maximum for most of a commercial – making it indeed louder for viewers. Advertisements can also be compressed electronically, speeding them up – usually by about 15 per cent. This adds to loudness density. Researchers have found that the human voice has the greatest impact between two and six kilohertz in frequency; engineers can manipulate voices in commercials electronically to keep them within that range. No other bureaucracy – anywhere – has sufficient ideological protection to be so intrusive on people's time and attention.

In the only independent and in-depth survey of Canadians' attitudes toward advertising on television, done for the Canadian Radio-Television and Telecommunications Commission between 1975 and 1977, 87 per cent of respondents thought there were "far too many commercials on television most of the time"; 87 per cent considered it "annoying to see three commercials in each half hour of programming" (there can in fact be twelve thirty-second commercials in and around a half-hour program; more if some of them are only fifteen-seconds long); 93 per cent agreed that "four commercials in a row are too many" (four is a typical commercial pod, and eight or more sometimes appear back to back); 86 per cent thought "commercials on television interrupt the program at the worst possible time"; 62 per cent found "the commercial breaks make it difficult to follow the program you are watching on television"; and 89 per cent preferred watching programs that had no commercial interruptions ("where commercials are shown only at the beginning or the end").

Similarly, 74 per cent objected to "the way some advertisers tell you that you can have the good life if only you would use their product." ("Lifestyle advertising" has become even more predominant in the interim.) A lesser but still majority 56 per cent considered that "television commercials rarely tell you anything useful about the product which is being advertised"; only 28 per cent disagreed.

It's an indication of the ideological protection of the advertising and marketing bureaucracy that the report was promptly shelved (indeed, an internal struggle was required to get the report made public at all), and that ways and means of checking the bureaucracy were never publicly discussed, much less implemented. This, too, when not only are there non-commercial ways of underwriting television but when financing television with commercials carries with it extraordinarily wasteful overheads.

Radio commercials impose themselves just as mercilessly. The sales promotions and gimmicks used in radio to sell advertising, are now pushing their way into television, raising the clutter and noise level. It's even becoming entrenched at the network level – McDonald's-NBC, K-Mart-CBS, and Coca-Cola-CTV cross-promotions, for example – television as "a platform for fevered promotions and sweepstakes," as *Business Week* put it.

Commercials have now pushed themselves into North American movie theatres, one of whose attractions was their freedom from commercials. The bureaucratic euphemisms for the commercials are "ad films" and "screen trailers." Their introduction in Canada, by Cineplex Odeon – which also carries commercials in its U.S. locations – was greeted by hoots and howls in some theatres, even popcorn tossed at the screen, but the movie-chain's chairman at the time, Garth Drabinsky, was sure people would get used to the idea. "Advertising is one of the greatest forms of education and enlightenment that I know of in this society," he said. In-flight commercials have invaded air travel, taking advantage of an audience as captive as they come. "Passengers can't escape ads at 40,000 feet," read a headline over a story reporting their introduction by CP Air (now Canadian Airlines International) in 1981.

If you can get ads onto movie screens before the movie, why not ads inside the movie, when nobody can escape? One fast-inflating advertising subsection spends its time and its clients' money placing products in movies – advertising in mufti. These cadres did not even exist as an organized bureaucracy until the late 1970s. By the mid-1980s, there were about thirty such companies operating in Hollywood. A number of prominent advertising agencies have also horned in. Coke and Pepsi have fulltime employees checking out movie possibilities. A "product-placement classic," *Back to the Future, Part II*, had at least twenty-five prominent product placements. Another, *The Wizard*, became notorious as "one long Nintendo commercial." "It's almost become embarrassing," admitted one shamefaced cadre.

Interrupt what you're doing and rush to the ringing phone expecting to hear the voice of a friend and it may be a totally strange voice, or a computer rigged to sound human, trying to sell you aluminum siding, magazine subscriptions, chimney cleaning, or some other product or service. The computer may be calling numbers at random, or your name may be on a specialized list procured from another source without your approval. There are an estimated 180,000 telephone solicitors in the United States, aside from computers, who intrude on people's privacy. The top ten telemarketing concerns in the United States had an estimated combined capacity of calling 100 people per second, as of 1988.

A 1987 U.S. survey found that 79 per cent of people were annoyed by live telemarketing calls, only 2 per cent liked talking to telemarketers, and 70 per cent objected to pre-recorded telemarketing messages. Computers and robot-like cadres in countless telemarketing warrens continue to intrude on people's privacy anyway. "The most annoying thing since the invention of the house fly," one American complained to a privacy advocate. When state legislators began bringing forward bills to reduce telemarketers' intrusions, U.S. telemarketers responded in the usual bureaucratic way: spending money on lobbying.

Buy or rent a video for some non-commercial television watching and you may run into a thirty-second or sixty-second ad when you start playing it. A video research company openly refers to the commercials as an "intrusion," which does nothing to shake its "[belief] in video as an ad medium and as a tool for advertisers." "Sponsorship" of videos is now on the rise, with joint promotion by the video's producer and the advertiser – Paramount and Pepsico, for example. Watch a sports video in the United States? It will probably have commercials and be sponsored by an advertiser – a brewery, for example – which will use the video for sales promotion purposes. Some entertainment videos are being produced directly by cadres, like *McTreasure Island*, starring Ronald McDonald.

If commercials can be inserted into television programs, why not make program-length commercials inserted into television schedules? Evangelical broadcasting in effect has been doing that all along. Now the format is being used by promoters of dwarf trees, ant farms, hair oil, get-rich-quick schemes, miraculous multi-vitamins, and similar ventures and products. "Infomercials," they're called, or, by cynical cadres themselves, "trash for cash." Usually they are shown in off hours, but not always; they are slowly moving into better time-slots. Part of their intrusiveness is adopting the guise of regular programs, with "program hosts" and "reporters" conducting "real interviews," so as to blur the line between regular programming and the commercials. Print does the same thing with its "advertorial" sections. Higher-class advertisers will sometimes use specially produced documentaries called "documercials" or "comdocs" – upscale infomercials.

Billboards proper have long interfered with cityscapes and countrysides. Now there are videowalls constructed out of twenty-six-inch television monitors, up to as many as 108 of them, for malls and intersections. They won't let your eye wander away.

One particularly ambitious American cadre, Christopher Whittle, is publishing short hard-cover books with advertising between the chapters. The books are put together as marketing packages, with part or all of each publishing run, depending on the series, distributed free to target audiences. A *Washington Post* columnist surmised that if the experiment succeeds, advertisements in regular book publishing may not be far behind.

Whittle has also floated a satellite-delivered television news and features package for school classrooms, packed with advertising, to reach kids twelve to seventeen years of age. Aside from bringing commercial propaganda into the classroom, it has a special intrusiveness bonus. When the kids watch television at home, they can go to the bathroom or get something to eat when the commercials are on. But this commercial package, as a St. Louis advertising copywriter herself protested, is "forced" viewing.

When California and New York state rejected the Whittle "educational" network, an editorial in *Advertising Age* called the school officials a "lynch mob." Another editorial suggested the scheme was a humanitarian effort. "Whittle's idea," it said, "is to donate valuable video equipment to schools." Video equipment was the carrot Whittle offered to get the package into classrooms. Whittle reached its initial target of 8,000 schools in about a year after launch. Such *quid pro quos* aren't a new idea. Pepsico donates sports equipment in exchange for vending- machine placements. Coca-Cola provides scoreboards. Some other national advertisers donate equipment or money to schools in exchange for collecting product labels, which helps school children make sure their parents buy the right brands. Consumers Union has identified marketing-service companies that specialize in product placements in schools and use "school as the new prime time to sell and tell." Schools, says their report *Selling America's Kids*, "are turning into an advertising medium." Even pre-schoolers in kindergarten are targeted. Guidelines are ignored. *Selling America's Kids* lists 234 companies that market in one way or another in classrooms. *U.S. News and World Report* quoted one estimate that put the total of companies and organizations marketing in U.S. schools at twelve thousand.

Telephone kiosks in some U.S. schools are now crowned by fourteen-inch screens playing silent commercials from such as Coca-Cola, Kraft, Pizza Hut, and Reebok (brought to you by Telephone Advertising Corp.). Make a call from a telephone in a college dorm? Hello, there are display ads on the wall (thanks to Collegiate Marketing & Communications).

Another Whittle project is a videodisk television package for doctors' waiting rooms, so that while patients are waiting to see their doctor, advertisers can take a special run at them. This was an add-on to a Whittle quarterly magazine for doctors' offices, which does the same thing. Half of Whittle Communications now belongs to Time Warner. The jargon for such advertising is "place-based": It gets people wherever they go. Inspired by Whittle's initiatives, U.S. media executives are looking forward to greater use of captive audiences – in offices, schools, health clubs (up to fifty TV monitors per club), airports, bus and train stations, banks, fast-food restaurants, and other places where the citizenry can't duck.

The new wrinkle in supermarket background music is lacing it with commercials. Grocery carts now have advertising. "The shopper sees [the message] subconsciously every time an item is put in the basket," a Canadian ad agency executive enthused. If placards on the carts weren't enough, a Chicago market-research firm is putting "VideOcarts" into supermarkets: electronic video screens mounted on shopping carts, with ads and other messages fed via rooftop satellite dishes and low-power retransmitters. The videocarts are programmed so that different advertising spots can be shown as customers reach predetermined points in each aisle.

Multiple television monitors or electronic signs, some as large as two feet by five feet, are being hung over some supermarket aisles and shelves, for shoppers visually to bump into. Computer technology, using motion, light, and colour, flashes on advertising messages. The use of in-store media generally is being stepped up. Reach for something on the shelf and your eye may be hit by a sales promotion card, dubbed "shelf talker." One gimmick being tested actually does talk: It automatically plays a thirteen-second commercial or jingle as you approach and dispenses a cents-off coupon or sweepstakes entry. Look up at the aisle directory: more ads. Avert your eyes to the floor? TheFloorBoard, a patented process, is about to put mini-billboards there, too. Go to the checkout and – the coming thing – you'll start running into a packaged television "chopped-news" (or "infotainment") channel, with plenty of commercials (taking up 30 per cent of the time). On your way out, you may hit another promotional bulletin board, just by the door.

Some cities, like London, The Hague, and Regina as of last report, have parking-meter ads. One promoter of the idea found, in his research, that men spend twelve seconds feeding coins into meters, women fourteen seconds, and that a pedestrian needs twenty-six seconds to walk by five consecutive meters. These few seconds of private time, he concluded, could be intruded upon. "It's quite like subliminal advertising," one user said. "People see it and see it." Drive down the Queen Elizabeth Way in Toronto and you'll see "corporate garden billboards" along the embankment. Go to the SkyDome for a Blue Jays baseball game, and the giant JumboTron television screen will pummel you with video ads every half-inning and with still-picture ads each time a new batter comes to the plate. Stop for gas? Television monitors on gas pumps (two per pump), blasting forth commercials, are being tested in the United States.

Taking a bus or streetcar is no escape, either. Not just the occasional transit shelter has ads. Ads are being put on bus-stop posts. Is there advertising on the inside and the outside of the bus? Now the whole length of the bus's exterior may be painted up as an advertisement. "Total paint," it's called – totally intrusive, which is the point. (Southwest Airlines has even done it with three of its Boeing 737s.) Ask the bus driver for a transfer? Depending on the city you're in, it may have an advertisement on it, too. So might your fare card. Ads on subway tokens have been suggested. Buses in the north of England have audio ads in case the traveller ignores the printed and painted ones. Commercials appear on television monitors hung in railway terminals. Agencies in Japan are using spaced images or laser projection, depending on the scheme, to produce video-like commercials on train and subway-car windows as they speed through tunnels.

Ads increasingly are being put on washroom walls and stall doors in restaurants, nightclubs, health clubs, and elsewhere; take a pee and you have to look at an ad. One firm that places these ads bluntly calls itself "Captive Audience." In the the United States, ads are being put in "jet johns"; relieve yourself while avoiding the in-flight movie commercials, and other advertising gets you.

Tee up at the golf course and check the sign beside you showing where the sand traps are; you may be trapped by an ad. Ball-washer boxes on some U.S. golf courses have ads. Markers with advertising are now also being put on the edge of fairways. Hole out on some U.S. course and an ad may be waiting for you in the bottom of the golf cup (courtesy of "Ad-in-the-hole"). Take up skiing instead, in disgust. The lift towers, lift buildings, time and message centres, lodges, cafeterias, and even ski-run maps may catch you with ads. Inevitably, television monitors with closed-circuit packages are now entering the scene; get into a lift line and the commercials will get you.

The U.S. advertising bureaucracy, in the form of a Virginia consulting company, has even put ads on the wrapper of U.S. Customs Service declaration forms, which all people flying into the United States (except those from Canada and Mexico), must read and complete. "The passengers are sitting with this for the entire flight and they have to look at it," exulted a company spokesman. "It's not optional reading." "Just when you thought the world was running out of places for advertising messages . . . . ," *Advertising Age* quipped. In Britain, advertising has stepped into postage cancellation. Metered-mail postage in most places has long carried messages from the company doing the mailing; the company's name is already on the envelope anyway. But the new postage-cancellation ads intrude on outside-party mail. Send a *billet doux* to your lover and it could arrive with an unsolicited advertising message on it. They'll even catch you when you prepare your *billet doux* for mailing to begin with: Ads are now beginning to appear on the "selvage" – the border – of sheets of postage stamps in Canada.

No object is too small or too fragile to be safe. Ad messages are squirted onto egg shells ("empty spaces just waiting to be exploited," *Marketing* magazine described them). Ads appear on paper clips.

Look up at the sky in despair, hoping that a dirigible or a balloon with advertising doesn't get in your way. That, finally, is no escape, either. A computer-generated corporate logo may appear on a cloud formation, thanks to the merciless combination of marketing bureaucracy and laser technology.

This dreaming up of new ways of intruding on people, via what the cadres call "non-traditional media," is now a regularized, expanding part of the branch. *The Economist* estimates that the average American now sees more than three thousand advertising messages a day.

The intrusiveness doesn't end with just the advertising. Advertisers and their agencies have long intruded on the other content of the media, particularly of television. They've censored programs. "Dollar censorship," Newton Minow, former chairman of the U.S. Federal Communications Commission pungently labelled the practice. They also have produced programs themselves, controlling them directly, an arrangement which went out of style for a while but is now coming back.

The mechanism by which advertisers pay for programming according to ratings has indirectly, but relentlessly, restricted the kinds of programs that appear in network prime time (almost exclusively entertainment programs) and the independence of producers and writers. Newton Minow called this "ratings censorship." The ratings dictatorship shapes programming style (more "jolts per minute"), affects how news is done, and determines the kind of programming thrown at children. It bullies and distorts television schedules.

The heavy hand of bureaucracy works in less direct ways as well. There has been a gradual meeting of minds, on public issues, by network and station operators and by advertisers and their agencies. The latter provide the former with their money. This limits the range of expression, not least in the way that the media deal with the advertising bureaucracy itself. Independent consumer information that fights the culture of brand-name advertising, for example, is largely beyond the pale. Except for the odd, incidental report or comment, the bureaucracy itself wonderfully escapes criticism.

The advertising and marketing branch isn't just an arrogant bureaucracy, fattening itself at the expense of the public. It is the rare case of a bureaucracy whose actual mandate is to take advantage of the public and work against it.

The bureaucracy is particularly antagonistic to people who flip through the pages of a magazine without looking at the ads or who avoid the commercials on television. Cadres also pull their hair with angst about how to combat "commercial wear-out" – the loss, through repetition, of a commercial's ability to hold the viewer's attention. In all, as Eric Clark commented, "it calls for a kind of warfare. The brain puts up its protective barrier. The people who create the ads have to come up with a way to get round, over, under or through it." The advertising branch has no compunction using mind-numbing repetition and manipulation to overcome the viewer's defences or critical notions. "Manipulate those around you," goes the corporate credo of Japanese advertising powerhouse Dentsu, which grew out of Japan's wartime propaganda machine. "In the end, the manipulative rise way above the manipulated."

One advertising commentator, in discussing the zapping of television commercials, argued that the only real protection the advertising bureaucracy had against it was "media weight" – more repetitions. "The more zapping that occurs, the more total impressions are needed to burn the spot (whatever the creative approach) into the minds of viewers and onto the commercial recall studies."

Games and artifices have been touted as a weapon against zapping. If, for example, an advertiser inserts clues for prizes or sweepstakes numbers within commercial clusters, viewers hooked on getting something for nothing will have to watch the ads whether they want to or not. Another trick is to fuse a commercial "billboard" at the head of a mini-program – during sports program intermissions, Ford's "Great Moments In Hockey," for example – so that anybody who wants to watch the mini-program is willy nilly exposed to the advertiser's plug.

"People might not like it," a leading U.S. advertising lobbyist said, of the manipulation of sound techniques in commercials, "but unless the guy gets in [a salesman gets his foot in the door], he hasn't got any chance at all." It's not that choice cannot be offered. Broadcasters, for example, could put an inaudible signal at the beginning of each commercial pod and another one at the end, and make available cheaply, on a mass-production basis, a set attachment that would automatically silence or blank out the commercials. Viewers could then decide whether and how they wanted to be irritated. The inaudible signal could also be used, in video recording, to excise the commercial time altogether. Of course, that is exactly what the advertising branch does not want us to do.

Action for Children's Television, a U.S. citizens' organization, pushed the idea of such an automatic deletion system for commercials directed at children, whereby parents could decide what was watched. Commercials directed at children are akin to letting a high-powered, manipulative salesperson into one's living room to get at one's children alone. The idea of an automatic deletion device to preclude that did not get far. An ad-axer device would undermine "the whole concept of a commercial system of broadcasting," the president of the National Association of Broadcasters declared. The commercial system of broadcasting needed its autocratic protection to keep afloat, he was saying, in so many words. The invocation of the "commercial system of broadcasting," however, drew resonance from the anterior ideology of free enterprise, which is sacrosanct, and behind which, in this case as with the New Bureaucracy in general, bureaucratic power hides.

Perhaps the cardinal sign of an entrenched and arrogant bureaucracy is that it freely imposes on others what it does not want for itself. Advertising cadres are an élitist minority inasmuch as they rarely watch commercials except as part of their work in the office. They just inflict them on others. Meanwhile, if anybody complains, the cadres call the complainers "élitist" and charge them with being against "ordinary people," reversing common-sense with the same self-serving smugness as the pigs in Orwell's *Animal Farm.*

A survey done in Britain in 1986, for example, found that most business executives watched commercial television less than a quarter of the national average, and a fifth watched no commercial television at all. When debate raged about whether or not the BBC should carry commercials, a survey was done of two hundred marketing and sales directors selected at random from a Dun and Bradstreet's directory of major British companies. In their bureaucratic capacities, a majority were in favour of commercials on the BBC, but "as a member of the public and a TV viewer," most were very much opposed to the prospect. In Canada, in 1973, a survey of business opinion by the *Financial Times of Canada* found that 64 per cent of business people considered advertising was untruthful or misleading, 61 per cent agreed it was intrusive and annoying, and 59 per cent agreed it was insulting to intelligence. Television commercials in particular were disliked. At a 1990 speech to three hundred top U.S. ad agency bureaucrats, the executive vice-president of one major agency asked for a show of hands of those who thought there was too much advertising. Almost everybody raised a hand.

Against this syndrome – where the cadres do things to the public they do not want done to themselves as members of the public – an awareness of advertising's manipulation, waste, grossness, and even injury has little or no effect. Absurdity piles on absurdity, as the bureaucracy follows its own rules. Cigarette advertising and marketing is a graphic case in point – the promotion of a practice which kills people. When efforts are made to eliminate cigarette advertising, ad agency spokespeople mutter about "a severe blow to the advertising industry" and "devastating" effects. Tobacco companies, meanwhile, throw large sums of money into the political battle.

When restrictions are finally legislated, the advertising bureaucracy goes to work circumventing them. If broadcast advertising is out, resources are shifted into print, or event sponsorship, or other sales promotion. When cigarette advertising on television was banned in the United States in 1971, for example, the advertising in magazines and newspapers was increased an extra 150 per cent. Promotional spending was pushed up dramatically, from 14.7 per cent of marketing expenditures in 1970 to 66.2 per cent by 1987; annual promotional spending in constant dollars multiplied by eleven times in that period. The four largest outdoor advertisers in the United States, using billboards and similar locations, are cigarette companies, according to Leading National Advertisers data. Cigarettes and tobacco, similarly, are the largest outdoor advertiser as a category, spending more than two-and-a-half times as much as the runner-up (retail).

Television has not been abandoned in the process, either. Sponsorship of sports events broadcast by television is used in place of prohibited direct advertising. A good example is the 1989 Marlboro Grand Prix, broadcast on NBC. The Marlboro logo was seen 4,998 times on small raceway signs, 519 times on large billboards, 249 times on the Marlboro car, 57 times on the start/finish overpass, 31 times on crew jumpsuits, and so on down to one Marlboro patch on the neck of a driver's wife. There were also eleven verbal references to Marlboro. Of 93.62 minutes of broadcasting, Marlboro was on the screen for 46.17 minutes or 49.32 per cent of the time.

Until the threat of legislation got tobacco companies to drop paid product placements, cigarette packages were also placed in movies in the usual way. Philip Morris once paid US$350,000 to have one of its brands prominently featured in a James Bond movie. In Canada, new legislation – still being fought over in the courts – prohibits cigarette-company sports and cultural sponsorship except under company corporate names (as distinct from brand names on cigarette packages). The tobacco companies simply incorporated new subsidiaries named after their brands and continued their promotions under those "corporate" names. By advertising the events, they carried on with advertising as well, also supposedly disallowed by the legislation.

Another trick, used especially in Europe, is to sell and advertise non-tobacco products with the same name, colours and/or logo as the cigarette package: from lighters, watches and clothes to car wax and video arcade games (obstacles in the form of Marlboro outdoor boards). Yet another trick is paying to get mentions of the brand name in magazine articles and on the radio. Advertising cadres take great pride in circumventing legislation and codes and finding loopholes.

"I work in an ad agency," goes an old ad-agency joke, "but I tell all my family and friends I play the piano in a whorehouse." The joke has more truth in it than the tellers of it realize. Piano players in whorehouses don't manipulate or hurt masses of people. Ad agencies, on the other hand, for all their creative directors and copywriters and glitzy cachet, are bureaucracies using the most refined techniques and testing mechanisms, systematically applied. There is nothing romantic or even illicit about them, just, in this case, the "banality of evil."

Cigarette advertising propaganda is only one instance of the branch's evil banality. There are an annual 100,000 alcohol-related deaths (of which 10,000 are homicides) in the United States and US$130 billion in economic costs from alcohol use. Meanwhile, about $2 billion a year is spent advertising and promoting beer, wine, and liquor in the country, the greater part of that by breweries.

The leading killer of sixteen- to twenty-four-year olds in the United States is alcohol-related traffic accidents. A quarter of eighth graders and 37 per cent of twelfth graders consume five or more drinks on a single occasion within two weeks. One of the two major targets of alcoholic-beverage advertising is youth. The lifestyle ads are especially targeted at youth who, of course, are exposed to them before reaching drinking age. The *Wall Street Journal*, with the aid of a college marketing service, once calculated that two-thirds of all national advertising in U.S. campus newspapers consisted of alcohol advertising. Promotional spillover, from sports sponsorship to product sidelines, also hits young people. The other top target group for alcohol marketing is heavy drinkers, who are also particularly vulnerable to advertising.

Restrictions are no match for the ingenuity of the advertising bureaucracy. " 'Lifestyle' alcohol ads banned in Ontario," read a 1978 *Toronto Star* headline. "Ads cannot glamorize drinking" and " 'Lifestyle' ads banned," read a headline and subhead in a 1983 issue of the *Vancouver Sun*. The restrictions were easily mocked and circumvented.

The advertising branch's function, after all, is exactly to take advantage of people. It does the same with children, against whom all of the machinery of research, targeting, and psychological manipulation is put to work. Cadres talk about "how to capture a child's mind." Research material on children, unlike other market research, isn't bandied around publicly by the cadres because of the outcry it might cause. Even older children who have learned to be sceptical about commercials prove no match in the end for heavy advertising campaigns. "Our advertising strategy," joked the vice-president marketing of Toys 'R' Us, "is nuke 'em till they glow." As for parents, they need to be circumvented and put on the defensive against their children.

Over 80 per cent of advertising directed at children deals with four categories: toys, cereals (primarily sugar-coated cereals), candies, and fast-food restaurants. One of the most notorious bureaucratic masterstrokes has been the introduction in the United States of programs based on toys – in effect, half-hour commercials. Sales promotion techniques and devices are also used, like television kids' clubs complete with newsletters or magazines where advertisers can do couponing as well as flogging brands. "Clubs disguise commercial messages," commented Consumers Union. "Kids are invited to join something that promises to be 'theirs,' but turns out to be a way of manipulating them to buy things." About two dozen major U.S. brand-name advertisers have also started kids' clubs of their own.

It's not surprising that in the most bureaucratically captive country, the United States, the advertising bureaucracy has the freest rein in manipulating children and that concerted and persistent attempts to do something about it have been beaten back.

One of the most heavily propagandized products is pharmaceuticals. Doctors are researched, targeted, and manipulated in favour of brand names and line-extensions, with all the bureaucratic meticulousness applied to market research in general. Despite the doctors' image of themselves as objective professionals, they succumb like everybody else. Sales promotion spending, largely for "detailers" who call on doctors, is huge. Marketing costs, including advertising and promotion, now eat up about 20 to 25 per cent of drug revenues, about double the percentage a decade earlier, and almost double the spending on research and development. Pharmaceuticals, however, are supposed to be chosen by doctors on the basis of scientific information.

The consequences were predictable: over-prescribing, unnecessarily high dosages, a discounting of side effects (detailers are instructed to play them down), unmeasured suffering and discomfort as a result, extra hospital admissions from overuse and adverse reactions, and inflated costs (because of both brand-name power and the high marketing expenses). Propaganda for over-the-counter drugs contributes to a quick-fix chemical culture.

The same propagandized distortion occurs with food, another health element. High-sugar, high-fat, and high-additive products are pushed indiscriminately.

Images of women as sexual toys, and hence as targets of abuse and humiliation, are still standbys of the advertising branch. Images of wholly or partly naked women have been crudely used all along in trade magazines and calendars, but brand-name mass-media advertising has added high-powered sophistication to the device. Specific images, cropping up in print ads or television commercials in different parts of the world, have ranged from more-or-less naked women in sexually provocative poses to bondage, telephone-number sex advertising, violent and overt phallic imagery (a knife, a bottle), suggested group sex (several men, one woman), and impending rape and other sexual violence ("S&M chic"; clench-fisted men glowering at their women). One notorious Argentine case involved a double-entendre invitation to punch a woman.

If you can use young women for the purpose, why not use underaged younger women? Jeans commercials have used fifteen and fourteen-year olds. And why not use children? A little girl in a bikini, with earrings, made up, looking sophisticated next to her sexy, equally naked mother; topless toddlers in mascara; pouty schoolgirls in lace; a young girl dressed seductively, lying on a table ("Innocence is sexy after all") and seductively posed boys sell suntan lotion and perfume. And, as clinical psychologists have observed, they also excite child molesters.

This exploitation of children and use of children is just a variation of the bureaucracy's propaganda over all – lies of association, suggestion, and omission, which is how the best propaganda works. Nobody has any illusions about this lying, either. Besides, as Northrop Frye has pointed out, advertising doesn't have to be believed literally to do its purpose. Much of advertising is fantastic – so fantastic it can't be taken seriously and criticized at the literal level. So viewers' critical propensity is suspended, while the imagery and exhortation go to work. This makes the advertising all the more insidious.

Waste, intrusiveness, and abuse are not the only consequences of this entrenched bureaucratic power, however. We think of other, foreign bureaucracies – Stalinist apparatchiks, Chinese mandarins, the old Spanish court – as being rigid by their nature and resistant to change, because change would destroy their power. The history of their increasingly bizarre behaviour intrigues and appalls us. The New Bureaucracy's advertising branch, with its whacko materialism in a world under environmental siege, is of the same order. Much worse, it passes on its "bureaucratic realism" – a reality which it doesn't even believe in – through pervasive mass-media propaganda, making whole societies rigid and the world less able to adapt to the environmental threat upon it.

Social fabrics are also damaged. The propaganda portrays the values of consumption, instant gratification, and self-indulgence, but not the values of self-discipline, co-operation, community, productive investment and livable neighbourhoods. Expressions of these values have a harder and harder time against the "bureaucratic realism." Intractabilities crop up everywhere. The most vulnerable to the bureaucracy are the most disarmed by it. Take, for example, a black ghetto in Chicago. The area is plagued by crack and other drugs, has high rates of unemployment and people on welfare, and is full of single teen-age mothers with poor educational achievement and job prospects. For the young, the quick money to get the latest thing comes from stringing for drug dealers. The community is disabled. People there do, however, watch lots of television, where they are flooded with images of beer, easy good times, "status" sneakers and fast cars.

In genuine democracies, on the other hand, different values are allowed to find their balance freely.

The principal device the advertising bureaucracy uses when attempts are made to curb its abuses – its waste is inviolable – is an appeal to freedom of speech and to the free-enterprise system. When steps were taken in the United States to eliminate cigarette commercials on radio and television, the tobacco lobby hollered that its "First Amendment rights" of free speech were being abrogated. The tobacco lobby in Canada has resorted to the same argument in its fight against the 1988 bill banning cigarette advertising. The alcohol lobby has cranked up the same defence. "Is there an unworthy cause in the land that will not try a free speech defence?" *Washington Post* columnist Charles Krauthammer drily observed. A catchy phrase was invented, using word association, to carry the argument forward: "commercial free speech." "Freedom of choice" is another loaded phrase often used.

Coalitions were formed for lobbying purposes, like a new well-heeled U.S. organization called "Libertad" (liberty and advertising; also Spanish for liberty), backed by the tobacco industry, the breweries, and others. It follows what is now typical New-Bureaucracy form – applying bureaucratic leverage over money to finance self-serving political propaganda and lobbying. One of its slick full-page magazine ads showed a pair of fingers pinching out the torch of the Statue of Liberty. "Censorship extinguishes the flame of freedom," said the ad's headline. The ad attacked "people who think they must control our freedom." Philip Morris mounted a campaign associating itself with the Bill of Rights, complete with a series of slick full-page advertisements in magazines and newspapers across the United States, with television ads, and with a national exhibition tour, also heavily advertised. The cost was US$60 million plus.

As the *Washington Post* columnist remarked, speech is already massively controlled on mass media. There are elaborate and strict censorship codes for television, for example. People are willing to make television speech a bit less free when there is an important reason for doing so. More pertinent, there is no such thing as "commercial freedom of speech." Advertising is an extension of selling. Restricting advertising isn't a freedom-of-speech matter at all, but a regulation-of-trade matter. It is possible, for example, to ban the actual sale of tobacco (the way the sale of marijuana, heroine, and cocaine are banned). Banning their advertising is a lesser prohibition. Freedom of speech, which is for matters of conscience, news, art, opinion, and democratic debate, does not come into it.

Even more fundamental an issue is whether one should be able to flood a society with propaganda simply because one has the money to do so, while others cannot do the same. The American ideology of free enterprise covers for the advertising bureaucracy again, because it militates against any restrictions on the use of property and wealth.

All that aside, the advertising bureaucracy isn't for freedom of speech and freedom of choice in any case – no more, in their realm, than were bureaucrats in communist countries. Advertising propaganda is exceptional in western societies in being one-way propaganda. This is how it gets its bureaucratic power. Unlike political campaigns where one party's propaganda has to face opposing propaganda from the other side, voices opposing the messages of commercials are not allowed in an equivalent format. The bureaucracy does everything it can to suppress such opposition.

Not that there is much opposition anymore. The public has given up, resigned to being pummelled. Fifteen or twenty years ago, television columnists used to inveigh against the increasing frequency and interruptions of commercials. Now they no longer bother. They know it's futile to protest. In the 1989 British satirical movie *How To Get Ahead in Advertising*, the hero, when he misses a deadline for a pimple cream company, cracks up, quits his job, and vows reform. In his moment of enlightenment, he sprouts a boil of his own, on his neck, which grows facial features and spouts advertising slogans at him. The allegorical device is reminiscent of eastern European political jokes about their communist bureaucracies, against which only cynical, private humour was possible.

The U.S. tobacco companies fought tooth and nail against the application of the Federal Communications Commission's (FCC) "Fairness Doctrine" to provide equal time for anti-smoking counter-commercials. The doctrine called for free speech and the presentation of opposing views. The anti-smoking commercials were "the first appearance of simple truth on commercial TV," FCC commissioner Nicholas Johnson commented at the time. The counter-commercials actively hurt the tobacco companies. They got so much attention, they also threatened to set a precedent for other commercials. Advertisers, agencies, and broadcasting companies decided it was better to let the cigarette commercials disappear, taking the counter-commercials with them, rather than to risk the example spreading.

The Fairness Doctrine, applied to advertising propaganda in general, would mean that counter-commercials proclaiming the deficiencies of goods and openly contradicting the original commercials would be carried free whenever consumers had objections to them. The U.S. Federal Trade Commission (FTC), in the early 1970s, actually made such a proposal to the FCC. "Our feeling is that advertising has been too much of a one-way street," the chairman of the FTC explained. "The advertiser presents just one side of what could be a many-sided question. Advertising may be the only form of public talk in which there's no general opportunity for public debate, for rebuttal, for airing opposing ideas. To us, that doesn't seem quite right." U.S. public-interest advocates brought forward test cases having to do with toys (misleading claims), large-engine cars and leaded gasoline (damage to the environment), phosphate detergents (also damage to the environment), and garbage compactors (antithetical to recycling).

The advertising branch realized what this would do to them, since a system of closed propaganda, on coming into contact with a body of free and equal speech, disintegrates, and everything dependent on that system falls to the ground. They turned up the lobbying screws, to make the Fairness Doctrine disintegrate instead. Under this pressure, the FCC brought out a "Fairness Report" declaring product advertising to be outside the bounds of the Fairness Doctrine.

The advertising bureaucracy has continued in this way to fight against free and equal speech and against choice. The U.S. breweries fought against their own commercials being banned, successfully, although a majority of Americans favoured the move. Then they fought against equal time for counter-ads. (They also, such is their love for free speech, fought against distillers being allowed to advertise on television.)

The bureaucracy's attempt to hide behind freedom of speech and freedom of choice is akin to the communist bureaucracies' hiding behind "democratic centralism" in the name of democracy. Free and equal speech would dissolve the advertising bureaucracy's entrenched power as quickly and easily as free speech broke up communist bureaucratic sway in Eastern Europe once it was allowed.

Free-enterprise ideology is the last refuge of wasteful bureaucracies.

8

The Culture and Sports Branch

If throwing millions of dollars into a Pepsi commercial isn't enough waste, and if pushing cigarettes with huge magazine and billboard expenditures (still permitted in the U.S.) isn't enough bureaucratic evil, the advertising and marketing branch has now overlaid its waste and intrusion on culture and sports as well. Given free-enterprise mythology which protects such bureaucratic growth, it was inevitable.

The inflation has been so rapid that the cadres who first got involved, and who feed the inflation in turn, can hardly believe their good luck. "Event marketing" is the jargon for this new bureaucratic layer. "Sponsorship" is another name for it. The idea is to buy "rights" to an event, or to buy or create the event oneself, and use it to market one's brand name. Olympic Games "sponsorship" is an example. The sponsorship simultaneously triggers additional advertising and sales promotion allocations.

It also represents another bureaucratic encroachment on liberties. The arts are supposed to be a free expression of the human spirit and imagination, at least in non-communist western democracies. Where there is a possibility that government might interfere, battle cries go up. State censorship is anathema. Since public money for the arts requires some kind of formal legislated mechanism, considerable care is given, in countries such as Canada, to keep the government bureaucracy at a distance. The distancing is called an "arms-length" relationship. The government and the bureaucrats who work for it aren't allowed to meddle in the operations of the CBC or the Canada Council, for example. If artists and journalists are in bed with the government and its bureaucracy, it is assumed they have compromised themselves.

The New Bureaucracy, on the other hand, protected by ideology, doesn't need to put up with an arms-length relationship. It jumps into the bed, having arranged for the recipients of its largesse to have intercourse with it.

Tied to this is what is known familiarly as "commercialization." The great quality of art, entertainment, and athletic prowess is that they express themselves in their own terms. Add commercialization – an extraneous, interfering element – and you turn, and sometimes poison, the wine. With event marketing, in short, creeping "bureaucratic realism" has gotten into every corner. It has even gotten into charities – "cause-related marketing," it's called, in the jargon. Big Brother Market Research is watching you, and you are watching the name and logo he wants you to watch.

Fifteen years ago, this bureaucratic branch, for all intents and purposes, did not exist. The first conference for its cadres in the U.S. wasn't held until 1982. In just a few years, it was growing at a "staggering pace," as one cadre put it. By 1991, total spending on event sponsorship in the U.S. and Canada together was US$2.9 billion. This staggering inflation, almost out of nothing, represents a bureaucratic coup. The rising expenditure, in turn, generates additional spending on advertising and promotion, pushing the link between the event and the brand name. Sponsors routinely put out as much for this "support" propaganda as for the rights purchase itself, and often much more. Many cadres call for at least a two-to-one outlay. For amateur sports – the Olympics, for example – a three-to-one ratio is common.

The heaviest spenders on event marketing are sectors whose aggregate market share is stagnant or declining – breweries, tobacco companies, liquor companies. At one point, the breweries in Canada bankrolled – read "subsidized" – half of the sports events reported by the media. They dominate sports sponsorship.

Given the multiplied spending on support advertising and promotion, only a relatively small percentage of the outlay helps finance the actual event. If a company were primarily interested in supporting some activity, it would hand over a donation anonymously or endow a foundation for the purpose.

The bureaucratic spillage doesn't end there, however. The "sponsor" corporation (part of the corporate branch) needs its own bureaucracy to make decisions on events and to oversee allocations. The recipient organization needs its own bureaucracy to hustle its events to "sponsor" corporations and to manage their intercourse. Participants in events who feed in this bureaucratic trough, mostly athletes, need their own bureaucracy (agents and managers). In the middle of them all, and providing the major bureaucratic impetus, is a separate new bureaucratic section offering specialist advice and linking "sponsors" to recipient organizations and vice-versa. These are the event-marketing consultants (sponsorship agencies and boutiques). Cadres in this section may also concoct and manage events for a "sponsor," screen requests for money, provide measurement services (research), represent athletes, and undertake any other tasks in place of in-house cadres. This consulting section, promoting event marketing – promoting its own make-work – has mushroomed.

This is the culture and sports branch proper.

One of the originals among the consultant cadres, and a leader, is the Cleveland-based International Management Group (IMG). It will not only manage sports and cultural events and series, it will also conceive and develop them to suit; stage an event or series from beginning to end; acquire rights for "sponsors"; make up a "sponsorship" package and represent the sponsor; package and sell television rights; sell and operate on-site "hospitality" services (including turnkey corporate entertainment programs, custom decorating, celebrity hosts); look after merchandising and licensing for an event; produce film and video of the event and of the sponsor's participation in the event; make programs of the event (and sell the advertising for the programs); and undertake promotion and publicity for the event and the sponsors connected to it. IMG now has sixteen divisions and operates through twenty-five offices around the world, including one in Toronto.

IMG and similar operations are just the first of many layers of event-marketing ranks in North America. Behind each brand-name or logo appearance seen by the public – for example, the American Express and Pepsi-Cola logos where *The Phantom of the Opera* is promoted – is a bureaucratic cadre unseen, in the above instance, a Toronto event-marketing boutique. Proliferation into bureaucratic varieties was predictable: shops specializing in sports events (among them, major sports management companies), entertainment, the arts, licensing, and public relations as well as those, like IMG, that try to cover the whole field. Advertising and public-relations firms build up special-events divisions. "Everyone is scrambling to make [event marketing] a part of their territory," a U.S. observer of the scene commented.

The ranks of sponsor-corporation in-house cadres grow in parallel. There are now such things as a "vice-president, event marketing," a "group manager, sports and special events," and a "community affairs manager." Brand-name managers and other marketing cadres get into the act. Other senior management (up to the CEO) and public-relations specialists (directors of communications and retinue) are pushed to get involved. Pollsters and market-research firms cross over into this branch. In the United States, there are more than four thousand major corporations now involved in sponsorship.

Most companies attach their names to existing events, but a growing number are also concocting their own events, trying to target their audience.

More than two hundred U.S. companies have established in-house departments responsible for nothing other than dreaming up such special events. Some have established operational subsidiaries to run the events. (Larger event-marketing agencies may also own some events themselves.)

Aside from the brand-name marketing inflation, other bureaucratic impulses are at work, on the corporate side. Sponsorship is used to increase visibility within the corporate community and to impress clients, a little like having a sufficiently impressive fleet of corporate jets. Olympic sponsorship is particularly good for such competitive emulation. Indeed, visibility among the corporate Joneses is used as a selling point in International Olympic Committee (IOC) sales pitches.

Best of all, sponsorship is executive indulgence and preening at its most gratifying. The CEO, for example, can choose to subsidize an event closest to his pleasures. It's a bureaucratic freedom to allocate moneys that would put to shame a corrupt commissar buying himself a *dacha* with public funds. Golf, corporate executives' favourite sport – almost an executive requirement – is one of the three most heavily subsidized categories of events, and not only because of its good marketing demographics.

The indulgence only begins there. Ross Johnson, while at RJR Nabisco, gained notoriety for the opulent hospitality offered to visiting friends and VIPs at the golf tournament sponsored by the company. A corporate tent at the National Football League's Super Bowl is another favourite. At Super Bowl XXV in Tampa in 1991, for example, forty-two corporate tents from 2,400 to 45,000 square feet in size covered some 500,000 square feet of parking lot. The basic tent package included AstroTurf carpeting, entrance canopy with corporate signage, elegant table linen, air conditioning, floral centerpieces, unlimited gourmet food, the best in bar service, and security. The cost for a 200-people tent package was US$59,000 or $295 per person, not including special theme decor, entertainment, private rest rooms, game tickets, hotel rooms, travel, gifts, and other incidentals that a sponsoring bureaucracy might throw in for its guests. At one Super Bowl, for example, in San Diego in 1988, a corporate tent featured a dance floor and the Count Basie band.

"Sponsorship" of artistic events allows for a different but no less pleasing bureaucratic ease and enjoyment. Take a sample event – a 1990 "fundraiser" for the Toronto Symphony – first, a concert with Liza Minnelli, backed up by the orchestra (nothing too heavy for the party-goers), and then a reception and dinner at the Metro Convention Centre. Tickets were $500 each. The evening was sponsored by Northern Telecom. Other companies bought tables of ten tickets. Helix Fragrances, which creates custom-made corporate perfumes, created a special perfume called Gala exclusively for the evening. Executives and their wives attended (all the executives appear to have been men). Names were noted in the social column of the *Financial Post*'s next issue.

Corporate sponsorships of various kinds allow executives and "corporate wives" (occasionally "corporate husbands" and "corporate lovers") to rub shoulders with literary luminaries, attend receptions to meet pop stars, eat of the best catering, "personally congratulate" (viz. rub shoulders with) the cast of performers at similar gala receptions, even participate in artistic events (say, as spear carriers in opera), and generally bask in an ambiance of sophistication, culture, and social standing – no mean bureaucratic perks.

Add to this good bureaucratic life the psychological perk of being thanked profusely for one's generosity (using shareholders' and, indirectly, taxpayers' money) as if one had forked up the money oneself from a wage-earner's income. Awards ceremonies, at which CEOs and minions, in black tie, pat each other on the back for donating company cash to the arts, also provide psychic and social satisfaction. Framed certificates and trophies are freely handed out.

Recipient organizations, which get the allocations and realize what is to be had, build up their own cadres, also with bureaucratically impressive titles: "director of development," "director of corporate development," "director of tournaments" (in the case of golf and tennis tournaments), "manager of corporate and sponsorship campaigns," and so on. These cadres, in professional sports organizations, were always marketers. In arts organizations, the cadres were more likely to have been conventional fund raisers asking for donations. Now they have become marketers, too. A new subsection, "fund-raising consultants," also helps out, for a price. The IOC, once a bastion of amateurism, has become a marketer. These new cadres pander to and flatter corporate executives, brand-name managers, and public-relations functionaries; adopt their bureaucratic notions and language; and by their weight in their own organizations, help modify their characters in the process.

These sections in turn have inevitably generated a seminar and publications subsection. In Canada, the *Financial Post* organizes periodic sponsorship conferences and an annual awards ceremony. The big sponsorship conference in the U.S. is organized by the International Events Group (IEG); one thousand apparatchiks from corporations, agency intermediaries, and recipient organizations (sometimes called "sponsees") showed up for the IEG conference in 1990. No detail on how to use events for marketing is too small or too manipulative to be left unexplained and undiscussed at these get-togethers. Pricey newsletters for the cadres report on the scene.

Corporate sponsorship provides a bureaucratic cover for a vast inflation of spending. There is, for a start, a direct flow-through of inflated compensation to athletes and performers, who play the role here, again, of fellow travellers to the bureaucracy. Take, as one example, the Grand Prix tennis circuit. It was founded in 1970 with just over US$2 million in prize money. By 1988 it had reached $30 million in player compensation. Prize money for other sports and events, like the PGA Tour in golf, tells the same story. An extra layer of endorsement income, on top of that, comes from wearing logos, which show up in the televising of events. For music performers, sponsorship of events and tours – Pepsi sponsorship of Tina Turner, Michael Jackson, and David Bowie tours, or Coca-Cola sponsorship of Whitney Houston tours, for example – adds another bureaucratic dispensation to already massive incomes.

These figures are just for the extra bureaucratic flow-through to athletes and performers. Costs only begin there. The Olympic Games are an example. The 1976 Montreal Olympics were plagued by construction-cost scandals and overruns. The 1988 Calgary Winter Olympics, on the other hand, were considered a model of restraint and efficiency and, most important, were "profitable." Yet the Calgary games came in at C$800 million, almost double the original projection and four-and-a-half times the cost of the Sarajevo, Yugoslavia, games just four years earlier. Part of the extra cost was paid for by $80 million in sponsorship rights and by the record $386 million in television rights from the U.S. network ABC (much of whose advertising revenue for the games would come, in turn, from corporate sponsors). Protected by ideology, this made the huge budget overrun perfectly acceptable.

If one added the overhead waste of related sponsor activity – television advertising prior to the games, radio and print advertising, sales promotion (like Petro-Canada's endless and ultimately insufferable Olympic Torch Relay), direct marketing (coupon booklets, etc.), hospitality, and not forgetting sponsorship-agency and corporate-in-house overheads – the Calgary cost becomes an even greater multiple of the Sarajevo figure. Then add to those costs the $140 million in sponsorship rights pocketed by the IOC for its overheads, including the overheads of selling sponsorships in the first place.

These costs came out of the North American economy and, marginally, other economies just as surely as if the Canadian and U.S. governments were called upon to throw in another $440 million in subsidies to make the games "profitable" and then spent an additional $440 million on sales promotion and advertising saying what good governments they were. In that case, of course, there would have been howls of criticism.

There had long been product sponsorship of the Olympics but it wasn't until the 1984 Los Angeles Games, with that country's entrenched New Bureaucracy, that the culture and sports branch became a major factor. It provided 34 per cent of the game's budget as compared to 1.5 per cent for the 1976 Montreal Games. This was exclusive of U.S. television rights (which covered a further 47 per cent), sponsors' sale promotion and hospitality expenditures, and sponsors' staffing of various game activities.

The "corporate Olympics," as the Los Angeles games were dubbed, were a strong impetus behind the future growth of the branch, and a marker of how it would continue to inflate. Single-company sponsorships ran as high as US$15 million. Advertising and promotion doubled or tripled the expenditure. The idea of "defensive" sponsorship, regardless of the cost and modest return, also took root at this stage. Defensive sponsorship involves spending whatever is necessary to buy up all the other opportunities – television, national Olympic committee rights, sponsorship of national teams, and so on – to pre-emptively exclude competitors from undermining one's main sponsorship and indulging in other "ambush marketing." There was a precedent set, too, for "venue sponsorship" – the new Olympic swimming pool and stadium at the University of California, built with a US$4 million donation from McDonald's, with the proviso that the installation bear the company's name. "McLympics," local wags joked.

The ideological rationalization that would be used later for Olympic sponsorship was set here. The games were "U.S. private enterprise at work," the public was told. When the organizers boasted they had found a way of financing the games "without costing the taxpayers a dime" – although they were costing taxpayers, as consumers, for every dime and nickel spent – nobody uttered a peep. The attached advertising and promotional waste was ignored as well. Corporate Olympic expenditures are now huge, with one company alone, Mars, spending upwards of US$200 million on marketing in connection with the 1992 games (Albertville and Barcelona).

Inevitably, in the bureaucracy, event marketing, created as an escape from advertising clutter and its spiralling cost, has itself becoming cluttered and expensive – particularly sports-event marketing. Everybody is getting into the act. Local events, or at least local teams, have always had sponsorship – say, a local merchant buying the uniforms of a baseball team. The culture and sports branch, on the other hand, brings into play its whole bureaucratic apparatus and its strategies of brand-name indoctrination. There is no refuge here for medium-sized sponsors, either. The sponsorship powerhouses – breweries, for example – are expanding into regional and local sponsorship, too. Sponsorship price tags are soaring as the territory becomes crowded and sponsorship is attached to anything under the sun. "[Sponsorship is] taking on many of the characteristics of media advertising," a vice-president of IMG Canada explained.

The resultant next step, as the IMG cadre put it so artlessly, is that "corporations will have to work harder to enjoy the benefits." That is, they will have to spend yet more money and allocate yet more time. Far from seeing this step-by-step inflation as a disaster, event-marketing cadres look upon it as a great opportunity for expanded professionalism, sophistication, and revenue.

The essential working element of the process is bureaucratic intrusion into events. The basic idea is for the name and logo of the sponsor to be seen and repeated as often as possible. A television commercial can always be silenced or zapped. A brand name on banners spread throughout a racing site, at finish lines, on clothes, on arena boards, or on equestrian jumps, on the other hand, are inescapable if one wants to watch the event at all, either on-site or on television. It is the anti-zapping device *par excellence*, and is touted in those terms by event-marketing specialists.

Pushing the brand name or company name into the name of the event itself – "title sponsorship," it's called – is another increasingly used device, especially helpful for getting the brand name or company mentioned and repeated in press coverage of an event. In Canada, there is the Molson Indy (car-race circuit), Player's Ltd. International (tennis tournament), du Maurier World Stage (theatre festival), the Air Canada Classics (symphony concerts), the Bank of Montreal Nations Cup (equestrian competitions), and so on, for major events. Second-tier and third-tier events get the same treatment, say the Smirnoff Grand Prix (tennis), Pepsi Junior Curling or the Esso Cup (swimming). Names can get awkwardly long when the original name of the event is already long and the sponsor's name is then attached to it, like the Federal Express Vancouver International Triathlon, the Husky Women's World Cup Downhill, or The Toronto Symphony Guaranty Trust Canadian Odyssey. With bureaucratic enthusiasm, the component words are strung together anyway. If that's possible, why not a corporate-name brand-name double whammy? Procter & Gamble's Team Tide Motocross Promotion is an example.

The next step is to impose one's name on a building. Canadians are familiar with this in an old form: Massey Hall, Roy Thomson Hall, Beaverbrook Art Gallery. Crass as it might be to name a concert hall after a compulsive acquisitor like Roy Thomson, however, the Thomson donation was made from a mixture of status-seeking (a demand for acknowledgement of achievement) and philanthropy. The new style of name imposition is for cold, bureaucratic event-marketing reasons – the McDonald's pool in Los Angeles, for example, or the du Maurier Theatre Centre at Toronto's Harbourfront. Names can also be attached to performing groups, like the Alcan String Quartet.

Once the intrusion into the name of the event is accomplished, the way is open for mass-media advertising (including full-page newspaper and magazine ads) and sales promotion to take advantage of it, especially valuable for cigarette companies in Canada, which are supposed to be banned from media advertising altogether.

The bureaucratic leverage of self-defined "sponsors" is such that they can impose their name on an event even when their contribution is minor. Most of the support for high-brow culture (symphony, opera, theatre) in Canada comes from the Canada Council and provincial funding agencies. A brand-name advertiser, with only an incremental contribution, can nevertheless, as a condition of participating – in a kind of financial arm-twisting – get its name into the event, become the sponsor, and/or take over the program cover and other display rights. If the major funding source – the Canada Council, for example – insisted that *its* name go on the event, the corporate and event-marketing cadres would lose their leverage, but that doesn't happen. The culture and sports branch of the New Bureaucracy rides on the back of public subsidy.

Imagine if events were called the Sports Canada Progressive Conservative Women's Downhill or the Canada Council/Department of Communications and Culture "Team Progressive Conservative" Symphony Classics; if the public monies accounted for only a fraction of the costs involved; if those names were plastered everywhere (fifty small signs and start and finish banners on a downhill course); if there were expensive full-page newspaper ads thanking the public for attending while featuring the "sponsors'" names (their real purpose); if a large, highly-paid bureaucratic infrastructure was devoted to exploiting events (and choosing them accordingly) solely to enhance the image and presence of the Canada Council, Sports Canada, and the government in power; and if their self-promotion expenditures were two or three times what was allocated to the actual events. . . .

Event-marketing specialists push sports-event marketing by citing how it can take advantage of people's emotions. People often relate to sports emotionally, as participants themselves or because they follow their heroes and teams. It has long been known, for example, that viewers watching games or meets on television – involved in the action – are sitting ducks for commercials. The insertion of brand names and logos into the event itself takes this exploitation of emotions one step further. So does the act of sponsorship – the association of a brand name with an activity that is part of people's lifestyles and emotional loyalties. Rock performances are also sponsorship favourites because, like sports, their audiences are easily targetable, emotionally charged and generally loyal.

In the United States, a handful of companies – Philip Morris, RJR Nabisco and a few others – control 80 to 90 per cent of sponsorship funds, according to an early 1989 estimate. In one year, 1987, RJR Nabisco was involved with some 1,800 individual sporting events. Anheuser-Busch, for beer alone, has sponsorship associations with twenty-three of twenty-four U.S.-based major-league baseball teams, six National Football League teams, twenty-five of twenty-seven National Basketball Association teams, thirteen of fourteen U.S.-based National Hockey League teams, three Major League Soccer teams, the U.S. Olympic Team, and the U.S. boxing, soccer and hockey federations. Local distributors handle sponsorship associations with college sports teams – at last count, more than three hundred of them. The brewery and its distributors together also sponsor about a thousand individual events, almost all with an Anheuser-Busch brand name inserted into the name of the event. In Canada, breweries are heavily involved in rock music, and to a lesser extent in other music and entertainment, as well as bankrolling sports events. Labatt's, for example, subsidized ("sponsored" and "underwritten" are the euphemisms) the five Canadian dates of the Rolling Stones tour in 1989, in exchange for their marketing quid pro quo.

The cigarette and beer event-marketing cadres exploit the possibilities ruthlessly. The Virginia Slims tennis-circuit sponsorship aims at young women, a special target group whose incidence of smoking has been pushed up. Sponsorship of inner city music festivals aims at blacks, another special target group whose smoking has been jacked up. R. J. Reynolds, under the cigarette brand-name More, used to be a sponsor of the Ebony Fashion Fair circuit; glamorous models, exiting the ramp, sometimes stopped to take a puff, while a sultry-voiced commentator joined in with a plug. Free cigarettes were handed out at these events.

The pretence of good works – of corporate bureaucracies being Medicean rather than Machiavellian – has fallen away as the event-marketing bureaucracy has become elaborate, professionalized, and entrenched. Traditional giving (donations) is on the way out. Market-driven, strategically managed, bottom-line event marketing is in, to the point where one Toronto event-marketing consultant could say that "virtually every sponsorship budget of which I'm aware is part of the corporations *marketing* budget." [Her emphasis.] The notion that philanthropy was behind such money was mostly a pretence to begin with. There was usually a quid pro quo required in the way of an acknowledgement – a public-relations pay-off. Now the "quid" in the quid pro quo has been stepped up and become bureaucratically calculated.

Du Maurier Arts Ltd. (ex-du Maurier Council for the Arts) shows the pattern. Its guidelines for applicants for largesse, detailing the required "commitment to du Maurier Arts Ltd.," read like a set of marching orders, with Imperial Tobacco as the field marshall. What happens in practice is illustrated by a 1986 Canadian Opera Company tour of Rossini's family opera *Cinderella*, as described by the company's national tour director at the time. At the last moment the company's fund-raising department announced that du Maurier had chipped in with a grant of $25,000. Although this was only 6 per cent of the overall budget of $400,000, the name had to be changed from the Canadian Opera Company production of Cinderella to the du Maurier production of Cinderella. Every publicity utterance and news release had to use that name. The original advertising and promotion concepts had to be scratched. Pink, the colour chosen for brochures because the tour was being aimed at family audiences, was replaced with the du Maurier red. A new and expensive house program, at a cost of almost three times the amount normally spent on tour programs, was produced, with du Maurier supplying the front cover, complete with logos (as well as the stipulated ad on the back of the program). Exact placement of du Maurier lobby signs was demanded so that the public would see the signs immediately on entering the various theatre lobbies. Open packages of du Maurier cigarettes and matches had to be placed at each table for the opening night reception.

The du Maurier Council was supposed to be terribly committed to the arts in Canada, but when anti-cigarette-advertising legislation was before the House of Commons in 1987 and 1988, the tobacco lobby, with Imperial Tobacco in the lead, made sure everybody knew that if they could not use cultural and sports events to market their products, the arts and sports communities could say goodbye to their money.

This "hardball giving" and its contractual requirements reflect how the culture and sports branch now wields its bureaucratic muscle. "Corporations want VALUE for their MONEY," blares a brochure from the Sport Marketing Council. The supplicant either comes across or it's out of luck. "Pay-back," "partnership," and "fit" are some of the terms used. An IMG-Canada apparatchik, observing his branch's muscle at work, foresees that in the future the promoter of a sports event (the people looking for sponsorship money) "will be much more in tune with the sponsor's needs and marketing objectives. . . . Commercialization will become totally accepted and necessary. . . . Promoters in essence will become better marketers and corporately inclined."

Under this pressure, they may end up so inclined to the point of distraction. In the case of the du Maurier contribution of $25,000 to the Canadian Opera Company, the tour director remarked, sardonically, that more than $25,000 worth of "staff time, hassle, bother, and aggravation" was put into the project in order to "service" the clients. "Those were the words used," he added, in exasperation. "We were servicing the client."

The analogy to prostitution is apt. Some of the practitioners even take to enjoying it, not least the IOC, which tutors clients on how to get the most out of their consorting and works hard at developing new variations like premiums. Elsewhere, a kind of grovelling and deference take place. A symphony fund-raiser, the wife of the orchestra's cellist, gives a little speech at a reception, thanking sponsors for their contributions – the bureaucratic equivalent of the gardener touching his cap. An American performing arts touring organization eagerly offers to name its various events after corporations in return for a contribution. Another touring program not only publicly touts the sponsor's support, but also echoes its corporate slogan; slick brochures explain that "the goal of the arts program, like NCNB [the sponsor], is to be 'in your neighborhood.'"

Workshop programs teach supplicant organizations how to bow and scrape appropriately. There is even an annual "student" award for it in Canada, given by the Council for Business and the Arts in Canada. In one instance, the winner, an actors' showcase troupe, "targeted" the local dairy. "They clearly understood that sponsorship is an effective marketing tool for business," gushed one judge. "Right in the covering letter they established the fact that they want to work as a team with the sponsor," gushed another. "I loved the slogan they used," chimed in the third. "'Nurturing growing minds and bodies' – what better combination than theatre and milk for young audiences?" The competing organizations are patted on the head.

The Canadian Women's Cycling Team put on lipstick and bare their shoulders for glamour photographs. "I tell my girls that we can't sit around and wait for somebody to give us charity . . . we have to make ourselves marketable," says the coach.

The obsequiousness is most pathetic when cigarette-company sponsorship is involved. When legislation was introduced in Canada to limit cigarette company advertising and sponsorship, several arts and sports organizations that received tobacco money lent their names and voices to the industry lobby fighting the bill. Others kept silent – in effect condoning the tobacco industry's prostitution of culture and sports. Arnold Edinborough, the head of the Council for Business and the Arts in Canada, became an apologist for the lobby.

Women tennis professionals, 95 per cent of whom hate cigarette smoking and hate cigarettes, according to U.S. tennis veteran Pam Shriver, express gratitude to Virginia Slims (Philip Morris) nevertheless and play the Virgina Slims circuit.

The media are supposed to be deferential, too. "If an event takes place because a corporation paid $100,000 to make it happen," declaimed an IMG Canada vice-president, "I contend that's part of the story – so report it. I think that corporations, through a variety of means, will bring pressure to bear on this point. In time the media will recognize this part of the story, much as consumers will in the same manner."

The next step is more complete bureaucratic control and censorship –

censorship if necessary although not necessarily censorship in the blue-pencil sense of the word. "What modifications are the organizers prepared to make to accommodate the sponsor's needs?" the senior vice-president of the Houston Group Communications Ltd., Toronto, listed as one of the questions sponsors should not fail to ask. "This isn't to suggest that the sponsor assume the role of censor," she went on, "or, in the case of the arts, any kind of artistic involvement, but rather, to ensure that – as in any successful partnership – there is a sense of 'give and take' to arrive at a product that ultimately totally benefits both parties."

So sports and the arts become "product," in this bureaucratic newspeak. They also have to satisfy Big Brother who makes the "sponsorship" dispensation. But – again in the newspeak – no censorship is involved, although conforming to the demands of a bureaucracy used to be understood, at one time, as censorship.

In classical music, the accommodation means a tendency towards the mainstream and away from the innovative and experimental. The more chilling wind, though, is on rock music, theatre, and, to a lesser extent, art, dance, and opera – forms that have lyrics, dialogue, story lines, or images, and that can have social and political content, including content about the corporate and advertising bureaucracies that subsidize them and ideas to which those bureaucracies are attached. It's a sign of how comfortably the New Bureaucracy is protected by ideology, and how entrenched it has become, that not only have arts organizations submitted meekly to this connection but also, like hungry puppy dogs, they scratch hopefully on corporate doors.

On top of this is another, broader kind of cultural conditioning, in which people and the world are no longer seen in a natural light. Event-related marketing commercializes everything instead – a kind of censorship by suffocation.

The next stage, for the bureaucracy, is to take over ownership of the events themselves, so that its cadres can shape the events directly according to bureaucratic *diktat*, without the nuisances of "give and take" and unpredictable artistic expression. Such ownership of events has become the latest fashion in the culture and sports branch, especially for sports and rock music. Ownership "insures that [companies'] financial commitments and marketing opportunities are being maximized," in the no-nonsense words of an IMG Canada cadre.

Outright ownership of events, teams, venues, and broadcast rights is common in professional sports. Molson, for example, owns Montreal Canadiens, the Forum, and a part of what used to be called "Hockey Night in Canada," including the production company. Labatt's owns the Toronto Blue Jays, the production company which televises its games, The Sports

Network, and a half of the sister French-language network. These arrangements provide the breweries with seamless control of chosen teams and events and, with them, everything from the brochures of team schedules to the final logo shown on the season's final telecast. Molson had the bureaucratic power to change the deep-rooted name "Hockey Night in Canada" to "Molson Hockey Night in Canada."

Labatt's has also moved into the impresario function. It now has a 45 per cent interest in powerhouse Concert Productions International (CPI). A new wrinkle in the United States is location sponsorship, like a deal between MCA/Pace Amphitheatres Group and Coca-Cola, by which Coca-Cola sponsors a group of locations built for the purpose, with its name attached. The first in the group: the Coca-Cola Starplex Amphitheatre (that's the one in Dallas). The deal also puts Coca-Cola's name in the lights, gives it trademark identification inside the amphitheatres, and gives it the right of first refusal to co-promote acts that play in the buildings.

Protests are no match for this bureaucratic power. In Britain, the well-known theatre manager and television producer Peter Stevens attacked this "poisoned chalice" and its destructive effect on artistic freedom and variety. The artistic director of the Theatre Royal Stratford East, talked about the "insidious self-censorship" and loss of self-respect that sponsorship brings with it.

In Canada and the United States, the bluntest criticism has come from the rock music scene. Toronto-born Neil Young in his video "This Note's for You" spells out in the lyrics that he, unlike some fellow musicians, won't sing for the likes of Pepsi and Coke, or anybody. He's not going to make a fool of himself playing their game, the song goes. Bruce Springsteen, John Mellencamp, Midnight Oil, U-2, and Bruce Cockburn have all stood up against the sponsorship connection. Sponsorship and appearances in commercials, declared Leslie Savan, advertising columnist at the *Village Voice*, "send the message to young people that selling out is cool, that it's hip to be square if you're cynical."

"If rock'n'roll can't survive without having to shill products, it ought to die," said Cockburn's manager, Bernie Finklestein. "Sponsorship has corrupted artistic values and is propping up lazy, inefficient businesses."

These holdouts are a minority, though. And unless they have the leverage of a Bruce Springsteen or a U-2, they end up trapped by the culture and sports bureaucrats whatever their convictions. Almost every major venue comes with at least one and often a collection of corporate sponsors attached. As Young's agent explained, if the performer doesn't agree to work the location, he would have to work for another promoter without corporate sponsorship connections and in lower grade venues, or maybe not at all. Promoters also run fewer ads for non-sponsored acts, claiming they can't afford them, which leads to smaller audiences, which leads to reports the act is in decline.

Soon "you're out of the game," Cockburn's agent summed it up acerbically. "Sponsorship gives the major advantage to those who accept it. The safer the act, the less it rocks the boat, the more it'll be sponsored. Before long, artists with a genuine point of view or a critical opinion will be weeded out of the system, unable to survive. There will still be music, but it won't be rock and roll."

MTV, in the United States, banned "This Note's For You." They also banned Cockburn's 1985 single "Call it Democracy." MTV constantly carries commercials of the products Neil Young spoofed. "Sponsorship," *Toronto Star* rock critic Greg Quill commented, "is so all-pervasive, such an omnipresent element in our daily lives that it has become a monster . . . too big and too strong to budge or displace."

The creation of dependency, and with it passiveness and obsequiousness, is an essential part of the bureaucratic hold. Money doesn't simply talk, in sponsorship, it also produces a psychology of dependence. When somebody criticizes sponsorship, the conditioned reponse is that, although it may be undesirable, one can't do without it . . . even when, in fact, one can do without it. Professional sports and popular music can and have existed without breweries and tobacco companies, for example. It might mean that participants would have to settle for less than hugely inflated incomes and that other emoluments, luxuries, and refinements would be scaled back. That's the point, however. Expenditures and waste have inflated to fill the bureaucratic possibilities. It makes sense, economically, to debureaucratize in order to reduce the expenditures and waste, and to get rid of the overheads of the sponsorship cadres at the same time.

Similarly, a study of arts funding in Canada in 1985 and updated data for 1989 both show corporate contributions averaging only 4 per cent of arts organizations' budgets (the performing and visual arts taken together). For the performing arts alone, the figure for 1989 was 7 per cent. From these percentages should be subtracted the overhead costs of dealing with the sponsors. The remaining margins are easily recoverable by public-financing mechanisms (which bypass the New Bureaucracy and its overheads). In any case, if the money is available in the economy for the arts, as it is, then it should be allocated with the least overheads and intrusion.

In Canada there are still small arts organizations hesitant to accept event-marketing subsidies and what comes with them. The cadres of the culture and sports branch consider these hold-outs as backward renegades – like Winston in Orwell's *1984* – refusing to accept the obvious correctness of the new regime and hence needing to be re-educated. "Attitudinal barriers" is the newspeak for the renegades' stubbornness. "Breaking down" these attitudinal barriers is the shiny event-marketing cadres' final mission. The time when Canadian arts organizations understood the importance of independence from bureaucracy, not much more than fifteen years ago, isn't talked about, as if that state of mind disappeared a hundred and fifty years ago or, being too preposterous, never really existed at all.

Inevitably, the culture and sports branch extended its intrusion to cover causes and charities as well. If sports and rock music raise emotions and loyalties to which the branch can fasten itself and fatten its ranks, causes do even better. Once the cadres realized this, there was no stopping them. Almost overnight, metaphorically speaking, "cause-related marketing" became a fad. Or, as an article in *Fortune* put it, without wasting words on elegance, "How to cash in on do-good pitches." "Cause-related marketing is a strategy for selling, not for making charitable contributions," the article explained, in 1986, when the range of its possibilities was just becoming clear. New bureaucratic cells developed to help advertisers do it right. There are now cause-marketing consultants.

Cause-related marketing applies all of the techniques developed for culture- and sports-related marketing, plus its own strain of memorabilia (lapel pins, visors, T-shirts, certificates) which helps keep the respective brand names around. In terms of allocations to the actual charity, the margin of bureaucratic overhead waste can be enormous. In a pioneering and, in the bureaucracy, famous 1983 promotion, American Express raised an estimated US$1.3 million for helping to repair the Statue of Liberty. For three months it dedicated one penny of every credit-card transaction and one dollar of each new membership to the cause. It spent another $4 million, however, on its advertising campaign featured in print, on radio and television, in direct mail and in point-of-sale promotion. The overheads were more than three times the charitable allocation. In a 1989 Smirnoff campaign, "Help Smirnoff end illiteracy in America," the overhead/charity ratio was 9 to 1.

If a campaign can tug at the heart strings or capture fears, all the better. "Continental Airlines' FlyAmerica program will help fight birth defects," *Advertising Age* reported admiringly of a Continental Airlines program in the genre (actually devised to boost declining passenger miles and make travellers forget about Continental's erratic service). Anti-drug and -alcohol abuse and standing four-square behind literacy are favourites. So is protecting the environment. Cause-related marketing in schools – getting them while they're young – is another favourite. (Naysayers who complained about one such Procter & Gamble program must be against charity, *Advertising Age* gibed.) As in other marketing, any intrusion goes. In Britain, brand names are now part of Boy Scout merit badges.

Cause-related marketing, crass by its nature – exploiting charities for profit – quickly degenerates into Kafkaesque bureaucratic absurdity. In one wonderful case, a Toronto brew pub promoted its in-house brands (Growlers Lager and Royal Dunkel) on the back of the Ontario Special Olympics for the mentally handicapped. Quaff the beer, went the line, to make a contribution to the mentally handicapped. As one protestor pointed out, "the idea that buying a beer in a bar should be considered 'making a contribution' makes a total mockery of the committed individuals who actually go right down to the bone, giving their time and energy to such worthy causes." Worse, she wrote, alcohol is a known cause of birth defects. The tie-in, while it might benefit the Special Olympics in the short term, "actually promotes a product whose ill effects the organization exists to combat!"

"If [supposedly philanthropic Philip Morris] are really interested in doing something [for society]," similarly commented an official of Washington-based Action on Smoking and Health, "they should set up a fund to compensate all of the smokers who are dying of tobacco-related disease." She knew, however, that behind all their showy philanthropy, Philip Morris wasn't really interested in doing right.

These case histories reflect the general absurdity of cause-related marketing. Its unremitting commercialization of anything and everything blocks the awareness and social commitment really required for changing things. It's no coincidence that the western industrial country most backward in helping the disadvantaged and with the greatest inequities – the United States – should spawn the gimmickry of cause-related marketing, or that societies with the strongest anti-commercialization ethos, like Sweden and Norway, are the most charitable and caring in the way they have organized their societies. The same goes for the environment and wildlife: The commercialization behind environmental-cause marketing feeds the materialist culture that ultimately destroys the environment.

Pitching brand names for consumer goods isn't the only function of event marketing. It is also used for burnishing corporate images, defending the status of companies and helping lobbying efforts – in other words, as a political tool, like advocacy advertising, for the corporate branch. Alcan's sponsorship of the Montreal International Jazz Festival, for example, helps it detract attention from charges that its smelter emissions are poisoning beluga whales in the Saguenay River. The corporate image-building, with its variable applications of whitewash, happens as a spin-off even when the event marketing is focused on boosting sales of a product: The association between the company and its ostensible good works is made over and over again.

Cause marketing lends itself particularly well to this political function, because of its emotional associations. Education causes are widely used.

The sponsor doesn't just launch a program and pay for it. It advertises its involvement and good works, for the political pay-off. The more harmful a sponsor's activities – say, a tobacco company's – the more that event-related marketing comes in handy for creating the desired image.

At one of the *Financial Post's* sponsorship conferences, in 1987, the sports editor of the *Toronto Sun* newspaper group exulted over the fact that at the previous world hockey championships, all the players had an AGFA emblem on their sleeves, even the Soviets and Czechoslovaks. He joked about it as a "somewhat different version of the dialectical materialism . . . introduced by Karl Marx." He was closer to the truth than he thought. He failed, though, to follow through on the analogy. We have avoided the communist cadres, only to end up with quite similar apparatchiks, protected by ideology in their case, too, and battening onto us in not so different a way.

9

The Dogma and Media Branch

Some wasteful, entrenched bureaucracies are extensions of dictatorships. Others hide behind ideology – in the New Bureaucracy's case, the ideology of free enterprise. The greater the dogmatic belief in the ideology, the more entrenched the bureaucracy can become.

Academics who cling to the ideology, especially economists, help prop up the bureaucracy. They are the equivalent of the Scholastic theologians of medieval church bureaucracy or the communist theorists of Soviet bureaucracy. The mass media, without even thinking about it, pass on the dogma, acting as popularizers. They also shamelessly indulge the New Bureaucracy in order to maintain and increase their own revenues; the advertising and marketing branch and the culture and sports branch have turned the mass media into bureaucratic clerks. In between the academics and the popularizers are the think tanks. These together are the dogma and media branch.

The New Bureaucracy doesn't just benefit by the work of the dogma and media branch. It feeds it at the same time. The two become entrenched and inflate together.

The most reliable cadres in the dogma branch are the economists – most reliable because they are the most doctrinaire. At least this is the case for American-style economists who now dominate economics. These cadres are dogmatists by nature. They are trained in free-market doctrine – what economists call, with the intellectual certainty of dogmatists, the "standard economic theory" and "normal concepts" or, in U.S. circles, "the American doctrine." They discount, or try not to think about, anything else.

"Economists who come off the orthodox assembly lines of the universities," commented economic historian Guy Routh, of this indoctrination, "are not of this world. An essential part of their training consists of induction into a world of fantasy, as remote from reality as the world of the Hobbits." In the economists' self-contained theoretical world, supply, demand, competition, and private enterprises interact in free-enterprise markets much like divine clockwork. The whole is governed by an "Invisible Hand." The perfection of these workings is based on a body of theoretical assumptions, not on observable fact or how people really behave. The idea of bureaucracy, on the other hand, falls outside the doctrine. Bureaucracy is only supposed to happen in government. In the private sector, competition eliminates bureaucracy, according to the doctrine.

When a bureaucratic phenomenon cannot be ignored, the economists' job is to work up an ideologically correct explanation, no matter how bizarre. Take the outlandish salaries, bonuses, perks and indulgences of CEOs and other senior corporate executives – a case of corporate bureaucrats taking advantage of their bureaucratic leverage. Devout economists describe it as the "market in executives," hence not only acceptable but desirable. "Market" is the key theological word. Fattened executive cadres could not ask for better apologists.

Or take the stock-market branch – the endless churning by the players, the chatter and guesswork by analysts, and the swings, and sometimes wild ups and downs, of stock prices. Economists, mostly at the University of Chicago's economics department, a centre of *laissez-faire* orthodoxy, developed the efficient markets theory (EMT) to explain it. The theory, you'll recall, holds that investors act rationally and stock prices reflect whatever information people have about the fundamentals, such as current and expected earnings. A look at the stock-market bureaucracy reveals a real world quite different from the theory, but that isn't the point. As Chicago's pioneering EMT theorist, Eugene Fama, once explained, the theory is "a matter of belief" to him. (Scholastics, in the same spirit, once believed they could reconcile faith and reason, and Soviet apologists believed they could reconcile democracy and centralism.)

The work of dogma cadres is to make sure all behaviour fits, even if, intellectually, the exercise is much like stuffing an elephant into a suitcase. When the stock market crashed in October 1987 and then recovered, while the real-world economy carried on as usual, it appeared the theory was blown out of the water. Not, however, for the most zealous dogmatists. They argued that the swings really were market efficiency at work, whatever the appearances. The rational factors at play were just too myriad and inscrutable for mere analysts and other human observers to decipher.

Dogma cadres don't, however, need to convince anybody they are actually right. Dogma works by filling intellectual space with exercises based on the assumptions of the doctrine. The implicit assumptions carry the dogma. Whether the theoretical exercises apply to the real world or not, the doing of them and teaching about them imparts higher doctrinal meaning, under which aura the sinful and wasteful carry on as usual.

Stock-index futures and options, which have proved such a bureaucratic bonanza, were dreamed up in Chicago and launched on their futures exchanges largely because of the impetus of the University of Chicago's theorists. They argued that the new "instruments" would make the stock market even more efficient. The dogma actually rested on an administrative difference between regular and futures markets. One could play in futures markets with as low as a 1 per cent cash coverage, depending on the contract, instead of having to meet a 50 per cent margin requirement. This left more room for speculators. Their greater sensitivity to taking losses – in the case of futures, they would have to sell to cover their exposure if the market went the wrong way – theoretically would add a finer calibration to the futures market's "rationality." This, in turn, would have a playback effect on the regular stock market. The sheer extra activity of the speculators – in options as well as futures – would also add to the two parallel markets' "rationality," according to the theory.

Some of the same thing could have been accomplished by simply lowering the cash requirement for buying actual stocks. But the 50 per cent requirement was established exactly to prevent overheated speculation and irrational runs on the market. Boosting speculation, on the other hand, was precisely the object of the dogma cadres. For them, speculators – pure, mercenary, impersonal, short-term, in-and-out market players – were close to divinity and essential to market efficiency. Here, like the Scholastics' ingenious marriage of faith and reason, was another theological triumph of the mind – the marriage of speculators and rationality. This was music to the ears of the commodity exchanges, which had always had to explain away the apparently useless, parasitical games of speculators who played futures.

The upshot was another layer of bureaucracy – of churning, yo-yoing, make-work, paper stratagems, and wasteful speculation. The commodity exchanges, meanwhile, had a high-sounding intellectual front linked to deep-rooted ideology (the free market), behind which they could expand, lobby Congress, and dress up their annual reports.

The doctrine of a "market in executives" also created problems for the dogma cadres. Executive self-indulgence in the U.S. was hard to overlook. The dogma cadres could not deny, either, that in widely held companies – a theoretical ideal – the entrenched executive could behave autocratically. So when corporate raiders began to describe their forays in evangelical terms – in terms of ousting second-rate management and revitalizing U.S. capitalism – the dogma cadres seized on the idea. It saved the doctrine at a vulnerable point. The cadres called the mergers and acquisitions game the "market in corporate assets." The "market," once more, if only left to itself, made things right. Even greenmail had the redeeming value of shaking up management. A few particularly devout cadres began to elaborate this new theology with latter-day passion, refusing to allow that the mergers and acquisitions wave itself was largely a paper, bureaucratic phenomenon.

That anybody should take economists seriously at all reflects how the dogma works. Economists, again, are much like medieval monks. The majority of them share the same central beliefs although belonging to different orders. Their adherence to doctrine, their narrow "theological" training, their otherworldly theoretical meanderings and use of mathematical constructs (the use of formulae is a ritualistic requirement) make them prone to silliness when dealing with the real world. "I don't know of any other science that purports to be talking about real world phenomena where statements are regularly made that are blatantly contrary to fact," noted Herbert Simon, a psychology and computer-science professor and a Nobel prize winner in economics for some independent work of his own. One irreverent academic economist wrote a spoof called "Life Among the Econ," describing this strange tribe's use of "myths" and "modls [sic]" of little or no practical use.

Except for ordinary empirical studies – the equivalent of monkish good works – the economists' order is a nuisance, and sometimes dangerous. Practical people keep economists at a distance. For example, until the 1970s there were only two PhDs in economics among the higher career officials of Japan's Ministry of International Trade and Industry, which led Japan's extraordinary postwar economic renewal. It was an economics ministry but not a ministry of economists. "We did the opposite of what American economists said," a top official once explained. For societies like the United States and, to a lesser extent, Canada and Britain, on the other hand, where the orthodox American doctrine is credo, utterings of economists are still accepted with deference. Lay people in these countries remain awed, and not a little intimidated, by the sect's dogmatic devotion to the higher doctrine. They are loathe to cross economists openly, even while poking fun at them behind their backs.

Think tanks or, more properly speaking, "dogma tanks," also help prop up the New Bureaucracy. The spectacular inflation of the bureaucracy in the 1980s took place in counterpoint to a similar inflation in the ranks of "dogma-tank" cadres – cadres subscribing to the appropriate ideology. "Dogma tanks" is a literal description, not hyperbole. U.S. organizations such as the Heritage Foundation, the American Enterprise Institute (AEI) and the Hoover Institution, or Canadian ones like the Fraser Institute are unabashedly doctrinaire. Their job is to elaborate the doctrine and promote its spread and application.

By the mid-1980s, the aforementioned U.S. think tanks had annual budgets of US$10-$12 million each, staffs ranging from 105 to 200 people, and ranks of adjunct scholars and associates. A good part of their revenues and endowment capital came from the corporate branch. The AEI, for example, had over six hundred corporate sponsors. In the late 1970s, corporate CEOs and their boards, many on the defensive, had decided it was advantageous to allocate money to these and other similar think tanks across the country. Separate foundation money was also available, to be allocated to these centres and to special projects. Organizations directly stemming from the corporate branch, such as the Business Roundtable (CEOs of large U.S. corporations) and the Conference Board, are part of this section inasmuch as they do research and publish papers on public policy.

In Canada, similar dogma cadres work out of, or are supported by, the C. D. Howe Institute and the Fraser Institute (both financed largely by corporate members and endowments), the Economic Council of Canada, and the Business Council on National Issues and the Canadian Conference Board (the last two act for corporate cadres directly). The Economic Council of Canada is publicly funded but, relying on economists and adhering to doctrine, it fulfills the dogma function nevertheless. In Britain, there is the Centre for Policy Studies, the Institute for Economic Affairs, and the Adam Smith Institute (the latter modelled on the Heritage Foundation).

Good dogma tanks don't just elaborate the dogma, they promote it. Given their stipend, in these cases, particularly the largesse from the corporate branch, they have the wherewithal to do so. The Heritage Foundation, for example, holds daily lectures, debates, and briefings; arranges meetings between corporate representatives and government decision-makers through something called the Washington Policy Roundtable; holds a special lecture series for young "conservatives" to discuss how to use the media; has a resource bank of scholars and policy experts across the country to provide the media and congressional hearings with suitable commentary; sends material to hundreds of newspapers, much of which ends up in editorials or news copy; and publishes books, monographs, policy papers, a quarterly journal, and several newsletters. The AEI, in addition to similar efforts, prepares radio and television programs for six hundred stations, holds special seminars for business executives, and provides all AEI publications free to libraries.

"Marketing is an integral part of [our] product," the president of the Heritage Foundation once explained, in describing its proselytizing. The Fraser Institute in Canada in particular has picked up on these dogma-marketing techniques.

These and other think tanks act as policy planners for government, especially in the United States – in effect, merging with the old bureaucracy.

When a sympathetic administration is in power, the connection can be very close. The Fraser Institute has worked with governments in British Columbia, Alberta, Saskatchewan, and Ottawa. In the United States, in the Reagan years, the connection was reinforced with personnel transfers, much as if the think tanks were a civil-service farm system. In Reagan's first term alone, fifty people came into the administration from the Hoover Institution, thirty-six from the Heritage Foundation, thirty-four from the AEI, and eighteen from the Centre for Strategic and International Studies. American writer Sidney Blumenthal, in his 1986 book *The Rise of the Counter-establishment*, compared these cadres – the "conservative intellectuals with think-tank sinecures, foundation executives, political operatives, and federal jobholders" – to the *nomenklatura*, the indulged bureaucrats of the Soviet system. (The word *nomenklatura* had previously been used by these U.S. conservative intellectuals to attack "liberal" intellectuals working in Washington.)

The rise of the new "neo-conservative" think tanks, with their doctrinal commitment to *laissez faire*, helped create a climate for the New Bureaucracy to inflate unimpeded. One particular neo-conservative tenet was that wealth was created by rich, risk-taking heroes, winning huge profits and then re-investing them. Anybody who could be squeezed into that category was endowed with "moral legitimacy and divine sanction," as writer Blumenthal put it. The Robber Barons of the nineteenth century were rehabilitated. America's original entrepreneurs, the farmers and frontiersmen, were forgotten in this revisionist history. So was most of the reality of economic development and enterprise – the role of corporations, the workforce, education, public enterprises, and public infrastructure, for example. This was the re-arrangement of history in the worst Soviet-Encyclopedia manner.

It also ignored bureaucracy. So that when corporate CEOs levered huge compensation for themselves, when M&A bureaucrats made that inflated compensation look paltry, and when even many stockbrokers and bond dealers (glorified clerks) made millions of dollars a year in largely circular exercises, well, they were in the private sector. They got endowed with moral legitimacy and divine sanction, by ideological overflow.

One inference, flowing from the dogma, was that nothing should stand in the way of the rich, especially not taxes. This was part of another, larger tenet, "supply-side theory." Supply-side theory held that the way to regenerate a stalled economy was to increase the supply of goods and services provided by the private sector. To do that, personal taxes needed to be reduced to increase the incentive for working and investing, especially for higher-income groups whose savings, the theory had it, translated into investment capital. Corporate taxes, for their part, needed to be reduced to allow for more re-investment. If, at the same time, public services and welfare assistance had to be cut back for lack of tax dollars, so much the better. The most ardent believers contended that such tax cuts would, in any case, so regenerate the economy that *more* taxes in aggregate would be collected. "Voodoo economics," cynics called the theory.

Aside from the gross inequalities and public debt that resulted when the "voodoo economics" were actually attempted, the dogma again played into the hands of the New Bureaucracy. Corporate officers were only too pleased at this ideological backing for corporate tax cuts, not to mention the personal tax cuts favouring high-income earners like themselves. Their support for the think tanks, they saw, was beginning to pay off. "By buying into that group we bought into ideological help and political inroads on the Hill," a presidential aide, pushing for the tax cuts, explained. "We had to graft their stuff onto our own program. It was easy to grab what was in place. They brought all of their [ideological] baggage with them, but that was fine." It was about as explicit a use of dogma cadres by a self-serving bureaucracy as one could imagine.

Many of the corporations that received the largest tax breaks actually decreased investment in the following years (1981-1983), a study by the Washington-based Citizens for Tax Justice found. Aggregate figures showed the same pattern. The fifty corporations with the lowest tax rates reduced investment in total while the fifty with the highest tax rates, ironically, increased investment. Rather than boosting investment, much of the increased cash flow from the tax concessions went instead to stepping up dividends, adding to cash reserves, funding mergers and acquisitions (inflating the paper-entrepreneurialism branch), raising executive pay (inflating the corporate branch), or increasing advertising budgets (inflating the advertising and marketing branch). This was contrary to supply-side expectation but not contrary to bureaucratic reality.

One of the most graphic cases of think tanks helping to feed the New Bureaucracy is the privatization of public enterprises in countries like Britain and Canada, where a substantial number of public enterprises have been sold off. Privatization is a holy cause for the dogma tanks.

There is no business logic in privatization for its own sake. Quite the contrary, it destroys a valuable and creative entrepreneurial current in western countries. What privatization does do, though, is add to the New Bureaucracy. A privatized company listed on a stock exchange increases the shares available for trading and hence the ranks of brokers, analysts, and exchange personnel and their income, wealth, and status. The prior advisory and underwriting stages of privatizations also provide the stock-market branch with a fat rake-off. The money-manager branch, too, is inflated: Fund managers have more tokens to play with, adding exponentially to the possible permutations and combinations, hence to their assumed role and status.

Privatization also inflates the rake-off of corporate cadres. CEOs and other senior executives suddenly have the leverage to award themselves the outlandish salaries, bonuses, perks, and golden parachutes of the bureaucracy's corporate branch. Privatization also inflates the lucrative public affairs and lobbying section of the corporate branch. A Crown corporation is limited in how much lobbying muscle it can use, and cannot contribute to political parties and to ideological think tanks. Once privatized, though, a company can indulge in all these bureaucratic ways shamelessly. The privatization of radio and television inflates the advertising and marketing branch and its structural waste.

Privatization itself comes about by the process of bureaucratic expansion. The bureaucratic ranks which are inflated in each of these cases take an active lobbying and political role in pushing privatization. They are only too glad to have economists and think tanks help pave the way with ideological rationalization. Because these latter cadres really believe in their dogma, moreover, they outdo even political consultants and public-affairs apparatchiks as apologists for this bureaucratic capture.

When, on the other hand, the dogma doesn't serve the bureaucracy, the dogma cadres maintain a courteous silence or indulge in make-believe. Brand-name marketing is an example – unremitting, massive one-way propaganda. This cultural indoctrination interferes with the market and with the allocation of resources. It also makes a mockery of political freedom, because counter-propaganda isn't allowed access and doesn't have the equivalent bureaucratic allocation to compete even if it were. Defenders of the dogma should be outraged. Dogma, however, accommodates hypocrisy when its own bureaucracy is involved.

When they need to, for their own reasons, the dogma cadres simply overlook reality.

The key part of the dogma branch is the mass media. They are captive to the advertising and marketing branch and help prop up other branches of the New Bureaucracy in editorial ways. Every so often, a flagrant case of kowtowing comes out into the open. In 1990, for example, the ABC network decided not to rebroadcast a controversial episode of "thirtysomething" during the summer rerun period because of advertising pressure. Threats from the alcohol industry to withhold advertising effectively frightened television stations in California who were considering an offer of free time to proponents of an alcohol tax measure. (The liquor companies and friends were spending millions for radio and television spots opposing the measure, making free time for response appropriate.) Of thirty stations asked to air a commercial critical of Procter & Gamble's buying coffee beans in El Salvador, only two dared accept; one had no P&G business and the other was duly punished by having nearly $1 million annual P&G advertising withdrawn until it made peace with the company. This is an old story. The chilling effect of cigarette advertising on media coverage of the harmful effects of smoking is particularly notorious. (One study covering the 1970s, for example, done by the *Columbia Journalism Review*, "was unable to find [in magazines that accepted cigarette advertising] a single article, in seven years of publication, that would have given readers any clear notion of the nature and extent of the medical and social havoc wreaked by the cigarette-smoking habit." A sequel study published in *Journalism Quarterly*, on women's magazines in the five years 1983 to 1987, found a similar pattern.)

However, it's not just a case of a newspaper, television station, or network caving in to pressure from a large advertiser, or alternatively resisting such pressure, albeit resistance is a sometimes thing. Anti-bureaucratic media would provide a lively, unshackled, aggressive check on the advertising and marketing branch itself, undermining – in fact, rejecting – its brand-name propaganda and forcing it to cut back its inflated ranks. But the media, of course, feeding on advertising, cannot do that. They have become part of the bureaucracy themselves.

It's a conflict of interest so broad and so blatant that if there were a counterpart elsewhere, it would shock people to their roots and bring on sweeping reform. Leading the reform would be the media themselves, pointing to the conflict of interest and digging out all its variations down to the slightest hint and suspicion.

"By 1990," Roy Megarry, then publisher of the *Globe and Mail*, predicted several years ago, "publishers of mass circulation daily newspapers will finally stop kidding themselves that they are in the newspaper business and admit they are primarily in the business of carrying advertising messages." But the subservience of the media to the advertising bureaucracy wasn't new. Television executives had long before made the same confession to themselves. It had become a cliché that television's job was to sell viewers to advertisers, not programs to viewers. It only made sense, in the end, that the president of Campbell's Soups in Canada should become president of CTV. Radio, in the United States, had been taken over by the advertising bureaucracy by the 1930s, almost as soon as the medium got on its feet.

Now the incursions of everything from "advertorial" supplements in the print media to promotional tie-ins for television and radio advertisers are easily embraced; the media cadres themselves, once they see the possibilities, become active collaborators and promoters of these tie-ins. Journalistic considerations are downplayed. The erasing of the line between editorial content and advertising in special advertising supplements is casually shrugged off. Magazines full of fluff, created exclusively as advertising vehicles, and the neutered copy they pass along, don't have to erase the line; a genuinely independent editorial side doesn't exist. In 1989, top U.S. national advertisers called a special meeting with TV station and group officials to push promotional tie-ins and other "needs." "Meeting of the Minds," the meeting was appropriately dubbed.

The media will often defend the bureaucracy when it is least defensible on other grounds. Broadcasting lobbies both in Canada and the United States helped fight off any ban of advertising directed at very young children, failing only in Quebec, where the provincial government passed applicable legislation of its own. The U.S. broadcasting lobby has similarly pitched in to kill other reforms: counter-commercials under the Fairness Doctrine, the banning of ads pushing highly sugared foods at children, and the banning of beer and other alcohol ads. It bluntly rejected the idea of an ad-axer for children's programming. U.S. broadcasters also opposed, unsuccessfully, the provision of equal time for counter-commercials on cigarette smoking, which eventually led to the end of cigarette advertising on television and radio. American print media are represented in front organizations, such as Libertad, which lobby against similar reforms; the CEO of the *San Francisco Chronicle*, for example, is on Libertad's advisory board.

The *New York Times* and the *Wall Street Journal* cater directly to the bureaucracy with neutered service journalism on the bureaucracy itself. They run a "Media Business" page (in the Business Day section) and a "Marketing & Media" page respectively, each with its own columnist. These pages are part of an attempt to earn revenue from media advertisers, by selling them adjacencies to the columns to reach ad agency media planners and senior marketing executives (so far, the *New York Times* appears to be winning). Readers won't see the columnists taking on the advertising bureaucracy the way that tough-talking political columnists get after governments. This friendly, tethered coverage in two prominent daily newspapers, over and above coverage in specialist advertising magazines like *Advertising Age*, adds to the cachet of legitimacy protecting the cadres.

The bureaucratic interconnection to the money-manager branch is somewhat similar. *Maclean's*, for example, runs an RRSP advertising supplement. The editorial copy in the supplement is provided by the advertisers, mostly mutual funds. The *Financial Post* and others run special investment supplements chock-a-block with mutual-fund, brokerage, and other investment-firm advertising, tied together with what is sometimes called "sympathetic" editorial copy, drawing heavily in this case on interviews with money-manager cadres. There is little or nothing, meanwhile, exploring alternative arrangements – increasing the role of pension and investment funds held in common, for example.

The excessive coverage of stock markets inflates the stock-market branch. Part of the excessive coverage is the page upon page of stock listings every day in ordinary newspapers, especially when compared to the almost complete lack of practical information on productivity, technology, and the organization of work. Such daily stock listings are barely justified in a specialist business newspaper like the *Financial Post*. They more properly belong in a separate publication like the *Daily Racing Form*, with the bureaucratic cadres picking up their information directly off their Quotron monitors. The same goes for the daily stock-market chit-chat, the frequent feature articles about the stock market in news magazines like *Maclean's*, and the look-aren't-we-sophisticated reports of "Venture" on CBC television. This coverage says, in effect, that stock markets are of enormous economic importance when, in fact, they are a waste-ridden bureaucratic adjunct with a minor function. The stock-market reports on radio and the flashing of stock-market averages on television – useless practically and silly journalistically – play the same false symbolic role, as do visuals of stock-market action thrown into television montages to represent business activity. Media, in this way, pander to the New Bureaucracy.

It makes little difference whether the reporting on stock markets is critical or not – for example, the endless coverage in the *Vancouver Sun* of wrongdoings in and around the Vancouver Stock Exchange. It still gives the false impression that stock markets, in this case an exceedingly wasteful, fringe one, have more importance than they do, and generates a wildly false image of what enterprise really is.

The working media also partake of the bureaucracy's fringe indulgences, like the most-enjoyable investor-relations junkets. Invited reporters eagerly joined the party of ninety that Hiram Walker took on a Concorde to Britain, France, the United States, and Canada.

The media indulge the corporate bureaucracy by carrying its advocacy and institutional advertising, for the revenue, without providing countervailing space, time and production money to other voices. At least a few media organizations had the grit to resist. The CBC, going back to the radio days, refused to sell time to companies or anybody else for their opinions or propaganda on public issues. To do so would have given wealth, including corporate bureaucracies, privileged access to the airwaves. The major U.S. television networks, although without binding their affiliates, had the same policy. "To permit this time to be purchased for propaganda purposes . . .," a CBS president put it, "would mean that those with the most money would get to talk the loudest." The rest of the media, though, have taken the cash gladly. The CBC, in the meantime, has turned its policy into a sieve.

Others enthusiastically try to get their nose into the trough. The *Globe and Mail*, in the early 1980s, produced a thirty-five-minute film and a thirty-two-page booklet, drawing largely on American advocacy advertising, in a special marketing campaign to drum up corporate advocacy revenue.

Maclean's ran a similar marketing campaign at the time, complete with ads in its own magazine and in its sister French-language magazine, *L'Actualité*.

The mass media have just as eagerly turned themselves over to event marketers, helping to prop up the culture and sports branch. The key prop is television tie-ins, with their repeated showing of brand names embedded in events and the repeated mention of the names in event titles. Television networks and stations have offered virtually no resistance to the abuses of these tie-ins, even when they involve, as in the Marlboro Grand Prix case, the mocking of the law prohibiting cigarette advertising on television. Indeed, the networks outdo themselves in indulging this bureaucratic fiddling. CTV, in its broadcast of an equestrian event at Spruce Meadows, Alberta, sponsored by du Maurier Inc., and its repeated showing of du Maurier and other placards, also carried an obliging interview with an Imperial Tobacco executive about the company's wonderful sponsorship. There was no question asked, of course, about Imperial Tobacco's exploitation of a loophole in the law banning brand-name cigarette sponsorship, and no question either about what the event marketing really was doing. Private broadcasters themselves play event marketer, attaching brand names and other sponsors to snippets of their own material. In hockey broadcasts, for example, the awarding of three stars, the out-of-town scores, home-team power-play opportunities, home-team goals, and opening face-offs each period can come with sponsors attached.

Even previously independent organizations have found themselves giving way. The CBC once tried keeping gratuitous brand-name mentions and displays out of sportscasts. No longer. It accepts sponsors for many of its own "prestige" programs – has made arranging sponsorship deals an important part of its advertising sales. It carried the independently produced series "He Shoots, He Scores," which was laced with in-program commercial placements, getting rid only of a cigarette ad in the players' dressing room. At a *Financial Post* event-marketing conference, the CBC vice-president was as gushingly obliging as any of the others. The BBC, which is supposed to have no advertising at all, has given way on the contraband advertising of sponsored sports events.

Collaboration and intimacy of this sort with an entrenched, self-serving bureaucracy would be denounced in a vigorous democracy. But since the media who have the responsibility for bringing the matter forward are the very ones in bed with the bureaucracy – one of the major reason for its entrenchment – the bureaucratic inflation and abuse continue.

10

One Big Bureaucracy

Much like money in Gresham's Law ("good money follows bad"), the old bureaucracy follows the New Bureaucracy – is forced to follow it. Senior civil servants' pay is pushed up to be within at least shouting distance of private corporate cadres' emoluments and perks. MPs' pay follows further back. Governments imitate corporate cadres' manipulative bureaucratic techniques, such as advocacy advertising. The revolving door whereby deputy ministers and regulatory lawyers look forward to moving into the New Bureaucracy's lucrative corporate branch corrupts public administration. The private corporate bureaucracy's bad habits infect the public service.

The New Bureaucracy's inflation moves even more relentlessly from the United States, where the cadres have mushroomed behind ideological cover, outward to other countries. Canada, just across the border, was first. Western Europe and Japan, and quickly the rest of the world, are following. This creeping bureaucratic inflation takes place like any other self-generating bureaucratic expansion. Ambitious U.S. cadres look to expand into territory where their counterparts are less experienced and sophisticated – where they might not even be aware of the possibilities. At the same time, cadres in other countries see how it's done in the United States, copy its techniques, emulate its indulgences (using them as benchmarks), and compete against the Americans for bureaucratic territory.

The fashionable cover-phrase for this is "globalization." Globalization doesn't mean free and open trade, which is an old and separate idea. It doesn't just mean companies owning subsidiaries in other countries, or buying up other companies abroad, also an old phenomenon, although becoming more widespread. What gives "globalization" its special, current meaning is the spread of the bureaucracy and its habits and the breaking down of national legislative barriers – of the community check – that contained them. We are heading for One Big Bureaucracy.

Canadian columnists never get tired of pointing to examples of public officials, including MPs, living high off the hog in "Fat City" Ottawa. Symbolic characters with humble titles like "working man," disgruntled anti-government Reform-Party voters in Alberta, and other people on the street are cited expressing their amazement and disgust at some of the pay-outs. Top-level deputy ministers get C$136,000-$165,500 and, if that weren't enough, an indexed pension, much reviled by main-street critics who don't have that protection and nowhere nearly that income to begin with. Members of Parliament get $64,400, plus a tax-free expense allowance of $21,300, plus extra stipends for cabinet ministers, party leaders, speaker and deputy speaker, house leaders and whips, plus "fact-finding" junkets around the world, plus subsidized restaurants, plus on-site services such as a gym, plus pension pay-outs from an enriched plan for every MP who serves more than six years (and payable, according to length of service, regardless of the MP's age and prospects on leaving Parliament). If the retired MP joins a pricey law firm or gets a patronage appointment, he or she still collects the pension. "Endless perks and sometimes-obscene largesse," a *Vancouver Sun* columnist called it.

Over in the agencies, one step removed from Parliament Hill and government departments, the pay-out is even greater. The most notorious case: the pay range of Bank of Canada Governor John Crow, who was insisting that Canadians restrain their wages to control inflation. His own pay, though, went up something like 55 per cent in the four years 1986-1990, (from $120,000-$150,000 to $168,800-$253,200). At the same time, Crow's high-interest-rate policy was throwing people out of work and producing recession.

One step further removed, in Crown corporations – actual business corporations – the pay got even higher, and not always in the most auspicious circumstances. In 1989, the pay of the five top CN executives went up an average 19 per cent, with president Ron Lawless, although getting only an 11 per cent raise, receiving $493,000. The railway's union employees, meanwhile, had settled for wage increases of 4.5 per cent for 1989, 4 per cent for 1990 and 4.5 per cent for 1991. The exact compensation of Petro-Canada's boss Bill Hopper that year was not publicly available, but the ceiling was $475,000.

Other odd items occasionally get publicity. In the spring of 1990, the *Globe and Mail* revealed that the sixteen board members and two officials of the Canada Ports Corp. had spent close to half a million dollars the previous year in meal and travel expenses, including dining at exclusive private clubs like Ottawa's Rideau Club, Le Cercle Universitaire, and the Vancouver Club. Chairman Ron Huntington, who spent $35,000 over a three-month period, entertained at the Rideau Club where, as the newspaper reported, a $16 Côte de Beaune Villages is marked up to $56 with tax. Then the Port of Montreal Corporation was discovered to have bought ten tickets at $500 each to a glitzy benefit gala starring Luciano Pavarotti and to have spent $6,253 for season tickets to Expos and Canadiens games. One item that particularly raised hackles was the patronage appointment of former B.C. attorney general Brian Smith to the chairmanship of CN at $180,000 a year, when somebody else, who was getting paid much more, was actually running the railway.

"Outrageous salaries pirated by gluttonous Crown corporation execs and fat-cat mandarins," complained a Spruce Grove, Alberta, correspondent to *Maclean's*, about CN executive pay. "The common rabble may eventually rise up – yes, even in staid and sober Canada – against Ceausescu-like self-indulgence."

If the Spruce Grove man and other protestors really wanted to rise up against Ceausescu-like self-indulgence, though, they should really have been striking out at the private sector and its New Bureaucracy. Brian Smith's salary was not nearly so outrageous when compared to, say, the compensation of diplomat Ken Taylor, when he moved from the Canadian public service to the New Bureaucracy (senior vice-president, government affairs, for Nabisco Brands) for US$600,000 per year. Mind you, Taylor was still far behind Jack Nicklaus who got $1-million-a-year pin money from the same company later on (it had become RJR Nabisco). Taylor also had the corporate jets, limousines, and golf-tournament blow-outs to help soften the rigours of the job.

The Port of Montreal Corp.'s booking for a fund-raising gala and its Expo and Canadiens season tickets were minor, routine expenditures in New-Bureaucracy terms, whether for corporate-image purposes, self-indulgence or stroking customers. The Canada Ports Corp. restaurant expenses wouldn't have even been noticed in the New Bureaucracy. An in-house gym and masseur for MPs, special as it is for most people, hardly rates with the in-house gym and seven professional trainers in a M&A law firm. What marks off the MPs' compensation and the Canada Ports directors' expenses is that journalists bothered to think about them and brought them to the public's attention, when none of them touched the Marie-Antoinette level of indulgence of the New Bureaucracy.

Something else is happening here, though – the spread of the New Bureaucracy's indulgent norms and culture from the private sector to the public sector. Doing the pushing is the private-sector bureaucracy itself. It does it first of all culturally. The corporate cadres, business commentators, the media generally, the bureaucracy's lobbyists and ideological flacks, and almost everybody else tout the New Bureaucracy as a model. It's not surprising, then, that Port of Montreal Corp., encouraged to act like a private corporation by the same pressures, should try to adopt its ways, and enjoy a few hockey and baseball games in the process, just like them.

The federal, Quebec provincial, and Quebec City governments casually threw away $2.86 million on the Rendez-Vous 87 hockey bash and its lavish ostentation – one journalist called it "Sun King-inspired decadence" – but corporate sponsors put up even more, and there was a business leaders luncheon, too. As it was mixed up with the New Bureaucracy's indulgence, not to mention inspired by it, the old bureaucracy's waste in this case was declared perfectly all right.

Politicians most committed to the covering ideology, and hence identifying most closely with the New Bureaucracy, are most prone to follow suit. The Canada Ports Corp. chairman with the Rideau Club expenditures was former Conservative cabinet minister Ron Huntington. Huntington, as a member of Parliament, was an obsessive critic of public-sector waste, real or imagined. He was also, however, a Vancouver businessman and ardent exponent of private-enterprise ideology. In New-Bureaucracy manner, he wouldn't see eating well at the Rideau Club as an untoward expense. Former cabinet minister Erik Nielsen gets from $131,000 to $159,000 as president of the National Transportation Agency while still collecting his pension worth 75 per cent of his former cabinet salary. Nielsen was another savage critic of public spending and led a highly publicized task force, complete with private sector advisory committee and private sector study-team members, to clean up waste in the public service. What could be more natural than to pile up his compensation and quite modest "golden parachute" just like those eminent executives?

In 1986, the government, at taxpayers' expense, forked over $2.1 million for lawyers and accountants for the finance minister, Michael Wilson, and the minister of state for finance, Barbara McDougall, for their appearances before the federal inquiry into the collapse of the Canadian Commercial and Northland banks. The expenditure seemed wild beyond belief. Wilson and McDougall weren't even facing charges. The outlay was only for preparing them to appear at the hearing, and each appeared for only one day. All they had to do, in any case, was to recount and explain what actions they had taken and their recommendations for the future, a simple enough matter akin to Question Period in the House. Moreover, politically, they were all too willing to cast aspersions on public-sector spending.

Wilson and McDougall, though, were also former investment-dealer cadres, had many close associations with the New Bureaucracy's corporate branch, and identified with its culture. In that culture, the retaining of prestigious, overpaid lawyers and accountants from top firms to sit through proceedings for innumerable days, regardless of the cost – just to provide maximum insurance against any remote contingency – was routine. The $2.1 million allocation wasn't worth thinking about.

The influence is more than cultural, however. The private corporate cadres' inflated compensation forces public administration, public agencies, and Crown companies to follow suit. Otherwise, they would not be able to retain people with the necessary, competitive know-how and competence, or so it is argued. And, again, it's the New Bureaucracy's private-sector cadres who, in their own image, push for these changes. The turning point was the Glassco Commission on government organization – predecessor to the Nielsen task force – which reported in 1962. It recommended that the salaries of senior civil servants had to be increased if the government was to retain good people who would do a good job. Not only that, but the differences between the top level and the level below it, and so on, had to be increased, to provide necessary status and incentive.

J. Grant Glassco, chairman of the commission, was a vice-president, and soon to become president, of Brazilian Traction, Light and Power (now Brascan), a renowned private-sector corporation. Most of the project directors and officers were also private-sector corporate executives. They were paid their regular corporate salaries by the government but, as the *Financial Post* quipped, they did have to do without their large private offices and private washrooms. This culture shock helped them to recommend better things for their civil-service counterparts. As for the substantial pay differentials they recommended at the top: The idea that modest top salaries and small differentials were actually good because they lent themselves to an open, co-operative *esprit de corps* – an entrepreneurial model the Japanese were perfecting – never entered their bureaucratic heads.

Despite the raises in senior public-servant compensation in Canada, the top rate now for deputy ministers is less than a third of the income required to make the *Financial Post's* annual corporate list (the "$500,000 club") and only one-seventeenth of the leading executive compensation, as of 1990. One solution is to cap top CEO pay, lower the pay generally of corporate bureaucrats, and raise income taxes for high incomes so that the difference between their compensation and senior civil-service pay is less important. The corporate cadres, however, don't countenance that kind of change.

In the old days, one could appeal to a public servant's sense of idealism, but a yawning compensation gap in effect tells the senior civil servant that his or her work doesn't matter that much. Status lies in the New Bureaucracy. Its dominant imagery adds burnish to the status. Also, the corporate, paper-entrepreneurial, and stock-market cadres glorify the idea of maximizing one's own compensation. They dress it up with elaborate ideological rationalization about incentives and reward – a rationalization that overflows into the public sector.

The revolving door, kept turning by inflated private-sector compensation, doesn't help either. When colleagues leave for the New Bureaucracy, where they may get multiples of their public-sector compensation – for doing work like public-affairs consulting or government relations, which is easy back-filling – those left behind get the message. One part of the message is not to damage one's own, later prospects by crossing up the New Bureaucracy. Better still, indulge the New Bureaucracy. This has a subtle corrupting effect on the public service.

The closer the public sector gets to the private sector in bureaucratic form, the more the private sector's leverage inflates the public-sector compensation. Hence the pay of John Crow – who is the governor of a bank, after all – is levered up more than the pay of a line-department deputy minister, although it hardly counts next to the take of upper-level chartered-bank cadres. Crow's pay hike followed the recommendations of the Advisory Group on Executive Compensation in the Public Service, chaired by James W. Burns, deputy chairman of Power Corporation of Canada. Its other members were also private-sector corporate cadres. The advisory group was established in 1968, to consist expressly of corporate bureaucrats, to set things right, which it proceeded to do, New-Bureaucracy style. As it explained in 1984, its recommended salary levels were designed to "follow rather than lead those found in the private sector." It did not bother to note that in any follow-the-leader game, the leader has to be watched.

Similarly, the leverage is strongest on Crown corporations. When it was disclosed in 1984 that Petro-Canada chairman Bill Hopper was earning as much as $400,000 a year, some people gasped. The director of compensation research for the Conference Board of Canada, on the other hand – one of the New Bureaucracy's organizations – said he was "surprised the public-sector salaries are so low." Most heads of Crown corporations, he said, could obtain higher salaries in the private sector. Similarly, the 1989 raises given to CN executives were the result of incentive bonuses recommended by private compensation consultants according to the usual New-Bureaucracy measures. The compensation still fell short of parity. CEO Ron Lawless's huge total compensation was only one-quarter the pay of the CEO of Inco and less than one-third the pay of the CEO of Seagram – companies with roughly comparable revenues that year.

In the United States, the chasm between outlandish New-Bureaucracy compensation and modest old-bureaucracy pay is so great that in the late 1980s the ranks of federal government executives and professionals began to hemorrhage seriously. The private sector itself complained about poor public administration and pushed for increases in public-sector pay at the top. Unfortunately, free-enterprise ideology got in the way of Congress actually daring to do something about it. Finally, in 1989, Congress snuck through a bill that allowed the pay of federal judges and senior government executives to go up, so that top pay would be in the US$125,000 range (top individual compensation in the New Bureaucracy that year was $54 million for CEOs and $120 million on Wall Street). Free-enterprise dogmatists denounced the raises. "What they are going for are the extravagant bonuses of entrenched corporate managements," one columnist wrote, in wild hyperbole. Senior public servants were already in the top of the income distribution, he shouted. This latter point was true. But as long as the New Bureaucracy rakes in inflated compensation, the public sooner or later has to allow the old bureaucracy to follow suit, at least a little of the way along.

The bureaucratic leveraging of compensation works its way from country to country as well – from the United States to other countries. Compensation consultants now do international surveys by which corporate cadres in other countries can see the gap between themselves and their American counterparts and can sorrowfully point out this gap to others. They can argue that their compensation is "uncompetitive" – a key code word. Bureaucratic manoeuvring then goes to work.

Given the economic success of countries like Japan, West Germany, and Sweden, which have relatively modest compensation differentials, change should be taking place in the other direction: closing the differentials in the United States. Critics of U.S. corporate performance invariably cite the lower differentials in pay in Japan, and hence the greater spirit of teamwork, as a major factor in that country's progress. Europeans also feel that an organization suffers when a CEO's pay is an astronomical multiple of an employee's earnings. Lesser compensation differentials are equally important for social and democratic reasons – perhaps more important, for those reasons. None of this, however, makes much of a difference against a kind of bureaucratic inevitability.

Extraordinary as the executive remuneration in Canada is, a senior partner in Toronto compensation consultants Sobeco Group Inc. excoriated Canadians for being so backward and stick-in-the-mud as to allow their compensation structure to lag behind the American one. Free trade will narrow the gap, he predicted with satisfaction. Another Toronto compensation consultant, a partner at Hewitt Associates, elaborated on the uses of the mobility clauses built into the free-trade pact. The clauses make it easier for U.S. companies to "raid" Canadian firms for their best people, unless Canadian companies respond with parity compensation. The already huge Canadian CEO compensation would have to be doubled for the purpose.

The gap between the U.S. pay-outs and European and Japanese compensation is even greater. American cadres used to marvel at this – not at the puffed-up U.S. pay which, for them, was the norm, but at what they considered the virtually poverty-level pay of CEOs and other executives abroad. "Peanuts" and "grossly underpaid" were descriptions. In some easily comparable cases, the American CEO might be taking in five, ten, twenty, or as much as fifty times the compensation of his European or Japanese counterparts in any one year.

Executives in Europe have noticed the discrepancy, too, and have begun introducing the rigged gimmicks, such as bonuses and stock options, that have propelled U.S. executive cadres' pay into the stratosphere. "Variable compensation" is the euphemism. It "could make hundreds of European executives very wealthy in the 1990s," predicts a New York compensation specialist cited in *Fortune*. Stock options were non-existent in Europe until the mid-1980s.

Part of the process is talking up the rationalizations for the new compensation schemes, using phrases like "adding incentive" and "helping to create shareholder value" – self-serving bureaucratic hokum, prefabricated in the United States. The idea is to make such talk fashionable. "Tickets to fortune," on the other hand, is what the schemes are called in compensation circles.

Corporate links to the United States act as an agent, bringing this "crazy spending for executives," as one European put it, into other countries through the back door. The links work both ways – through U.S. subsidiaries abroad and through European and Japanese subsidiaries in the United States. The heads of the big French banks, for example – and the banks are very big – often earn less than the managers of U.S. subsidiaries around the corner. Or a European CEO, after a takeover, may end up with a U.S. subsidiary where his subordinate earns much more than he does, sometimes twice as much. This happened to the chairman of British Petroleum, whose compensation was promptly levered upwards with the usual gimmicks. Hanson PLC, a British conglomerate with holdings on both sides of the Atlantic, claimed to be on the verge of losing executives to American competitors, so the company moved to a "global pay scale," the euphemism for "inflated U.S. pay scale." The move also helped justify the Hanson chairman's own pay, US$2.4 million at the time (1987).

"The constant cranking in the U.S. [of CEO pay]," a *Fortune* feature reported, "is starting to ratchet up pay around the world." Even though American bosses might be overpaid, the magazine conceded a few months later, they weren't likely to cut their own pay and "the gap is too huge to last." Globalization, in this way, carries the bureaucratic process with it like a virus.

In Britain in the 1980s, the inflation of corporate bureaucrats' pay had extra help from U.S.-style ideology, which is essential cover for really high rake-offs. Paying senior corporate administrators huge amounts and cutting their taxes at the same time were hallowed by Thatcherism as a fundamental part of liberating private enterprise from socialism and returning Britain to greatness. There was status involved, too, in the boosted remuneration: It was a token of Britain's ability to keep up. True, the model for this bureaucratic privilege – the U.S. corporacy – was in disrepute. Also true, the lessons from Western Europe and Japan were quite the opposite, and those countries were even then leaving Britain behind. But none of this could get through the ideological screen. In one way, the British cadres did catch up, bureaucratically, to the Americans: The bulk of top corporate salaries in Britain for the year 1989-1990, two surveys showed, was unrelated to corporate performance.

Other costs to the British economy followed. Huge CEO raises on top of already fat compensation and tax cuts undercut the government's preaching of restraint to wage employees, in the government's effort to control inflation. This difficulty led to higher interest rates than otherwise would have been necessary, in an attempt to keep inflation down. The higher interest rates, in turn, contributed to economic slowdown.

Rich golden parachutes inevitably came along in the bureaucratic train. *The Economist*, a devout exponent of the covering ideology, was nevertheless unhappy, and denounced the "nonsensical generosity." The magazine recommended shareholders do something about it. But golden parachutes are just another bureaucratic privilege taken. If the cadres ever had to surrender them, they would arrange a compensating adaptation.

The corporate branch's habits spill over in all directions. The use of mass-media political propaganda (advocacy advertising) has spread outwards from the U.S. corporate branch to corporate bureaucracies elsewhere and to governments – another case of private-sector bureaucracy inflating public-sector bureaucracy. The progression has been from Mobil Oil (the pioneer of modern-style corporate propaganda), to other U.S. corporations, then across the border to Imperial Oil and the rest of the oil industry in Canada, then to other Canadian corporate bureaucracies, simultaneously to the Quebec and federal governments (remember those Canada geese television commercials pushing Canadian unity, *circa* 1980?), then via oil companies to Britain, and subsequently, through different channels, to other Canadian provincial governments, to the British government and beyond.

The advertising and marketing branch perfected the techniques of advocacy advertising as it went along. The mass-media bureaucracy, having gotten away with carrying the corporate propaganda, did not hesitate to carry the state propaganda as well. Governments in Canada and Britain, for their part, seeing that the corporate branch was getting away with it, guessed that they could, too, and could also get away with spending public money for the propaganda.

Probably the greatest user of advocacy advertising among governments in Canada was Social Credit in B.C. Its mass-media propaganda campaigns date back to 1982. The 1989-1990 B.C. News Update series – sixty-two different television commercials – would have made any propagandist proud. The Social Credit regimes of Bill Bennett and Bill Vander Zalm also published a monthly good-news newspaper about the government, *B.C.News*, distributed to every household in the province. In Britain, the Thatcher government launched massive, pervasive mass-media campaigns pushing several of its privatization schemes. Both governments in these cases were exponents of doctrinaire free-enterprise, anti-statist ideology, but they saw no irony or contradiction in using public money and statist propaganda to condition public thinking. The propaganda was just an extension of what the corporate bureaucracy, which it ideologically defended, was already doing.

How close this connection is was illustrated by a conference on advocacy advertising organized by the Conference Board of Canada in 1981. A federal cabinet minister rationalized his government's use of this propaganda in tandem with the same kinds of rationalizations offered by the corporate bureaucracy, represented by cadres from Imperial Oil and Mobil Oil. The Association of Canadian Advertisers announced that only two out of 124 member-respondents in a survey had a problem with treating government propaganda just like corporate-branch propaganda.

The lobbying bureaucracy also spreads by bureaucratic example, in a globalization pattern. Many Americans have been outraged at the way the Japanese have indulged in influence buying in Washington, their thorough application of cash, and their public relations (giving money to good causes and selected local election campaigns). The Japanese, however, have simply expanded a bureaucracy that was already in place, improving on it the way they have improved on American automobiles and American semi-conductors. The Japanese, at the same time, could not help but learn from the Americans – how, for example, to buy influence without breaking the law or risking scandal.

Similarly, American-style public affairs firms are springing up in the lobbyist bureaucracy in Europe, adding their refinements – and increased costs, and increased counter-costs – to what was already a large lobbyists' layer. American firms themselves, going global, and American law firms *cum* lobbyists, are joining in as quickly as they can pack passports. New York megafirm Hill and Knowlton is one of the fastest growing groups of

Euro-lobbyists. Brussels, the locale of the European Commission, the administrative arm of the European Community, is a growth-centre for lobbyists. As of 1989, and leaving aside translators and interpreters, there were perhaps seventeen thousand civil servants in the European Community, divided among Brussels (the Commission), Luxembourg (the Council), and Strasbourg (the Parliament). Brussels' lobbying population, meanwhile, according to *Management Today*, was a conservatively estimated twenty thousand, or more than one lobbyist cadre for each civil servant in the EC as a whole.

The mergers-and-acquisitions, stock-market and derivative-paper bureaucracies also spread outwards by bureaucratic cell division. In the 1980s, British merchant banks (investment dealers), seeing how the U.S. M&A bureaucracy had developed in the 1960s and 1970s, and the huge fees it was raking off, began their own expansion. A bar graph measuring the value of takeovers in the U.K. from 1981 to 1988 resembles an ascending staircase rising into the sky. Behind the merchant banks were the commercial banks and syndicates that lent money for the takeovers. The bureaucracy evolved to the point where it could handle big deals, and started "minting money."

U.S. investment banks and commercial banks, both as advisers and lenders, moved into the U.K. and Europe and made rapid headway. The aggressive pitch of the U.S. cadres in London forced their British counterparts to follow suit – touting for new business, for example, although the practice never reached the wild intensity it had in the United States. As the deals got larger, divestiture activity increased; the swallower in a large takeover would usually want to get rid of part of the prize. This divestiture recycling – bureaucratic double-dipping – generated added fees. Leveraged buy-outs (LBOs) and management buy-outs (MBOs) expanded with divestitures, on the buying side. The LBO idea was imported from the U.S. at the end of the 1970s. Later, as some of those LBOs ran into trouble, there would be refinancing work.

These LBOs were mostly friendly. They also, however, generated the cadres and infrastructure for managing hostile LBOs. A few hostile LBOs eventually followed. One, the 1989 takeover of Britain's third-largest supermarket chain by a shell company, hit the $4 billion mark. Another which didn't quite make it, a raid on conglomerate BAT Industries by long-in-the-tooth shark James Goldsmith, was in the $25 billion range. "How Europe is learning to love the American LBO," *Business Week* reported.

Transborder activity expanded the bureaucracy. U.S. investment banks, taking advantage of their familiarity with the U.S. scene, went to work getting British and European companies interested in acquisitions in the U.S. Some of the largest, messiest, and most bureaucratically costly M&A

deals in the U.S. were hostile takeovers by U.K. companies. The most spectacular part of these deals may have been the legal fees. In one case, BAT Industries' raid on the Farmers insurance group, Farmers' New York legal counsel entangled BAT in legal actions in twelve states, demanded depositions from countless BAT employees, and otherwise threw paper at BAT. Before it was over, advisory and legal fees were estimated to have exceeded US$100 million. A *Sunday Times* full-page feature on this and similar battles, instead of talking about the companies and the logic or illogic of their deals, focused on the lawyers instead. The most pungent criticism of the takeover companies, cited in the article, wasn't for their getting into the deals but for choosing the wrong lawyers.

Conferences and seminars were held on "Acquiring in the U.S." to help pump up activity. The fees that were being generated by this U.S.-U.K. transborder work encouraged the British merchant banks to try to occupy some M&A territory in the U.S. themselves. The British cadres had also branched out into Europe, preceding the Americans. A British merchant bank acted for Nestlé, a Swiss company, in its controversial snaffling of the venerable British firm Rowntree.

A strange pattern began to evolve in the late 1980s whereby the more developed the M&A bureaucracy in any one country, the greater was the sell-off of its enterprises to other countries. By the same token, the more backward the M&A bureaucracy in a country, combined with a vigorous real entrepreneurship, the more that particular country might snaffle other countries' companies while hanging on to its entrepreneurial home base. The paper-entrepreneurialism branch appeared to be primarily a sell-off bureaucracy.

The United States, for example, with the most advanced M&A bureaucracy, saw company after company being sold off to foreigners. The biggest acquirer in the United States, by country, was Britain. Its takeovers there far outdistanced U.S. takeovers in Britain. The M&A bureaucracy in Britain, on the other hand, while trailing the United States, was much more developed than in Europe. The loss of British companies to Europe, as a result, was considerably greater than takeovers flowing in the other direction. Britain, with its growing M&A cadres on hand, became the top target for transborder European acquisitions.

With all the LBO money now floating around in LBO funds in Britain and Europe and in bridge-loan facilities, the money began chasing deals – just as it had in the United States. Specialist LBO cadres beat the bushes across Western Europe. And with all those cadres trying to make work, fees, and bonuses for themselves by scaring up deals, they flogged transactions that never should have been made – just as their predecessors had in the United States. A growing number of transactions in France and Italy were "priced somewhere between aggressively and insanely," a British merchant banker commented in amazement. As for the increasingly huge size of corporation that was being created by the large multibillion-dollar transborder mergers, nobody stopped to think about it.

The required ideology also spilled over from the United States into, particularly, Britain. The quality of corporate management would deteriorate sharply without the threat of takeovers, went the rhetoric. Takeovers in general weren't adequate, it was explained further. One needed hostile takeovers. *The Economist* went so far as to attack friendly deals for stunting the buy-out market, by not allowing enough room and financing for hostile takeovers instead. Meanwhile, in Germany, Switzerland, Japan, and elsewhere where hostile takeovers were virtually taboo, corporate management did not look as if it were deteriorating. The M&A bureaucracy, by the process of bureaucratic cross-fertilization, slowly began to penetrate those countries anyway.

The American bureaucracy also helped inflate the stock-market bureaucracy elsewhere, especially in Europe. The buying and selling of European stocks by U.S. mutual funds and pension funds, as they began looking for new turns in the 1980s – a fashionable "globalization" item – fuelled the rising turnover on what had previously been small and sluggish European exchanges. U.S. investment banks on the spot, with their aggressive trading habits, added to the churning. "These foreigners are very active, thank God," the managing director of the Frankfurt Stock Exchange exclaimed in 1985, despairing of his fellow Germans by themselves ever making the exchange into a large and growing bureaucracy, New-York style.

The ideology propping up the American bureaucracy also played a role. Privatization in Britain and France expanded their stock-market branches with share issues and new share trading. Part of that process was ideological glorification of stock markets, inspired by the American example. The media gushed about the bureaucratic particulars – how to buy and sell shares, the routines of analysts and brokers, the newsletters – as if they were heroic. *L'Express* in France ran a reverential interview with William A. Schreyer – "his friends call him Bill" – CEO of Merrill Lynch, portraying him as a prototype and seer of globalization, bringing American cadres and methods to capitals around the world. (Tactfully, there was no mention in *L'Express* of the US$3 million Schreyer had taken off the top in compensation that year, 1986.) The interlisting of American stocks on European exchanges, especially London – shares in big companies that people were familiar with – itself helped the make-work and inflated the mystique of the exchanges.

What with interlisting of many U.S. and European companies among several exchanges ("globalization" of stock markets themselves) and sheer bureaucratic envy, the European stock-exchange bureaucracies began fighting each other for territory. London was in the lead in Europe, but Paris, Frankfurt, and others had their pretensions. Here, too, modesty and economy had to give way to waste and inflation, for their respective bureaucracies to keep up. Frankfurt couldn't keep pace with London if it only traded for two hours a day while London was open for six; in one particular month, more shares in Siemens, a major German company, were traded in London than on all the German stock exchanges combined. Other arrangements had to be changed to indulge the paper shufflers. Paris, Milan, and the German exchanges didn't have continuous pricing until the mid-1980s; in other words, the price of shares changed only from day to day. This wasn't much good for encouraging brokers and speculators to play the market back and forth in the course of a day and increase volume, or recapture it from another exchange like London. Minute-by-minute stock indexes – the totem of continuous pricing – were also introduced. These administrative changes are known as "adapting to international standards." By making this adaptation, one German investment manager declared with satisfaction, you "will automatically increase the volume [of trading]."

The bureaucratic rivalry, pushed by globalization, also helped get rid of the turnover taxes in most cases. Several countries, such as Britain, Germany, and Japan, had small turnover taxes on share transactions, from 0.5 per cent to 1 per cent. "Stamp duties" was another name for them. The taxes made money, but they had another function as well – they were a tax on the wasteful shuffling back and forth of paper. They were also a token reminder that the original idea of buying shares in a stock market was to invest – a long-term matter – not to play continuous bureaucratic games. Interlisting of stocks, on the other hand, meant that any stock market without a turnover tax could take traffic away from one where there was a tax. Gradually, in a delayed domino effect, the tax was dropped or lowered by one country and then another, as they tried to attract trading from each other. Only the occasional country like Sweden kept its tax – indeed, Sweden doubled it when brokers in the 1980s bull market began pocketing outsized incomes.

Countries that resist the bureaucracy are regularly chastised by apologists of globalization and the dogma behind it. West Germany has been a particular butt of their ire. Its stock-market turnover was too low, the attack went. The number of listed companies was far too small (only 234 domestic companies were listed on the Frankfurt Stock Exchange in 1987 compared to 1,147 on the Toronto Stock Exchange in a much smaller economy). The capital represented on West German stock markets was shamefully low (less than one-twentieth of Japanese stock-market capitalization, as of the end of 1987). The "notorious" stockmarket turnover tax was a monkey wrench in the works and should be abolished (abolition was eventually planned).

"Slaves to some defunct economist," *The Economist* thundered. Another heresy that stuck in the critics' craw was company pensions, which in West Germany are part of the invested capital of each particular company. This meant there were no pension-fund managers to speak of, actively trading shares back and forth and propping up not just the money-manager branch but the stock-market branch as well.

The fact that the German economy was eminently successful was disregarded. The idea that this success was in part attributable to its keeping down both the waste and influence of these bureaucratic cadres was disregarded, too.

Derivative-paper shuffling also globalized itself. Everybody who was bureaucratically anybody had to have a futures or options exchange. The enormous bureaucratic inflation of the Chicago commodity and options exchanges – their dazzling success in creating make-work out of nothing, for nothing, and their ability to protect it behind pomposities, dogma, lobbies, and earnest theoreticians – was hard to ignore. The NYSE, Amex, Philadelphia, Pacific, Boston, Toronto, and Montreal stock exchanges had all tried establishing themselves in this make-work territory before Chicago monopolized it all. Amsterdam, similarly, began trading options in a futile attempt to inflate itself into an exchange powerhouse. London, which had long had a variety of commodity exchanges, opened trading in options once it saw that Amsterdam had actually done it. A financial futures market, modelled directly on Chicago, was also established in London. The Swiss began looking into futures and options and eventually established a futures exchange. They realized there was no pressing demand for either futures or options but, at the same time, they saw Amsterdam and London hard at it.

Hong Kong had a futures market which managed to pump up trading in Hong Kong index futures to forty thousand contracts a day until it collapsed with the October 1987 crash, when speculators refused to honour their commitments. France established a futures and options market for government bonds. Before long there were financial futures markets being planned from Dublin to Lisbon, to occupy some of London's territory. In a little more than a decade, 1978-1990, twelve futures exchanges sprang up in Europe from nothing. London, like Chicago when faced with shrinking territory, was obliged to turn even more assiduously to dreaming up new products, in order to keep expanding in the face of all the newcomers. Singapore and Sydney, even New Zealand, now had futures exchanges of one kind or another. Link-ups between futures exchanges in different parts of the world added to the "products" available in any one place and expanded the opportunities for paper shuffling from fixed hours in one location – Chicago, for example – to twenty-four hours around the clock. The CBOT trumpeted the arrival of "a new breed of international trader." "Globalization" and "global market" became favourite buzzwords in exchange annual reports and at the annual convention of the Washington-based Futures Industry Association.

The most telling aspect of this bureaucratic progression, though, has to do with Germany and Japan. West Germany was staunchly opposed to futures and options. It regarded futures trading as nothing more than gambling, which it was, except that it had become routinized and bureaucratized by computer trading strategies. The Japanese also looked down on derivative paper games. In fact, when the U.S. occupation forces reopened the Tokyo stock market after World War II, they specifically banned futures trading. This was a carryover from the 1930s, when a primitive kind of trading in financial futures ended in scandals and manipulation. Until fairly recently, Japanese investors could not even buy gold. In the mid-1980s, the Japanese had ten kinds of investment categories ("products" in U.S. jargon) compared to more than two hundred in the United States. At the same time, Japan and West Germany were at the forefront of productive investment and innovation. It was as if their productive frame of mind protected them from these new kinds of bureaucratic waste. They were also protected by freedom from ideological dogma. Neither country subscribed to the silly American doctrine that anything dreamed up according to market rules was next to godliness, no matter what an idiotic waste of time it was. Both countries got along famously without the waste and distraction.

But, ultimately, bureaucratic envy got to them, too. The West Germans couldn't bear to see futures trading, especially in West German marks and government bonds, going to places like London, however unnecessary and circular the trading might be. By this time, the late 1980s, there was a well-established bureaucratese about "the volatility of global financial markets," "risk management," and "innovative financial instruments," which could be plugged into conferences, meetings and advertisements to give a new futures and options bureaucracy the patina of respectability.

The Japanese gradually gave way, as well. One of the steps was to allow Japanese institutional investors to trade in futures abroad; there had been foreign pressure, especially from the futures exchanges in Chicago, to get some of the growing pool of Japanese money coursing through their bailiwicks. This had a domino effect. Japanese brokerages and banks, watching Chicago inflate, could see how lucrative similar trading might be in Japan. The brokerages bought memberships in the Chicago exchanges and used Chicago as a training ground. They also used it – again copying the Americans – to create a new array of "products," which they could then sell to their Japanese clientele.

In counterpoint, the Chicago futures bureaucracies opened offices in Tokyo to direct more paper shuffling to Chicago. The New York investment banks, already in Tokyo, did even better. As soon as trading in Japanese stock-index options and futures was allowed in 1988, they began pushing their snazzy Wall Street trading strategies and exotic derivative concoctions to the Japanese. The Americans also used their big computer programs to trade on their own account. The centrepiece of the new make-work was index arbitrage between futures and stocks, made possible by the existence of futures to begin with; this puffed up both futures and stock trading. Another part of the process was getting Japanese fund managers interested in the new bag of tricks. The Japanese brokerage firms, trying to catch up, raided U.S. investment banks in New York for savvy program-trading (quant) cadres, paying top dollar, to strengthen their New York ranks, where they were also behind, and then to apply the expertise back home. Several European banks, seeing the derivative operations in New York expanding exponentially, followed suit.

The derivative-paper cell division did not end there, either. Where cadres can get enough futures trading going, they can also lever managed futures funds on it, and create another layer of fees and cadres. Several European futures brokerage firms and fund managers had already launched offshore futures funds trading in the United States, clamped on to the Chicago activity. Now, with regulations loosening and all those futures exchanges popping up at home, they turned an eye to launching additional futures funds based in Europe. The inherent waste and futility of these publicly offered futures funds had already been demonstrated in the United States. But that wasn't the point or, rather, that was exactly the point. The funds generated fees, and if it could be done in the United States, why not do it in Europe as well? In Britain, the idea was promoted by Whitehall (the government) itself, in order to strengthen London futures markets. One wasteful bureaucratic section is concocted to help feed another one.

In the money-manager branch (pension-fund management and mutual funds) the U.S. cadres also set the fashion for the new cadres elsewhere. Investment advisers in Britain play against each other, as funds under management became a bigger part of the market, and, like the Americans, they have little to boast about. The majority of their funds almost always do worse than an ordinary stock index. Like the Americans, too, the British investment cadres have consultant cadres tracking them and letting them and their sponsors know how useless they are. And they have other consultant cadres – inspired by the American consultant subsection, some-times the American consultants themselves – telling them how to get out of their fix. American bureaucratic wrinkles, like "risk analysis" consultancy and the use of high-quant computer models, have spread into Britain and beyond.

For mutual-fund cadres in particular, the Americans are especially to be emulated. The most elaborate of the American mutual-fund operators, Fidelity, with its heavy advertising expenditures and its trick of adding new funds, has set up in Britain and elsewhere in western Europe, providing an example *in situ*.

For country-to-country cell-division by the bureaucracy, though, nothing quite compares with the advertising and marketing branch and the culture and sports branch. American advertisers, pushing their brand names abroad, lobby against advertising and marketing restrictions. Subsidiaries of American advertising agencies join in. Local advertising agencies get into the act. Advertising agencies in different countries open foreign offices, buy pieces of each other, take each other over, or form alliances – globalization of the bureaucracy – drawing the country-to-country connections tighter. This process, covering also market research, public relations, direct marketing, and sales promotion, accelerated sharply in the 1980s.

The sheer money that this bureaucracy can make available adds to its power to destroy its containment. In Western Europe, for example, non-commercial or commercially restricted television used to be the rule. On the other hand, anybody who could break apart the public financing of television and have commercial television introduced, and get a piece of it, could share in the advertising bureaucracy's dispensations. One just had to look at the Americans; they showed how far the bureaucracy could go. This was a powerful lobbying incentive, for some. Satellite television, carrying commercials across borders, had its own bureaucratic inflationary power.

The spread of the advertising branch's presence in television happened by an almost routine bureaucratic progression. Territories close to the United States – South America and Canada – were easy to fasten on to, although Canada showed some resistance. Western Europe, with its ideological balance and public-service tradition, was more difficult. But in Britain, with the help of the U.S.-based J. Walter Thompson agency, the advertising lobby managed to get one commercial television channel in 1954.

Italy followed in the 1970s. The embryonic Italian commercial channels could prop themselves up with cheaply acquired U.S. television blockbusters, series and movies. This had a chain effect. In order to compete against the U.S. programs, the public networks in Italy needed more money. This was difficult to arrange through the accountable public process, but easy to arrange through the self-inflating advertising bureaucracy that had raised the ante in the first place. So the public networks, which had had limited advertising, boosted their advertising revenues. France followed with commercial channels in the mid-1980s. As in Italy, once a foothold was established for the advertising bureaucracy, it self-inflated. France once limited commercials to eighteen minutes a day per channel. That mushroomed to twelve minutes per hour. The progression worked in this way, from country to country and from commercial channel to public channel.

At the end of the 1980s, the European Community's bureaucracy in Brussels, planning Europe's own "globalization," issued a directive whereby any one country had to open its transmission network to foreign channels within the EC, as long as they adhered to certain minimal rules (for example, no more than twelve minutes of spot advertising per hour). This eliminated any last possibility of a check on the advertising and marketing branch. That, in fact, was the object of the directive: The branch wanted more access for brand-name propaganda and, as *International Management* magazine put it, the directive was issued to relieve this pressure. Globalization and the imposition of brand-name propaganda went together – were, in a sense, the same thing.

Scandinavia was the last region to surrender. Sweden and Norway both had no television commercials. A Swedish-based company then began broadcasting into Sweden, via satellite, from London in 1988. This pushed the Swedish government into allowing commercially financed channels on its own territory (one conventional channel and several using satellite), to capture that revenue at home. This in turn pushed Norway into allowing commercials, on both television and radio. Most Norwegians can pick up Swedish channels. The government was afraid that advertising expenditures would flow out of Norway to Sweden if it didn't do something.

No provision was made for counter-propaganda of the same frequency and with equivalent production values. What this meant, in terms of bureaucratic inflation, was obvious. The chairman of German media conglomerate Bertelsmann, for example, estimated that the value of advertising in West Germany would explode from 9.8 billion ECUs in 1989 to 20 billion by the end of the 1990s. Zenith, a subsidiary of Saatchi & Saatchi, predicted the same rate of inflation for television in Europe. In other words, Europe's advertising bureaucracy would be artificially inflated to double its size in a decade. The cadres "are already salivating," *The Economist* reported.

As in the United States, the mythology of free enterprise, or at least corporate enterprise, hides how bureaucratic the process really is. Take the case of Italy. The Italian bureaucrat who led the inflation was Silvio Berlusconi. Berlusconi got his start building suburban housing outside Milan. By aggressively playing the politics of television and using cheaply bought American programming, he ended up with ownership of three television networks, a major advertising company, pieces of French and German television, a Spanish channel and numerous other properties. He is described as a "TV magnate," "media baron," and "flamboyant capitalist," evoking the symbolism of individualistic capitalism and free enterprise. His television and advertising fortune really rests, though, on his having attached himself to an existing bureaucracy and bureaucratic process – one, moreover, already entrenched, especially in the United States.

The bureaucracy, as it inflates by this process from country to country, expands its lobbying resources correspondingly, by which it can protect and feed its further inflation. Organizations such as the U.S.-led International Advertising Association, the European Advertising Tripartite, and the European Association of Advertising Agencies, as well as individual agencies and advertisers and local associations, have joined together to fight possible European Community restrictions. "Global lobbying," *Advertising Age* described it. Restrictions banning or limiting cigarette, alcohol, toy, pharmaceutical, food and similar advertising are denounced. Attempts to restrict program interruptions are vilified. The political techniques pioneered by the U.S. lobbying cadres spread outwards in the process and themselves become globalized.

The worst of bureaucratic evils, moral indifference, also spreads outwards on the back of the bureaucracy's globalization. Philip Morris and other U.S. tobacco companies are using their high American cash flows and their U.S. advertising techniques to push cigarettes offshore, especially in Asia.

Once a new bureaucratic section, such as direct marketing, has been inflated to clutter-level in the United States, the bureaucratic impulse pushes the inflation outwards to other countries, stepping up their clutter and waste towards the density already reached in the U.S. "Responding to the maturing U.S. market and anticipating the united European market in 1992, the nation's largest direct-response agencies are seeking more fertile turf overseas," *Advertising Age* reported enthusiastically in 1989. By 1989, Ogilvy & Mather Direct, the largest global direct-response agency network, had forty-six offices worldwide and was planning to add more, probably in Asia and Latin America.

The equivalent, in the old bureaucracy, would be a state highways department adding layers of pavement to perfectly good highways two or three times and then, not being able to do it any more, setting up offices in France and Italy, adding extra layers to their perfectly good highways two or three times, and obliging their economies to pay for it.

Other waste and manipulation is similarly globalized. Huge payouts for phony endorsements proliferate country to country. In Japan, the use of western movie *su-tahs* is particularly heavy. There is a special bureaucratic irony here. Movie stars rarely do commercials in the United States because it risks tarnishing their images and their future film marketability. Japan, on the other hand, is considered far enough removed. Besides, the pay-outs are great – US$500,000 to $1 million for top American and European film actors, for a couple of days work.

Sales promotion and sponsorship bureaucracies are also transmitted by globalization. No place is immune. In Taiwan, for example, Coca-Cola uses assault-level "point-of-sale marketing" (translation: in-store sales promotion), a regular fusillade of other promotions, baseball and basketball seminars around the island by American coaches, and concerts by pop artists such as Stevie Wonder, plus stepped-up advertising, to push aside local sarsaparilla and lemon-lime drinks. The secondary and tertiary layers of cadres – from makers of television commercials to printers producing cents-off coupons – inflate correspondingly.

Eastern Europe, having lost its Communist-Party chastity belt, is virgin territory for the New Bureaucracy – wonderfully susceptible and naive, easily occupied now, and much coveted and talked about by the New Bureaucracy's eager apparatchiks. The now-globalized advertising agencies quickly opened shop in Eastern European countries, either with new offices, by buying up a piece or all of small start-up shops already there, or by forming alliances with locals. Their western clients, like Procter & Gamble, Unilever, Colgate-Palmolive, Coca-Cola, Kraft General Foods, McDonald's, RJR Nabisco, and Philips are moving in with them. *Advertising Age* has begun running specially flagged Eastern European items. Part of the process is opening up broadcasting and newspapers to brand-name propaganda – with the advent of propaganda-financed television channels, for example.

The irony of this new bureaucratic encroachment on Eastern Europe was illustrated by some thirty-second Adidas ads on Czech TV in 1990. Irate letters showed up in local newspapers, complaining about the frequency of the Adidas spot – twice during each ninety-minute World Cup soccer game. For propaganda-beaten Canadians or Americans, that kind of repetition is old hat, and passively endured; what's the point of complaining? The Czechs, though, saw the brainwashing fresh. The letter writers also objected to the commercials' content, with their vacuous use of lifestyle images, devoid of useful information. East Germans, market research showed, also had trouble with lifestyle ads.

"People here are not used to the type of advertising known in the West," the commercial director of a Czech ad agency explained, almost apologetically, to *Advertising Age*. Once the New Bureaucracy becomes entrenched, though, Eastern Europeans will get used to it whether they like it or not. They will have thrown off one bureaucracy only to be captured by another. New bureaucratic realism replaces socialist realism.

Advertising under Communist regimes at least had one saving grace. It was unslick. Viewers could compare reality against the propaganda, and make their own judgements. The much more effective and insidious propaganda of the advertising and marketing branch, on the other hand, is deliberately devised to avoid comparisons with reality and to get at people's minds despite themselves. The Eastern Europeans are now getting the real thing.

Naturally, the tobacco companies are in the pack. Led by Philip Morris, they've drawn a bead on Eastern Europeans. The incidence of cigarette smoking in Eastern Europe is rising. R. J. Reynolds Tobacco put up a huge Camel billboard at Checkpoint Charlie, at a spot formerly known as the "death strip." The location of the billboard said more than the company's advertising agency intended.

Because Eastern Europe is on the rebound from communism, almost anything that can be connected to free enterprise, even speciously, can hide behind its mythology. Consequently, the nascent advertising bureaucracy in Eastern Europe is protected by free-enterprise ideology even more securely than it is in the West. Meanwhile, in the United States, the cadres cite events in Eastern Europe in an attempt to protect themselves at home. The editors of *Advertising Age*, trying to discredit legislative moves in Congress against cigarette advertising, wrote an open letter to Gorbachev, congratulating him on opening up the Soviet media, and denouncing a reformist U.S. Congressman for heading in the old Soviet direction, as they grandiosely described it. This is typical.

The culture and sports branch proliferates outwards, helped along by the commercialization (really "bureaucratization") of television. Event marketing had already made inroads beyond the United States and Canada by the late 1980s. In 1986, 360 hours of sport on TV in Britain were "sponsored" by tobacco companies alone. By the end of the decade, brand-name proprietors like Coca-Cola and McDonald's were into everything from NBA videotapes sent to the Soviet Union to a soccer series in Brazil launched as a sponsorship vehicle. Heavyweight corporate sponsors, among them Volkswagen, Kraft General Foods, and American Airlines, were lined up for a precedent-setting women's tennis tournament in Leipzig, East Germany, just a few days before unification.

This bureaucracy, too, was quickly being globalized. The Leipzig deal was put together by Advantage International Inc., a Washington (D.C.)-based sports-marketing cell. The original, Cleveland-based International Management Group (IMG) had long since set up operations around the world. Other U.S. sports-marketing cadres, like Washington-based ProServ, have moved into Europe. Europe also has its own sports-marketing cadres, like ISL Marketing AG of Lucerne which acts as marketing consultant for the International Olympic Committee and the national Olympic committees of each country.

At the same time, the bureaucracy goes to work changing television – gradually, arbitrarily eliminating anything that doesn't fit, just as it did a long time ago in the United States, Japan and South America, where financing by propaganda has long been entrenched. Japan is an even better example of what happens than the United States. The predominant and powerful Dentsu advertising agency, with a finger in every pie and intimately connected to the powers that be, virtually dictates to media. "The hidden media boss," journalist Karel van Wolferen calls it, in his compelling book, *The Enigma of Japanese Power*. The "editing bureau," program makers jokingly refer to it. Needless to say, the media in Japan, dependent on advertisers and advertising, don't take on the advertising bureaucracy itself.

In Western Europe, on the other hand, the heavy hand of the bureaucracy had been kept at bay in many countries. This independence is being lost now, too. As new commercial channels come on-stream, public channels, competing for audience and sometimes advertising revenue, push risky, difficult, and commercially doubtful programs out of prime time. The public-service model of broadcasting is forced to the margin. The programming of small countries like Belgium and the Netherlands, which don't have the resources to compete, simply takes it on the chin when it comes to holding viewers. Pooling of resources in co-productions that can be sold everywhere in Europe and possibly in the U.S. and elsewhere isn't much of a solution. Such co-productions, like Canada-U.S. co-productions, are not going to pay much attention to the smaller countries' individuality.

The line separating broadcaster from advertiser is also being crossed. In Britain, that line was always very clear. The broadcasters made programs for viewers. The advertisers bought time but had no influence, particularly since the commercial stations (ITV and its offshoot, Channel 4) had a monopoly over advertising availabilities. Now sponsorship is being allowed to intrude, where advertisers and broadcasters package program ideas together with their marketing possibilities in mind. The contract between broadcasters and viewers is destroyed.

Advertising agencies are hiring television executives to identify sponsorship opportunities, to set up the required bureaucratic machinery, and also to produce sponsored programs. Some ITV stations have their sales departments searching out sponsorship, sometimes with a separate unit. Its proponents talk about the need to recognize the importance to sponsors of "below-the-line activities" – that is, the importance of combining television sponsorship with sales promotion and direct marketing. The most insidious below-the-line activity is cause marketing. To oblige, some ITV stations are linking up their sponsorship units with their community and educational departments. Product placement is next – a "new era for consumer marketers," crows a U.S. public-relations agency, looking at Western Europe.

The U.S. bureaucracy being recreated in Europe – "the Dallasisation and McDonaldisation of the world," as the chairman of Heinz put it –

carries with it the promise of entrenching major American and other leading brand names, too, wiping out local differences wherever possible. But that's the whole point of globalization: set up machinery by which advertising bureaucrats can overrun local differences.

The advertising and marketing branch has inflated the old (government) bureaucracy as well, and not just with government advocacy advertising. Its bureaucratic methods and norms, especially its use of market research and mass-media propaganda, have been applied to the electoral process, most indulgently and wastefully in the bureaucratic heartland, the United States. A non-bureaucratic society would have made parliamentary-style arrangements for elections and political parties. Free-time party political broadcasts on the CBC are an example, where no one party or candidate can dominate the other by spending more on propaganda. In the United States, however, the bureaucratic rules of the advertising and marketing branch hold sway. Expenditures and propaganda inflate exponentially in political versions of the cola wars or the beer wars or, alternatively, where moneyed congressional incumbents simply sideswipe challengers with inflated television and other media spending. The result has been the degradation of politics, "increasingly polluted by money," as political historian Theodore H. White (*The Making of the President*) put it in 1973, with the really inflated waste yet to come.

Market-research spending, which is an integral part of television propaganda campaigns, has inflated here, too. The electioneering propaganda wars have less and less to do with a parliamentary debate of issues and more and more to do with sheer bureaucratic weight and refinement. The campaign consultants, pollsters, media advisers, and their retinues, in the United States, have come to constitute a section of the advertising and marketing branch in themselves. There are leading firms, just as there are in advertising and public relations. If congressional politics is flat, they try pumping up business at the state level. There is even a magazine tracking the bureaucracy and reporting its developments – and helping to maintain its rake-off. There is, of course, an American Association of Political Consultants. In the last presidential election year, 1988, they and the rest of the election campaign machinery, at all levels, ran through US$2.7 billion, a 50 per cent increase over the previous presidential election year, 1984, and a 400 per cent increase over 1976. The various layers of bureaucratic cadres have fastened on to their share of this take and can be counted on to resist any attempt to cut their numbers back. Television station owners, for example, complain bitterly about any attempt to restrain spending for election propaganda or to reduce its costs.

There is no escaping the New Bureaucracy – neither its overweening corporate self-indulgence, its M&A paper games, its stock-market nattering, its futures make-work, its anguished investment advisers, or its propaganda and harrassment. Think tanks and media owners, and even astrologers, eagerly service them, catering to their bureaucratic power while battening on to it; the mark of bureaucratic power is that it intrudes everywhere and makes others dependent on it, so that criticism doesn't get far. Ranks of make-work bureaucrats proliferate, protected by an ideology that is supposed to be anti-bureaucratic, which makes it the finest bureaucratic protection of all.

The cadres are most entrenched and intrusive in the United States where questioning the ideology is considered unpatriotic heresy. Canadians next door, themselves captured, meekly go along. Now this new bureaucracy is also entrenching itself in Western Europe and the rest of the world by a process euphemistically called "globalization." It also infects and corrupts the old bureaucracy (parliamentary government) as it goes along. Stop by the Paris Bourse, walk down a street in Taipei, watch an American television channel. It touches everything, watches over everybody – One Big Bureaucracy.

Acknowledgements

I first discussed the idea of doing this book with Lynn McDonald, whose interest and encouragement resulted in my undertaking the project. My research assistants, Jane Oglesby, Lona Manning, and Barbara Maclellan, who worked on respective stages of the book, canvassed many subject areas for me and searched out even the most hidden of details. Barbara Maclellan also did some key editing work at a crucial juncture. The librarians at the University of British Columbia Main Library, where most of the research work was done, were unfailingly helpful. Innumerable people with specialized knowledge – mostly in the United States, in Canada, and occasionally in Europe – gave me their time to discuss different aspects of the subject matter, or to provide background on work they had done or statistics they had developed. Freelance editor Jennifer Glossop took on the task of bringing the lengthy draft manuscript down to publishable size, no mean assignment. My agent, Denise Bukowski of the Bukowski Agency, quickly understood the importance of the book and managed the business particulars with her usual dispatch. Dinah Forbes, senior editor at McClelland & Stewart, skilfully kept the editorial process in hand, as well as offering much useful advice along the way. Finally, my thanks to my wife, Marguerite, whose judgement and editorial acumen helped see the manuscript through to publication.

Index